GERMANY

Yesterday and Tomorrow

PETER H. MERKL

New York   OXFORD UNIVERSITY PRESS   1965

25490

GERMANY
Yesterday and Tomorrow

To Elisa

FOREWORD

This book is the quintessence of the writer's personal experience combined with an attempt to understand and to generalize about one of the most baffling national histories of our age. Large parts of it were written in dialogue in order to demonstrate the difficulty of searching for truth when faced with such large and fundamental questions. The dialogue form allowed the writer to speak his mind in turn through the mouths of four different principals, all the while leaving final judgment to the reader. It also made it easier to concentrate on the salient issues of German history and to proceed in an analytical rather than a historical fashion. The other parts of the book reflect both the preoccupations of a political scientist and the reactions and thoughts of an expatriate who, after an absence of seven years, returned to his native land. Seven years may not seem long in most cases. But it is in post-war Germany, and it seemed an eternity to the writer, who as a youthful refugee had left the burden of guilt of two generations and returned to find his erstwhile compatriots in better condition than he had anticipated.

It is often said that you can never go home again, or that one cannot recapture the past or right its wrongs. Western Germany today is full of the talk about the "unmastered" or "undigested past." Yet there is a power of understanding, a penetrating light that will make even the darkest corners knowable and familiar, and the deepest recesses of the human mind less frightening. Writing this book has helped this writer to come to grips with the burden of a collective past he has felt for many years. Reading it, he hopes, may help others to understand and forgive. It is possible to condemn hateful deeds even while forgiving the people in whose midst they were done, or at least forgiving their children.

Owing to the fundamental nature of the questions and the personal involvement of the writer, a debt of gratitude should really be acknowledged to an endless list of persons whose writings have helped shape the ideas expressed in this book. The bibliographical notes at the end of the book shall serve to acknowledge at least the more immediate debts. Gratitude is also due to the many persons in different walks of life and of different national origins with whom the writer conversed about the questions discussed in this book, teachers at whose feet he sat, and persons not of the teaching profession who taught him by example over many years. Acknowledgment is also due to Henry A. Kissinger of Harvard University, at whose invitation the writer attended a conference of specialists on German affairs at a point when this manuscript was almost completed. The discussions among the fine minds assembled helped to confirm or clarify many a salient point and concept.

Special thanks are due also to the cartoonists of the *Algemeen Handelsblad* of Amsterdam, Fritz Behrendt, and of the *Sueddeutsche Zeitung* of Munich, E. M. Lang, for permission to use their delightful cartoons for the book. Credit is due also to Mrs. Helen Barreto and Miss Karen Buss, who typed the manuscript with loving care. Last but not least, the writer owes the sincerest gratitude to his family, and especially to the person to whom this book is dedicated. Without her forbearance, patience, and moral support, this book would never have come to be.

Peter H. Merkl

Santa Barbara, California
June 1965

CONTENTS

GERMANY
Yesterday and Tomorrow

THE UNDIGESTED PAST

The scene is a brilliantly illumined theater foyer in a large West German city. The play has ended and well-dressed crowds are about to leave, waiting for taxi-cabs or heading for their own Mercedes in the parking-lot. The show has been a great success and was sold out to the last spot of standing room. But nobody in the crowd laughs or chatters excitedly. The ladies have red eyes and telltale streaks in their make-up. Their escorts are pale and look strained and tired. The play was *The Diary of Anne Frank,* or perhaps *The Wall,* a chilling dramatization of Hitler's "final solution" for the inhabitants of the Warsaw Ghetto.

Another time it may be a lengthy television series about the rise and the misdeeds of the Third Reich which the family watches with glum fascination on the recently acquired television set — a status symbol in the newly affluent West German society. The middle-aged parents follow every word of the narrator and every change of scene as closely as a fan might watch a ball-game. They do so with a breath-less suspense that springs from half-conscious memories and recollec-tions, almost as if they are discovering in the chain of past events a

3

historical turning-point at which they might have caused the Third
Reich to wither before it unfolded fully. They act like a man who
made a terrible mistake in his youth without much thinking, and in-
curred a crushing burden of guilt; who then spends the rest of his life
trying to figure out just which thoughtless step first put him on the
wrong path.

Our parents also read religiously the numerous feature stories in
the daily press and in news magazines like *Der Spiegel,* in which liberal editors and intellectuals tirelessly remind them of the gruesome
past or call on them to commemorate the gallant July 20, 1944, assassination attempt on Hitler. Their avid interest is also fed by the
horror story of Adolf Eichmann, by the continuing series of trials of
Nazi mass murderers who have but recently been ferreted out, and by
a growing stream of books about the Hitler era and the Second World
War, including a German translation of William Shirer's *Rise and
Fall of the Third Reich.*

Not long ago, in a broadcast from Radio Munich, dozens of young
men and women reported what happened when they asked their parents to explain how it had been possible for Hitler to come to power
in Germany. Uniformly, the parents proved incapable of giving even
the most general explanation. They tended instead to trail off into
personal excuses or exclamations of "I just won't be able to make
you understand."

Some parents have urged their almost adult children to devote their
attention to examining the unhappy past as they themselves have. The
young generation under 25, however, senses behind the urging of
their elders more than just the desire to protect them against the same
mistakes under very different conditions. With the wariness of any
young generation in taking on the burdens of their parents, they suspect they are being drawn into the maelstrom of guilty feelings for
activities for which the younger people cannot be blamed. Generations come and go. At the present time, only about 40 per cent of
West Germans between 21 and 65 today were of age under Hitler.

The past rears its ugly head most intensely in people's private
recollections which they cannot put aside but would rather not share
with anyone, even if there is no personal guilt involved at all. It could
happen to anyone: grocer, farmer, bureaucrat, doctor. For example,
a man awakens with a groan in the middle of the night in the

bedroom of a luxuriously furnished villa on Lake Lugano in Switzerland, where many West German business tycoons have built summer residences. Our successful businessman with the smooth and well-groomed appearance wakes up from a horrid nightmare, one of many that have troubled his sleep in the last fifteen years always leaving him tense and awake for the rest of the night, brooding over scenes that would not remain forgotten. Perhaps he was dreaming about the indescribable violence and bloodshed that took place during the last phases of the war on the Eastern front when no quarter was given on either side. Perhaps his subconscious conjured up infernal pictures of past activities he would rather forget: reprisals for underground activities against the civilian population of an occupied country; or service in one of the *Einsatzkommandos* which did the dirty work for Hitler, Himmler, and Eichmann; or, perhaps, one of those experiences of personal cowardice or helpless connivance with the evil worked by the Nazis which might well burn itself indelibly into the memory of a sensitive person. Next morning, our businessman, who usually radiates energy and efficiency, will look like an aging woman with a migraine. He can try to throw himself into his usual routine of ceaseless activity in order to forget; but when he stops to rest the tormenting scenes return to haunt him.

This is what West Germans call the *unbewältigte Vergangenheit,* the undigested past. It is a phase of the groping emergence of the Germans west of the Elbe river from the long tunnel of helter-skelter modernization which goes all the way through from the traditional culture and society of eighteenth-century Germany to the rude awakening of 1945. Dazzled by the penetrating light outside the tunnel, many dare not quite open their eyes as yet. They do not want to chart the course ahead nor do they want to look back upon what appears to them a hopelessly confused labyrinth. All they can grasp about the past is that much confused feeling, thinking, and violence somehow occurred, often passionately willed and supported by them, but for reasons and under compulsions they can no longer understand.

It would be incorrect and very simple-minded to believe that the undigested past of the West Germans of today represents simply a case of moral indigestion over the great crimes committed by Germans under Hitler, a kind of collective guilt feeling. It is not only far more complicated than that, as will soon be readily apparent, but also far more extensive. Many Germans, indoctrinated by nationalistic and Nazi historians, consider their country's history to be a straight line, starting with the wars of liberation against Napoleon I and ending with World War II and the Nazi concentration camps. Now no one in his right mind ever thinks of history as following a straight line anywhere. Yet this erroneous view is held by many Americans and persons in other Allied countries whose propaganda in the two World Wars was in the fortunate position of being able to quote at length from the inanities and labored misinterpretations of many German right-wing writers. For Germans whose eyes had been opened by the great collapse of 1945 and the subsequent disclosure of German misdeeds, this view of their own history created a strange dilemma. One way out was to disavow completely the entire past, at least from Bismarck to Hitler, if not before, as something done to the decent German, Catholic, liberal democrat, socialist, or civilian, by the bad Germans, militarists, reactionaries, or demented maniacs. Another solution was to maintain a stiff upper lip and to insist on German solidarity in triumph and defeat, admitting only to crimes and excesses, but not a basic perversity in German character.

Both of these extreme answers to the German question contain some elements of the truth. The first recognizes the fate of many different groups and subscribes to the nature of a cataclysmic history. But this answer also gives those who opposed Nazism, or stood aside from it, an undeserved halo, for if they had participated in German life then, they might have helped modify a course set for disaster. The second approach affirms a common nature in German history, at least from 1870 to 1945, from which no German can quite detach himself, no matter how carefully contrived his excuse or how minimal his role or how much opposition he displayed to the events of those fateful seventy-five years. Even émigrés or people obviously victimized by German regimes remain painfully involved in the undigested past, precisely because it is not just a case of moral indigestion, but rather an enormous piece of existential experience. The undigested past encompasses all memories that cannot be pushed aside or communicated to others, whether of misery and deprivations suffered in vain, of self-hatred and self-pity, or of friends and relations painfully lost to the war and its aftermath, to the concentration camp or, worst of

all, to a monstrous Nazi career. Pity the mother whose son has turned
out to be a mass murderer. And then there are also the living skeletons, the Nazi criminals who have survived and escaped detection by
weaving a clever web of lies, or because others in weary forbearance
do not give them away; and they all tumble out of the ubiquitous
closets of Germany or have to face final judgment some day.

How does anyone ever "digest" his past? Is such "digestion" necessary for one to control both present and future conduct? Germans
have built a church on the site of the concentration camp of Bergen-
Belsen, near Hannover. They have reimbursed survivors, paid reparations to Israel, and yet they know they can never do enough, for they
cannot undo the past or revive the dead. A few German youths have
found one way by going to Israel to work in a kibbutz and thus face
the people Germans have so gravely wronged. But for obvious reasons this way is open only to a few. A person can digest his past only,
it would appear, by understanding himself, his character and aspirations, the circumstances which frustrated or propelled him, his attitudes toward himself and others, and the actions which sprang from
his motivations. But understanding should also lead to forgiveness. A
very naïve person, such as a Puritan moralist or a victim still deeply
embroiled in feelings of hatred and revenge, thinks of guilt feelings as
a thing of only one dimension: the remorse of the evil-doer about his
deed. But the vast majority of Germans who suffer today from the
undigested past cannot point to any specific deeds for which they can
atone. All they have to blame themselves for are past attitudes and,
perhaps, a failure to resist or to act which it would be easy to rationalize from the circumstances of the time involved if it were not for that
vague, general guilt feeling — the undigested past.

Guilt feelings serve as a key to the mysterious, pathological subconscious of unmentionable desires and their repression. A criminal
who feels guilty about an act of violence is just as likely to commit his
crime again as he is to repent and to sin no more. In the subconscious
of those committing violent crimes, in the meandering ways of their
erring hearts, the victims emerge as saints, as morally superior to and
mentally more intact than their tormentors, who have ample reason
to envy them. The tormentor or murderer is the tortured wretch who
commits his crime because of feelings of unworthiness and self-hatred
which he projects, of course, onto the victim. Once he has committed

his crime, this outlet for his self-hatred may become fixed, and so he
goes on committing his deed, or hardening his conscience by reaffirm-
ing and rationalizing it in his mind. Needless to say, the opprobrium
and cry from his fellow men, who can thereby project a little of their
own feelings of unworthiness on him, only harden his resolve to commit crime instead of breaking the vicious circle in his mind. Only
through rehabilitation can the corroding effect of hatred and self-
hatred be ended, the feelings of unworthiness alleviated, and a halt
called to the endless chain of mutual revenge and retribution which
allows hatred to continue to proliferate and blight ever more lives.
The great crimes of the Nazi era should serve as a lesson to all the
world and teach future generations the horrible consequences of limit-
less, systematized hatred. But this lesson would quite miss its point, if
it merely serve to perpetuate the hatred and desire for revenge which
existed in the past.

The undigested past is such a broad and encompassing phenomenon in West Germany today that it can fairly be called a touchstone
of political orientation. To be sure, many politicians prefer not to talk
about it. Some cater to right-wing attitudes by avoiding giving offense
to veterans' organizations. However, this vague guilt feeling exists
everywhere today. One can orient oneself in West German politics by
the simple device of gauging the reaction of individuals and groups to
the manifestations of the undigested past. To the left of center, the
guilt feelings engendered by the German past are freely acknowledged, and there is a great willingness to make amends and to bring
to justice whoever has so far escaped the grand reckoning. On the far
left, the guilt feeling is externalized and projected with a self-
righteous vengeance onto ex-Nazis, their one-time sympathizers, and,
quite often, on everybody who is to the right of their extreme position. At the center, there is an embarrassed willingness to make
amends, coupled with the healthy realization that life must go on and
that one cannot reckon with the past forever. To the right of center,
individuals and groups are exceedingly touchy about the subject.
There are guilt feelings, but they are veiled behind defensive attitudes,
ranging from the valiant efforts of conservatives to salvage what still
seems unsullied in such emotional values as historical traditions, the
flag, duty and obedience to authority, to paranoid sallies in defense of
the indefensible. While the experience of the undigested past may

vary among different people and may have begun to weigh on some earlier than on others, there is hardly a German alive who has not in one form or another fallen heir to the collective shame of the Third Reich.

On a different plane, the experience of the undigested past can also help us to understand both the character of the present West German Constitution and the consistent course of policy of that admirable and often misunderstood old man with the craggy face of an Indian chief who has headed the government throughout most of the post-war years. The West German Constitution of 1949—the Basic Law— was the result of much soul-searching by its framers into the reasons for Hitler's rise to power. Their work was preceded by a vast religious revival in the wake of the collapse of Nazi totalitarianism. The most significant upshot of this revival was the rise of a powerful political movement, Konrad Adenauer's Christian Democrats (CDU), which set out to reinfuse religion into a society suffering from the ravages of totalitarianism. At the same time, prominent German historians and intellectuals carried out a great reappraisal of German history since the days of Bismarck and unequivocally condemned national aspirations as the first and primary error from which all further errors sprang. Against this background, the framers of the Basic Law attempted in a modest way to draw up a constitutional framework for West Germany that might help the people avoid past mistakes. The result of their labors was a constitution so cautious and conservative that one may hesitate to call it democratic. To be sure, the framers of the Basic Law had every intention of laying the foundation of a stable democracy. But how could they trust the masses of people who had so willingly flocked to Hitler and supported his regime to the bitter end?

They decided, therefore, to establish a framework of governmental institutions which would limit popular participation in government to voting for the federal legislature and which would arm future democratic governments against the possible resurgence of subversive movements on the right or the left. To achieve these purposes, they first established a strong executive. They made it more difficult for the federal parliament, the *Bundestag,* to overthrow the Chancellor (premier) than in such countries with parliamentary governments as France and England. Instead of a simple vote of no-confidence, the

Basic Law requires the opposition in the *Bundestag* to elect a successor to the incumbent Chancellor before it can vote him out of office. By this device, the framers hoped to reduce to manageable proportions the turnover of governments and to forestall the kind of crisis that existed in the last days of the Weimar Republic, when Nazis and Communists joined forces to paralyze the government. Little could they know that in the strong hands of Chancellor Adenauer, democracy in the Federal Republic would fall so much under the sway of the chief executive that it would become known as "Chancellor Democracy." Secondly, the framers of the Basic Law favored the time-honored checks and balances of federalism. German federalism not only divides power between the federal government and the states, which since World War I have been called *Laender*. But, unlike American federalism, it allows state governments a strong voice in national affairs through the federal council, the *Bundesrat,* in which their representatives can pass upon federal legislation, the budget, and the federal administration. The *Laender* governments thereby exercise a potent check upon the federal government. The third and perhaps most significant feature of the new West German Constitution was the creation of the Federal Constitutional Court as a powerful guardian of the constitutional liberties of the Federal Republic. This court has, among other things, formidable powers to enforce civil rights, strip subversive agitators of their constitutional rights, and to outlaw political parties and organizations hostile to democratic government. During the first decade of its life, as a matter of fact, the Federal Constitutional Court outlawed a neo-fascist movement, the Socialist *Reich* Party (SRP), and the Communist Party, while exercising wise self-restraint in regard to isolated crackpot groups or juveniles who smeared swastikas on the walls of synagogues.

When the West German constitution-makers had finished their Basic Law, there were some critics who voiced dismay: this Constitution, they claimed, is oriented exclusively toward the past. Instead of looking ahead to a brighter future, it is preoccupied with past problems and dilemmas which are rather unlikely to repeat themselves in quite the same way. But when viewed today with the benefit of hindsight, there can be little doubt that the framers of the Basic Law were most successful in creating a framework of stability within which a democratic body politic could slowly mature.

This orientation toward the undigested past has also been the distinguishing mark of Chancellor Adenauer's policy. Toward the beginning of his post-war career, he was overheard to say to a British journalist: "My God, what will become of Germany when I am no longer here!" And he went on to explain that he still harbored fears of a return of aggressive nationalistic forces in Germany which might once

Deutschland, Deutschland ueber alles!

more take the country down the road to war and disaster. He considered it his foremost task, therefore, to commit the West German Republic so thoroughly to the West, and so entangle its army in the North Atlantic Treaty Organization and its economy and government in a United Europe, that his successors would lack the opportunity to make the same mistakes again. Adenauer's policy may not have been very flattering to the judgment of his successors, but it bore spectacular fruit. Today, West Germany is the only NATO member to have put all her armed forces directly under NATO command. Her coal and steel production, once a crucial element in Germany's capacity to wage aggressive war, has been under the control of the European

Coal and Steel Community for more than a decade. The rest of the resurgent economic strength of the country is coming increasingly under the control of the Common Market. The day may be near when a political union will flower from this Common Market, and a federal government run by Frenchmen, Italians, and, perhaps, Englishmen as well as Germans will have power over the policies of Western Germany. When that day arrives, and to a large extent even today, that Old Man in Bonn will have triumphed over the ghosts of the undigested past. They will finally be buried, never to rise again.

Many Americans, too, feel the shadows of an undigested past with regard to Germany, a feeling which a Washington columnist recently characterized as the "strange times" of today when one could see President Kennedy embracing the Germans on the television news show, while on the late show we were still shooting them. Twice within living memory the United States has been at war with a Germany that rebelled against the whole Western and democratic tradition we stand for. Many Americans bore arms in those wars and remember all too well the bitter hostility when the antagonists shoot to kill each other. Many also remain influenced by the vast amount of war propaganda put forth in both wars. Others painfully experienced a conflict of loyalties: they would much rather not have been involved in these wars at all or may even have found themselves accused of disloyalty or lack of patriotic zeal. Today, most of the Germans the Americans once fought are in the West German Republic, which is supposed to be one of America's most important allies in the Cold War. Marshall Plan aid raised Germany from ashes and ruin. American foreign policy caused the Germans to be rearmed and supported their integration into the Western alliance.

All this is much food for thought, much of the past that still needs to be digested. Americans want to know how to account for Germany's behavior in the past. They are entitled to as much information as possible about the new Germany: Have the Germans really changed? How does the present regime differ from the Germany of the past? What about the alleged resurgence of Nazism, militarism, and anti-semitism in Western Germany? What about the Communist claims that it is only West German revanchism and belligerence which prevent the Cold War from thawing and produce recurrent

crises over Berlin and over German rearmament? From the stand-
point of Soviet foreign policy, both toward Eastern Europe and
toward the West, Western Germany offers a convenient scapegoat.
By reminding the Eastern Europeans and their erstwhile Western Allies of German actions and policies in World War Two, the Soviets
can skillfully reactivate everyone's undigested past and project it onto

Taking the foreign aid collection: "No buttons, please!"

an external "enemy," and in the process they can unite their own bloc
and drive wedges between members of NATO.

In recent years American public opinion toward Germany has increasingly tended to split into diametrically opposed camps. On one
side stand the numerous groups and persons genuinely interested in a
relaxation of world tensions and a thawing of Cold War hostility, particularly between the Soviet Union and the United States. This idea
has great merit, but the Soviets have so far refused, for reasons of

their own, to support in any significant way * the countless attempts
at disarmament and the re-establishment of peace. In their frustration, advocates of an understanding with Russia have blamed their
own government for the failure of these attempts, and occasionally
government officials advocating a hard-line policy have confirmed
their suspicion. Since these peace-seekers had to grant a certain
amount of good will and reasonable judgment to their own representatives, they turned instead to Western Germany as the villain of
the Cold War. The Federal Republic appeared to be the most likely
culprit, both because of its recent history and its geographical location, and because Russian propaganda pointed an accusing finger at
Bonn. One spokesman for this point of view even prefaced his book
about peace and the German problem with questions from his nine-
year-old son, reflecting the boy's confusion about which side America
has been on in World War Two and in the Cold War, the Russian or
the German side. Such false alternatives, of course, contribute little to
the understanding of the complex problems at hand, quite apart from
the danger of confusing the undigested past with undigested pablum.
Yet it is a sad commentary on the poverty of international understanding in those who profess it most, if they can extend it to one nation only by taking it away from another nation.

On the other hand, there are numerous groups and publications on
the right and even the far right who in recent years have clasped Western Germany, West Berlin, and the Adenauer administration to their
bosom and rise to their defense on the most unlikely occasions. The
two otherwise opposed camps hold a dismaying consensus about the
nature of the new Germany. Both appear to agree that the new Germany is dominated by old nationalistic reactionaries and more or less
unreconstructed Nazis. Right-wingers rejoice at this assumption,
which endears Adenauer's Germany to them. With friends like this
the Germans hardly need enemies. And the left wing is likewise glad
to look at it from this perspective, since it makes it so much easier for
them to understand why the Cold War has not yet dissolved in sweet
reasonableness. Both camps choose to ignore the democratic West
Germany which was actually resurrected and set on its way in 1949

---

* With the exception of the recent ban of nuclear tests above ground, which
in itself is no more than a first small step. Only time will tell whether there
are going to be further steps in this direction, much as we should like to see
them.

under the tutelage of the Western Allies, notably the Americans, and rearmed only at the insistence of the Western Allies, again most notably the Americans. This situation would seem to have the makings of the same tragic dilemma faced by the first German parliamentary democracy, the luckless Weimar Republic, whose democratic leaders were frequently humiliated by the Western democracies, only to discover later that the Western democracies fawningly gave to Hitler what they had grudgingly denied a democratic Germany. Fortunately, as we shall see, the new democratic Germany of today has much firmer foundations and fewer enemies within than did the Weimar Republic.

To the extent that understanding may be capable of helping Germans to master their "undigested past," and of vicariously aiding anyone else who feels involved in that past, this book is an attempt to throw more light on the chief issues at stake. To this end it will first present an informal discussion among proponents of various points of view regarding German national character from about 1850 to 1945 in order to unravel some of the extraordinary complexities of the German problem from the beginning. Those taking part are Kurt, a young German Social Democrat; Kenneth, a British Conservative intellectual; Jochen, a young German Christian Democrat; and Bernie, an American civic leader of liberal persuasion. Their characterization is, of course, quite subjective since there is no such thing as a typical German Social Democrat, a typical American liberal, indeed a typical anything. But it is hoped that such discussion will help to define the welter of arguments and points of view on German affairs about which no final answer is possible without gross distortion. Then will follow a similar discussion of the causes of the fall of the Weimar Republic and of the rise of Hitler. This second discussion has been deliberately separated from the first in order to avoid the misleading impression of historical causality or teleology from Wotan to Hitler which so many books about Germany create. After this comes a monologue about the economic and social transformations that have taken place in the Federal Republic under Adenauer. Then, the discussion will resume and deal with such subjects as the ex-Nazis, neofascism, anti-semitism, and militarism today, and will touch on the problems of disengagement, reunification, Berlin, and a United Europe. Finally, the political developments and forces of post-war Germany will be considered in some detail and some conclusion drawn about the outlook for post-Adenauer Germany.

The purpose of mastering the undigested past is to prepare for a better future. It is not a panacea for all the conceivable and inconceivable problems that this future may present. But it should prevent people from committing the same errors and making the same mistakes over again, either because they never quite understood why their assumptions were wrong in the first place, or because they react with a willingness to add new wrongs to the wrongs already suffered.

"The extent to which people act with a clear idea of their ends, knowing what effects they are aiming at, is easily exaggerated . . . to a very great extent people do not know what they are doing until they have done it, if then."

R. G. Collingwood, *The Idea of History*

"Great economic and social forces flow like a tide over half-conscious people. The wise are those who foresee the coming event and seek to shape their institutions and mold the thinking of the people in accordance with the most constructive change. The unwise are those who add nothing constructive to the process, either because of ignorance on the one hand or ignorant opposition on the other."

John Stuart Mill

1

THE GERMANS IN HISTORY

The little *Bierstube* near the railroad station in Munich was almost empty as the three men sat down at a heavy oak table near the window. In a far corner, under the mounted antlers and pictures of hunting parties, sat a group of men talking loudly and laughing as one of them attempted to stop the giggling waitress from leaving their corner. Outside, streetcars came and went, spewing out and then swallowing crowds of people on their way home from work, wearing raincoats and with the inevitable briefcase in hand, their faces set with a sense of purpose from a day of work well done.

One of the three men, bald with a fringe of white hair and quick brown eyes under bushy eyebrows, looked out the window and said: "Look at them: Germans at work. That's when they are really happy. Or Germans at play." He inclined his head in the direction of the far corner where the chubby waitress had finally broken away amid raucous laughter. "*Arbeit* and *Gaudi,* why can't they just stick to that. They are lovable that way."

The person sitting closest to the window, an older man in tweeds with greyish-brown hair and a pipe, chuckled and added: "I have been in and out of this country now for more than forty years. Every time I come to Germany, I am struck anew by the many surface similarities between what people do here and the way many of my countrymen in England talk, act, and live. This whole social atmosphere seems so familiar. You don't find this in France or in other Latin countries. I bet this is the reason why many American GI's think they like it here. Don't you think so too, Bernie?"

The bald man laughed with an undertone of derision and said: "Yes. It's like meeting your good-looking girl cousin for the first time and being taken in by the family resemblance. And then you find out the old girl's got a mean disposition."

The door opened and a young man with tousled blond hair appeared. He was greeted with a handshake by the youngest of the three, a very properly dressed dark-haired young fellow with glasses, who turned to introduce the newcomer: "This is Joachim Kahler. Jochen is a journalist connected with the trade unions. He has just come back from a conference tour in America. And this," he pointed to the bald man, "is Bernie Neisser, a politician from America."

Bernie laughed and protested: "Having been in the United States, Kurt, you ought to know better than to call me a politician. That's an insult. Call me a statesman, or a civic leader, or an organizer of enlightened causes, or something!"

Kurt went on to introduce the Englishman. "And this is Professor Kenneth Stearn who teaches German literature at a British university." Stearn shook hands with Jochen and proposed: "Since all of us seem to have spent some time in America — Kurt as an exchange student, Jochen on a conference tour, I myself on a research assignment, and Bernie from birth — why don't we just call each other by our first names? Jochen, Kurt, Bernie, Kenneth: what do you say, *Herr Doktor* Kurt Jaeger?"

Kurt blushed and nodded. Jochen turned to him and said in a low voice: "Don't you teach at the university here?" Kurt's embarrassment grew and he quickly replied: "I am only a teaching assistant in psychology." Then he turned to Bernie and asked: "Well, now, you were going to tell us all about why the Germans have always behaved like Germans, weren't you?"

Bernie said, "Well," and took out a piece of paper and his ballpoint pen, visibly trying to collect his thoughts. But before he could begin, Jochen had started to speak: "I hope this isn't going to be the usual list of charges such as the one that the Germans invaded France three times in seventy-five years."

Bernie gave him a startled look. "They did, didn't they? What's wrong with this charge?"

Jochen replied amiably: "It is a typical example of how nationalistic historians of any nation can distort history. This particular statement cuts off history at a very convenient point. If you went back farther, you would get to where Napoleon occupied the German states, and still farther, where Louis XIV had his generals invade the Palatinate, take away Alsace, and burn down Heidelberg." Bernie did not reply and Jochen went on. "I also hope that you won't come up with the stereotype account of intellectual predecessors and antecedents 'from Luther to Hitler.' "

Bernie raised one of his dark, bushy eyebrows like a *circonflex:* "What about Luther's authoritarianism and what about Frederick II of Prussia, and what about Hegel's cult of the state? Weren't these men typical of the Nazi approach? Weren't they figures of tremendous influence among generations of Germans? Can you deny that their thought represented the first stirring of that spirit that gave birth to National Socialism?"

The waitress brought glasses of dark beer for everyone at the table and set them on flat papier-mâché coasters, embossed with the insignia of the brewery. Kurt began to play with his coaster, turning it over and over between two fingers. Finally, he blurted out: "This pedigree-hunting has always bothered me. It's like a gentlemanly sport in the United States, like a fox hunt, and the fox is well marked ahead of time and hasn't got a chance of escape. You pick out a few writers and statesmen from the broad panorama of German history, carefully avoiding, of course, those who do not fit your pet theory."

"Oh, come now," interrupted Bernie. Kurt turned to him and asked: "Why don't you ever mention Leibniz, Lessing, Goethe, Schiller, the Humboldts, Rotteck, Welcker, Bebel, and the many other names that stand for the best Germany has produced?"

Bernie did not answer and Kurt continued: "You take these men out of their historical context so that people won't realize that in Luther's day, everybody was authoritarian, including, for example, Calvin or, for that matter, the Catholic Church. Or that the task of starting a reformation in such chaotic times required Luther's reliance on friendly princes and his violent rejection of the lunatic fringe that used his noble call for reform as an excuse for license and outrages. If Lutheranism is such a bad influence, then what about the Scandinavians and the American Lutherans?"

"He has a point, Bernie," Kenneth intervened. "In spite of its emphasis on faith rather than good works, Lutheran Protestantism had, perhaps, even more potential for liberal developments than Calvinism. Calvinism became allied with self-government and democracy thanks to the favorable setting, namely a strong, independent bourgeoisie rebelling against royal power and the established church. Such an independent bourgeoisie was never really strong in Germany, partly because of the terrible devastations of the Thirty Years' War (1618–48) and the suffocating *Kleinstaaterei,* the petty territorial states with their oppressive feudal autocracies. It was the petty princes and lords, and the authoritarian climate of their society, which stifled the progressive tendencies in German Lutheranism — not Luther's authoritarian tendencies that spoiled the people. In the nineteenth century, when the old society threatened to break up, even the Catholic princes followed suit in bottling up social progress with a union of throne and altar."

Bernie looked embarrassed and would have liked to rephrase his argument. But Kurt began again, somewhat stridently: "It is the same with some of the other charges. Why don't the pedigree-hunters preface their remarks with the statement that, for example, anti-semitism has been a widespread disease throughout medieval and modern Europe, or that Thomas Carlyle also was a hero worshipper and that Hegel's doctrines have significant parallels in the writings of such saints of the Western tradition as Edmund Burke and Jean-Jacques Rousseau. Rousseau's influence on Germany, for example, accounts for some of the anti-rational tendencies you often criticize. And how can you consider as typical a man such as Frederick II of Prussia, who considered himself a Frenchman ruling over barbarians and refused to speak German because he thought it a language fit for horses?"

"That is not quite to the point," Jochen interrupted Kurt and turned to Bernie. "You people always forget that during most of the eighteenth century almost no enlightened thinker seriously advocated democracy or thought that the illiterate and boorish lower classes could be entrusted with governmental power. The leading liberal doctrine of that day — regardless of what you may think of it now — was enlightened absolutism, rule by an all-powerful, but wise and benevolent king, just like Plato's philosopher-king in *The Republic*. And it was because Frederick II of Prussia and also Joseph II of Austria were regarded as the epitome of enlightened philosopher-kings that liberal Germans, Frenchmen, and many other European nations admired them. Napoleon even built a monument to the *roi philosophe*, Frederick. If later on German nationalists tried to build up a different image of Frederick as a military hero, well, that is another story."

"Well, so enlightened absolutism was the rage in the mid-eighteenth century," Bernie countered quickly. "But then there came the French and the American revolutions, not to mention John Locke and the English upheavals of the seventeenth century. Why didn't any of this movement for human rights and free government leave a mark on Germany?"

Jochen thought for a while, then he replied: "During the English revolutions, I am afraid, Germans showed no response at all. Maybe this was because of the terrible devastation of the Thirty Years' War when half the population died and many towns burned down. While the English people made great strides in every respect in those days, Germany was just about going to the dogs. And the French Revolution? Well, there was some initial enthusiasm from many German thinkers, at least until the reign of terror began. But then when Napoleon came here to serve up the French Rights of Man with the tips of the bayonets of his armies, the sentiment turned. And most of the old enthusiasts of the French Revolution became its most scornful enemies, rejecting everything even remotely connected with it. Not unlike many pre-war admirers of Hitler in England, France, or the United States who would rather reject everything German today than admit they once made the same error of judgment as many Germans." He looked around defiantly, but none of his interlocutors raised any objection. Finally, he continued in a resigned voice: "After Napoleon was defeated, of course, there was a good deal of popular agitation for constitutions, parliaments, and bills of rights. In the small and medium-sized states it was quite successful. Only in Prussia and Austria, where government had long ceased being enlightened or benevolent, did the old forces of autocracy keep the upper hand. And then, of course, Prussia took over all the other German states save Austria."

"If I understand you right, Jochen," said Bernie, "then your ideal of enlightened absolutism corresponds to what some people have called the German idea of freedom, namely that the individual citizen enjoys the highest form of freedom by surrendering his own will to a supremely moral and rational state. And this state, to qualify as the equivalent of a philosopher-king republic, has to be run by a highly efficient bureaucracy of simon-pure ethics. Well, I admit that such a bureaucracy may be a good thing in this age of Big Government. But that it should be regarded as all-wise and that it should be given an all-powerful position — no, I cannot accept that. Never mind Plato. I have always distrusted that man."

"Don't call it *my* ideal," protested Jochen. "All this lies generations behind us. We have had too many irrational and even immoral governments to set our trust in philosopher-kings. And, this so-called 'German idea of freedom' you can also find in a slightly different form in Burke and Rousseau, as Kurt pointed out before."

Kurt was quick to take up the cue. "I grant you that this idea of freedom was in large part a rationalization by a handful of intellectuals of our failure to gain control over our own government. Maybe this is one of our big national vices, stubbornly to rationalize our shortcomings until they look like great virtues. This idea of freedom, of course, also plays a role in legal philosophy. But on the level of broad popular sentiments, I believe, we tend to identify it quite erroneously with the ingrained sense of moral duty of the typical nineteenth-century German. Well, this sense of moral obligation, or inner-directedness, if you will, you can find among the older generation almost everywhere, and especially in America. But this sense of duty cannot explain away Nazism for us which arose precisely from the disintegration of old-fashioned moral scruples. This is the reason why the whole attempt to search for intellectual precursors of fascism completely misses the nature of a fascist movement whose desperadoes and agitators surely do not get their motivation from poring over Hegel's abstrusities or even less from studying their Lutheran catechism. Jochen, you know your labor union members. The working class is about one half of the German population. What percentage of them, do you suppose, reads Hegel or Nietzsche? How many understand their writings?"

Jochen shook his head: "Very, very few, I am sure, though not for lack of trying. Most blue-collar workers and even white-collar employees lack the formal education to receive and be influenced by such complicated intellectual messages, even those few who are yearning for art and culture. The pedigree-hunters are really using a Hegelian method of analysis, here, trying to reduce the complexities of social movements to crude sketches of the development of an idea."

Kurt looked at him in surprise, as if he wanted to say "and where did you learn so much about Hegel." There was a brief silence, then Bernie said mildly: "You may have a point there. But you are aware, I am sure, of the vast literature by Nazis, Nazi sympathizers, or the proponents of 'conservative revolution' in the 1920's which has linked the familiar doctrines of the *Fuehrer* cult and racial superiority with exactly these figures in German history."

Kurt nodded approvingly and added: "This is not only true of much of the German literature of the 1920's and 1930's but even long before. Ever since the Germanies tried to become a nation-state in 1848, self-appointed German nationalists and historians with an uncontrollable urge to find more grist for their mills have reinterpreted and simplified German and European history. They scoured the misty origins of the early Germans in search of the spirit of their *Volk*. They romanticized and falsified the Middle Ages. They brutalized and idealized historical figures in order to make national heroes out of them, making their human shortcomings into shining virtues and the narrowness of their place and time in history into a national symbol. But just because Richard Wagner and some Nazis claim, for example, that Germans are anti-semitic by nature, that doesn't make it true, does it?"

Kenneth, who had listened all this time, quietly sucking his pipe, interrupted him: "All nations create their own folklore and early history as soon as they have emerged from the cultural shell of the traditional past. Think of the French historians of the nineteenth century and their Celtomania, trying to make out the roots of French national history long before the Gauls of Caesar's day. Or of George Washington and the cherry tree. These things are all pure invention for the sake of giving the people of a country a patriotic education."

Kurt looked dismayed: "Maybe so. But then, the story of George Washington is only a harmless fib which makes the man more human and understandable to young people. There is a difference between exhorting a child never to tell a lie and telling him to emulate barbaric Nordic warriors, isn't there? So much of our political literature of the last ninety years has been deliberately wrongheaded and perverse."

Now it was Bernie's turn to be surprised by the sudden agreement in which he found himself with Kurt: "Now we are getting some place. For a while you two had me thinking you were unreconstructed Nazis."

Kenneth chuckled without taking the pipe out of his mouth: "Didn't you notice how Jochen was putting the arguments into your mouth, setting you up as a strawman only to knock you down? You fell into a well-baited trap." He paused. "But it serves you right for trying to defend the stereotypes of war-time pamphleteering on the Allied side."

Kurt broke in to say: "You can't really blame him for repeating these charges. They were all taken from these wrongheaded reinterpretations of German history made by Germans."

"Yes, yes," Kenneth brushed aside the interruption, "but if we really want to come to grips with the causes and circumstances that drove the Germans into the arms of Hitler, we have to forget about the blanket indictments written in the wrath of two world wars. We must be far more specific and beware of such easy shortcuts as identifying the German masses with the morbid rationalizations of a handful of nationalistic intellectuals. Why don't you try to develop your theme of national character on the basis of the people at large, Bernie, rather than of books and writers read by only a small stratum of the population? We don't even know to what extent those who read them were converted by them. This Hegelian flimflam of understanding a people by the books that some of them write is really too crude."

Jochen had already finished his beer while everyone else's glass was still half-full. He ordered another beer and turned to Kenneth: "This concept of national character has long been shot full of holes by sociologists. It is just one of those big words that anyone can fill with laudatory or polemical verbiage as the spirit moves him. Besides, you cannot possibly speak of a German nation in the days of Luther or of Frederick II of Prussia. It just did not exist. There were the Germanies, German-speaking provinces and states which included at one time, for example, the Netherlands, the German part of Switzerland, Alsace, and German Austria along with Hungary and Czechoslovakia. This whole complex of territories was almost as diverse and separated from one another by state sovereignty, different cultures, and different dynastic policies as Germany and France are today. To attribute a common national character to all these territorial populations is a misinterpretation of history. It would force you to explain, for example, why Switzerland and Holland did not develop a native National Socialism to the same degree as the Germans. Even after the foundation of a German nation-state in 1871, there were still great regional variations between, say, East Elbian Prussia and the Catholic Rhineland or the liberal South which make it difficult to describe this so-called national character in terms specific enough to derive Nazism from it."

He paused to take a deep draft from his beer, as Kenneth cast a wry glance at him and said: "I think it's true that national character is a very elusive concept which can easily be abused for some Hegelian type of analysis of the soul or spirit of the *Volk*. It's also true that it can change very rapidly. Just think of the French reversal of attitude from the belligerence of 1914 to the mutinies of 1917. Or Voltaire's statement early in the eighteenth century, contrasting his stolid, conservative Frenchmen with those radical Englishmen who staged revolutions, beheaded their king, and undertook to reconstruct society and government on principles of natural law. Less than seventy years later, the roles were reversed and Edmund Burke made exactly the opposite comparison between his British countrymen and the French revolutionaries." He took out some pipe tobacco and began stuffing his pipe. "However, this is no reason why we can't look at the motives and conditions of the people inside Germany within the borders of, say, 1919 during a particular period, say, from 1871 to 1933. If we do this conscientiously, we ought to be able to understand the reasons for the triumph of the Nazis."

"By conscientiously," Kurt interjected with an air of importance,

"I take it, you mean that we should start out with a balanced analysis of what things were like in the years from Bismarck to the fall of the Weimar Republic. And only then will we look for the immediate causes of Hitler's triumph and for the extent to which the German background may have led in a straight line and with causal necessity to National Socialism. Most interpretations of the Hitler era with an air of scientific causality put the effect before the cause. They start out with the takeover of the Nazis and then quickly beat the preceding German history into shape until it can be completely identified with carefully selected and tremendously magnified 'causes' or manifestations of German national character. Then they crow to the world that the causal nexus has been undeniably established and that National Socialism is nothing but the most complete expression of that horrible German national character they have just derived from Nazism with the benefit of hindsight. I think a balanced interpretation of the period from 1871 to 1933 can be made only if we postpone all references to Hitler's triumph until later.

Bernie had been busy writing key words on his piece of paper in order to organize his attack. He conceded: "That seems a fair enough request which should help us to avoid prejudging the issue of whether German history runs in a straight line with utter logic from Bismarck to Hitler, as a number of writers are claiming currently.

"Now, let's get started on specifics about the condition of the German people in that pre-Hitler era. Is it not true that the Germans in those days were militaristically inclined to a very high degree? I am thinking, for example, of the delightful story of the Captain of Koepenick, the ex-convict who learned the military commands in jail and then used this knowledge and an old uniform to call out the guard, arrest the mayor of Koepenick, and abscond with the city treasury. I can hardly think of a better demonstration of how the general reverence toward the military way of life penetrated the whole German society before World War I."

Jochen kept his eyes lowered as he replied: "This charge is true enough, I guess. Let me explain it this way: When the attempt of the Frankfurt Parliament of 1848 to unify the German states on the basis of a liberal, Western-style constitution collapsed, there was tremendous disillusionment with the whole Western approach of reason and persuasion. Then Bismarck used the military might of Prussia to engineer the wars of unification, including the one against Austria and the southern states, and then the common war against France. In the excitement of national unification, I guess, the aroused patriotism became almost synonymous with the Prussian military tradition."

Kurt added: "Prussia was dominated by the aristocracy which had one of its strongest positions in its monopoly over the officer corps. With the victory of Bismarck's policy of 'blood and iron,' the aristocracy won complete ascendancy again over the bourgeoisie; and its feudal and military outlook was widely imitated."

"Except by the Catholics, you might add," Jochen interrupted him impatiently. "And they were a pretty significant minority in opposition to the policies of Bismarck and the Prussian king, I mean the *Kaiser,* and to their nationalistic and militaristic cohorts."

"Well, for that matter, the trade unions and the Social Democrats didn't go militaristic either," Kurt protested. "And by 1912, the Social Democratic Party was the largest of the parties in the *Reichstag.*"

Bernie had followed this exchange with great interest: "Didn't you tell us, Kurt, that Jochen had connections with the trade unions?"

"Yes, the Christian trade unions," Kurt replied with an undertone of malice. Jochen gave him a sidelong glance and said in a low voice: "And you're a Social Democratic egghead?"

Kurt ignored him and turned to Bernie: "You see, the failure of liberal democracy in pre-Hitler Germany can be described from beginning to end as the failure of the bourgeoisie to accomplish what the classical bourgeoisie did in England and France, namely to push aside the feudal aristocracy and to establish a constitution and parliamentary government. The liberal revolutionaries of 1848 failed because they could not agree on what they wanted. The left-wing Liberals were waiting for the street mobs to help them and the right-wing Liberals preferred to call in the forces of reaction than to come to a compromise with their more democratically-minded confreres. That was the crucial point and from that moment on the reactionary aristocracy stepped in and called all the shots."

Bernie bent forward: "And then about a million Germans had to emigrate, most of them to the United States, in order to escape harassment and repression, right?"

Kurt nodded with a frown: "Yes, that was the vent that let off the revolutionary pressure, and they left their own country in the lurch."

"Well, now," Bernie said, "don't be so severe. My granddad was a *Revoluzzer* of 1848 who came to the States just ahead of political imprisonment. You can't blame a man for saying 'to hell with my country, if my countrymen are so benighted that they don't want to live in freedom.' So you think that this forced emigration drained off the politically most active part of the bourgeoisie and thereby left only unpolitical duds and those who accommodated themselves to the return of the feudal aristocracy?"

Kurt nodded eagerly and said: "Have you ever noticed that in German, in contrast to English, the word 'feudal' is a word of approbation? Everybody here likes the thought of living in a 'feudal' or 'feudally furnished' home while everywhere in the Western liberal democracies 'feudalism' is considered a dirty word. This desire to live like an aristocrat in riding boots, lording it over inferiors has been deeply rooted in the minds of so many middle-class people since that day that it is no wonder they flocked to the Pied Piper and his Master Race. Every man a feudal lord!"

Kenneth had allowed his pipe to go out while listening to Kurt and Jochen. Now he said: "You yourself insisted that we should leave out Hitler for the time being." He lit his pipe again, and dropped the burnt match in the ash-tray. "What about German Liberals after the debacle of 1848? You aren't saying that the liberal movement completely disappeared, or are you? They put up a pretty good fight in the Prussian diet in the 1860's. And there was strong opposition to Bismarck among the left-wing Liberals, the *Freisinn* and the Progressives, not only on the part of Catholics and Socialists."

"Well, yes. But the right-wing Liberals were largely identified with the Bismarckian national state and later with the imperialistic expansionism of military figures, Naval Leaguers, and Pan-Germans. Even their great industrial build-up never made them an independent middle-class force, because they were always leaning on the nobility and on the state bureaucracy."

Kenneth still looked doubtful: "I think you have to take into account the great odds against which the German bourgeoisie had to struggle in contrast to France and England, where the monarchy had long ago done the job of national unification for them. In nineteenth-century Germany the old aristocracy was particularly strengthened by the survival of many of their feudal bailiwicks as quasi-sovereign states. I rather doubt that the Frankfurt Parliament would have succeeded against the particularism of the German states even if the framers of the Frankfurt constitution had not been bickering for so long over the bill of rights. Their failure at Frankfurt gave German Liberals a clear choice between national unity and constitutional liberty. Under the circumstances I am reluctant to condemn them for having chosen the former. They had very little choice. This triumph of a liberal bourgeoisie over the old order is not as easy as you make it sound. Just think how long the French with a far stronger bourgeoisie took from the Great Revolution of 1789 to 1875 when republicanism finally won out over monarchism. Or think of the long road from our Glorious Revolution of 1688 to the electoral reform of 1832 or the repeal of the Corn Laws in 1846. And your impatient Liberals expected to defeat far greater odds in one year or two. You people give up far too easily." He sucked on his pipe to keep it from going out again. "Of course, German Liberals in the Bismarckian Empire also had an additional handicap that had not occurred in the West until Englishmen and Frenchmen had pretty well accomplished politically what they wanted. By the 1870's liberalism everywhere had split into at least two hostile wings, such as the German National Liberals and the Progressives. There are fitting parallels in England and France for the antics of your National Liberals and assorted imperialists. Think of the Social Darwinists in America, or the KKK, or the Spanish-American war. Or Joseph Chamberlain and social imperialism in England, the cult of the Empire, and the White Man's Burden. Or think of the Dreyfus affair in France, or of the *Action Française,* or the *Camelots du roi.* Why, those Frenchmen were actually ahead of the Germans in producing authentic fascists. I really think too much has been made of the particular perversity of pre-Hitler Germany." He puffed again. "But I digress. What about the Liberals of the Weimar Republic? Didn't they co-operate with the Social Democrats and the Catholic Center Party in establishing what was meant to be a model of liberal democracy?"

Kurt conceded that this was so. "But that was true only of the left-wing Liberals, the Democratic Party (DDP) of the Weimar Republic. The other wing was hostile to the Republic from the beginning." He made a deprecatory gesture with his hand. "It was just as if all the bourgeois parties were sticking together against the Social Democrats and the liberal democracy they associated, of all things, with the labor movement. Organized labor, in fact, was the only reliably democratic force in Weimar Germany. Already before and during the First World War the poison of annexationism ate its way into the minds of some left-wing Liberals. Even Matthias Erzberger, the leader of the Catholic Center Party, was on record as an annexationist according to recent research." He threw a significant glance in the direction of Jochen, who chose not to contest the point. Instead, he ordered another beer. Kurt went on: "Parts of the grand bourgeoisie, as you know, actually gave their money to Hitler, and if you examine carefully the election statistics of the Nazi landslide of the early 1930's, you will find that the voters who had previously supported both left- and right-wing Liberals defected *en masse* to the Nazis. Small wonder that one of the first Nazi actions was the outlawing of the Communist and Social Democratic Parties, and the dissolution of the free trade unions."

By that time Jochen had regained his speech and seized the opportunity to take the floor: "Much of what you said about the spread of Prussian militarism and the moral failure of the bourgeoisie in selling out to nationalism and Social Darwinism may be true. But I still feel that you are barking up the wrong tree. The moral decline of the bourgeoisie, nationalism, the worship of national power, technology, and military might, these are all but aspects of the fateful process of the secularization of public life which replaced God with public idols and threw away all social ethics in exchange for moral relativism and grasping materialism. How else, do you suppose, did we get from the image of moral man of, say, St. Thomas Aquinas to the biological idea of nationality and race? Or from St. Augustine's spiritual purpose of civic life to aggressive imperialism against weaker nations? And Karl Marx with his call for class-consciousness and his economic determinism, along with all his Communist and Socialist disciples, is certainly a key figure in the process of secularization."

Kurt was all set to give him a similarly heated answer when Bernie hastened to intervene: "I think both of you have a point. If Jochen means his indictment of secularization as a clarion call for a return to the Middle Ages, I am all with you, Kurt, in regarding this as just another sterile issue which can only lead to reactionary political results. But at the same time, the talk about the dangers raised by secularization represents a sound piece of sociological analysis, once you grant that this secularization has already largely taken place and can never be undone." He looked at Jochen, who winced in dismay, and continued quickly: "By secularization in the sociological sense I mean the process of modernization by which traditional cultures began to break down in many Western countries and, for that matter, throughout the non-Western world today."

"What do you mean, they broke down?" Jochen interjected. "What culture broke down in Germany?"

"Well, call it whatever you wish," replied Bernie. "In art and architecture, I guess they call its last form the baroque. In society, it was the hierarchic structure, the different estates, the high clergy, the aristocracy of many tiers, the bourgeoisie divided into many callings, and the peasants. In politics, it was the sacred monarchy and the universal empire, or *Reich*. In philosophy, it was a unitary world view with theological overtones. All this had lasted for hundreds of years. It was sanctified by religion, enforced by political authority, and accepted by everybody without much thinking as traditional cultures always are. Everyone quietly accepts his role in them for they seem to give a sense of purpose and meaning to his life, no matter how low his station or how arduous his calling. Then all of a sudden, perhaps as a result of violent changes or experiences, this sense of meaning begins to break down in some people and they begin to question things and to strive for a better niche for themselves in society. That's how you get the *nuovi uomini* of the Italian Renaissance, the condottieri and artists, the new men of science, the early captains of industry and the industrial proletariat, or the imperialists of the late nineteenth century. In most countries, I suppose, this cultural decay is slow enough not to frighten people too much and not to produce too many of the rootless new men at once. Now in England and France this decay had gone on for a long time, even before the great revolutionary upheavals occurred. Still, the civil wars and revolutions were tremendously upsetting and produced extremely violent and irrational reactions by drawing further numbers of people into the experience of the cultural breakdown. Great wars and, in particular, the industrial revolution have been major factors in making secularization a mass experience."

"But the breakdown of this traditional culture in Germany did occur gradually, too," Kurt interjected. "The baroque turned into rococo and then Biedermeier, and unitary philosophy into German idealism. And then there was the rise of cultural and literary nationalism."

"Well, yes," Bernie defended his thesis, "some of the cultural change went on gradually and without producing acute anomie and despair among the masses of people. But consider, for example, the enormous changes since 1810 when Madame de Staël, in her book *De l'Allemagne,* described the Germans as the impractical people of poets and thinkers, or the descriptions of Germany in 1800: overwhelmingly rural, even the towns preoccupied with agriculture and forestry, with unpaved streets and very poor transportation, all this of course no different from other European countries except for the headstart of England and France. Then the rural idylls began to be disturbed by early industrialization in the Rhineland, in Westphalia, and in Saxony, accompanied by the impressive rise of scientific research and technology. Finally, and after political unification cleared the path, the great push of full industrialization occurred within a single generation, from about 1880 to 1910. No other country, except perhaps the United States and the Soviet Union, went through this transformation at such a dizzy pace. Such a great push demands its toll in human happiness. Just consider urbanization. In 1800 there were only two German cities with more than 100,000 inhabitants — Berlin and Hamburg — in 1870 eight, in 1910 forty-eight and in 1939 sixty-two. During the peak generation between 1880 and 1910 this meant the uprooting of millions of Germans from the rural life of countryside and small towns, endless migrations to the big cities and industrial centers, and initiation into an entirely new world of struggle for existence, slum living, and a breakdown of the old customs and mores of the rural society. This was the time when masses of people experienced most dramatically the many regional dialects of Germany, the different folkways, the unflattering stereotypes of Hessians, Swabians, Silesians, and what not, the frictions between regional groups and the first big stirring of projected images of love and hate. When members of a regional group of new city-dwellers found themselves discriminated against or made fun of, they probably said, in their own defense, that they were Germans and just as good as the Germans of any other regional origin. And as an afterthought, they probably added, 'if you must hate someone, why don't you pick on the aliens, or on foreign nations, or on the Jews.' So this is, perhaps, how the urban masses become nationalistic and may even have developed some of their xenophobia and anti-semitism.

"And as for the growing materialism, I suppose, the breakdown of the village mores also includes religious observances. German peasants are a pretty materialistic lot, anyway. Once the migrants to the city find out that the god of their fathers does nothing to protect them from starving, from unemployment and exploitation, from seeing their children go bad, their health suffer, their husbands drink and what not . . . once they experience that God does nothing and the Church, at least the Lutheran one, only promises salvation in the next world, they become bitter and disaffected. That's when they come to say, as in Brecht's *Threepenny Opera: Erst kommt das Fressen und dann erst die Moral* (First comes the grub, and only then morals)."

Jochen seized the fraction of a second during which Bernie had to draw breath to protest: "From the way you talk about secularization, one would think these people had lost only a mess of potage rather than their moral values and their belief in God."

Bernie shook his head: "No, no. These are false alternatives. The new generations which emerge after the breakdown of traditional culture are not necessarily without religion and moral values. As a matter of fact, the emancipated individual may have a much deeper personal sense of moral obligation and participate far more actively in religious worship than those in culture-bound societies do. But he does it because he wants to and not because he has been brought up not to question the cultural system he imbibed with his mother's milk."

Kurt had been listening with growing interest. He added with animation: "You talk like an American. Nothing impressed me more during my years as an exchange student in the United States than the vast amount of conscious and deliberate direction with which Americans take control of their own lives. The way you conduct your community affairs, your church life, and your politics, or the way marriage and child-raising problems are popularly discussed and incorporated into customs and mores! Why, this is social science and practical psychology in action, understood reasonably well by vast masses of the population! Your whole educational system is geared to equipping the emancipated individual with an understanding of himself and of the social relationships necessary for a full and happy life.

"In comparison to you, we Germans are such helpless clods, at least on a mass level where our social science just has not penetrated the fog of traditionalism and prejudices at all. The German population at large is quite unaware of Freudian and other types of everyday psychology. They are prone to forming cliques and in-groups and projecting their feelings of unworthiness upon some outsider or out-group simply because they never learned to understand these elementary psychological mechanisms at work. They give in to all kinds of abnormal psychological impulses without even realizing how cruel they are being to others."

"You mean, when a people leaves the traditional mold, bad habits of prejudice, negative projection, and discrimination develop as a matter of course, unless militant advocates of tolerance go to work to civilize these new savages?" Bernie asked with raised eyebrows.

"Exactly," came the reply. "Many people have wondered how such a highly developed educational system as that of Germany could produce barbarians like the many mass murderers with doctorates in Hitler's genocidal apparatus, or the countless cynical opportunists among German scientists, top-echelon bureaucrats, judges, and officers who sold their souls to Hitler for a little promotion when they should have known better. The reason is simply that German schools have naïvely trained the mind, while leaving moral character to the corruptions of maladjustment in a changed world. Ignazio Silone in *Bread and Wine* touchingly described the failures of a traditional education to prepare people for life in the world of today. Psychologically speaking, German society has also long been in limbo between smoldering resentments or ill-understood agonies of the mind and the recognition that there is a very considerable streak of insanity in various forms in all of us. Germans like to call each other crazy or insane at the slightest hint of eccentricity, but they will never take it seriously as long as they refuse to acknowledge it in themselves."

"How large a percentage, would you say, is in need of psychiatric help in West Germany today?" asked Bernie.

"The last figure I saw was 600,000," Kurt replied. "But I suspect it's much higher."

"Are you aware of the current wave of criticism of 'life adjustment' in American education, Kurt?"

"Yes, I am. But this need not detract from my thesis that German schools ought to adapt their charges better to modern life. Americans have decided to tone down the emphasis on life adjustment in the schools today, but that has to be considered against decades of thoroughgoing adjustment of the entire educational setting and the teaching methods on all levels. You might say they are giving up only a little of something of which we have nothing at all. Besides, much of the noise of educational reform in the United States is due merely to the impact of Soviet space technology and to the ever-present right-wing agitators who are exploiting the uneasiness over education along with the fluoridation of drinking water and the abolition of the income tax." He had broken his papier-mâché coaster in several pieces and discarded it in the ash-tray. "But this cannot affect the need for life adjustment here where people are so helpless and in so many ways incapable of directing their own lives. The very words 'adjustment' or 'orientation' are completely alien to a German school teacher."

"Or, for that matter, to a Frenchman or Englishman," threw in Kenneth. At this moment the men at the table in the far corner got up. Two struggled into their overcoats while the third put on a Tyrolean hat decorated with a kind of brush which looked like a shaving brush. One by one, they filed past the table, cautiously maneuvering their short, portly figures between the chairs on their way to the door. The man with the shaving brush was the most obese of the three, but he had a jolly smile and the green stripes and oak leaves on his grey suit along with the rustic buttons gave him a rural appearance. Bernie thought of the antlers on the wood paneling of the restaurant, the hunting pictures, bookstore windows full of books about health fads, resorts with mineral waters which cure every malady known to man, or books with pictures about the wondrous sights of nature. He remembered going, with German friends, for a picnic in the woods, his friends deeply inhaling the forest air and exclaiming, as they walked upon a carpet of fallen pine needles and moss: *"Wunderbar!"*

Kurt had followed Bernie's glance, and he chuckled: "If they can't keep their own weight and appearance under control, what must their politics be like?" But Bernie was reluctant to share his own thoughts with the group, in part because Jochen was wearing the same kind of rustic suit with green ornaments as the fat man before. How can people live in the big city and yet feel so beholden to touches of rural

life, he thought. Could this rustic character have made Hitler's ideas
of racial breeding more plausible to the Germans? How can they live
in the bustle of city life and yet be so tradition-minded? The French
would not wear such rustic things in the city. Italians perhaps, and
even then only in northern Italy where people were still half Austrian,
anyway.

Kurt again interrupted the silence which had fallen: "And another
thing that shows how helpless people are here in comparison to the
supposedly so 'lonely crowd' in America. You'd be surprised how
lonesome most Germans are in the big city where about one out of
two spends his or her life. Young women who would like to meet a
nice boy, young men who would like to settle down to start a family,
retired widows or widowers, even people with something to sell or
something to give away. There are practically no regular channels
through which a boy meets a girl in a nice way; there are few
neighbor-to-neighbor relations between the distant rituals of formal
politeness and the accident of close friendships, and very few senior
citizens' clubs except for some highly specialized hobby clubs.
Maybe, I am over-simplifying the many reasons behind this paucity
of human contacts. But it seems to me that much of it is due to the
inability of many of these people to come out of their little shells, to
tackle their problems of loneliness by the habits of association and
joint activity so common in the United States."

"Now wait a minute," Kenneth interrupted him. "I always thought
Germans were a nation of joiners who belong to innumerable dog
clubs, hunting associations, sport clubs, rose-growing societies, student fraternities, and all kinds of historical costume outfits. This is
part of that famous social atmosphere that tourists find so *gemütlich*
in Germany."

"Well, the public social atmosphere perhaps. In private, people are
kind of shy and introvert here," Jochen said.

"Maybe so," Kurt agreed, "but I prefer calling it helpless. The
clubs you are referring to, Kenneth, are either highly specialized or
they are purely traditional in orientation. You'll rarely find civic associations, neighborhood improvement or self-help groups, or anything
as functional as the League of Women Voters, or Alcoholics Anony-
mous, or Junior Achievement. Also," and he turned to Jochen, "this
shyness can be dangerous. Germans of all classes tend to be isolated

in their own small group, their family, their few friends, or their associates at work. They are too self-centered to care much about the life of other groups, except that their ignorance and lack of contact promotes mutual suspicion and distrust. Hostile, stereotyped images of other groups and classes often take the place of firsthand knowledge and a hatemonger of Hitler's or Goebbel's stripe has an easy time manipulating the images and channeling the latent hostility against a scapegoat like the Jews. This isolation makes many Germans fear and distrust well-meaning leaders and their own government, and yet gives them a naïve confidence in total strangers and sometimes demagogues who know how to make themselves folksy and how to appeal to the secret yearning of lonely hearts."

"Germans sound much like Americans in this respect," Bernie added pensively, while Kenneth knitted his eyebrows. "You have just described much of the popular following of our right-wing demagogues."

Kurt continued: "I remember vividly my first exposure as an exchange student to American social customs. I learned a whole new vocabulary of words of human association and communication for which the German language has no equivalent. For example, Jochen, how would you translate such phrases as 'to contact somebody,' or 'dating,' or 'a social mixer'?" Jochen smiled vaguely, but it was not certain if he understood the words well enough to be aware of the problem. Kurt went on: "Well, if there are no words for it, the facility just does not exist. With the sole exception of his family, friends, and kin, the urban German is a stranger among strangers. And being far less individualistic than a Frenchman or an American, he is not at all happy about it. Germans are very nostalgic about group life and like to fancy having lost some primordial community in which they felt as secure as in their mother's womb."

"This is the reason, I suppose," interjected Kenneth, gesticulating with his cold pipe, "why Germans fell for Hitler's fraudulent *Volksgemeinschaft* (people's community). Even now when public opinion pollsters ask them to name anything good about the Nazi era, some come up with this confounded fraud."

"Well, that's what I am saying," insisted Kurt, "people are so helpless. They prefer dreaming of sham communities to going out and creating new ones to suit their purposes. There are so many things a person can do once he really takes control of his life . . . I once met an American couple who started going to church in their thirties for the simple reason, as they told me, that they expected this to be a wholesome influence on their children. And it did not matter to them which of the many churches in America they were joining. They just picked the one most conveniently located."

Jochen was shocked. "But this seems so unnatural, so artificial. This is not the same as introducing your children to your own faith and to the faith of your fathers."

"I don't think we should use the word 'natural' for anything done by human beings except for purely biological functions of the body," Kenneth said with a frown, pointing his pipe stem at Jochen. "Of course, human society is artificial whether it is traditional in character or emancipated. What you must have meant by 'natural' was really 'traditional.' This word 'nature' is one of the most ambiguous in the whole modern German literature. People have used it for all kinds of things close to their hearts; for the forests and lakes where they like to be, for all kinds of fantastic cures with mineral water and strange herbs, for the romantic imagination, or as a rationalization of power politics, of class distinctions and of German superiority over the Slavs, and for all kinds of curious prejudices. Hitler used to consider expressionist art, democracy, and intermarriage between Jews and 'Aryans' unnatural. This word is just a smoke-screen for whatever you want. It may even serve to hide your prejudices and desires from yourself."

"Exactly," said Bernie, wiping away the beads of perspiration over his bushy eyebrows. "The word 'natural' is a typical catch-all that hides the enormous confusion of people when traditional culture breaks down. And," he turned to Kurt, "thank you for expressing so well what we Americans are trying to do. We may sometimes fall down on the job and every so often we have our own problems of cultural lag and social maladjustment. But this is really what we are aiming at, enabling individuals to take control of their own lives in every way."

"You are more advanced in this direction, I think, than any other nation I know of," Kurt noted. "Here in Germany even the intellectuals are not yet, for the most part, fully aware of the artificial character of society which has long been cut loose from its old cultural moorings and has been at the mercy of human actions for better or for worse. If they had only realized that they had to take full control rather than rummaging around in their cultural memories for old, outworn ideas, while *Junkers* and power-hungry militarists and racists like Hitler seized power by default!"

"Very good," said Bernie. "That is just my point. The Germans at large have simply failed to take control when their traditional culture began to collapse under the battering ram of historical events from the Napoleonic conquest and the popular wars of liberation to the upheaval of 1848, the national unification by Bismarck, and, most of all perhaps, the rapid industrialization and urbanization of the new nation-state. In Germany, the traditional cultural shell was intact far longer than in England and France. In terms of its acceptance by vast numbers of the population, it lasted at least until the first or second decade of the Bismarckian Empire. And then it broke down all at once."

"But there were German writers, political leaders, and entrepreneurs who broke with the traditional culture, if I understand you right, long before the 1870's and 1880's," Kenneth objected.

"Well, yes," Bernie conceded, "however, you must not imagine this process of cultural breakdown as something that happens for all the members of a society at once. For the individuals affected by it, the breaking of the spell may take years or even more than one generation. In society, it proceeds layer by layer, from the cities to the countryside, quite slowly, if there is sufficient time, or cataclysmically, where rapid industrialization, urbanization, and war experiences mobilize the masses — as in Germany. Naturally, intellectuals and political leaders experience it long before it becomes a mass phenomenon. The appearance of the new men of business or of politics, who contemptuously cast aside the traditional taboos and rules of the game in pursuit of their advantage, of course teaches those of whom they take advantage the same disregard for the moral rules of traditional culture. Thus, competing groups infect one another, classes corrupt each other — if you regard this as corruption — and imperialistic nations help to break the spell of traditional culture in their colonies, as we are witnessing today. In this fashion the breaking down of all the cultural myths, or secularization, if you prefer this word, can speed up tremendously and thereby make the adjustment of the people to a new life very difficult, if not impossible."

"I am beginning to see what you are driving at," said Kenneth, sucking his cold pipe. "But how can you be so sure that the experiences with the passing of traditional society in underdeveloped countries of the most diverse sort will help us understand what happened in Germany when the spell of the old culture wore off? After all, cultures differ widely and here you are dealing with a culture of very considerable past achievements in art, music, philosophy, and social organization."

"Well, let me try it, anyway," Bernie replied. "After all, our anthropologists and sociologists who are studying the passing of traditional society in the Middle East, in Latin America, Asia, and Africa have always acknowledged that these developing nations are in many ways merely recapitulating the stages of modernization of Western societies. In fact, many of the concepts that are being applied to the understanding of modernization and social mobilization in the new nations were derived from what we know about these phenomena in Western societies. The study of growth and modernizing processes everywhere, of course, deepens our understanding of how we ourselves came to be as we are. Naturally, there are differences in style and reaction depending on the particular cultural pattern of an area. There are different circumstances as well, which have to be accounted for in applying the insights about some of the new nations to Germany's modernization in that crucial period.

"The case of Germany is obviously not one of Westernization or colonialism. Except for the short-lived Napoleonic reforms in West Germany, German modernization was not introduced from outside, although the English and French headstart may have invited invidious comparison and hastened the process by a sense of competition. This may explain somewhat the xenophobia and extreme nationalism in Germany, in analogy to these manifestations, say, in Egypt, Brazil, or China today. And the developing Germans did not have the benefit of the aid and advice of more developed countries or an international organization. On the contrary, by the time the Germans had definitely made up their minds that their development was going to be very different from that of their Western neighbors, say by about the first two decades of the twentieth century, if not earlier, enough hostility had built up between them and the Western democracies to perpetuate their only tentatively anti-liberal and anti-modern stance. And this was still before the German and Allied war propaganda machines during World War I fixed their two antagonistic positions: the German position, according to Thomas Mann, of 'the warriors' fighting off the inroads of 'commercial civilization' upon their *Kultur,* and the Allied position, in Woodrow Wilson's phrase, of the 'crusaders to make the world safe for democracy.' "

At this point Kenneth interrupted him excitedly while an expression of discovery spread over his face: "Ah! That's it. You have just revealed the formula that explains the anti-modern stance of Germany before 1914. It's at the confluence of two vital processes: one of them is the process of modernization which always splits society into more advanced groups and more tradition-bound segments and often leads to conflict between the two, with the crusaders of modernity and debunkers of tradition on the one side, and a traditionalist revolt on the other. The other process comes from the international alignment, the rivalry and competition of the great powers which in this case aligned Germany with the other Central powers, Austria and Turkey, against the more advanced West. As the two elements coincided in time, the power alignment then simply forced Germany into a reactionary stance and lent strong support to its traditionalistic elements which were rationalized with the aristocratic warrior image; just as the Cold War with the Soviet Union today has pushed such a liberal and modernistic country as the United States willy-nilly into a reactionary stance in which hard-lining leaders enjoy broad popular support."

"There's something to be said for this argument, Kenneth," Jochen agreed with a sidelong glance at Bernie. "I think that most Americans and many Englishmen have difficulty understanding the tremendous impact of foreign policy considerations on the political attitudes of continental Europeans. Until very recently, you people have never felt constantly exposed to the threat of attack by neighboring powers as we have from time immemorial. You were always protected enough to work out your internal problems unbothered by international politics."

"Maybe so," Bernie conceded. "But let us not forget that, international alignment or not, Germany under the *Kaiser* was run by a firmly entrenched clique of reactionary Prussian aristocrats, bureaucrats, and feudalized big businessmen who had rigged the political system to their advantage by means of the Prussian electoral law, the systematic exclusion of Liberals and Socialists from administrative office and high staff positions in the army; and by the Prussian position in the federal constitution. The *Kaiser*'s Germany was modern only in its industrial and military technology, and maybe in some of the groups and movements that were so carefully excluded from sharing power. But all social and political modernization was effectively bottled up by the Prussian ruling class whose rule, it seems to me, *was* accepted by most Germans with little grumbling. I simply cannot alter my impression that the Germans as a nation were more conservative than other nations; that is to say, they were lacking in the inner resiliency, empathy, or flexibility required to adjust their social and political life to their changing technology and to the rising level of urbanization and industrialization."

"But the old Prussian conservatism was not what you seem to think," Kurt objected, "a creed of military violence, or of aggressive war. It had a high code of ethics, a noble sense of duty and austerity rooted in Protestantism which definitely set it off to advantage from the pseudo-conservatives and neo-Prussians of the Weimar Republic, not to mention Hitler's storm-troopers."

"I know that," Bernie replied firmly, "and I recognize the distinction which you are drawing here. But the real problem of German conservatism is this: the fellow who is too rigid and unyielding to adjust to the changing world around him ends up paying a terrible price. Underneath his unbending moral stance there are psychological forces at work which eventually prove his ethics brittle. Just consider, for example, the growth of outspoken anti-semitism among German conservatives from the small beginnings in the 1870's to the end of the 1920's when the anti-semites finally controlled the bulk of conservative groups, from aristocratic, farm, and veterans' organizations to the white-collar and small-business segment of German society. This surrender to a scapegoat philosophy along with the cry for a man on horseback and the general radicalization of these groups I see as a path of moral, and ultimately mental, disintegration. Once rampant prejudice and the projection of images of love and hatred have overcome all pretensions of rational self-control, conservative ethics disappears, and fascism takes its place."

A deep furrow had appeared between Kenneth's brows as he pondered these candid words. Bernie continued: "There are, of course, similar processes of moral and mental deterioration going on among the traditionalistic diehards of other countries in the throes of modernization which may account for the upsurge of right-wing extremism, except that most other nations have within them powerful antibodies of religious restraint or liberal conviction which saved them from the worst.

"It was no coincidence at all, as Jochen here, I am sure, will agree, that the Nazi gospel never got very far in Austria, the country of its birth, or even in Bavaria where Hitler's movement grew up. Only when it hit the Protestant parts of Germany, where the bulk of this disintegrating conservatism lay, only then did Nazism move into the big time and close to victory. There were, apparently, no strong antibodies there to stop the raging fever. Instead, rabid stalwarts of the old order would begin to babble the slogans of the gutter which they had so long despised along with many sound doctrines of the emancipated new society."

Jochen nodded, somewhat uncertain of how to express the fact that he agreed with some but not all of Bernie's assertions. But Kurt had followed Bernie's explanations with rapt attention and said now:

"On an individual level, perhaps, one could compare this process to the difficult adjustment of generations of mothers and daughters of respectable society to the emancipation of women: The unemancipated mothers express their own fear of emancipation by hundreds of hints and unspoken clues from early toilet training to the maternal attitude toward friends and suitors of the girl. The daughters then get the idea that there is something terribly wrong about physical uncleanliness, sex, and certain kinds of undesirable people, such as gypsies, transients, foreigners, workers, Jews, Negroes, Bohemian artists or writers, and what have you. Where this kind of miseducation succeeds, and it will with weak characters, there emerges a mentally crippled woman who combines frigidity with violent, hysterical phobias against one or several of these categories of people.

"Or take as an example the industrialist of the old school who has closed his mind to the suffering and deprivation of his own workers because he considers himself something much better than they are. He stubbornly persists in this attitude despite the growth and modernization of his plant, the utter dependence of his business on other parts of the economy and on governmental policies. He still won't sit down at the same table to bargain with his 'inferiors.' As labor becomes organized in trade unions and in a Socialist Party, he develops an acute phobia about 'outside agitators,' foreigners or foreign ideas, and a subversive conspiracy of international proportions. Finally his phobia reaches a fever pitch when he discovers representatives of his 'inferiors' in the government. He reacts with frantic calls for violence, counter-organization, and counter-revolution and is likely to collapse into the arms of the Bolsheviks of the right who have gotten around his mental block by persuading him that theirs is an anti-Marxist, 'national' socialism."

There was a long pause while Kurt fingered another coaster. Finally, Bernie said:

"I shall gladly grant also that this German culture at the time of the great transformation was highly developed and had made many admirable contributions to Western civilization in such fields as philosophy, science, and music. However, it seems to me that high development may well become an obstacle to finding one's way in a changed world. A primitive people living in mud huts will more easily find modern civilization something worth having and gladly leave their old Adam behind. But in highly developed cultures the modern urban-industrial way of life may not look very attractive at first glance. Just think, for example, of the threat of modern industrialism to the old trades and crafts. At least to those on a high enough level to enjoy the cultural rewards and pleasures — and that was a very large minority in Germany — this commercial civilization must have looked ugly and impoverished in lasting values. Furthermore, a highly developed culture by definition inculcates in its people habits of thinking in abstractions, images, and symbols which are placed between a person and the world around him. If the environment begins to change rapidly, I presume, the adjustment of people to these changes follows confusedly along two levels. On the level of symbolic abstractions, floundering efforts are made to mine the cultural tradition for guide lines for the unprecedented present and future. On the level of emotional adjustment, the absence of the guide of reason allows wild and woolly maladjustments to smolder and to be translated into unmotivated resentment and hatred.

"Looking at the course of German history from 1800 to the Nazi era, I cannot help feeling that there has been a steady deterioration from generation to generation. Bismarck's policy of blood and iron comes as a shock after the ages of Lessing, Goethe, Kant, and Heine. But he appears as a sensible, peace-loving old diplomat when compared with the generation of power-hungry imperialists who followed. They again were mere pikers, if we contrast them to the annexationists of World War I and the extremist desperadoes of the 1920's who in turn were dwarfed by the monstrous generation of mass murderers under Hitler." Kenneth mumbled something about "sweeping mass indictments," but Bernie brushed aside his interruption. "This whole development illustrates what I mean by these two levels of adjustment. From one generation to the next, the ideological rationalizations went into more desperate gyrations at the urging of the alienated and unbalanced emotions, at first unable to see that new values would have to come from outside the dying cultural tradition, and then increasingly nihilistic to compound the earlier error. And while Nietzsche and the German scientists of the turn of the century may still have had noble and reasonable answers to the question of nihilism, the discontented masses already called for the 'cleansing thunderstorms of steel' of a monstrous war to wash away their unspeakable agonies in victory, or to end it all heroically in one great *Götterdämmerung*. This heroic nihilism which boiled up from the mistreated and misled German soul finally led to the gates of concentration camps and of World War II. As the song went, *es zittern die morschen Knochen der Welt vor dem grossen Krieg* (The rotten bones of the whole world are trembling before the great war). Only heroic nihilists, filled with an inexplicable but elementary destructive rage, could sing a song like that, longing for chaos and death."

Bernie had talked himself hoarse and, disdaining the rest of his beer, waved to the waitress. He asked for a cup of coffee. The waitress raised her eyebrows. Kurt explained that the little *Bierstube* did not serve coffee. Bernie finally settled for a tasteless, bubbling drink that purported to be lemonade. In the meantime, Kurt began to point out that a comparative analysis of the economic growth of various nations, such as Walt W. Rostow's *Stages of Economic Growth,* clearly showed the parallel nature of the economic development in such diverse countries as the United States, England, France, Germany, Russia, and Japan. "And Rostow sees in Germany's turning to aggression in the twentieth century a typical phenomenon of the fail-

ure of an industrialized Western society to move on from industrial
maturity to the stage of high mass consumption. This failure he attributes to a combination of bad leadership, a kind of miscarriage of
nationalism in reaction to outside powers, and the determination of
the *Junkers* and their grand-bourgeois helpmates to maintain their
dominant position in society, both by restricting competitive mass
production with cartels and by trying to take advantage of the less
developed populations to the east."

Bernie took a diffident sip from his glass of lemonade. "An economic interpretation can be very helpful, except that it's rather obvious in this case that the important factors are all non-economic —
bad leadership, a nationalistic reaction to foreign rule, the efforts of
aristocrats to maintain their status, and the differential in political
and economic development between Slavs and Germans. That's exactly why I prefer the sociological and anthropological approach. Not
only is the economic development only one aspect of the whole evolution, but it is actually a distinctly modern aspect. When a new nation
has decided that its salvation lies primarily with economic development, it is already ahead of Thomas Mann's fictitious warrior who
considers the cash nexus a menace to *Kultur*."

"But you are relying on the assumption that there is some inevitable progress going on, with a capital P, which will bring us into a
technological utopia," said Jochen with growing impatience. "This
assumption has not only long been proven a preposterous fallacy,
but it is one of the notions that led to twentieth-century totalitarianism, to Hitler and to Stalin. This is just a dangerous piece of liberal
mythology."

"And what you're saying there," Kurt interrupted him, "sounds
more like a dangerous piece of Christian Democratic mythology. For
almost a hundred years now the aristocratic-bourgeois ruling class of
this country has made schoolchildren write essays on such topics as
'There is no such thing as progress' and 'Technology is the enemy of
Kultur,' or of nature. What reactionary doctrines! Why, this is just
like solving the problems of the industrial revolution by smashing the
machines. If technological progress is bound to lead to totalitarianism, then why didn't it do so in England, or in the United States
which developed further and farther than Germany?"

Jochen looked very startled. He apparently expected no objections to his assertions which he seemed to regard as self-evident. Kenneth tried to assuage his feelings by saying: "We are not advocating progress with a capital P when we note that there have been far-reaching changes in all Western countries during the last century and a half. These changes are a matter of record. There has been industrialization, urbanization, a vast increase in communications, the rise of mass media and political parties, and so forth. You may bewail this, if you must, but I am quite certain that it is completely impossible to undo these changes and to go back to the family farm and other manifestations of traditional culture."

"Talking about traditional culture," said Bernie, impatient to continue his line of argument, "let me finish what I was going to say before. I believe there is ample evidence from the study of cultural change in such highly developed cultures as China, India, or Egypt, that some nations in transition have a much harder time than others. Take Egypt as an example of a country which finds the transition to modernity exceedingly difficult and in part so, because its middle classes and leaders are living in a dream world of symbolic goals and problems. As President Nasser himself has pointed out, his country has to bring off at the same time two revolutions which in Western countries came separately, one revolution to achieve national independence and then a social revolution to abolish the unequal social classes. Substitute for national independence the fight against Napoleon and national unification and you have the same in Germany. There is also the same separation between *Macht* and *Geist* as once in Germany, between those who make the decisions and those who are the guardians of knowledge. There is also the same 'academic proletariat' of unemployed or poorly employed university graduates hovering between intense frustration or rebelliousness, and rank opportunism."

Kenneth interrupted him: "There are in Egypt more than ten times as many university graduates in proportion to the population than in Great Britain, I understand."

Bernie nodded. "And there are the urban nomads, the uprooted who now live in the streets of the big cities, illiterate, without jobs and homes, peasants and tradesmen who moved there in search of a better life. You might compare them to Hitler who after years spent in flophouses in Vienna, fell to his knees to thank God at the outbreak of World War I, because he had found something to do."

"But you can't just compare a Middle Eastern street mob with Germans," Jochen protested.

"Oh no?" countered Kurt. "I grew up in a neighborhood here in Munich just one block from a public housing project for what they called the shelterless, or the 'large families.' You should have seen that place. They had scores of dirty children in ragged clothes who used to form mobs of fifty and more, invading our middle-class neighborhood and throwing rocks and sticks at us handful of boys. The manager of our block of apartment houses, a big woman with white hair, used to drive them away singlehandedly, swinging a broom and shouting abuse in her heavy Hessian dialect."

"Of course, there are differences in degree and shadings," Bernie assuaged Jochen. "But there are basic patterns in this outer fringe of city life, or the subculture of urban poverty, as sociologists call it, that recur around the globe and especially wherever large numbers of people leave the farm and move to the city. You find them today in Mexico City, Rio, Caracas, at various periods in parts of Chicago, New York, Los Angeles, London, Frankfurt, Munich, Calcutta — you name it. This is one of the great social upheavals of our time. In Germany they appeared in particular during the thirty years from 1880 to the beginning of the First World War. Most of these marginal city dwellers, of course, don't find the fulfillment of the dreams that brought them to the big city. They become proletarians along with a lot of other unhappy souls, tradesmen who have lost their independent shops or whose trade or craft was taken over by machines, city folk of the lower fringes who have never been able to make good, domestic servants who are tired of the petty tyranny on the job. But the migrants from the farms are among the most disappointed and resentful about the precarious existence in squalor and crowded conditions, in depressions, unemployment, depredation, and exploitation. They find city life rather overwhelming and hardly know how to help themselves. And life in the subculture is grim. There is crime, despair, and suicide; alcoholism, sexual promiscuity, illegitimacy, a cult of raw masculinity, and of physical courage. There is violence, fighting, wife beating, and paternal authoritarianism."

"Let's not make it too dramatic," Kenneth interjected. "The chief point is merely that these people are leaving the tranquility of traditional rural life, stirred up by the great dreams of social advancement, of getting rich, or of growing beyond the station accepted by their forebears during a thousand years of rural slumber. And once they get to the city, they breathe a new air of freedom and opportunity and become aware of a whole new world they have never known. The road to advancement is open to them. In your country, Bernie, some of these farmboys grow up to be President."

"But in Europe they don't," Bernie objected heatedly, "not as long as the class structure lasts. They arrive with the glint in their eye and immediately find themselves pegged as proletarians, on the lowest rung of the ladder of social mobility, and denied further advance. And herein lies the political significance of the whole story. These frustrated social climbers are still hayseeds with their rural background. They are prone to accepting, as if awe-struck, sweeping, simplified explanations of everything, such as Marxism or racist ideologies. They are still of an authoritarian cast of mind and are suckers for a raving demagogue, or for a psychopath on horseback."

"But people like that don't participate in politics," Kurt objected. "They are just not interested in it. Besides, they distrust the governmental authorities and the politicians of the upper classes."

"Well," Bernie replied after some reflection. "It's true that they don't often participate in the discussion of issues or in voting and modern party politics as we know it. But I'd hesitate to call them apolitical. They have their own kind of violent populistic politics of demagogic dissent and indignant eruption. Even their non-voting lasts only as long as they are not threatened by some catastrophe, such as war or a great depression. And since they are not accustomed to our kind of politics they bring to the emergency all their private feelings and maladjustments. They expect a political leader to solve, at least symbolically, their private problems of how to grow up or how to get along with women. They expect him to carry out their wildest prejudices and aggression, and also to express their fears and hatreds of members of the more refined upper classes. They were delighted, I am sure, when Hitler started his speeches with the egalitarian formula 'when I was still a simple private in World War One'; or when he said that the word culture made him feel like drawing his revolver."

"I am glad," said Kenneth, "that you are attributing these manifestations to a certain status in urban life and not simply to the much maligned petty bourgeoisie as a class."

Jochen, pleased with the turn of the conversation, added: "I recall my mother telling me how storm-troopers in 1938 smashed some of the fine Jewish homes in our part of town. They did very little looting even though most of them were poor devils. But they shattered antique mirrors and vases and chopped precious pieces of furniture into tiny splinters with a fiendish abandon. It is frightening to think of this vast destructive rage against anything cultured and valuable boiling up from the depths of anarchic nihilism and frustration."

"Well. Don't think the storm-troopers had a monopoly on destructive rage," said Bernie. "It figures in all extremist movements and hate groups. You should see the extreme right in the United States. Or the diehard segregationists who'd rather close down the schools than share them with colored children. People like that, of course, need some scapegoat group they can safely hate or to whom they can feel superior; someone they can kick around when their spirits are low. Or they need a conspiracy they can blame for their frustrations, like Wall Street, the international financiers, the Communists or Socialists, the Free Masons, the Jews, or the British.

"This takes me back to the Egyptians. You see, there, the unassimilated urban masses have put all their frustrations into anti-British and anti-Israeli sentiment, egged on by the stream of radio propaganda from Nasser's *Voice of the Arabs* which unsettles and unites them at the same time. Just like the Germans before 1945, the Nasser regime has put off its social revolution, the reconciliation among the social classes, and instead expanded its political revolution into a sense of mission of Pan-Arab or Pan-African leadership. Instead of promising the Egyptian masses opportunities for advancement, Nasser has channeled their revolutionary energy into a hatred of Britain or of Western colonialism and into a kind of imperial mission, as if these sentiments could do something to relieve economic misery in Egypt."

"This is as if the growing sons of an authoritarian father did not have the courage to assert themselves against him," commented Kurt, "and let out their inhibited revolt on the neighbors instead. Or as if they victimized a neighborhood boy who happens to look different from them."

"I think Freud is right there," Kenneth joined in eagerly, pointing his pipe at Kurt. "German hegemonialism and aggression were an *ersatz* social revolution, just like the hegemonial drive of Napoleon's armies. German nationalism developed and unified the nation in response to French conquest and rule, and later in rivalry to the British, not unlike Egypt today. And the mumbo jumbo of Aryan superiority and anti-semitic ravings falls into the same category. The Third Reich was the final miscarriage of the social revolution in Germany."

"Tell me," Bernie inquired, "do you get any feeling that there is a reasonable likeness of the way things developed in Germany in what I have been saying about Egypt, Kurt? The basic processes of modernization and the fundamental tensions and dilemmas which it brings at various stages, after all, are identical in all nations. And what is happening in many developing countries today can provide us with a veritable laboratory of firsthand observations about the great transformation which took place in our own societies several generations ago."

"I agree with you, Bernie," Kurt said. "Most of the points you have made, in fact, have opened my eyes about angles and connections of which I had not been aware. In particular, the logical link between the great transformation and nationalistic xenophobia, or rather between the traditionalistic rear-guard and prejudice, that is now clear to me. In fact, I am beginning to understand now, how the rise of political anti-semitism ties in with the process of modernization in more than one way."

"How is that?" Bernie asked.

"Well, I realize now that I need not account for the whole German nation, but only for the traditionalistic rear-guard, for those parts of pre-industrial society that could not adjust to the modern life and, for that reason, were looking for an 'out-group,' a scapegoat, upon which to project their negative affects. I have always asked myself why German Jews should have been singled out for this purpose and now, I think, I have an explanation. Since the Jewish emancipation of the eighteenth and nineteenth centuries did not in most European countries remove barriers to most traditional occupations, such as the crafts or agriculture, young Jews tended to crowd especially into the few careers open to them: journalism, law, and medicine, the fine arts, science and technology, business and banking of the new, large-scale type, middleman operations, and, of course, political careers. Every one of these occupations without exception is among the chief agents of the modernization process which caused such anxiety to the inflexible people of the traditionalistic rear-guard. And seeing such a disproportionate number — in terms of the Jewish share of the total population — of these by and large very competent Jews among the harbingers of modernism, they jumped to the conclusion that the Jews were *causing* this frightening process of modernization. This, I think, is how it started, back in the 1870's when only a very small segment of Prussian society — the small farmer element mainly — was actually suffering from modernization. The bulk of the traditionalistic rear-guard did not need to stoop to such excuses as long as it succeeded in holding power. Only when the old regime collapsed, in 1918, did the anxieties of the traditionalistic rear-guard really become extended to the whole conservative establishment."

"We can come back to this problem of anti-semitism tomorrow when we talk about the Nazi takeover," Kenneth said and turned to Bernie: "Do you have any more points left on your agenda?"

"Just two more, authoritarianism and anti-semitism," came the reply. "Let me start with the first one. One of the chief features of the great transformation, as you will recall, is the leveling of the hierarchic distinctions of traditional society, or the coming of equality, as you may also call it. Such a social revolution involves by necessity the destruction of most relationships of authority between what were once superiors and inferiors on many levels. As authority begins to break down in the throes of modernization, the declining upper strata of course try desperately to assert their position. The lower strata, without guidance and experience in the use of their new freedom, often tend to succumb to the blandishments of the old authority or of new men on horseback who know how to combine some modern appeals with old-time paternal authority. This is the setting for the kind of authoritarianism which has characterized most of the objections shown by other Western nations to Germany, in my opinion: arrogant *Junkers* insisting on their privileged status as against commoners, the authoritarian state dominating submissive subjects, the bourgeoisie striving to impress its superiority on tradesmen and workers, city folk lording it over the country bumpkins, fathers tyrannizing their children, husbands their wives, and the educated asserting their authority over the lower classes. All German society seems to hinge completely upon authoritarian relationships between petty tyrants on a hundred anxiously maintained levels and servile underlings so devoid of civil courage that they will carry out any order no matter how inhuman just because 'an order is an order.' And everybody clinging to titles, aristocratic, academic, or official, titles which are claimed even by the wife who insists on being called *Frau Geheimrat* or *Frau Doktor.*"

"Just a minute, Bernie," exclaimed Kurt, "you are attaching so many different meanings to the word authoritarian that it is going to take me all night to disentangle this confusion. Let me take up your charges one by one. The first one was about the class structure — that the lower classes have been particularly fawning and obsequious toward the ruling classes."

"Yes," said Bernie. "In fact, I have heard Germans themselves criticizing their compatriots for acting like bicyclists who bend their backs toward the powers above them and viciously trample on those who are beneath them."

"This is a charge often made," conceded Kurt, "but somewhat exaggerated in my opinion. You should bear in mind, I think, that the spell of the traditional culture vanished very late in Germany and that therefore the traditional class structure also did not begin to break down until quite late in the nineteenth century. As the different classes became emancipated, however, they moved with determination to better their place in society. The bourgeoisie may have been cringing before the *Junkers.* The working-class certainly was not exactly obsequious. In fact, it was filled with revolutionary sentiment for most of the period before 1914."

"Peasants and petty bourgeoisie didn't cringe either, when they threw their weight behind protest movements and, finally, behind the Nazi landslide," interjected Jochen.

"What about the authoritarian claims to superiority of each class toward the one immediately below it?" Bernie began again. "And what about the general clinging to a social order of superiors and inferiors, and to the perquisites and titles that denote status?"

"I can suggest an explanation for this," Kurt answered after some reflection. "First of all, we should perhaps bear in mind that the traditional social structure was infinitely more complex than our image of aristocrats, bourgeoisie, petty bourgeoisie, workers, and peasants. Each of these groups contained dozens, even hundreds of fairly well-defined gradations. There was by no means only a relationship between upper and lower groups, but also countless divisions into occupations, trades, professions, or callings. And there was a certain amount of social mobility which might allow a boy from an artisan family, for example, to rise as a prosperous tradesman or entrepreneur, or as a famous artist, or to become a class-conscious blue-collar worker or a white-collar clerical employee or salesman. Or, as his personal luck and pluck would have it, he might end destitute or on skid row. Well now," and he turned to Bernie, "under the spell of traditional culture, as you were saying before, everybody pretty much accepts his fate and, in fact, derives his purpose in life from his particular calling or role. But when the spell wears off, everyone gets restless and develops the ambition to improve his own social position."

"A kind of revolution of rising expectations," Kenneth threw in while he lit his cold pipe; "especially, if it happens on a massive scale."

"You might call it that," Kurt agreed. "Except that you have to remember that, while everybody would like to move up, only very few succeed in doing so to their complete satisfaction. The masses probably move together and at such a slow rate that most of them hardly feel they are moving at all."

"Aha!" Kenneth exclaimed between violent puffs which brought tears to his eyes and caused Bernie to cough again. "Expectations rise faster than the men and women who have them. And then they start envying each other. The Nazis used to claim that envy was one of the chief things wrong with the Germans. Envy everywhere. And, of course, the less successful people were, the more envious." He drew another mouthful of smoke and let it out with a long low hiss.

"And, of course, age has something to do with it, too," Kurt added. "A person dreams of the fulfillment of his potentialities when he or she is young. That's what we popularly call 'the illusions' here. As he grows to manhood and finds out that he will never set the world on fire, a tremendous disillusionment sets in. It seems to me that many of the great popular errors of recent German history were made of the same stuff. From Wagner to Hitler, some fool or knave would always supply these youths with some romantic, nationalistic, or heroic way out of their disillusionment."

"You were going to explain why Germans are so anxious to impress their title or status on their inferiors," Bernie reminded him.

"Oh, yes. Well, when disillusioned people have found out that they are not among the vanguard of the social climbers, they not only envy those who are. They start fighting a rear-guard action of constantly reminding those who are still behind them of their status, class, and title. Since the 1880's, just about every class in Germany, city and country, every profession, occupation, and walk of life has begun to view enviously the real and fancied progress of others. Well, if you have a series of great crises, it is small wonder that this social malaise engulfs the whole nation. But I am sure Germans are not the only ones who have these status anxieties. What Germans do with titles, others do with other status symbols. One theory of right-wing activity in the United States, I understand, also connects it with this form of anxiety. Now, if you want to call this authoritarian, this really strikes me as stretching the meaning of the word beyond recognition."

"But then," Kenneth interjected, "there is also the matter of the apparent German predilection for such a hierarchical, one might almost say, Platonic society in which everybody is supposed to stick to his little niche. I am frankly doubtful about your argument that this is merely due to the late breaking-down of traditional society. No other highly industrialized and urbanized nation has clung quite so tenaciously to this traditional image of social order. I have another explanation to offer, though you may not like it. Germans, in my opinion, have always been rather different from the rationalistic Frenchmen and the pragmatic Englishmen. Read their literature over the past two centuries and earlier, and you can hardly fail to note the emphasis on emotional experience, even mysticism. Even the neo-humanists in the footsteps of Goethe were really aiming at *Innerlichkeit* above all, the cultivation of the inner life, the beauty and wholeness of the soul rather than at rational control. Or take German idealism and literary romanticism. Germany lies in more than one sense between France and Russia. The farther you go east, the more it is the soul, the sentiment, the inner sense rather than reason which is called upon to integrate the personality of an individual. And this inner sense tends to be far more attuned to the call of tradition, to group ways rather than to individual reflection, to social harmony rather than to individual self-interest."

"Germans are obsessed with order," Bernie interrupted him impatiently, "whether it is in government or in street traffic. They would never cross a street against the red light. A revolutionary mob trying to storm a railroad station, if ever there occurred such a disorderly thing here, would probably first ask for the station-master's permission to pass through the turnstile without a ticket."

"I take exception to that," Kenneth said between puffs of smoke. "That's pure myth. Germans are among the most disorderly people I know. I have never seen so many negligent, careless, law-breaking, and maniacal automobile drivers anywhere. Do you know that Germany's rate of fatal accidents per car is almost four times as high as in the United States, and twice as high as in France? And when do Germans ever queue up voluntarily for a bus or at a ticket counter? If you think the Germans are too orderly and law-abiding, then what are you going to say about the British? And why do you suppose German tourists are unpopular in other countries? Because they always complain, get drunk, are disorderly, loud, boisterous and that sort of thing.

"Germans seem to suffer from a peculiar kind of formlessness and an inability to see themselves as others see them," continued Kenneth. "That's what makes them so unpredictable. That is also why they have not been able to establish the general norms of behavior and attitude that we associate with the word gentleman the world over. Of course, there are occasional exceptions. But even the German aristocrats have been by and large a coarse lot, and among the other classes there are frequent lapses of judgment, tact, and demeanor so severe as to border on the pathological. Think, for example, of the excessively vituperative polemics of some of the academic controversies among German scholars, or the vicious filth poured over enemies by some of the journalists of the Weimar Republic or, for that matter, some contemporary politicians. If people go in for such unrestrained verbal aggression, then how can you expect them to act when they have power over life and death? I cannot help thinking behind these manifestations must lurk a chaotic emotional life. If Germans are obsessed with order, social or otherwise, it must be because they fear the aggression of their own chaotic desires, and with good reason. If they constantly search for forms and norms in antiquity, among the early Nordic tribes, in the Middle Ages, in philosophy, or in other countries, it must be precisely because they lack a natural or indigenous form, because there is no German archetype.

Maybe this is why they find it comforting to be a part of a hierarchic class structure. Perhaps, this also explains why militarism became the rage in Bismarckian Germany. It offers the insecure a set of standards and forms."

"And that makes the desire for order pathological," Bernie interjected triumphantly. Then he turned to Kurt. "So much for the social structure. Do you also have an explanation why educated Germans, and especially intellectuals, are so convinced of their superiority over the less educated masses? I have heard fishmongers on the *Viktualienmarkt* in Munich argue with each other, each insisting with a stream of abuse that she was an educated woman whereas the other fishwives were not. I know that academic titles confer high prestige here, even in politics, very much unlike the United States. I have never understood why this should be so. It seems undemocratic, somehow."

"Kenneth, I believe, used the word Platonic before to describe the complex vertical and horizontal divisions of the traditional German society," Kurt replied. "That very aptly describes also the notion that the guardians of knowledge should form the highest social class, and that their chief exponents should rule the country. The latter, of course, took place in Germany only in small part since the aristocracy and later the business oligarchy had no intention of stepping aside in favor of a group of eggheads. Barred from the powerful position promised to them by the inner logic of the social order and the influential Platonic philosophy, the representatives of *Geist,* the intellectuals, clamored for *Macht* (power) and, in their frustration at not getting it, they turned radical."

Jochen nodded eagerly: "There is also another angle. It is the Platonic idea that there can only be one authentic truth and not a pluralistic multitude of subjective truths. This reminds me vividly of the time when a professor in Missouri told me about the old midwestern farmer who had said: 'Son, there are twenty-four ways to skin a muskrat and everyone of them is right.' I always like to tell that to my countrymen because it really sets them thinking. They are convinced there can be only one right way of doing anything and that he who knows how, the expert, ought to give the orders. Naturally, this cast of mind tends to discourage compromise and pluralism and to promote doctrinaire ideological thinking, a kind of philosophical radicalism of rigorously applying abstract principles to the complicated social reality."

"Another thing that's difficult to understand for an American," Bernie said after a brief pause, "is the authoritarian relationship of Germans to their officialdom or to the state in general. As soon as a German sees a police uniform or the letterhead of a government agency, all his courage seems to leave him. He capitulates whenever faced with a *Respektsperson,* a figure of authority."

"Well, now. I am going to have to break up this subject into two parts, before I can discuss it meaningfully," said Kurt. "One aspect has to do with German attitudes toward the state and its authority, the other with the courage to face bureaucrats; policemen or, for that matter, the occupation authorities.

"You see, when one talks about 'the state' in Germany one has to explain first which state. The best entrenched bureaucracy in Germany is that of the old territorial states, Prussia, Saxony, Bavaria, and the others. These state bureaucracies in the old traditional system represented the authority of the princes over mere commoners. You can compare them to the French bureaucracy in many ways, including the loathing felt by the citizenry for the bureaucrats behind their little windows."

"Loathing?" interrupted Bernie. "There was a time when a *Beamter* (civil servant) was regarded as a great catch by marriageable girls of the bourgeoisie."

"Before the Nazis, perhaps," replied Jochen. "Because in those days civil servants were the only people who in their old age could expect a comfortable pension for themselves and for their widows. But in the days of the Weimar Republic and especially right after the Second World War, when so many people became dependent on public handouts and on the rationing of all goods and housing, people came to loathe the bureaucrats and their haughty behavior. I suppose civil servants still have some social prestige and political influence, but if you meet them behind their little office windows you despise them."

"The central bureaucracy of the *Reich* and now of the federal government," Kurt added, "is still a rather recent growth whose rights are constantly questioned by the state bureaucracies. The federal bureaucracy also has very few contacts with the public, its main concern being the conduct of foreign relations and defense, and the drafting of federal legislation."

"But isn't it true that, at least during the period we are discussing here, Germans have worshipped the state and turned to it for help in every conceivable emergency?" Bernie interrupted again.

"This general notion of the state is totally misleading," Kurt answered, "although I won't deny that this is the way most German writers have referred to it. What they really meant, however, that is another question. It hinges on *whose* state they are talking about.

"You see, way back in the centuries when the territorial states evolved, 'the state' was the power of the great territorial potentates whose rise was often welcomed by people as an antidote to the misgovernment and petty tyranny of many a small feudal lord. Even in the nineteenth century, for example, Prussian administration was infinitely more efficient, orderly, and fair than, say, that of the Hanoverian dynasty it replaced, and the Bismarckian *Reich* administration was more equitable and well-qualified than that of any of the states, even of Prussia."

"Could it be," Bernie asked, "that you people expect too much of bureaucracy? Why does your bureaucracy have to measure up to the exacting standards of Plato's philosopher-king?"

"You may have a point there," came the reply. "But so much of it is just a struggle of various local group interests against each other. The cities of Hanover, for example, may definitely prefer Prussian administration, because it paid more attention to their commercial interests. The aristocracy and the peasants of Hanover, on the other hand, may feel more attached to a separate Hanoverian state simply because the old dynasty favored them. To describe the attachment of both of these groups as worship of 'the state' strikes me as ridiculous.

"Bismarck's *Reich* also wasn't just 'the state' to everybody. The Social Democrats roundly rejected it as the state of the bourgeoisie and as the bourgeois instrument for holding down the working class. The Catholics suspected it of being the state of the Protestant King of Prussia, the *Kaiser*. The Liberals thought of it as the embryo of a constitutional state which would in time shed its aristocratic trimmings and become a constitutional monarchy with parliamentary government like Great Britain. And the aristocratic princes of the states and the *Junkers* and other conservatives thought of it as a mo-

narchic confederation of quasi-sovereign princes led by the most
powerful of their houses, the Hohenzollern. And the state of Weimar,
as you know, was accepted neither by the extreme left nor by the entire right wing."

"Somehow you are trying to slip through my fingers," Bernie said,
with one bushy eyebrow raised and his lips pursed in concentration.
"These are not the alternatives I see."

"Being an American," Jochen interrupted him, "you just have the
typical anarchistic bias. American civilization started after all not too
long ago with settlements in virgin wilderness. You hardly needed a
government at first and even today a person just cannot convince
some Americans that one is necessary now.

"You Americans are learning only now what most Europeans have
experienced for centuries. In a densely settled country with complex
social organization there is never a dearth of powerful people and
groups whose decisions determine much of your life, whether you like
it or not. The real issue is not whether government and taxes are necessary. It is whether these oligarchs can be brought around to following the public interest, or at least the interests of a majority, or
whether they will just govern in their own interests."

"Listen to this young whipper-snapper," chuckled Bernie, pleased
with this formulation. "You'd think he had invented democracy."

"Regarding the second charge of German submissiveness to authority," Kurt resumed his rebuttal, "it is a great fallacy to ignore the
changing times. So long as the traditional culture lasted the authority
relationships were part of the general cultural system and should not
be held against the people under its spell. Later on it was largely the
failure of the revolutionary intellectuals to persuade the German
masses to follow them into revolt, a problem somewhat comparable
to that of the Russian intelligentsia under the Czars. In their frustration German intellectuals began to taunt their countrymen, calling
them cowardly and too timid ever to make a revolution. This charge
was echoed abroad but hardly gained in meaning thereby. Kenneth
will agree, I am sure, that one should not confuse voluntary co-
operation with timidity. It means consent and not submission. If people consented to the wrong thing, or let it go by default or out of ignorance, or if they later claim they had no choice or did not know,
that is immaterial; they are guilty of co-operation as long as there was

not, on a mass scale, any real necessity or force involved. No one in his right mind, except of course a frustrated intellectual, will ask people to be rebellious or to stage revolutions just for the sake of revolutions. That is a childish thing to ask of an adult. As long as you cannot demonstrate a desire for the gains of revolution, you have no case. This is a typical example of many of the pairs of charges of which one accuses us. One critic will ridicule us as being too reasonable while the other will call us too irrational."

"Well, can you name cases of popular revolt in recent German history?" Bernie asked with a grin

"Why not?" Kurt replied. "What about the popular uprisings just prior to the war against Napoleon, the local uprisings in 1848, when the bourgeoisie almost brought off the great coup; or the refusal of Catholics to follow the draft for Bismarck's Franco-Prussian war, the uprisings in 1918 which led to the establishment of Soviet Republics in some German states, the general strike that ended the Kapp putsch of 1920, or the street mobs of Nazi and Communist revolutionaries during the Weimar Republic, not to mention the bombings and murders in some rural areas; and last but not least important the East German uprising of 1953? Most of these didn't do much good either, but here at least you can feast your eye on violent rebellion, if this appeals so much to you. But perhaps these revolts were not big enough or bloody enough for you, or maybe the wrong people revolted against the wrong thing and for the wrong reasons."

Kurt paused and looked around, but none of his three listeners seemed ready to question his assertions. He continued: "These charges are just like the pair of accusations popular immediately after World War Two. At that time many foreign observers and self-hating Germans called the war-weary German population cowardly for not developing a militant Nazi underground against the Allied occupation. Others again, at least more in keeping with the avowed Allied goals, blamed them for their failure to repent their immediate past on a large enough scale. You see, we are damned if we do and damned if we don't."

Kenneth felt that the discussion had become too heated and quickly intervened: "It is getting late. Maybe we should turn to the next point on Bernie's agenda."

"Oh, all right," Bernie responded and looked at his list. "Now what about authoritarianism in the home? Is it not true that in a typical German home neither women nor children have any share in the decisions that are made and are trained from the very beginning to accept the authority of the father and husband, as if he were some kind of god? The series of authoritarian leaders from Bismarck to Hitler, and now Adenauer, is merely a parallel of political father-figures, each worshipped by his flock just as *Vati* (Dad) is supposed to be at home."

Kurt shook his head impatiently: "This is just another tendentious statement bending the evidence to the purpose of proving your pet theory. It is erroneous on several counts. First, because you ignore how recently the emancipation of women took place in all Western countries. Germany had its roaring 'twenties, too, and such indicators as women's suffrage, the admission of women to universities and to the professions, or their legal status show German women to have advanced at about the same time and pace as the women of other nations. And as for the charge that German fathers and husbands were tyrannical, you ought to read the accounts of German family life by such American anthropologists as Robert H. Lowie or David Rodnick.* Rodnick actually makes out a frequently dominant position for wives and mothers and describes German childhood as particularly pampered and sheltered, although he is also trying to show Germans as submissive. Cases of domestic tyranny, wife beating, or abuse of children are rare and obviously deviations from a healthy norm."

"I wouldn't be so sure about that," Jochen mumbled, scratching the back of his head. "My old man still belongs to a generation in which most men seem to have had a pasha complex. Understand, it's not that he ever meant to be brutal or sadistic toward his wife or children, though some of his contemporaries may have been. Just kind of heavy-handed. But I have always had the impression that it was really his temper. He is actually a very sensitive man, almost morbidly so, and easily offended. And when he gets angry, he can lash out at you with a vengeance. Never an apology afterwards, even if he hit you much harder than you deserved." He took a long draft from his freshly filled glass of beer, and wiped the foam from his lip. "Just as if he meant to tell you: You know my temper; watch yourself."

Kurt had listened to him with visible annoyance while his ears

* See bibliographical notes.

turned a deep pink. He burst out: "Your father is in his seventies, I suppose." And as Jochen nodded, he continued: "Would you agree that this pasha complex, as you call it, was peculiar to that particular generation but that it is practically non-existent now?"

"Yes, I agree," said Jochen.

"Well, in that case," Kurt concluded with satisfaction, "this particular generation may well be one that was particularly hard hit by the emotional stresses of the great transformation. I'd be inclined to say that the same explanation applies to the cases of emotional instability and ungentlemanly conduct that you mentioned before, Kenneth. This was a generation of hero worship, exaggerated militarism, romantic fantasies, and high-flying ideologies. They tried to interpret dialectically the vast social transformations as national, class, or race struggle. It was a generation of maladjusted intellectuals, both here and abroad, whose arrogance and warped judgment were generally mistaken for the revelations of genius. It was the generation of Hitler and of the men who fell for him."

"I am wary of these doctrines which make a parallel between domestic discipline and political liberty," Kenneth added. "They are often little more than dogmatic assertions by a handful of far-out psychiatrists, progressive educators, and ultra-liberal politicians. Athenian democracy did very well without their womenfolk. So do the Swiss, who have a rather patriarchal family structure. Much of English, American, and French family life has been distinctly authoritarian, often father-oriented, without appreciable damage to democracy. Just think of nineteenth-century American democracy. Also, I have met some exceedingly emancipated and bossy Nazi women who wore the pants in the family, assuming that any husband even wanted to stick it out with them. Likewise, the typical Hitler youth leader was far more likely to be a strong-willed rebel in his own family than a meek, submissive son or daughter. Again, we should guard against the fallacy of mistaking voluntary co-operation for submission." He waved his pipe-stem about and Jochen and Kurt nodded agreement. "And as far as the education of children is concerned," Kenneth continued, "did you by any chance see the public opinion poll a few years ago according to which 70 per cent of Englishmen believe that children should get a whipping every once in a while? Mind you, I am not saying that this is good. But if your theory was correct, Bernie, then Sir Oswald Mosley should long ago have become our great and glorious leader by an enormous landslide."

"Oh, but there *is* a relation between democracy and domestic life," Bernie insisted in the face of Kenneth's skepticism. "A democratic home life creates people of equal self-assertiveness rather than bullies and submissive natures, or hammers and anvils, as the Germans call them, who tend to create authoritarian relationships."

"What about your mother, Jochen," Kurt interjected. "What is she like?"

"She passed away a few years ago," Jochen answered pensively, leaning on his elbow, chin in hand. "She always tried to make up to me for what my father had done. She did not love him, although she was completely devoted to her family and especially to the children. I think she regarded him as not masculine enough. She'd sometimes say nostalgically that she wished she were living back in that age when a man could be depended on to take care of a woman completely and in every respect. She often used to lapse into a state of depression, starting to cry about trifles, yearning for affection and security and feeling that everyone was against her. She also had this strange idea that a woman constantly has to fight for survival against other rapacious females. I guess," he added after a few minutes of silence and without noticing Bernie's rapt attention, "she belonged to that generation, too."

"Did your experiences with your father predispose you to like a man like Adenauer as the head of the German state?" Kenneth mockingly asked Jochen, who had finished his seventh glass of beer and began to look around for the waitress. Kurt had noticed the increasing signs of intoxication in Jochen and interceded: "That's an unfair question, a loaded question if I ever heard one."

Bernie looked at his watch and rose to his feet. "Good heavens. It is almost midnight. I am sorry to have to leave you, gentlemen; I left my family waiting at the hotel. Could we meet again tomorrow at the same time and place in order to finish this discussion?"

The other three nodded their assent. Kurt reminded Bernie not to forget the last point — anti-semitism. Kenneth, also rising, took his hat to leave with Bernie.

Jochen clutched his newly filled glass and looked up at Kurt who had arisen to put on his coat.

"You are leaving, too?" Jochen said to him in German. "I suppose you think I shouldn't drink so much in this company, don't you?"

"Never mind your drinking. That's an old German vice. I'd appreciate it, if you didn't always knife me in the back when I am trying to explain something. But it's really because I have a splitting headache that I want to go home now."

"You talk as if this whole discussion was strictly an academic debate or a propaganda battle," Jochen sighed. "You have no idea what a storm of emotions I have been drowning in my beer." He looked up and Kurt saw something glistening in the corners of his bloodshot eyes. Kurt gave his arm a compassionate squeeze and took his leave, mumbling something about feeling the same way. As he opened the door of the *Bierstube* to step into the cold night air, he still heard Jochen saying to himself: "How was it possible? How could they? How, just how could it happen?"

"... immediately after the end of the World War—our country was full
of saviors, prophets and disciples, of presentiments about the end of the
world, or hopes for the dawn of a Third Empire. Shattered by the war,
in despair as a result of deprivation and hunger, greatly disillusioned
by the seeming futility of all the sacrifices in blood and goods, our people
at that time were lured by many phantoms ... Bacchanalian dance
societies and Anabaptist groups, there was one thing after another that
seemed to point to what was wonderful and beyond the veil ... At that
time so many prophets sprang up, so many secret societies with Messianic
hopes appeared and then disappeared again leaving no trace."

Hermann Hesse, *Journey to the East*

"... we Germans have produced the greatest philosophers and the
most excellent artists. We have shown ourselves to be most capable in war.
Why should it surprise your Excellencies, if we are asses in politics. There
has to be a shortcoming somewhere."

Prince Bülow in 1908

2

HOW COULD IT HAPPEN?

The other three were already at the *Bierstube* when Kenneth arrived
the next day at twenty minutes past seven. The restaurant was
crowded and filled with smoke so that he could not see his friends at
first. They were sitting at a different table. Jochen waved his hand to
attract Kenneth's attention and soon the four were sitting around
their glasses of beer again. Kenneth took out a small notebook and
said: "Being a bachelor who can burn the midnight oil without interference from my family, I sat down last night and tried to summarize
our discussion. I shan't promise you that I remembered every point
that was made or that I succeeded in eliminating my own prejudices
from this summary. You can always correct me if you like. In any
case, I thought that giving you this résumé would be like having minutes of the last meeting and would start us off nicely on the climax of
our discussion: how could it happen in Germany?"

The other three indicated their satisfaction with this proposal and
Kenneth began by opening his little notebook and peering at the numbers and words written in a small, neat hand.

"We started out, I believe, with the decision to concentrate our analysis of the German problem on the popular motives of Germans between about 1850 and 1933, after rejecting such alternative subjects as the intellectual meanderings of German writers or the historical distortions of nationalistic historians and war propaganda on both sides." He looked at Bernie who seemed a little unhappy but raised no objections. "Oh yes, and we also agreed to omit all causal inferences linking our discussion of German national character with the rise of Hitler until today.

"Now, how did we approach the popular motives of the Germans during this crucial period? We followed three approaches. The first was along the familiar lines of analyzing the failure of the German bourgeoisie to wrest power from the *Junkers* and to establish constitutional liberty in Germany. Now, let me be honest about this. I have read and heard many accounts of this sort under such titles as the *via dolorosa* of the civilian spirit, the sell-out of the bourgeoisie to reaction, or the erosion of bourgeois morality by imperialism and Social Darwinism. As applied to Germany, frankly, these interpretations are beginning to bore me because they explain so little. The German bourgeoisie, in comparison to that of other Western countries, was in a weak position from the outset and at a hopeless disadvantage when faced by the well-entrenched princes and aristocrats. Its inner divisions and moral crises the German bourgeoisie shared with other Western middle classes. It was no worse and no better." He looked at Kurt who looked dismayed and wanted to interrupt him. Kenneth quickly continued: "Let me finish this point first, Kurt. We have not even mentioned so far the greatest moral crisis of the bourgeoisie. I believe it makes a reasonable alibi. I am referring to the enormous ground swell of anti-bourgeois sentiment which started with the Marxists, spread through the working classes, and finally engulfed the war veterans and the right wing in one huge front against bourgeois culture, bourgeois morality, politics, art, everything. The bourgeois world was ground to pieces between extremes, an obvious victim of the neo-barbarian revolt that led to Hitler, but hardly its instigator. So, now you can protest, Kurt."

Kurt was so taken by surprise by this new argument that he begged off in order to think about it. Kenneth continued:

"Our second line of approach was this theory of cultural breakdown, or the passing of traditional society in Germany, which was rather new to me and, perhaps for that reason, held a particular fascination for me. Of course, I have read a great many fictional accounts and memoirs by Germans and, for that matter, Englishmen and Frenchmen, about the momentous transformations of a few decades and their impact on the lives and the peace of mind of the writers. I myself was too young before the First World War to have noticed the first warnings of change, the menace in the air; but after the war I clearly recall the sense of a whole world of bourgeois certainties and moral verities collapsing around us. I was in Germany at that time, attached to the occupation and really having a very good time myself. I met many Germans of all classes and know of the agonies and frights they were going through from one day to the next. I am deeply aware of all of the simplistic distortion of the choices open to them and the polemical misinterpretation of their decisions a later generation of harsh judges have made with the benefit of hindsight. I am pleased, therefore, to find a comprehensive explanation of the German state of mind in the 1920's which, instead of placing the guilt for everything on a particular class or group of fools or knaves, finds broad social causes to blame for the growing sense of chaos among the German masses.

"If I understood you right, Bernie, the crucial thing about the breakdown of traditional culture is the speed at which it occurs for the masses by and large. If it happens too fast, as with industrialization and urbanization in Germany, many people affected by it cannot adjust to their new life. They develop tremendous anxieties, latent hostility toward one another, perhaps also a high incidence of political extremism, and of mentally deviant behavior, etc. In particular, their awakened hunger for personal advancement exposes them to terrible frustrations and a sense of failure which become the chief fuel for corroding envy and ill-will, a kind of stock-car race syndrome which induces a man to begrudge and frustrate the success of anyone else as well. Of course, the reaction to these strains varies greatly from person to person. Some people respond to being uprooted from village or small town with a virulent anti-modernism, chauvinism, and xenophobic anti-semitism. Others again rise to the very same challenge with a splendid display of moral leadership and constructive thinking. If I may digress for a minute, the rabid French nationalist, revanchist and anti-semite, Maurice Barrès, for example, spent his boyhood in Lorraine trying to prove to himself and others that he was not a German. The late Robert Schuman, who also grew up there, became a peacemaker and the architect of Franco-German rapprochement and of a United Europe. It's the same with the different reactions toward economic crisis and frustrated social advancement. Some respond by developing stomach ulcers or a corroding hatred and envy which can turn them into harpies, while others seem to be ennobled by suffering and become more humanitarian in reaction to their own humiliation.

"The crisis of the cultural breakdown is compounded also by the failure of such groups as churches, schools, or the intelligentsia to supply new meanings and ethical goals when the old ones had evidently collapsed. Thus Germany became a classical example of cultural lag, a land of industrial and military giants and of ethical infants who preferred to leave politics to the giants or the experts. When people fail to take control after the passing of the old cultural precepts of personal conduct, the new generations grow up as rank barbarians, savages hiding behind uniforms, titles, or pious traditional appeals, or easily misled primitives who are too naïve to know their own hearts. I also found your comparison between Egypt and Germany rather instructive, especially the part about the imbalance of society: too many intellectuals and the miscarriage of social revolution into an imperial mission with the help of anti-British and anti-Israeli sentiment."

Jochen interrupted Kenneth at this point to express his admiration for the résumé. "I strongly agree that we should not look for fools or knaves," he said. "I have always been revolted by the standard historical accounts which make everything depend on what von Schleicher did, von Papen said, or von Hindenburg failed to do. Instead we ought to ask ourselves how men like that ever came to occupy such pivotal positions, or to look at the voting statistics of these years and at the motives which in 1932 induced more than 50 per cent of the German voters to vote either for the Nazis or for the Communists. The Papens and Hindenburgs will never come again, I am sure. But how can we keep the voters from losing their minds again and selling us out to the next paperhanger from Austria?"

"All right, I agree," said Kenneth somewhat impatiently. "But let me finish my summary first. Our third approach was the analysis of the German problem in terms of authoritarianism which Bernie professed to see in the class structure, in the role of women, in education and the relation between parents and children, in the prestige of knowledge and of the educated, and in the role of the state and the citizens' attitude toward bureaucrats. You may, perhaps, disagree with me on some points, but I was under the impression that, with the exception of elements that dovetail neatly with Bernie's theory of the rapid breakdown of traditional culture, there was preciously little left of the whole thesis of German authoritarianism at the end of our discussion. In other words, it is nonsense to see pathologically authoritarian relationships in the hierarchical forms of traditional society, for these relationships were present in the traditional culture of other Western countries as well, not to mention most new nations. One should likewise distinguish between, say, a Prussian of the old feudal-military tradition and a neo-Prussian or neo-militarist who tries to pour his insecure and shapeless personality into this rationalized mold in order to get a hold of himself or to give socially acceptable form to unacceptable aggressive urges. I for one look upon the stereotype excuse of some of Hitler's henchmen, *Befehl ist Befehl* (an order is an order), with great skepticism. Perhaps, some of these people delude themselves about the chaos within their own bosom. I guess it is no different with the other manifestations of authoritarianism, whether we are dealing with religious fanaticism after the old religion breaks down, or with fanatical adherence to an ideology, a quasi-religious crusade for some 'one and only truth,' or with a great attachment to the authoritarian state of old. It seems to me, that this German authoritarianism which is so often blamed for the rise of Hitler, was a transitional phenomenon and followed upon the all too rapid passing of traditional society. It was no more a permanent attribute of German national character than of French or British or anyone else's character. Once the transition is safely behind us and people find their bearings in their new lives, authoritarianism will pass with the other infantile disorders of modernization and social mobilization."

Bernie had ordered a small dish of *Bratwurst* sausages with sauerkraut and a roll. When Kenneth paused, he quickly interjected with raised eyebrows: "I can see that I should never have gone into this passing of traditional society. Incidentally, this is not 'Bernie's theory,' of course, but just a composite of modernization theories of various sociologists and anthropologists."

Kenneth smiled and said: "I'd be inclined to conclude from my summary that there seems to be nothing especially wicked or even unusual about the Germans as a nation before World War I. They showed signs of strain no different from other nations undergoing the great transformation, including a tendency toward political extremism and toward pursuing their own idea of 'Manifest Destiny.' "

"Now, wait a minute," Bernie interrupted him, gingerly wrapping some sauerkraut around his fork as if it were spaghetti. "I resent this identification of the American expansion toward the west with the German drive to conquer and enslave all of Europe. We were not trying to take away anything from anybody."

"Only from Mexico, Spain, Russia, England, and the Indians," Kenneth laughed. "But you're right. The land you grabbed was practically empty and there was very little resistance that you had to overcome by force. You're lucky, you see. In Europe, any land that you might want, any wealth and any resources are always and without exception owned by somebody else who will not relinquish them without a fight."

"Try to understand the psychology of the new German nation-state, Bernie," Jochen interjected pleadingly. "To the politically interested during and after the regime of Bismarck, the German position seemed very precarious and surrounded by hostile powers that had had a considerable headstart in economic and international strength. Germany was the latecomer, so it felt insecure and vaguely inferior. The great imperialistic rush for colonies, markets, and spheres of influence was already in full swing, and many Germans felt a curious moral ambiguity in the face of all this international greed and shameless power politics. They felt that perhaps they were being too decent, too naïve, too inhibited by moral scruples to take advantage of the opportunities for a fast gain. They secretly wished to become more ruthless and yet felt somehow morally superior to their greedy international competitors. I guess this is the same feeling that small businessmen have in a booming economy, a mixture of self-pity and a secret desire to make a killing through fraud since they believe that nobody ever gets rich by honest effort alone.

"The economic muscle of a nation and its position in international affairs, as you can see, are as intimately wedded to each other as the new riches of a tycoon and his craving for social prestige. During the brief thirty years preceding the First World War, Germany had become a newly rich society carried along on a pink cloud of boundless optimism and rising economic and political strength. Hence, when the Great War broke out, the Germans were absolutely positive that they would win, and within a very short time. It was not that they started it — this theory is, I think, rejected by all reputable Western historians today — or even that they wanted it to come about. Instead they waxed morally indignant at the encirclement by hostile neighboring powers who wanted to stop Germany from rising to her due place in the sun."

"But underneath," Bernie exclaimed triumphantly, "underneath, they were really spoiling for a fight. And as soon as they were in the war, they began to draw up plans for ever greater annexations, eastern France, Belgium, large territories in the east . . ."

"Let him finish, Bernie," Kurt interrupted. "Jochen is about to develop the main theme that led to Hitler, if I am not mistaken."

"Let us say that German public opinion indulged in the same moral ambiguity as I described before. The annexationists represented the half-acknowledged, half-repressed greed underneath the self-conscious stance of respectability.

"As you know, the war did not end in a short time. Instead it became the most horrible, exacting, never-ending nightmare the participant nations had ever been through. The first all-out war of masses of men and matériel for four grueling years, a devourer of men and of human sanity, a school of violence and destruction for a generation of marked men of whom many would never again find their way back to a civilized society. This war finally broke up the rest of the old society and the Bismarckian system of government. Worst of all, it was lost in what seemed to many a last-minute backstage maneuver that happened so quickly that people hardly grasped it."

"The truth of the matter," Kurt interjected with passion, "is that the German High Command had lied with such conviction and for such a long time to their own people and even to the *Reichstag* that hardly anyone realized the desperate situation of the German armies until General Ludendorff himself gave the sign to sue for an armistice. A short time later, that same Ludendorff had the gall to claim that the German army had been 'stabbed in the back' by traitors and conspirators at home. Talking about fools and knaves who are to be blamed for the rise of Hitler . . . Let me show you some . . ."

"All right," Jochen cut him short with a gesture, "let me continue describing the stage on which Hitler set foot. At the outset of the Great War there was a wave of popular enthusiasm inspired by the only popular remark the *Kaiser* ever made: 'I no longer know parties, only Germans.' Even the Social Democrats, who for years had planned to undercut any European war with international proletarian brotherhood, were swept off their feet by the exhilarating flush of patriotism. For the first time in their history, or so it seemed, all Germans felt united in one great national community, for better or for worse.

"Well, as you know, it got worse, and worse, and worse. Difficulties began to mount, casualties sky-rocketed, and the Allied blockade brought rationing at starvation levels. Also, Allied war propaganda felt compelled to depict their German adversaries as huns and devils in order to make the protracted conflict and mounting losses plausible to their own peoples. The Germans reacted to all this by splitting into two sharply defined camps. On the one hand, there were those in power who wanted to fight the gigantic struggle with all available means to the final victory whatever the cost. These were especially the military men, conservative aristocrats, and big businessmen. They gambled on the rewards of that final victory: annexations and war indemnities. Of course, the French made the same gamble, hoping that *le boche payera tout*. But they won and we didn't. The other political camp held out for an early end to the senseless slaughter, a peace by reconciliation among the warring powers, and no annexations for anyone. It was based on the return of the Social Democrats to their pre-war thoughts of international solidarity, and they were soon joined by the Progressive Party and by the Catholic Center Party."

"The two blocs called each other such endearing names as 'war prolongers' and 'cowards,' respectively," added Kurt. "And, of course, much of the bitterness between the two camps also stemmed from the fact that even if Germany won in the end, the common people were expected to suffer and to die most patriotically in the war, while the upper classes would reap the spoils of the final victory."

"Well," Jochen began again, "the popular sentiment under the strain of war shifted decisively from the right to the left, producing an increase of about 25 per cent of *Reichstag* seats for the Democratic and Socialist parties in the Constituent Assembly of 1919. The crest of this landslide of electoral opinion happened to coincide with sudden defeat in World War I, with the signing of the armistice, and the fall of the monarchies of *Reich* and states, as well as with the birth of the ill-starred Weimar Republic. It was spearheaded by revolutionary mobs which briefly established Soviet governments in Berlin and in Munich and had to be suppressed by force of arms."

"And that was the point at which the Social Democrats called in the infamous Free Corps to suppress their own confreres on the left," Bernie interrupted excitedly, raising his finger in admonition; "the Free Corps, many of whose members later became Nazi storm-troopers. In their typically German fear of disorder and anarchy, the Social Democrats made the same mistake as the moderate Liberals in the Frankfurt Assembly of 1848, who called in the troops of the old regime to protect them against their left-wing Democratic confreres. Won't you ever learn how to make a successful revolution?"

"You make it very easy for yourself with the benefit of hindsight," retorted Kurt angrily, since he believed these words were addressed to him. "What would you have done? Allow a totalitarian dictatorship of the Soviet type to establish itself? Or slide into civil war between the Reds and the Whites who were already organizing armed protective leagues and vigilante groups to guard against a Bolshevik coup. Besides, the Free Corps was needed to repel the Polish invasion. This *was* the best choice of policy under the circumstances."

"The Free Corps of that period has been an object of curiosity and suspicion for good reason," Kenneth intervened in a professorial tone. "Its members and those of the innumerable anti-Communist protective and vigilante organizations symbolize perhaps more than any other group the lost generation of the Great War: young men with no political program, no convictions, trained only to march and fight endlessly, even senselessly, spoiled for such pedestrian, bourgeois pursuits as holding down a job and raising a family, the pathetic products of the war experience; also the tens of thousands of non-commissioned officers left out in the cold by the limitations of the peace treaty on the size of the *Reichswehr,* hangers-on to the regular army whose livelihood depended on Free Corps assignments, assorted non-military jobs, and participation in illegal *Reichswehr* units. Naturally, these men wanted German rearmament, which to them would have spelled economic security and a future for the only way of life they knew. Hitler was one of these hangers-on after the war until the *Reichswehr* gave him a job as a kind of indoctrination officer."

"Jochen was going to tell us about the scene when Hitler entered German politics, wasn't he?" Bernie said

"I shall, if you let me proceed," Jochen began again. "You see, the great landslide which brought the three Weimar parties into power and determined the democratic character of the Weimar Constitution was dramatically reversed within a year. Immediately after the war, for example, the German Nationalist Party, the successor of several conservative pre-war parties, was so cowed by defeat that it did not even dare to advocate openly the re-establishment of the monarchy. By the time of the 1920 elections, a substantial number of voters had left the Democrats and the badly split Socialists again and returned to the opposition camp of German Nationalists and the right-wing Liberal People's Party (DVP). This strong resurgence of the right wing meant, in effect, that the leading elements of the old war party, the annexationists and 'war prolongers' of World War I, had rallied their popular support and could resume their strident clamor for a final victory. Of course, the rug was thereby pulled out from under the Weimar Republic, because the nationalistic opposition believed in part in resurrecting the monarchy and the privileges of the old ruling classes or, at least, felt nothing but contempt for democracy. And this retrogressive landslide to the right, in my opinion, was clearly due to two momentous events that occurred in the first half of 1919: one was the Communist uprisings and the establishment of Soviet-style workers' and soldiers' councils, which created a major Red scare; and the other the signing of the Peace Treaty of Versailles which, despite the promises implied in Woodrow Wilson's Fourteen Points, saddled Germany with guilt for the war, took away a good deal of German territory and all its colonies, and imposed substantial reparations, based, of course, on the assumption of German war guilt.

"Understand me right; I am not trying to place the blame on anybody or to rake over the coals of the Treaty of Versailles. I only want you to understand the psychological reaction of many Germans to

Versailles. It drove them back into the arms of aggressive nationalists. On hearing about the terms of the treaty they would have to sign,
lifelong pacifists and Socialist leaders swore that it should never be
signed, and everywhere the moral indignation felt at the beginning of
the war boiled up again at the thought of having to agree to a war
guilt clause contrary to their knowledge. The annexation of German
territory further confirmed the impression that the imposed treaty was
the product of the victorious chauvinism of French, Belgian, Italian,
and Slav nationalists. And, like all nationalists, the old German war
parties had absolutely no understanding for any annexationism and
national egotism other than their own.

"It was in this charged atmosphere of violent emotional reaction
and smoldering hatred that German revanchism was born, crystallizing about the 'stab in the back' legend, and spreading like an epi-
demic until Hitler was put in charge of bringing to a victorious conclusion what some historians have called the 'Thirty Years' War' of
the twentieth century."

"But why?" Bernie exclaimed. "I still don't understand why the
Germans felt they had to conquer the whole continent of Europe, if
not the world."

"Look," Kenneth interrupted him, gesticulating with his fountain-
pen, "you have a similar phenomenon in the United States. Don't you
remember the painful collapse of the American illusion of omnipo-
tence and invincibility at the time of the Korean armistice? Just like
the Germans, who were deceived about their own limitations until the
sudden collapse, the American right wing refused to believe that the
decline of American dominance could have taken place without the
aid of subversion, espionage, and conspiracy on a gigantic scale.
Even respectable American politicians have frequently accused the
leadership of Congress and the executive branch of pursuing a 'no-
win policy,' of a lack of determination and will-power to end the Cold
War with an all-out victory for America."

"A 'no-win policy' — " Jochen nodded eagerly, "excellent. That
was it, precisely. In fact, there is a propaganda film of Hitler celebrat-
ing his final triumph. He called it *The Triumph of the Will,* the will to
win. At its most strident, the nationalist propaganda line accused the
left-wing movements of having betrayed the country in its most sacred effort at winning its place in the sun. 'The November traitors,'

the nationalists called the leaders of the parties that took control after the fall of the monarchy. Hitler, who became the 'drummer' for their cause, was discovered by his *Reichswehr* employers and by other conservatives to be a spellbinding orator with an uncanny knack for verbalizing the frustrations of thousands of common people, veterans, officers, aristocrats, and traditionalistic conservatives of all walks of life. In an hour's speech, he could mobilize their energies and enthusiasm and launch them emotionally on a fervent campaign to win the final victory. And this victory, as he never failed to point out, had to be won in two stages: the internal liberation from 'the Weimar system' and its politicians, and the external liberation, the final victory in war. Naturally, these enemies of a 'no-win policy' had utter contempt for the liberalism and democracy of the Weimar Constitution in which they professed to see further alien influences foisted upon Germany by the November traitors. It is surprising that the Weimar Republic even lasted as long as it did with this chorus of opposition from the right, including many high civil servants, diplomats, and judges, and the entire *Reichswehr,* not to mention the revolutionaries on the extreme left.

"A typical example of the corrosive hatred of the nationalistic groups was the campaign of vilification against Matthias Erzberger, the Center Party politician who had been instrumental in the implementation of the armistice and who convinced the reluctant government that it would have to sign the Versailles Treaty in order to forestall the threatened Allied invasion and partition of Germany. After this, the right wing hounded him relentlessly in a concerted campaign of character assassination and petty harassment, finally destroying his political career. After several attempts on his life, two young officers shot him down like a hunted animal."

"Such a personal hate campaign, I suppose," Kenneth interjected, "is complementary to hero worship, both being panaceas to pathological minds. The hero or great leader is expected to solve all your problems; the elimination of the hate-figure which personifies all the hostile elements is supposed to end all your trials and tribulations at one stroke.

"There are some criminal urges in varying degrees in all of us, I suspect. But during times of great political emotions, crises, and frustrations, that's when the criminal tendencies really come out under the protective cover of political idealism, or even patriotism. In wartime, at least, you can channel all the personal aggressiveness toward the enemy. But in peacetime, when the wildest expressions of chauvinism are no longer considered respectable, then what?"

"There are always hate groups," Bernie answered glumly, thinking apparently of personal experiences, "and campaigns of character assassination, even against persons of the greatest integrity. I could name some masters at this sinister art back in the States. And when there has been enough of a hate campaign, a mob or a confused young man of criminal bent appears from nowhere to commit a dastardly crime, an act of terrorism, or a bombing. In the American South, in fact, emotions have been running so high over the race issue for the last ten years that violence is touched off by the smallest of causes. All it takes to call out the hoodlums is a hint of official connivance with lawlessness by an ambitious politician who is out for another term in the state house. And after the horrible deed is done, you still find the haters gleeful over the vicarious execution of their crime. It is disturbing to see how the good people of the South allow their emotional reaction to eat its way into common decency and respect for law and order. I guess, the climate of opinion in the Weimar Republic must have been similar."

"I am sure it was," Kurt agreed. "There was also plenty of official connivance by judges, police, and bureaucrats with right-wing violence. But it was not only the impact of the Versailles Treaty that poisoned and corroded all social and political relationships. A combination of issues and grievances provided the fuel for the rise of Hitler, not any single cause. I agree with you, Jochen, that German revanchism was the main factor that brought Hitler to power. But this was true only after he and the nationalists had succeeded in focusing all other grievances and popular discontent on this one issue. Among these other grievances were the severe economic crises suffered by various groups of German society, especially the Great Depression, which triggered the final collapse of the Republic. Another source of massive discontent was the traditionalist revolt, the political reaction of elements of pre-industrial society to the manifestations of the twentieth century. A third motive was the rise of the masses to political self-consciousness, however awkward and gullible; and a fourth the presence of vast numbers of disoriented, lost souls, especially among the young generation, who were drawn into the extremist movements by the tens of thousands. Finally, the ability of Hitler to appeal to the legions of discontented and frightened and to rally their support behind him at a crucial moment, as well as his skill in hoodwinking the old military and conservative elites who helped him into power, were major factors in bringing about his totalitarian rule. It was the combination of all these factors, not any single cause, that did it."

"I noticed that you have not even mentioned the explicit rejection by a majority of German voters of parliamentary democracy in favor of authoritarian dictatorship," Bernie interjected, wagging an admonishing finger. "Don't you think that this decision was also very significant in bringing Hitler into power? After rejecting democracy the Germans got the government they deserved."

"I don't think this interpretation is entirely fair to the facts, Bernie," Kurt said after some reflection. "The way things really happened, there was never a clear contest for or against democracy, except, perhaps, at the beginning of the Weimar Republic. Even then, Germans were really voting against the old regime rather than for democracy. Perhaps, they never really understood democracy as an alternative to authoritarian rule or to totalitarianism. In the early 1930's, likewise, they were voting for Communists and fascists largely as a protest against the glaring failure of the parties and leaders of the Republic, to give them jobs and orderly government. Even the anti-democratic right was not very much concerned with fighting democracy as such. It just scorned it and considered it part of 'the system' of which it wished to rid the country."

"If I may add my twopence worth to Kurt's remarks," Kenneth added, "we Westerners should be more aware of the fact that there is nothing inevitable or obvious about the arrival of democracy in a developing country, which, of course, Germany still was. We should also take seriously the fact that the Germans have generally been confronted with democracy in the most undemocratic manner, namely by the bayonets of a victorious army.

"What's more, we should not be so smug about the failure of Germany to develop a working constitutional system under the Weimar Republic. After all, how many countries were there in those days that had succeeded in evolving a stable system of responsible popular government?" He counted them off on the fingers of both hands. "There

is Britain, with her unique advantages and habits; the older dominions; the United States, which had the benefit of maturing in isolation; the Scandinavian countries, with their relative isolation and their
felicitous habit of sitting down to talk over their problems and reach
a compromise; Switzerland, the Low Countries, and Czechoslovakia.
France had great difficulties throughout the nineteenth century and
also during the early Third Republic, under the shadow of royalism,
anti-semitism, and revanchism, a period very much like that of the
Weimar Republic, except for its economics. Today the French are
again in an acute state of political crisis, and I would not call their
government an example of responsible popular government. The
change from authority, monarchy, and empire to popular self-
government is always fraught with great dangers, especially if economic crisis and war aggravate the normal stresses of transition.
Look at the list of casualties in the period between the wars: Italy,
Portugal, Spain, Austria, Poland, Hungary, Bulgaria, Yugoslavia,
Romania, not to mention Russia, many an Asian or African nation
today, or the Latin American countries. Germany was simply another
failure on the list.

"And the reasons for its failure are by no means obscure, nor need
we search for glaring abnormalities in the German national character
to explain it. With the exception of the issue of revanchism, the reasons for the failure of Weimar are similar to those which caused
many of the other failures to establish responsible popular government."

Kenneth made a dramatic pause in order to take a deep draft of
beer while holding the attention of his listeners with an eloquent gesture of his left hand. Then he continued:

"Look at the countries which succeeded in the great transformation without succumbing to the lures of extremist demagoguery on the
way. Every one of them had a well-established pattern of political co-
operation and group compromise, usually resting on a system of political parties or other representative devices in which the political leaders were accustomed to co-operation in solving their common
problems and resolving their conflicts. Such a system of political co-
operation is like a game with roles and well-defined rules. The object
of the game is to put the common problems and group conflicts
through a procedure which is designed to give the contending parties

a fair chance to present their claims and views, and which will bring each case to an authoritative conclusion.

"Now, you know how important gamesmanship is to us British, in politics as well as in everything else. Well, from what I have been able to observe, the Germans are not only poor sports, bad losers, and worse winners, who seem to have little sense of fairness and are rarely willing to leave well enough alone; they also seem to be quite unaware of the point of it all. In the days of the Weimar Republic, for example, the favorite definition of politics among German writers and politicians was that it is a struggle for power. Instead of thinking of it as an orderly game they thought of it as a free-for-all. Their parties, consequently, were organized more like military organizations, with thorough indoctrination and militant intransigence, than the representative devices of responsible popular government that they should have been. Toward the last days of the Republic, the chief antagonists among the parties even had large para-military formations with banners, uniforms, and arms, a telling reflection of this struggle-for-power idea. Or, let me cite another example: I believe most Germans of that day were more interested in politics than they are generally given credit for, but that again they had the wrong idea about its nature. They assumed very poetically, or romantically, that almost anything could play a role in it, the army, para-military organizations, would-be saviors, knights in shining armor, half-religious expectations of utopia, big lies, dictators — anything at all that seemed capable of swaying men's minds.

"But politics in the sense in which I am using the word is a very limited and restrained game which has little use for all this poetic license, this metapolitics of irrationalism, deceit, and force. The mistake the Germans made here is about the same as that of a young man who confuses marriage with unlimited love life between the sexes. Undoubtedly, a limited political game or a monogamous marriage holds less appeal to the senses and to a lively imagination than the other alternatives. But there's sanity in self-restraint. Oh, all right, so I am a bachelor and should be quite ignorant of what it means to be married," he quickly added with an undertone of annoyance, seeing the grin spreading over Bernie's face.

Then he went on: "The biggest shortcoming of the Weimar Republic, I suspect, was the lack of communication between the different political parties and the many social and economic groups, who were all in trouble as a result of the common predicament but were simply too selfish and too short-sighted to try to solve their common problems together. This is where the remaining class distinctions, the doctrinaire ideological commitments, and the caste spirit of the different groups really produced disaster and led to universal friction and hatred among all. It was a prime reason why no game of politics ever developed and no consensus evolved about the rules of the game, least of all on the foundation of the Weimar Constitution. Without a game of politics, of course, the Weimar system was ill-equipped to handle the many problems which needed to be solved.

"Of course, the failure to develop such a pattern of political cooperation and compromise politics goes back to the pre-war policies of the monarchy, of the conservative parties, and of Bismarck who deliberately chose to exclude the vast majority of Germans from any share in political authority. This disastrous and shortsighted policy, like so many open sores of pre-war days, had been forgotten during the times of prosperity and political strength. But after the disastrous defeat, and with the *Kaiser,* the monarchic buttress of it all, in ignominious flight, this failure to establish a political consensus came back at the Weimar Republic with a terrible vengeance. Instead of a well-established system of party government which could integrate the demands of the various social and economic interests as far as possible into the general public policies, the Germans then called for an authoritarian state and got utter chaos; with all the political, social, and economic groups fighting each other to the death, fantastic schemes of social revolution and utopian Third Reichs mobilizing vast masses of people, and violent street fighting and coups d'état taking place on repeated occasions. The Weimar Republic really broke down long before Hitler took power."

"Don't you think, though," Jochen pleaded, "that the rise of Hitler could have been prevented, if the monarchy had continued to be there or had been restored as a focal point of legitimate authority, an element of continuity, something to cling to in confusion and crisis? I am not saying this out of a preference for monarchy. But just look at the historical parallels: how the French fell for Napoleon as a substitute for their beheaded king, or for many another man on horseback after that. When Hindenburg was first elected President of the

Weimar Republic, I think, many Germans regarded him as an *ersatz Kaiser* and had confidence in him because he symbolized some of the old pre-war glamor."

"Why not in President Ebert, his Social Democratic predecessor?" Kurt queried sarcastically. "Or do you object to him as an *ersatz Kaiser* because he was only a saddler by profession?"

"That is hardly the point," Kenneth intervened. "Jochen's suggestion has merit, I believe. As long as the crusty old general was willing to uphold the constitution and as long as he was capable of playing his role with circumspection, he was certainly preferable to Hitler. At least he gave repose to the mind of the average middle-class burgher who was disturbed by the unaccustomed spectacle of warring parties and interest groups."

"I like the way you qualified your endorsement with the words 'as long as he was capable of playing his role with circumspection,'" Kurt retorted with bitterness. "That's just the point. He wasn't for long. He appointed Hitler. It was he and the German monarchists and nationalists who actually helped Hitler into the saddle."

Jochen and Kenneth both rose in protest. Bernie tried to mollify them and induced them to sit down again.

Finally Kurt said, in order to change the subject: "I suppose, the Weimar Republic would have survived also in one way or another, if the Great Depression with its vast amount of bankruptcies, unemployment, and other economic crises and miseries, had not occurred?"

"Really now," Bernie objected, "this is another point I have never been able to understand. I can still comprehend German revanchism. But why should a whole nation go berserk because of an economic crisis? Why should they want to go out and take more *Lebensraum* from others who were just as much in the troughs of depression as they? The British and the French . . ."

". . . also responded with a great surge of political extremism to the depression," Kenneth interrupted him quickly and added: "And so did Americans, if my knowledge of recent history doesn't deceive me."

Kurt gave Kenneth a grateful sidelong glance and said: "There are several factors which you must consider, Bernie. First of all, Germany's industrial build-up had been particularly rapid and had reached a very high point of development, which made an all-out depression all the more catastrophic. The war years had already brought a major reversal of the pre-war boom, and defeat destroyed many a fortune and caused painful economic dislocations, armies of unemployed veterans, and an inadequate food supply for masses of people. Then there was the runaway inflation culminating in the frenzy of 1923, when people committed suicide right and left as they saw their savings wiped out, their businesses destroyed, or their families reduced to utter penury."

"My mother still has a cigar box full of inflationary bank notes from that time," Jochen interrupted. "There is a big wad of 500 billion mark notes in it for which you could buy something like one loaf of bread apiece at the height of inflation."

Kurt smiled and continued: "And throughout there was also the lingering farm crisis, bankruptcy among farmers and small businessmen who could no longer meet the competition of the big businesses. Germany was so full of groups of every conceivable sort afflicted by one grave economic crisis after another that their economic nerves lost all resistance to the buffeting of fate. By the time the Great Depression struck, German society was so softened up that large sections of it panicked into the irrationalism of extremist parties at the first touch of another collapse.

"And what a total collapse! Up until the elections of 1930 the Nazis had been a group of the lunatic fringe with no more support than similar groups elsewhere — well, except for the year of the great inflation when their vote was large, and the general crisis and the French occupation of the Rhineland almost produced a conservative dictatorship. In 1930, the number of Nazi representatives in the *Reichstag* rose to almost ten times what it had been in 1928. Most of their new supporters belonged to the middle class: shopkeepers, white-collar employees, civil servants, also farmers and a great many youthful voters who had never voted before, a whole wave of frightened, often unpolitical victims of the economic crisis."

"They were afraid of being demoted from the middle class to the status of proletarians, of blue-collar workers, weren't they?" Bernie probed with an undertone of disapproval.

"That's a very misleading formulation," Kurt replied. "And it is based on a misleading picture of German society. With industrialization, the enormous increase in population and the impact of the war on many middle-class fortunes, a typical shopkeeper, civil servant, or white-collar family became quite dependent on the current income of the breadwinner. Then, if he lost his job, or if his shop was closed down, or if his income declined substantially, they had nothing to fall back on. They became public charges or had to beg from their relatives. And it was this rather than the dread of the prospect of a blue-collar job, for there weren't any. Mass unemployment soon ran into the millions. There was no possibility of 'stepping down' into blue collar work. You also must not imagine these social classes as one below the other in this sense. A successful blue-collar worker often led a richer and more rewarding life than many a struggling white-collar man. If you were a bankrupt shopkeeper, a laid-off salesman, or a jobless artisan, you were a flop and simply joined all the other flops on the welfare rolls, in beer halls, and on street-corners.

"By 1932, of course, millions of unemployed workers began to vote for Hitler, too. Or for the Communists. Once you are down in the economic doldrums, with little regard for the height from which you came, you become a part of the vast, nameless sea of despair. The elemental discouragement is all the same whether it comes from being disinherited, frustrated in the middle of your career, or dispossessed of the future that all young people crave to see in front of them. There is an all-pervading feeling of social malaise. Something basic must be wrong with society. The whole society is conspiring against you. There has been a terrible, fundamental betrayal somewhere where no one suspected it. Capitalism, if you will, has welshed on its promise of economic affluence, or the rationalistic modern civilization has betrayed itself. The magic of technology has proven to be hollow. Mothers and children are starving. The family farm, the natural way of life, the genuine German way of life is dying. Small wonder if people in the doldrums begin to follow the saviors of the right and of the left — Nazis and Communists. It no longer mattered which.

"A big depression puts a man completely at the mercy of this great beast, economic society. During successive stages of industrialization this economic society first destroys all hereditary status and then eats up all wealth until vast masses of people live solely from their income. Their income, of course, is determined by their function in society, their usefulness to society. And then one day," Kurt made a dramatic gesture with both hands, "one day a great depression breaks out and the great beast tells you that your function, your usefulness to society, is worth *nothing*. You lose your income, your shop, your job, your self-respect. You are at the end of your rope."

A pall of silence fell over the group. Finally, Kenneth spoke up and said: "I guess you are quite right in emphasizing the psychological aspects of a depression over the purely economic effects. There is nothing so well-designed to lure the skeletons out of a man's mental closet as unemployment and failure. I realize, Bernie, why you are reluctant to accept the fact that Germans should react in such an extreme fashion to the great economic collapse. But just think of the peculiar nature of life in modern industrial society, where everything is staked on a person's economic success. I am also reminded of the year 1923, the rehearsal for the rise of dictatorship in Germany, when economic and other crises had the peculiar effect of bringing scores of self-appointed saviors, sectarian movements, and fantastic schemes of reorientation and reorganization to the fore. Crisis seems to make people so gullible and receptive to saviors and panaceas. And there's never a want of demagogues or fanciful appeals. I was not in Germany at the time of the great Nazi landslide, but I imagine it was similar."

"Perhaps even worse," said Jochen. "There was a basic difference between the plans for military coups and for a 'March on Berlin' of 1923 and the upheaval of the early 'thirties. In 1923, despite the deep crisis and the employment of Hitler's talents as demagogue to win the people to the conservative cause, the masses of the people were not involved and simply sat it out on the sidelines. Between that time and the 1930's, however, this changed. The masses became mobilized, and there was a great surge of mass democracy, of egalitarianism that challenged the remaining old elites, the aristocrats, and even the fat cats of the middle class. This surge of the German masses actually dated back to the egalitarianism of the war experience, but received new impetus during the economic crisis of the Republic. And Hitler very skillfully intercepted this surge of the masses for his own purposes."

"Wait a minute," Bernie interrupted him. "Did I hear you say that the growth of egalitarianism and democracy in Germany led to Hitler's rise?"

"Well, yes," Jochen replied. "You see, when you Anglo-Americans use the word democracy, you really mean constitutional democracy, or what Kenneth called a well-established game of politics. But this aspect of orderly rules and procedures cannot be taken for granted in most countries where the lower classes are just beginning to flex their muscles. These lower classes are the *demos,* the people, at least numerically, and when they begin to take over, you get a kind of democracy, but not your kind. Without good leadership, or Kenneth's game of politics, you get instead mob rule, democracy by plebiscite, Bonapartism, or at least a very emotional and often nationalistic populism that is more likely to hurt itself by its own immaturity than to make responsible decisions."

"Immaturity is too charitable a word," Kurt interjected bitterly. "The rising German masses were true to their symbolic figure, the German *Michel* with the nightcap; how they allowed the wool to be pulled over their eyes! I agree that it is most important to distinguish between the leader and the misled masses in such a case of colossal fraud. But did they really have to be so incredibly stupid?" Turning to Jochen, who looked dismayed, Kurt continued: "The French in those days had their right- and left-wing demagogues, too. But the French masses were much too suspicious of the demagogues' personal motives and their secret sources of financial support to fall for any of them on such a large scale. The French also had a sound horror of dictatorship for which I look in vain among my countrymen even today. If there were any aspersions cast upon the character or the financial backers of Hitler by anyone, I just know what the typical German reaction would have been: his followers would be furious about seeing their own dreams of their hero destroyed and would turn angrily upon the 'dirty mind' of the cynic who exposed him. Germans love to be enthusiastic about anything, no matter what; and they think it's a mark of a low mind to be matter of fact about the objects of their cult."

"True enough, Kurt," Kenneth said, cleaning out his pipe. "But you should also take into account that this was a time when a lot of elaborate new techniques for organizing and bamboozling the masses were just being invented and turned loose on the inexperienced populace. Advertising slogans, handbill campaigns, house-to-house canvassing, totalitarian propaganda, and cell organization—this vast array of new manipulatory techniques, supported by psychological insights into the role of symbols and myths, and by new media such as the radio, had just begun to appear. Men like Lenin, Stalin, Mussolini, and Hitler, in fact, devised many of these techniques and avidly learnt from one another. German social scientists who kept abreast of these inventions were unable to forewarn the public of what was happening. Hitler revealed a hideous stroke of genius when he discovered that the best way to build up a powerful totalitarian mass movement was to use a Big Lie, a freely invented ideology of hate, a demonology, but at any rate a lie so big that it can be accepted on faith or rejected *in toto*. This created the black and white picture that appealed so much to the mentality of the followers of such a party.

"All this was just evolving and the public had not yet built up the immunity toward advertising or skepticism about publicity campaigns that exists today. Especially in Germany, the country of Platonic education and good government, people believed anything that appeared in print, in particular if it was sanctioned by governmental authority. Germans are very literal people. In this setting it made an enormous difference that Hitler and his henchmen were openly favored by such old authorities as judges, bureaucrats, police magistrates, and military notables. Also, that he was legally appointed by Hindenburg and endowed with extraordinary powers by an Enabling Act passed by the *Reichstag*. Germans are accustomed to governments that make no mistakes and, least of all, commit such a disastrous error. It seems to me that the President and his advisers and the *Reichstag* majority were far more culpable than the gullible masses."

"But why didn't the masses revolt, or the groups which installed him, once they found out what a mistake they had made?" Bernie asked, doubtfully raising his bushy eyebrows.

"Hitler was a clever man," Kenneth answered. "He was very careful (during the first years) not to arouse any opposition except from his declared scapegoat groups. It was not until a number of years later, when he had thoroughly consolidated his position and subordinated all rival groups and powers, such as labor or the army, that he started such infamous deeds as the persecution and eventual murder of the Jews and the launching of World War II. I should also emphasize his astonishing initial success in reducing the catastrophic unemployment and restoring, with the co-operation of many foreign powers, the international position of Germany. It would be very unfair on our part to condemn the downtrodden masses for lacking the fore-sight to look beyond the immediate relief of their misery until it was too late. Then there was also the great mass of opportunists who joined the bandwagon. Once the design for totalitarian control of the whole society was completed there was hardly an opportunity for any opposition to organize, especially not during wartime."

"Let's come back to the subject of the Big Lie," Bernie suggested. "If I understood you right, then the campaign against the 'no-win policy' of the Weimar governments, against the 'stab in the back' by the November traitors, and the Treaty of Versailles and the men who had signed it — those were all important parts of Hitler's Big Lie which appealed to the Germans. What about anti-Communism, was that a part of it, too?"

"Yes, of course," answered Kurt. "Anti-Communism and anti-Socialism, and anti-Marxism in general. And it suited the compulsive consistency of Hitler's more paranoid followers that you could simply reduce the German defeat in World War I, Versailles, and the 'no-win policy' to the activity of Marxist revolutionaries and subversives who were now holding high office in the Weimar Republic."

"What about anti-semitism? Where did it fit in?" Bernie queried. "Was Hitler's anti-semitism a major attraction to the German electorate?"

"I don't believe it was, to answer your last question first," Kurt re-plied. "It did fit in nicely with the Big Lie for those minds that were inclined to go for it. For paranoid consistency you could always re-duce Marxism and the Socialist movement further to a worldwide Jewish conspiracy, and for the traditionalistic elements, say of small business, agriculture, and the civil service, you could throw in capital-ism, international finance, and the whole twentieth century as further manifestations of that worldwide conspiracy. In fact, you could even claim, with pseudo-scientific overtones, that at the bottom of it all there was a creeping corruption of the blood, of the vitality of West-ern man. Thus everything in the world could be made to fall into a logical framework that could supply certainty and peace to disturbed minds."

"Well, that's an old trick of anti-semites everywhere to polish off Moscow and Wall Street in one stroke," Bernie observed. "But what about support for these views among the German population?"

"That's a long story," Jochen hastened to say, "and it is difficult to answer in quantitative terms, because you cannot, in practice, identify all the Hitler voters of 1930 or 1932 with anti-semitism, or even divide people neatly into anti-semites and philo-semites. This is due, in part, to the many varieties of anti-semitic sentiment that have appeared in the course of modern history and the link between outbreaks of anti-semitism and social or economic crises."

"Many varieties of anti-semitism?" Bernie asked suspiciously. "Just what are you trying to prove?"

"I consider it fundamental to an understanding of Nazi anti-semitism to draw these distinctions," Jochen replied with great seriousness. "Of course, all varieties of prejudice are ignoble and immoral, some pathological. But behind each kind of prejudice stands a different, and non-interchangeable, mentality, and it is simply not true that one kind leads to another. A person prejudiced against all religious faiths as well as Judaism is not a racist. And people with an intense prejudice against strangers, foreigners, or other people who are different, including some Jews, are very typical of the great transformation from a rural to an urban way of life. Then there is also an economically motivated prejudice which springs from the stresses and strains of the evolving industrial society and channels many different kinds of frustration and failure into hostility against a particular minority. Farmers in some regions would associate Jews with the disliked middlemen between producers and consumers, small businessmen linked them with the competition in a contracting market, while both groups singled them out as the scapegoat for their fear of Big Business and banking. Some of the less successful members of the professions saw in them all-too-able competitors." Noticing Bernie's skeptical look, Jochen interrupted himself and began to plead: "Look, Bernie, I am not trying to construct an alibi for what Germans have done to the Jews. I am in full agreement with you that this is the most horrible blot on the German record. But how can I ever explain how it could happen, if you won't listen?"

"Jochen is right, Bernie," Kurt added. "You should not jump to blanket conclusions until you have heard him out. The long history of religious intolerance in Germany as well as elsewhere is no real precedent for Nazi anti-semitism, although it may have neutralized some of the potential opposition of Christians to the inhumanity of the Nazis. I am thinking, for example, of the recent West German play

The Deputy, whose author accuses the Vatican of failure to resist and protest against the Nazi persecution of the Jews." He cast a sidelong glance at Jochen, the Christian Democrat. "And religious intolerance is still as strong in Germany today as it ever was in the Middle Ages. Just a few years ago, the Jehovah's Witnesses held a congress here in this city. Both churches, the Catholics and the Protestants, promptly distinguished themselves by appealing to their flocks not to rent any rooms to the Witnesses. I could tell you many stories . . ."

"All right; who's talking about being knifed in the back?" Jochen interrupted him in a low voice while his ears had turned a bright crimson.

Kenneth intervened and admonished the two in his professorial voice: "Let's stick to the subject now, shall we? I also thought Jochen's points were well taken. During the earlier stages of the great transformation in many countries, pride in the national development often conflicts with the tensions and frustrations common to a modern industrial society. A worker takes pride in the industrial muscle of his country, in the creative leadership of the management, and yet he cannot but hate the factory-system, the low wages and working conditions, and the enviable status of owners and management. A small businessman also cannot but admire the power of the big fish in the economic pond, even though he fears them and hates the system of competition which delivers him helpless into their hands. This conflict of feelings is inevitable and becomes aggravated whenever depressions strike, especially among the business failures and the unemployed. The most convenient way out of this confusion of emotions is to put the blame on a minority of the people — in this case, the Jews. The Nazis had even refined this solution to the point of distinguishing between Aryan capitalism, which was said to be creative, and Jewish capitalism, which was branded a destructive and corrosive element.

"A minority never has it easy. In the case of the German Jews, matters were complicated further by their small number and by the provincial cast of mind of most Germans, many of whom hardly knew any Jews or did not know them well. Most Western and Southern European nations have had infinitely more contact with foreigners, far-off cultures, and other races. The land-bound Germans and, I suppose, also many East European peoples lack the sophistication and experience which comes from a long seafaring, trading, or colo-

nial tradition. Many well-meaning Germans I know speak about
other races and minority problems, if ever they do, with an embarrassing lack of tact and empathy which seems to indicate that their
minds never quite left the countryside or little towns."

Bernie smiled, thinking of the rustic trimmings on Jochen's jacket
the night before, when he noticed that Jochen was wearing a fashionable blazer without lapels. Jochen looked up in surprise at Bernie's
apparent interest in his clothes. Somewhat flustered, Bernie began to
speak: "I grant you that perhaps they are awkward and tactless about
minority relations, but I would certainly prefer a well-meaning but
naïve provincial to a vicious but polished urbanite like Josef Goebbels. Prejudice indeed feeds on failure, frustration, and maladjustment. Show me an anti-semite, or any other hater, and I'll show you a
person who in some important way has never quite realized his potential as a human being, a failure of one sort or another. And for a
Goebbels to channel all the resentments and to turn them on a minority for a scapegoat, why, that is like kicking a man in the teeth when
he is already lying on the ground. I guess," he added after a short
pause, "this is about as good a definition of fascism as any: Kicking a
man in the teeth when he is lying on the ground."

"But I really meant to say that the kind of anti-semitism that motivated Hitler and his henchmen was of a very different sort from the
religious, xenophobic, or economic types that I described," Jochen
objected timidly.

Bernie was startled and asked with an undertone of long-held suspicion: "What do you mean, it was different? Different in what way?
Do you mean that they were rank opportunists who just used anti-
semitism as their Big Lie, in order to climb to power?"

"Not entirely," Jochen stuttered. "I mean they were, of course, extremely opportunistic in the sense of exploiting religious intolerance,
xenophobia, economic frustration, or crisis reactions, and in the sense
of using every trick they could to play on the emotions of the masses.
But then, they were really a small band of fanatic sectarians, dedicated to the point of complete abandon to a few pseudo-scientific
ideas about race and history. Like other ideologies, I guess, their kind
of racism consisted basically of a few half-baked shreds of sociological insight grasped with quasi-religious fervor. Well," he turned to
Kurt, the Social Democrat, "perhaps Marxism is more sophisticated,

but its basic ingredients are the same: a handful of outdated sociological insights defended with religious fanaticism. And the followers are of a similar frame of mind: people so deeply disaffected from the society around them that they cling unwaveringly to fixed ideas and are willing to do almost anything to further their cause. What kinds of twisted minds or criminal tendencies may have been lurking beneath their disaffection, I suspect, varied widely from person to person."

Kurt, who had listened to Jochen's diatribe against Marxism with an amused smile, now eagerly agreed: "This is actually the most fascinating question about such a movement. One would expect people of such profound disaffection from society to be quite dumb about politics and how to manipulate people. Some are. Others again have a veritable power complex that drives them to seek publicity and influence, and a large number of these extremist minds on the right as well as the left possess an extraordinary touch for politics and for manipulating people. Evil geniuses such as Hitler and Goebbels are a formidable menace even though they may be as deeply disturbed themselves as some of their most demented followers."

"Yes, this is a very important distinction," Jochen nodded, "and in the development of the sect into a political movement the more power-oriented, the more effective orators and organizers naturally go to the top of the movement. But the fanatical core remained essentially as I have described it, a mere handful of zealots striving for power, except that the great economic crisis temporarily gave them a vast landslide of popular support. It was just beginning to recede when President Hindenburg made the fatal mistake of appointing Hitler Chancellor.

"And I am fairly certain that the huge mass of Germans who decided to vote for Hitler in the early 'thirties was only in very small part attracted by his anti-semitism, even granting the psychological effects of the crisis. After all, there was another large party, the German Nationalists, who were anti-semitic and also beat the drums for traditionalism and nationalism. No, the Nazis had some special additional trump cards which no other party possessed in quite the same manner. For one thing, they possessed a superb propaganda machine and a well-geared organization unlike anyone to the right of the Communists, from whom they had copied it. Secondly, they took great pains to offer to every group exactly what it wanted: the welfare state and socialism to the workers, the abolition of unions to management, credit and a boost for the morale to the farmers, monarchy to the monarchists, populism to the rabble, nationalism to the nationalists, a bigger army to the military, and so on. Thirdly, they presented the image of Hitler as a man of the people, the simple private who had become almost a kinship figure, an *alter ego* to many a small guy struggling for survival. And fourthly — not counting the three issues mentioned above, anti-semitism, revanchism, and the traditionalist revolt — after a decade of partisan squabbles Hitler offered an image of energy and decisiveness that few Germans could withstand. In the atmosphere of economic crisis and the political turbulence, Germans were frightened by all this belligerent pluralism of groups fighting for spoils and for power. Hitler instead offered them a totalitarian utopia where no conflicts would ever occur in society."

"But if anti-semitism was not the most important selling point for the Nazis," Bernie began to probe again, "then why was it not a deterrent to Nazi popularity? What do you think would happen to a party or a politician in the United States who advocated anti-semitism? They'd be beaten, that's what."

"This yardstick does not seem to apply to avowed anti-Negro politicians in the South," Kenneth interrupted sarcastically, puffing on his pipe. "No, regarding the German situation in 1930 or 1932, the truth of the matter seems to be that the German masses were neither particularly anti-semitic nor were they liberal enough to balk at the open anti-semitism of the Nazis. I realize that what I am going to say will make your liberal soul cringe. I believe, the Germans simply did *not* take anti-semitism very seriously. They regarded it, as do many people in England, as a gentlemen's vice, too vulgar, perhaps, to be talked about by others, but basically a private idiosyncrasy that was nobody else's business. You might say, they simply did not understand its significance and dynamic portent, either as an indication of mental aberration or as a blue-print for genocide. And, mind you, the Nazis never let on what was in their minds.

"It is true that there were vulgarians such as Julius Streicher from whose ravings one might have feared results of mayhem and murder. But this fear was hardly compelling even to those directly threatened by Streicher's speeches. I remember talking to two Jewish writers in 1938 and being told, 'My dear friend, you are seeing ghosts.' There is a vast gulf between mere talk of racial superiority and systematic genocide, just as there is between Karl Marx's call for the 'expropriation of the expropriators' and Stalin's mass murder of the *kulaks*.

"And as for the Germans, I have already mentioned how provincial they were and how inexperienced in the dangers of group hatred and hate-mongering. In America, perhaps, you have a general popular awareness of the problems involved and a healthy fear of hate groups. But in Weimar Germany and elsewhere in Europe, I have found not only ignorance, but also a vast callousness toward social injustice in many forms, a kind of unconcern for such temporal problems which is as timeless and ancient as the venerable old cultures etched into the beautiful, but cruel face of the continent."

Bernie looked Kenneth in the eye and, after a little pause, said: "I believe I know what you mean by inexperience mixed with the callousness of old civilizations. I have seen examples of this in India." He relapsed into his silence. Finally, he turned to Jochen: "Could you tell us more about what you mean exactly by calling the Nazis a sectarian movement?"

"Well, now," Jochen responded, "of course, it would be very presumptuous of me to make this assertion without emphasizing that most Nazi voters and, in fact, many party members had very little, if anything, to do with this sectarian anti-semitism. During the Weimar years, many of Hitler's 'old fighters' were just that, bully boys, or eternal adolescents, or the 'eternal marchers' of World War I. The heterogeneous origin of the Nazi party, the issue of Versailles, and the opportunistic leadership encouraged many other lost souls to join. Besides, any full-blown mass organization tends to develop a rationale of its own, with group loyalties, individual ambitions, and other motivations that have little to do with the ideology the movement professes. In fact, some of the sectarian anti-semites were in other groups, such as the so-called folkish conservatives or the German Nationalists where they played an increasingly important role in producing the decline of the Republic. Some may have stayed out of political activity altogether. After Hitler came to power, moreover, thousands of high-ranking party members were merely opportunists, though far from innocent, but at any rate not at all deeply committed to sectarian anti-semitism.

"The sectarian movement actually goes back to the nineteenth century and to the ethnic fringe areas in Imperial Austria and Germany, where an upper class of German merchants had for centuries dominated a rural, Slavic population. In the nineteenth century, this dominance was threatened simultaneously by a general awakening of the Slavic nations accompanied by the appearance of powerful, messianic ideologies such as Pan-Slavism, the rising nationalisms of particular Slavic nations, anarchism in many different varieties, and Marxist socialism. These messianic ideologies flourished especially in what Austrian historians have called the 'European underground.' "

Seeing Bernie's questioning glance, Jochen interrupted himself to explain: "The European underground around the turn of the century was made up of vast legions of intellectual vagabonds, declassés, and free thinkers of many sorts who lived lives of rebellion somewhere between *La Bohème* and the underworld of crime and prostitution, outside of bourgeois respectability but not outside the intellectual and political world of the day. These were the men who by choice or necessity were the outcasts of the old society, the most concrete symptom of its disintegration, the dreamers of social revolution and utopian salvation who hotly debated their fantasies in the cafés and flop-houses of great European cities from Vienna to Madrid, and from Paris to Berlin. You can hardly miss this peculiar environment, if you study the lives of the great anarchists, the nationalists and socialists in exile, or even of the avant-garde artists and writers, of which Berlin and Munich had more than their share despite the provincial atmosphere of the rest of Germany.

"The real forerunners and teachers of Hitler's sectarian anti-semitism were such men as the Austrians Georg von Schoenerer, Karl Lueger, and Lanz-Liebenfels, who concocted an explosive political religion from a phobia about Jews, Negroes, Slavs, Latins — even of all dark-haired and dark-eyed persons — together with paranoid suspicions of the Catholic Church, of an invisible government of Free Masons, Marxist socialists, or Zionists and of anything so international and cosmopolitan as the Hapsburg monarchy. Here, elemental sentiments and irrational fears emerged as fantastic race theories eulogizing the old Germans and their hypothetical Nordic master race of demi-gods, theories which you can also find in milder form in the writings of Houston Stewart Chamberlain, Count Gobineau, and Richard Wagner, the great showman whose magic supplied one of the formative experiences of Hitler as a young man. The young Hitler was a disciple, in particular, of the 'theo-zoology' of Lanz-Liebenfels, an apostate Cistercian monk whose magazine *Ostara* is supposed to have clarified Hitler's ideas from a pseudo-scientific anthropology of race to the quasi-religious interpretation of world history as race struggle."

"What did you call this theory, 'theo-zoology'?" Bernie interrupted him incredulously. "This is all quite new to me. I was under the impression that the claims to racial superiority were just a widespread illusion among Germans."

Jochen laughed good-naturedly. "I am sure, some Germans who needed some such boost to their morale fell for it after it had been propagandized in a more harmless form, that is without a call for the castration, enslavement, or outright genocide of supposedly inferior races which you can actually find in *Ostara*. The respectable public opinion media of the day, of course, never dignified these perverse preachings about race and God by discussing them or refuting them. This may have been a big mistake, but in those days you simply didn't talk about such things in polite company, just as the Berlin police forbade the performance of Gerhart Hauptmann's play *The Weavers* as late as 1897. This play was considered morally unedifying because of its subject — the suffering of the weavers during the early industrial revolution. Hitler's racism, along with working-class problems, free love, Marxist socialism and anarchism, various strange religious cults, health fads, astrology and various pseudo-scientific doctrines, were all part of this unrecognized world of the European underground. Socialism was the first to surface and, to the horror of conservatives of every description, became wedded to the labor movement and hence strong and respectable. The sudden conversion of the German Social Democrats to patriotism in 1914 and their espousal of liberal democracy and of the Western-style constitution of the Weimar Republic at the expense of militant, revolutionary, and chiliastic socialism, even in armed opposition to it, that was the price they paid for respectability."

"The rise of socialism from the unrecognized sphere of social reality, if I understand you right," Kenneth interjected between puffs on his pipe, "was like the baring of the human stomach and its demands in a world of Victorian prudery. And the surfacing of racism, finally,

laid bare even more intimate spheres of the human body, having to
do with sexual reproduction, breeding, and supposed miscegenation."

"Except that it was a distinctly perverse sexuality, not just one
with an exclusive emphasis on the biological nature of man," said
Kurt, who have followed Jochen and Kenneth with rapt attention.
"Racists and their theories are the delight of psychological interpretation, for they epitomize father-hating Oedipal complexes and the
externalization of sexual guilt feelings."

"Translation, please, Mr. Freud, for illiterates like me," Jochen
asked with a puzzled smile.

"A typical racist, and I think this is generally borne out by actual
case histories," Kurt responded, "suffers from a childhood fixation to
have his mother all to himself. He looks upon his father, who of
course is in his way, with a mixture of admiration or envy and with
mortal hatred. This effect is later projected upon, say, the Jews to
whom the racist will simultaneously attribute admirable power, both
sexual and political, and a depravity worthy of hatred and destruction. The mother-figure and later mother substitutes, on the other
hand, are idolized as demi-gods of Nordic purity and virtue . . ."

"Or as the Southern white woman," Bernie interjected quickly,
"the epitome of breeding and virginity."

"But at the same time, the man with the Oedipal complex has
learned not to trust his mother's loyalty to him," Kurt continued.
"Not only does he fear the superior power of the father or other powerful males to cast a spell over her; he also knows that she is weak
when faced by the father's charm. And so the typical racist suffers
from a kind of anti-Lady Chatterley stance, a positive horror of
emancipated women, of women's rights and freedoms. He prefers to
build his pedestal for his mother within a cage of enforced purity, as
it were."

At this point Jochen began to nod vigorously, thinking apparently
of racists with whose lives he was familiar. Kurt continued: "You can
also explain the morbid seeking for a heroic death which underlies so
much of the psychology of storm-troopers and Nazi leaders in terms
of the guilt feelings associated with the Oedipus complex. Since the
racist prototype feels very uncertain of his own attraction to mother
and later mother substitutes, and, of course, many racists are sexually
deviant anyway — he dreams of himself as a romantic knight in shin-

ing armor, as a dragon-slayer and savior of princesses; or, perhaps even more important, as the sentinel of the people, or the guardian of the race. This may well be the secret behind the driving political ambition of a Hitler, and others of his sort."

"This and the desire to rival the 'invisible government' of the supposedly inferior race, the substitute for the hated father, as you explained," Jochen said. "Some of the racist teachers of the Nazi movement also used to motivate their anti-semitic sentiment with a desire to substitute the hypothetical Aryans, or the German race, whatever that is, for the 'chosen people' of the Bible. Others again, including Hitler himself, wanted his fascist supermen, his Aryan heroes, to take the place of the rival quasi-religious movement of Marxist socialism, so that a fascist conspiracy would be substituted for a Communist conspiracy, or a fascist 'invisible government' for that of an interchangeable and intimately associated Jewish, Marxist socialist, or liberal-democratic 'system.'

"As you can see, the method behind much of this madness is not even specifically biological or tied to a remotely scientific concept of race. Only a paranoid mind could find it so easy to class together such disparate things as Marxist philosophy, liberal-democratic constitutionalism, the working-class movement, and its own racial phobia."

The four sat around their table, abandoning themselves to their thoughts or staring into their beer, while Kenneth puffed on his pipe. Finally, Bernie broke the silence: "Look, I realize it sounds silly after two solid hours of explanations. But I still don't understand how Germans could fall for this weird line of racism and fantasy. Most of the sentiments you have named before, such as the economic crises and the rise of the masses, or the revanchism, monarchism, and nationalism of the conservative right, well, all these motives seem relatively rational and understandable, even if they led the Germans into starting the Second World War. But this, the racist ravings and the underlying sexual perversity, and the sado-masochism of craving a dictatorial leader, a man on horseback — this is so sick, so psychologically abnormal, that these rational problems that may have vexed the Weimar Germans simply don't explain it. What was the matter with the Germans, for Pete's sake? Did they all hate their fathers and worry about the weakness of their mothers, wives, and sweethearts toward hypothetical seducers? They must have been at least temporarily insane to fall for the Nazis in such numbers, 37 and even 44 per cent of the voters in 1932 and 1933."

"In a sense, perhaps, they were," Jochen said with furrowed brow. "But I believe that the religious overtones are far more important for an understanding of how and why it happened than the fact that racism was the cause, or that Jews became its chief victim. I just read a fascinating book by Norman Cohn, *The Pursuit of the Millennium,* which gives a detailed account of chiliastic movements and revolutionary eschatologies throughout the history of Western monotheistic religion. Time and again, according to this book, such movements have sprung from similar settings of social and economic crisis, a breakdown of legitimate authority, a waning of the faith among new and unassimilated masses of men, an underground of pagan or heretic beliefs and practices, and half-mythical leaders around whom the lost souls rally like lemmings heading for the cliffs. And, of course, every time there was a vast amount of senseless violence and slaughter, fanaticism, brutality, and scapegoats. You are probably acquainted with the analogous interpretations of Russian Communism as a kind of perverted Russian orthodoxy by Berdaev, Fedotov, or Stepun. Of course, no chiliastic movement before the twentieth century was ever of such technological proficiency and therefore so powerful as our totalitarian regimes of the right or the left. But the energy behind Nazism, or behind Communism, still remains clearly a perverted religious fervor of the worst kind. And don't let the presence of atheism or nihilism deceive you. They are profoundly religious affects, too.

"I cannot but conclude that there was at the core of the Nazi movement a sectarian movement not unlike many of those Cohn describes in his book. And this leads me back to what I said earlier about the secularization and the breakdown of social authority in our time. In spite of your smug secular pride, gentlemen, I still insist that secularization has merely led vast masses of people to worship idols and to pursue such violent and perverse faiths as racism and Communism. Man continues to have a religious sense, a spiritual need for ultimate commitment."

Kenneth took the pipe out of his mouth and said dryly: "You made your point, Jochen. Let me come back to Bernie's question, though, about how Hitler could ever convince nearly half of the German voters of his absurd 'theo-zoology.' The answer is simple: he never even tried. In fact, a large part of his movement was never completely initiated into the genocidal implication of Nazism until they caught glimpses of its being carried out, if then. The ignorance of many party members, not to mention voters and other outsiders, regarding the ultimate goals of the movement, was deliberately fostered by the totalitarian organization and propaganda of the Nazi movement. Allow me to give credit for this explanation to a brilliant woman, Hannah Arendt, who first explained it to me. I hope I am not misrepresenting her original meaning. According to her theory, a totalitarian movement is organized into many carefully separated layers, from the leadership through secret police, storm-troopers, and concentration camp guards on out through Orwellian inner and outer parties, auxiliary organizations for youth, women, and other groups to the welter of front organizations, the general public, and foreign observers. These layers are differentiated by how much they know about the real intentions of the movement and by how central their own motives are to those of the leadership. Totalitarian propaganda, then, comes by no means as a uniform message for all, but it is pitched separately to each layer according to its degree of knowledge and to what it might like to hear. I am sure you have heard how well-intentioned people and groups have been turned into unwitting puppets or front organizations by the Communists. The Nazis operated in the same manner, appealing to each group only in terms of what this group might desire and how little it could be permitted to know about Hitler's real aims.

"Hitler's evil genius, in contrast to other racists, lay in his ability to assess with great accuracy how much of his racism a particular group could be expected to tolerate. Most Germans and many foreigners would forgive him a little private race phobia, if it was hidden behind a genteel facade of propriety. Some would stand for the ousting of Jews from jobs and positions which they hoped to inherit, but not for murderous persecution and brutality. A still smaller number would abandon itself uncritically to the wave of emotions aroused against the scapegoat and join mobs, or participate in pogroms. Even they might feel ashamed later and definitely recoil from the idea of systematic genocide. Only the sectarian zealots themselves and the scores of sadists always attracted by hate groups could really be allowed full knowledge of what the leadership was planning to do once it was securely in control. This limitation, of course, in no way kept the Nazis from implicating people in crimes and acts of hatred far beyond their original level of tolerance. Men who had reluctantly agreed to tolerate racial prejudice of the mildest sort found themselves swallowing the infamous principles of the Nuremberg Laws and finally had the horrible blood of the 'final solution' on their consciences. In this respect, the progress of Nazi totalitarianism was one of never-ending moral corruption, moral salami tactics over a period of years. There was no lack of Canossas of the conscience, capitulations of abject cowardice between the whip of brutal terror and the carrot of hard-to-pass-up rewards. There were some martyrs, but not many. Most of them paid for resistance with their lives.

"The initial process of persuasion, however, to come back to Bernie's question, took place with the help of issues that were quite secondary to sectarian racism. Nationalism, for example, was one of the chief selling points of the Nazi party, and they whipped up a feverish frenzy of 'national rebirth' among the German people, even though Hitler himself considered nationalism outdated and too closely associated with liberal democracy to be of much use. Nationalism, of course, served them well with the voters, who associated it with fatherland, glory, unity, and revenge for humiliation and defeat. Their peculiar, multi-layered propaganda structure made it possible for the Nazis to be considered a nationalist party by probably some 80 per cent of the voters and the foreign press. Conservatism, or the traditionalistic revolt of the pre-industrial elements of society against modernism and rationalism in economy and politics, was another big drawing card with the voters, who somehow hoped that prosperity would return along with other features of the good old times. The Nazis obligingly denounced capitalism, parliamentary democracy, constitutions, freedom of the press, labor unions, internationalism, and the League of Nations, women using lipstick and claiming individual rights and freedoms, abstract art and supposedly un-German literature, and racy entertainment in the big cities. Many of these issues, to be sure, added grist to their mill, although they rarely forgot to include 'reactionaries' among the devils on their never-ending list of people they accused or regarded as their enemies. But the point is really that this pseudo-conservative agitation succeeded in convincing vast masses of Germans that the Nazis were conservatives. Large numbers of conservative civil servants and judges, for example, who had always waxed indignant about government by political parties, were made to believe that Hitler would reinstall the centralized state headed, perhaps, by a monarch or president. As you know, Hitler hated the state and subordinated it immediately to his totalitarian party. States' righters were persuaded to back him as a determined foe of Berlin centralism, only to see him abolish the states altogether and set up a regime more centralized than even the leaders of the Weimar Republic had ever dreamed of. Aristocrats joined him in the hope of re-establishing their privileged position and discovered too late that he intended to replace them by a new aristocracy of Aryan heroes. Farmers and small businessmen voted for him in the vague expectation that he would restore the rural and small town idylls of a distant past but instead found themselves caught in the gears of a war economy which made them more dependent on national planners and administrators than they had ever been on the capitalists and banks of the big city. Conservative military men, business oligarchs, and other feudal authoritarians had been certain that they could use Hitler to beat down their own opposition and then discard him at will. They were perhaps the most deluded of them all."

Kurt nodded vigorously and interjected: "The conservative controllers of power who let in Hitler, the Trojan horse of totalitarianism, are a perfect example of the futility of the traditionalist revolt. They ended up going over to the enemy with flying colors, and to the wrong enemy. The same thing happened as with my psychological simile of the daughter wrongly educated by an unemancipated mother, whose stifled sexual energies led to a hysterical race phobia. And racism, as we have seen, is a symbolic act of sexual aggression, and sexually perverse in character. Likewise, the traditionalist revolt, however sincere its motives, is far more likely to lead to totalitarian utopias than to a genuine return to the past."

"Well spoken, Mr. Freud. Couched in the proper phrases," Kenneth chuckled. "I might add to this that such a traditionalist revolt may also derive some of its vigor from guilt feelings associated with intense selfishness or high living, especially among a bourgeois society barely emancipated from authoritarian or Victorian restraints such as the Weimar society of the 1920's. Call it escape from freedom, self-punishment for high living, or whatever you will. Anyway, the illusion of Nazi conservatism obscured its real character to large masses of voters and to scores of political leaders, not to mention the foreign press.

"Finally, the same thing was true of the image of anti-Communism and opposition to Marxist socialism which the Nazis tried to present to bourgeois and petty-bourgeois voters as well as to conservatives. Of course, they were bitter rivals of the various socialist groups. But their relationship to them was by no means their chief concern nor were they very sincere about their opposition to Communist totalitarianism, for the simple reason that there was a basic kinship between them and the Communists. I used to know several members of a Communist shock troop unit who had joined the Nazis after 1933, as so many Communists did, and boasted that they had been running after the red flag even before there was a swastika in it. The Nazis always considered former Communists their best recruits because they already had the right mentality and outlook on political action. There is much evidence of Nazi-Communist co-operation, and even tacit collusion during the last years of the Weimar Republic. As for socialism as an economic system, as welfare state, or as a system of collectivism, the Nazis were advocating this themselves in the hope of appealing to workers and to the innumerable economic casualties of the Great Depression. Really, the more I think about it, the less am I impressed by the anti-Communism of the Nazis. To them, this was just another smokescreen to hide what they really were doing.

"All this, I should think, goes to show that the Germans in the early 'thirties, and even later, were hardly aware of the nature of the movement they were voting into power. Instead, each group of Germans and, perhaps, every individual was deluded by a different and generally positive image of the party and of its leader. Now, of course, you will ask why the different groups did not get together and discover that their images did not agree with each other and even less with the reality they thought they perceived. Good point. But you must consider the fragmentation of German society by the traditional class and occupational status lines, not to mention the ideological divisions and new social fragmentation of a modern industrial society. And once the Nazis took control, they established a monopoly over all public opinion media and pursued all dissenters and doubters, thereby intensifying the fragmentation of society and the isolation of the individual by creating a reign of terror."

"Are you saying now that most Germans did not know what the Nazis were doing to the Jews?" Bernie exclaimed in alarm.

Kenneth shook his head. "You are asking the wrong question, Bernie. No honest man could answer that in the either-or fashion of whether or not they knew. I am sure there were some, the instigators and executors who knew everything or at least enough to be fully accountable, but these were a very small number of persons highly placed in the party, in the military, and in the administration. According to the latest trials of Nazi criminals in Frankfurt, Hitler employed about one thousand genocide specialists, and they appeared in every mass murder. Then again there must have been a fairly large number of Germans who were too remote from political life in one way or another, geographically or psychologically, to see the handwriting on the wall. Even the most advanced modern society has a large minority of people who are too overwhelmed by their private lives to know anything outside of their most direct concerns in job and family, if there. And Germany, of course, was still in the throes of modernization, as we have seen. Between these two groups, I should venture to guess, lay the majority of Germans along many gradations of partial knowledge. Just about all of them knew, to give examples, that there were concentration camps in which political enemies, Jews, gypsies, and so-called asocial elements were forcibly detained and often roughed up. Very few persons in the general public knew that there were extermination camps and mass executions in the occupied eastern territories. And the real mass murders were carried out mainly there and only in wartime. Many must have caught occasional glimpses of storm-trooper violence and brutality, of political arrests, or of concentration-camp inmates working in defense plants or on the road. But such partial glimpses are rarely enough to prompt a man to action, especially if he is forbidden to confirm and discuss them with others and knows that protests will get him and his family into very deep trouble. Then also, the human mind is quick to seize on rationalizations of various sorts: suppose, the victims or inmates you saw had really done something to deserve their fate? How would *you* know? And what can *you* do, anyway? How many instances of human nastiness do we witness every day — and the Nazi murders

were, of course, not witnessed by the public — and then forget with
the comforting thought that they are none of our business? And then
there is the nagging fear of brute violence which can turn many a civilized heart to jelly. Adenauer's wife, I once read, betrayed her husband's hiding place to the Nazis when they threatened her daughters.
Normal people are too frail for heroism, Bernie, and not angelic
enough for martyrdom. That's why abnormal personality types in politics are such a menace."

Bernie still looked dismayed but could think of nothing to say.
Finally, Kurt broke the silence and returned to Bernie's question about
the state of mind of Hitler's voters: "I would also agree with Jochen
that the men and women who voted for Hitler in the early 'thirties
were indeed half out of their minds. But I don't think one needs to
bring religion into it. The sociologist Emile Durkheim, in his writings
on suicide, offers a concept which explains quite adequately the national suicide committed by voting Hitler into office. He speaks of
anomie, a state of society where large numbers of people seriously
lack the kind of integration with a stable framework of social institutions which their emotional well-being and the smooth functioning of
the social system require. *Anomie* is also typified by people losing
their sense of purpose and by a confusion of expectations, symbols,
and values such as are most commonly associated with what we have
called the great transformation, or modernization. With the shifts of
status and social structure, the replacement of monarchy with parliamentary democracy, and of the pre-industrial way of life with the
crises of industrial society, and the many competing ideologies and
political creeds, no wonder increasing masses of men grew desperately insecure, disoriented, and disaffected, prone to suicide or to
'over-determined' aggression toward scapegoats and hatred toward
social stereotypes, such as the 'greedy middleman' or the 'dirty
foreigner.'

"We should also consider the differences in the rate and degree of
modernization between different areas, groups, and persons which
became increasingly apparent and further split society into warring
camps of traditionalists and the advanced and emancipated. You
know how even the most emancipated people retain latent misgivings
about some aspects of modern life, a smoldering uneasiness which
can spring into open flame when they are confronted with personal

failure of any sort. Goebbels and Hitler never failed to exploit these feelings of hatred for Berlin, the glittering cosmopolitan city with its avant-garde art — they called it decadent — its naughty amusements, its sharp-tongued press, and its melting pot of regional groups and nations. Here again you have two competing value systems which might well induce anxiety or 'over-determination.' And you also get the 'over-determined' modernistic crusader or debunker as well as the 'over-determined' zealot for tradition.

"Another important factor and, perhaps also, an effect of social *anomie* in Germany, was the emancipation of women, which went hand in hand with the revolutionary transformation of the old patriarchic family and the crumbling of the social class structure. The emancipated woman was a formidable new force whose demanding 'cry for a child' was quite enough to chase an insecure young male into heroic fantasies or membership in a para-military organization. Along with the revaluation of sex went a trend of vitalism and biologism in thought and political action which made racism and the cult of leadership far more plausible than they may seem today. Just think of Oswald Spengler's immensely popular theories of cultural decline and you get a glimpse of the dominant feelings of many.

"The best gauge for the rise of acute *anomie* is usually the behavior of youth, which has an uncanny ability to reflect the hidden uncertainties and silent despair of their elders. Already before World War I there had been the widely ramified Youth Movement, loosely organized groups of German middle-class youths who rebelled against the materialism and rationalism of their elders, and against the increasing mechanization of their lives. They had no real alternatives to offer, but sought to escape from *anomie* into a fantasy world of romanticism, nature hikes, camping, and tales of medieval knights and Christian-Germanic faith and love. Above all they discovered group life, comradeship among young men, and a kind of collective idealism which was beyond rational self-criticism. The war experience and the Free Corps gave German youth still more comradeship and more cause for disaffection from society, while their capacity for idealism and selfless sacrifice went begging for want of a cause.

"Those were also the days when scores of literary heralds of *anomie* called for a 'conservative revolution' and wallowed in irrationalism and in impassioned calls for a Caesar and a Third Reich.

Or when famous poets wrote fantastic allegories about a secret society of servants which was destined to rule the world.

"In this situation of ever-worsening *anomie* appeared Hitler, the
'drummer' of many causes which he at least considered interchangeable — conservative revolution, revanchism, national rebirth,
anti-Communism, and a futuristic racism of unlimited potential. With
his charismatic magic, his electrifying oratory, his sophisticated
mass propaganda, and unceasing determination, Hitler was a one-
man wave of the future, an irresistible force which rallied and unified
the German youth into a phalanx of enthusiasm as nothing had before. His fanatic certainty that he was right, his somnambulant self-
confidence, his utterly sincere megalomania had a magic effect on the
many smitten with *anomie:* it mobilized them and gave them a sense
of national purpose.

"Young people under 30, even under 25, made up the bulk of the
various para-military organizations, of Nazis, Communists, and
Nationalists, as well as of the innumerable militant societies and vigilante groups. They also played a disproportionate role in the two extremist parties. As early as 1930, incidentally, the Nazis had
whopping majorities among the university students. This enthusiasm
for political extremism among German youth suggests that they saw
this as a practical way of acting out their youthful tensions and hostility, a substitute for juvenile delinquency, if you like. Of course, juvenile delinquency again is a reflection of acute *anomie.*"

As Kurt stopped talking, a stillness made itself felt in the little
Bierstube. All the other patrons had long left. Kenneth's pipe had
gone out, but a pall of cold smoke still hung over the tables and between the wood-paneled walls. Kurt took off his glasses and began to
rub his eyes. Bernie noticed for the first time that Jochen had only a
glass of lemonade in front of him. He felt tired, and it seemed to him
as if the hours of discussion had somehow failed to lead up to a conclusion. Finally, Kenneth spoke: "Somehow, I cannot help feeling
terribly dissatisfied with all our talk about classes, crisis phenomena,
anomie, economic causes, and other fancy concepts. Why Nazism triumphed in Germany still seems such an elusive topic that all our
efforts to trap it verbally seem pointless and in vain. I am tempted to
say that only a poet, a novelist, or a man reminiscing about his own
past can even come close to capturing the essence of how a human

being turns into a fascist, and that only at the price of much distortion.

"I've been a Tory all my life, which may explain my distrust and disrespect for your neat little formulae and demonologies. I lived through this period and came face to face with Nazism, in Germany, in England, and even among old and close friends of mine.

"Perhaps I don't strike you as a person of deep experience with the human predicament, having remained a bachelor and a man of the academic ivory tower and all that. Perhaps, you would not think of me as a sound judge of men or of affairs. But I think that fascism is a thing of character, of human failing on the deepest personal level. A personal failure which may lurk in everybody's life from childhood on, and in all developing countries — and what country is not still developing? — though perhaps in some more than in others. It is a personal failure, in fact, that threatens especially when a person grows up to adulthood and again when he reaches the point in his life that he must face his own limitations and settle for his own station in life."

At this point Bernie tried to interrupt him impatiently, but he was silenced by Kenneth's remark that, of course, only people of rare judgment and maturity were capable of recognizing when their mental grasp fell short of the goal. "You have a son of 25, don't you, Bernie?" Kenneth continued. "Just think how difficult it is to raise a son right in these changing times.

"The demands of modern life and politics on our human judgment are so enormous. Just growing up into a responsible adult can be an insuperable task. It is difficult to say just where fascism starts in the life of the individual, nor even if he is entirely to blame for it. It can start as a kind of egotism, a hard-heartedness, a stubborn refusal to forego inherited privilege or station, no matter what the price may be, a lack of empathy or inability to think of yourself in the other fellow's shoes. It may be a lapse in the firm grasp of the social reality around us, or a willingness to accept social stereotypes in place of real people, or even an incapacity to relate to individuals which hides behind projected group stereotypes of love and hate. It could also be an inability to realize your own limitations, an excess of expectations toward life, an exploitative attitude toward others, or a propensity to substitute for reality fantastic dreams that feature oneself as a glorious hero. When a whole people in dire straits loses touch with reality, you get such a tragicomedy, or rather, despite the overtones of a comic opera, a horrible tragedy for millions of innocent victims and continents of peaceful nations, as was the Hitler era.

"It can also be an exercise in the power of positive thinking, if you will pardon the expression, in asserting with a fierce mien, until you have convinced even yourself in spite of all evidence to the contrary, that Germany really won the First World War, that Germans are clean and honest while foreigners are dirty and crooked, that German women are the epitome of purity and that Jewish men can think of nothing better than chasing them . . . Of course, you can substitute Englishmen or Americans for the Germans, and Negroes or Orientals for the Jews, if you like.

"If you come to think of it, only the finest of lines separated British Conservatism from fascism, a line so fine that many contemporaries could not tell the difference. Only the benefit of hindsight shows the chasm that really lay between them. There were countless men and women in the 1920's and 1930's, people of high station and, as everyone thought, of sound judgment, who were taken in by the Nazis, by Hitler's magic, and whose joining swayed the opinions of thousands of others who had implicit trust in their judgment. Members of royal families, famous scientists, and writers fell for them in a manner that now seems incomprehensible. Or think of how Sir Oswald Mosley and Benito Mussolini were very prominent Socialist leaders in their respective countries until they all of a sudden turned fascist. What a thin line divides fascism from so much that is legitimate and sane.

"The dividing line seems to lie in, . . . in," he paused, searching for the right word, "in a kind of nobility of character, in a refusal to take unearned advantage, in a reluctance to deceive or to accept deception as an easy way out, even when vast masses of men crave it from the bottom of their hearts.

"Hitler had, above all, a frightening talent for showmanship, for histrionics, for projecting his image as that of a man to be trusted. So much so, in fact, that there are still Germans today who attribute all the evil deeds to his henchmen and not to him. 'If the *Fuehrer* had only known,' they think . . . He also had the strange ability to impart to the minds he swayed a sense of purpose, a piece of his charisma, if only for a day or two, an affect of moving intensity however negative, a glimpse of authenticity in an increasingly artificial life. At a time when people were suffering under the mechanization and bureaucratization of social life, when they craved meaningful activity with a thirst too impatient to bother about the little observances of loyal citizenship and neighborliness, a thirst that could be quenched only with heroic action, however pathetic; when their hearts were so full of a painful void, their nerves so taut they could scream for violent release, the anarchy in their minds so menacing, that calling for a dictator seemed the only response left; that's when he appeared and gathered a whole nation into his genocidal net.

"He had the hypnotic will power to sweep them off their feet when millions of the downtrodden longed to be carried away into the irresponsibility of group life and group action. Hitler fooled the Germans about himself and his movement, indeed. But then how large a percentage of the people you know are unfailing judges of character? There is an impostor in every fascist. Perhaps, there is one in all of us. Hitler was the very epitome of a fascist, and, with his campaign, he succeeded in mobilizing in vast masses of Germans that same element of the impostor, of irrationality and self-delusion, giving them a way out of the oppressive necessity of having to face themselves in all their unadorned smallness, every day, in the mirror of their own minds and in the mirror that is society. He could have become a German Cecil B. DeMille, a grandmaster of illusion and spectacle. Instead he was possessed by an insatiable lust for power, a craving for conquest, for imposing his perverse kind of order on the whole world; although he was an apocalyptic creature of chaos and destruction if ever there was one."

Kenneth paused reflectively and fingered his glass of beer. At last, he lifted it and said: "Let me offer a toast to the real hero of our democratic age, the little man, or rather, the lesser man from the vice president on down. The man who knows how little he is and yet would rather settle for what he is than aggrandize himself at the expense of others — to him I raise my glass. For he is immune to this creeping disease of fascism, whatever the circumstances may be."

We may smile at Kenneth's single-minded preoccupation with individual motives for fascism, "whatever the circumstances may be," after hours of discussing precisely the circumstances that tricked the

Weimar Germans into the arms of Hitler. Which comes first, the hen or the egg? Individual propensities or the fateful circumstances of economic crisis, societal breakdown, and the agonized search of a humiliated people for a sense of identity?

From a historical perspective, the crucial question whether the Germans have really changed is very difficult to answer. It is far easier to find out whether the fateful circumstances are different today. Has the German industrial economy overcome the catastrophic tailspin of the Great Depression? Has it finally begun to meet the rising expectations of the masses for a better life, fulfilling thereby the promise industrialization holds out even to the most lowly? Have the Germans finally come to terms with the disintegration of class structure and found their balance in the more mobile and egalitarian world of status symbols and pretensions? What persons and what values have replaced the old warrior caste that had such a pernicious influence on the German cultural and political development? In what direction, pro- or anti-West, individualistic or collective-authoritarian, has the search for identity been going in Western and Eastern Germany? Only after we have answered these questions about the basic foundations and social orientation, can we turn to individual motivation and understand how West German politics has markedly changed in the course of two or three decades.

> "We come now to the age of high mass consumption, where . . . the leading sectors shift towards durable consumer goods and services: a phase from which Americans are beginning to emerge; [and] whose not unequivocal joys Western Europe and Japan are beginning energetically to probe . ."
>
> Walt W. Rostow, *Stages of Economic Growth* (1958)

3

AN ECONOMIC MIRACLE?

It is peculiar to man's fate in modern industrial society that his peace of mind and political rationality are linked to a disturbing degree with his individual and collective economic success. As long as there is prosperity and continuing economic growth, each participant in the national economy, from the cliff-dweller of our big cities to the coupon-clipping old person and the "scientific farmer," can pursue his own career of growing affluence, and new jobs are made available to the burgeoning population. The steadiness of this one-dimensional world of economic success seemingly enables people to pull themselves together, to be friendly to their fellow men, and, as a political community, to face their common problems rationally. But as soon as serious economic misfortune strikes the national economy, all its stockholders, so to speak, suddenly become aware of the precariousness of their lives on the rungs of the ladder of personal "success." The gaping spiritual emptiness of modern life assaults them all at once and shatters the self-control, the human relationships, and the rational attitude toward politics of many. If a large enough number of people falters, allowing the skeletons in their own mental closets to get the better of them, or turns all its energies to the persecution of witches, then the time of political catastrophe has arrived. Unless deeply ingrained popular traditions of democracy and of constitutional law and order can stem the tide and help a country weather the storm; and unless broadly based and well-led popular forces man the dykes and beat back the rising floods erupting from the chaotic depths of mind and society, as has been the case in the Western democracies on such occasions, even a civilized people can all too easily be inundated through the appeal of a Hitler by the destructive waves of emotion within and around.

Some of this reasoning probably lay in back of the impressions of many foreign and domestic observers who have reported on the economic progress of Western Germany since the days of 1945. Even before the mid-'fifties, in fact, they began to speak of a *Wirtschaftswunder,* an "economic miracle," to describe the drastic changes they had witnessed. Yet at the same time there was a consensus among journalists and scholarly experts on German affairs that democracy and political stability in Western Germany depended upon continued prosperity there. In fact, some observers felt that the ghosts of political extremism and especially of aggressive nationalism could be banished only by the new prosperity and would return with a vengeance with the first serious economic reversal.

Today, twenty years after the catastrophic condition of 1945, the significance of the economic development of Western Germany presents a rather different picture. To begin with, the "economic miracle" appears at second glance to be still astonishing but hardly miraculous. The alleged dependence of German democracy and political stability on prosperity, moreover, is no longer a fact, if it ever was. In the subtle transition during the Adenauer years, though not only because of him, the West Germans seem to have discovered new sources of inner strength that will enable them to survive most crises. Some American observers, both to the right and to the left of the political center, have tended to misinterpret this new inner strength according to their own respective frames of reference: reading into West German economic policies their own predilections, conservative Republicans blithely ignored the elaborate welfare state in Germany as well as the prominent role of government in the German economy. Ultra-liberals fancied they perceived in these policies pure reaction and a bias against labor and the Social Democratic opposition, which they could tie in with their related assertion that the West German government was militaristic and implacable toward the East. The economic aspect of these misconceptions ignores not only the traditional welfare state in Western Germany, but also the importance of satisfying the innumerable social welfare claims at the end of a lost war as a chief motive for a concerted effort at economic development; it also fails to acknowledge the substantial co-operation of organized labor and of the Social Democrats, without which the economic recovery would have failed. Finally, there is the application of Rostow's thesis about the stages of economic growth to the German situation. According to Rostow, a nation in the throes of industrial growth undergoes a long and difficult period of inner unrest until it reaches the stage of mass consumption. Prior to this stage, inner tensions, together with burgeoning industrial strength, may drive a nation into a propensity for inner upheavals or imperialistic aggression against its neighbors, as they have indeed done in the cases of Japan, the United States, and Germany in the past and may still be doing in the case of the Soviet Union today. But once a nation reaches the stage of mass consumption — apparent in Western Germany by the late 1950's — the newly affluent society lacks the motivation for belligerence and political extremism. If Rostow's thesis is correct, then it makes little sense to seek the cause of Cold War tensions with West Germany or other Western countries rather than with the Soviet Union.

Let us take a closer look at the course of those changes often referred to as the "economic miracle" and at the economic policies of the erstwhile occupation powers and later of the West German government. No one surveying the sorry state of Germany from 1945 to 1948 could have predicted anything but decades of slow and painful reconstruction under conditions of extreme scarcity and deprivation. Most German cities were half-destroyed by air-raids, and sometimes also by the fighting during the final conquest of Germany. Along the roads from the east came a never-ending stream of rag-tag refugees and expellees — eight million by 1946 — mostly women, children, and old people who were fleeing ahead of the Russian army into the Western zones, pennyless, hungry, and often unable to work. The food supply for the inflated population of the Western zones was so inadequate that frequent shortages interfered even with the paltry rations of as little as twelve hundred calories daily for adults. Even in restaurants one had to use the coupons from ration cards for dismal meals. On public beaches it was easy to spot the well-fed American GIs among the hordes of undernourished German youths. Germans learned to hate the words "rationing" and "calories" so much they used to say: "Hitler made us eat vitamins [in allusion to the vitamin campaigns of the Nazis], the democratic government is giving us calories; when are we ever going to get something to eat?"

A large part of German industrial capacity was destroyed. Much of what machinery was left by the war was confiscated for reparations. The German currency, the *Reichsmark,* was almost worthless and little inducement for any effort on the part of anyone. The only real currency was American cigarettes which dominated the "black market," the only flourishing exchange for goods and services. The black market involved such a vast number of people to a greater or lesser extent that law enforcement against it was as much of a mockery as was U.S. Prohibition during the roaring 'twenties. The regular market of goods was disrupted not only by the bad currency and low production, but also by the omnipresent system of rationing, and price and rent control which undertook to distribute what little there was through an enormous bureaucratic apparatus to a select few who happened to be high on the list of priorities. The damage and poor state of repair of roads and vehicles, railroads, and other means of transportation were further compounded by shortage of fuel and spare parts and by the division of Germany into four occupation zones, which inhibited commerce and exchange among each other.

Finally, the German authorities were faced with never-ending claims and welfare cases arising from the Nazi period, the war, and its after-effects. Not only the surviving victims of the Nazi regime and former enemy countries submitted claims, but there were tens of millions of disabled veterans, families of war casualties, refugee and expellee families, persons who lost everything in air-raids, or through enemy action in the final conquest of Germany, or whose quarters were requisitioned by occupation troops, not to mention the vast number of orphans, widows, and elderly people who were left with no other recourse but the state. The demands were insatiable, the supply, from food to housing to clothes, hopelessly inadequate. Small wonder that all the three major political parties licensed by the

Allies, the Christian Democrats and Free Democrats as much as the Social Democrats, all favored socialism in one form or another during the three years after the end of World War II. Even the occupation authorities of the three Western zones saw no other alternative for their German charges but to continue rationing and a controlled economy for an indefinite period to come.

This was the sad state of Germany at the time when the outbreak of the Cold War between the Soviet Union and the Western Allies induced the latter to change their policy toward their erstwhile enemies. For the West Germans it was sheer luck that their geographical location should make their co-operation so valuable to the West as to compensate for the bitter feelings engendered by the misdeeds of the Nazi regime and the hostilities of the Second World War. The change of Allied policy manifested itself in three important ways: the Marshall Plan, the currency reform of June 1948, and the establishment of a common German government for the Western zones of occupation. Marshall Plan aid pumped close to one billion dollars into the despoiled and broken-down economy, where it served as one of the major sources of initial investment, often enabling businessmen to buy the latest industrial equipment in place of the obsolete machinery claimed by destruction or reparations. Bitterly opposed by Communists everywhere and right-wingers in the United States, it was, perhaps, the best investment ever made abroad with the money of the much-abused American taxpayer. Without the Marshall Plan, West German recovery would not have got off the ground and the impoverished population might well have been tempted by the alluring promises of Communism. The currency reform was carried out by the Allies with the intention of liquidating the *Reichsmark* system and of creating a new and trustworthy foundation for economic growth. It froze bank acounts and devalued cash holdings of *Reichsmark* in the proportion of ten to one, allowing each man, woman, and child a limited quota of spending money until their first pay checks in the new currency would arrive. The effect of the currency reform was dramatic. The black market disappeared and hoarded goods of all descriptions flooded the market in quest of the new currency. The *Deutsche Mark* (DM) also drove hundreds of thousands of people who had not been willing to offer their services for the old money to look for employment. The creation of a West German government and, prior to 1949, of a Bizonal Economic Administration also meant that now the West Germans were able to make their own economic policy, unfettered by zonal differences, occupation objectives, and divergent points of view among the three Allied zonal administrations and the eleven West German state governments, which until 1949 had been the highest German authorities in occupied Western Germany.

The economic development of the West German republic has followed so completely the economic theories of one man that it would be a great injustice not to give credit to the fateful decision by which he set the West German economy on its course. Professor Ludwig Erhard was a disciple of the Freiburg school of economic liberalism of the late Walter Eucken who placed his full confidence in the beneficial effects on the whole society of a free market, while admitting that the economic structure of a market economy — though not the economic processes themselves — may at times require extensive corrections, such as anti-trust legislation. After the war Erhard had joined the new Christian Democratic movement and took over the economic leadership, first of the Bizonal Administration and then of the cabinet of the new Federal Republic. Faced with the vast extent of post-war misery and the innumerable claims on the social welfare policy of the new federal government, he decided to put off the satisfaction of all these demands for the time being. If your blanket is too short to cover your whole body at night, his argument ran, you will improve matters little by trying to stretch it or by cutting it into small pieces to cover the most sensitive parts. What you need is a bigger blanket. Thus Erhard decided, in the face of angry criticism not only from the opposition Social Democrats but from large sections of his own party and of the occupation authorities, to throw all the available energy of Western Germany behind building up the production of goods. Marshall Plan aid and the currency reform were welcome contributions to this end. He added many further measures, shrewdly calculated to give an incentive here, to brake a development there, to correct defects in the basic structure, and to deal with the many different situations and minor crises one by one as they arose. Not until 1952 did he have the satisfaction of a generally favorable public response to his policies. Until that time, he faced many a crisis of confidence and the recurrent charge that his so-called Social Market

Economics was more "market economics" than "social-policy-oriented."

The success story of Erhard's policy could, of course, be documented with a vast array of statistics. For our purposes here, just a brief indication of the rising levels of production, employment, and living standards will suffice. Total industrial production, which in June 1948 was at less than half the volume of 1936, passed this pre-war level by the end of 1949. The gross national product of Western Germany caught up with the 1936 figure by 1950. By the time of the federal elections of 1957, the gross national product had doubled again, progressing with an average stride of about 10 per cent a year, a figure several times as large as the American growth rate. Since 1957, industrial production has risen again by more than one-half, with a growth rate held back somewhat by the labor shortage. Such an indicator as the steel production also tells the story in its rise from 14.8 million tons in 1936 to 23 million in 1956 and 34.4 million in 1962. During this period, employment figures rose to more than one and a half those of 1948, mirroring the absorption of millions of unemployed refugees and further millions of new workers from among the young, women, and handicapped or over-age men into the productive process. The booming economy also featured impressive gains in productivity and an increasing turn to automation. Yet despite these labor-stretching devices and the great influx of refugees and new working men and women, an increasing labor shortage has begun to make itself known in recent years, and so hundreds of thousands of Italian, Greek, Spanish, and even Turkish workers were recruited. By 1964, unemployment in Western Germany had dropped below 0.4 per cent of the labor force; nearly one million foreign workers had followed the lure of West German wages; and yet there were still over 500,000 job openings vacant.

What was the secret of the West German success? There is no simple explanation such as ascribing it all to the government policies or to the willingness of Germans to work hard, though work they did. Among the various factors favoring the West German "economic miracle" were the very high rate of investment, first sustained by Marshall Plan aid and then by "self-financing," i.e. the reinvestment of a large part of the profits. By deliberate government policy tax inducements were provided for reinvesting profits. An overwhelming and insatiable demand for consumer goods allowed a generous profit margin from which capital could be plowed back into production. At first the demand represented only a desire to replace items worn out and lost during a decade of wartime and post-war rationing. But soon it turned into a vast acquisitive urge for a higher living standard and goods, such as automobiles, washing machines, and refrigerators which the average German had never been able to afford before. Another factor was the universal eagerness among owners of businesses, management, and labor to co-operate in the economic reconstruction of the country and in the recovery of its foreign markets. The trade unions especially were willing to restrain the demands of labor for higher wages and shorter hours during the first years for the sake of improving the competitive position of Western Germany on the world market. Finally, there was also an element of luck in the gaining of new foreign markets whose demands often happened to fit what the German industry could supply, in the vicissitudes of the international situation which often favored German business expansion, and in the long years of low German defense expenditures at a time when foreign competitors suffered from the handicap of their own defense efforts. Needless to add, there was also a vast pool of well-trained and willing manpower lying idle at the beginning and just waiting to reconstruct and develop pre-war industrial capacity.

While there may be little doubt about the spectacular rise of production, we can still ask how the population at large benefited from the economic boom. After all, in the earlier phases of German industrialization, a high rate of economic growth often went together with unrelieved misery of the masses. The West German recovery is reflected clearly in the income statistics. Adjusting the German figures and converting them, in the ratio of four to one, into post-war United States dollars, the real *per capita* income in Germany underwent the following changes: falling from a pre-war level of about $450 *per annum* in 1936, it stood at $335 in 1949. By the middle of the Korean war, in 1951, it had already passed the pre-war mark, with about $465. From there it rose steeply from $615 in 1954, $765 in 1956 to $1030 in 1960. By the end of 1962, West German *per capita* income was estimated to be well in excess of $1200, which meant that it had almost quadrupled since the beginning of the new economic policy in 1948. To be sure, this amount still places the West

Germans at only a little better than half of the American national average, but they are already catching up with the *per capita* income of some of our poorer states and may well be able to buy more with their marks than the exchange rate would suggest.

Since these figures do not reflect differences in the cost and standards of living in the two countries, the question must also be raised what the West Germans can buy with their money and whether this new rise in purchasing power extends all the way down to what once used to be the lower classes in Germany. The following are the impressions gained during a visit to Germany several years ago. The typical housing for a West German family is still a small, overcrowded apartment which on the average costs no more than about twenty-five to thirty dollars a month, or about one-tenth to one-sixth of the family income. The rents are lowest in old housing, where they have been under government control for decades, which means they are usually in a poor state of repair. There are also new apartments with three to five times as much rent as this average and a down payment in the neighborhood of one thousand dollars. There are generally no suburban subdivisions yet as in the United States, but one can find three-story "row houses" (*Reihenhäuser*) which share the same roof, but have each its own staircase and driveway within a twenty-foot frontage. They correspond in space and price approximately to $20,000-subdivision homes in the United States, except that down payments of four to six thousand dollars place them completely beyond the reach of the average family. Certain services in Western Germany are also less costly than in America. For example, higher education and medical care, items which heavily burden American family budgets, are negligible expenditures in Western Germany, where the state pays for a large part of both out of tax revenues. With housing and these services so inexpensive, and food about as high-priced as in the United States, the average West German family still has enough income left to indulge its own kind of a revolution of rising expectations.

The acquisition of refrigerators, washing machines, cars, and television sets by an increasing number of West German households has been the most obvious manifestation of the yearning for a higher living standard and its satisfaction by a steadily widening group of people. In the gradual rise of family incomes since 1948, a particular point seems to have occurred around 1957 when the income level began to allow the broad masses of people to acquire these objects of their desire. In 1950, for example, only three out of a hundred West German families owned a refrigerator, only five a washing machine, and only three an automobile. In the following half dozen years, the percentage of owners of these items rose only slowly beyond this limited top layer of beneficiaries of the "economic miracle." But then came the labor shortage and a succession of annual advances of 10 and 12 per cent in the average level of wages. Between the years 1958 and 1960 alone, the percentages of families with refrigerators rose from 17 per cent to 42 per cent, and with cars from 17 per cent to 23 per cent. Twenty-nine per cent owned washing machines in 1960. By 1958, West German roofs had also blossomed forth with television antennas; eleven out of a hundred families owned television sets. By 1963, television-set ownership stood at 44 per cent, refrigerators at 58 per cent, and car ownership at 35 per cent of West German families.

If there was any doubt left about the distribution of the affluence of the "economic miracle" to the broad masses of the people, a closer look at the statistics of car ownership will dispel it: between the years 1954 and 1961, the number of privately owned passenger cars rose from 380,000 to 3 million. Business and professional people in Western Germany increased the number of cars in their possession by about 70 per cent. In the same period, however, white-collar employees in the public service and in private industry raised their car ownership sevenfold, and the blue-collar workers their number of cars twenty-seven times. This meant, in effect, that the traditional upper 20 per cent of West German society, the business and professional class, lapsed in its share of ownership in this foremost status symbol of West German affluence from 37 per cent in 1954 to 8 per cent in 1961, while the lower 60 per cent of society, the blue-collar workers, improved their share from 13 to 46 per cent. The white-collar groups, which make up another 20 per cent of the gainfully employed, changed their share only a little in this social upheaval, from about 50 per cent to 46. It is true that these figures do not reflect the great variety in size or cost of the automobiles acquired by the different social classes. But there is a far greater social gap between non-ownership and owning a small car than between small- and big-car owners. It should be noted also that blue-collar workers, for example, bought about one-fourth of all the new cars in 1961, while the white-collar employees bought another 30 per cent. This further confirms the evidence that West Germans by and large have finally arrived at the stage of mass consumption.

With understandable pride, the Minister of Economics — architect of the "economic miracle" — could write in 1959:

> Not only the steadily rising incomes and living standards of our people, but also the welfare achievements in old age, sickness and disabled veterans' pensions bear witness to the fact that our free enterprise policy is the best social welfare.

The high public revenues derived from all the new affluence indeed enabled the federal and state governments of Western Germany to be generous in their compensation toward those who were not able to avail themselves of the opportunities offered by the great economic boom. With the increasing success of his economics of the free market place, Erhard now shifted more emphasis to the social policy part of his "Social Market Economics." His anti-trust bill, in the making since 1952, became law in 1957. The construction of public and co-operative housing was stepped up and stock of denationalized enterprises like the Volkswagen works made available exclusively to small investors, who responded with enthusiasm. As another aspect of the "property policy" (*Eigentumspolitik*) of this "popular capitalism," the federal government offered attractive savings premiums which can double the little man's savings over a period of five years. Again the public response is evident from the astounding average of three thousand marks ($750) which West German families had in the bank in 1961. Ludwig Erhard had every reason to be proud of his achievements, which were marred only by creeping inflation and a rising defense budget.*

Americans reading this story of economic growth and rising levels of mass consumption may be tempted to view this as an "economic miracle" in view of their own record, although they may have noticed

* The West German federal budget of 1963 allotted approximately 32 per cent of its expenditures to defense and 19 per cent to social welfare. The rate of inflation has fluctuated between about 1 and 3 per cent a year.

the recent decline of the West German economic growth rate to 3.5 per cent in 1963 and about 4.5 per cent in 1964 as a consequence of the saturation of foreign and domestic markets and various other factors. However, periods of rapid economic growth seem to occur at markedly different times for different countries and there is really little justification for comparing West German development during the last decade with that of the United States which is at a more advanced stage. A better frame of reference might be other European countries which also have only recently reached the stage of mass consumption.

A cursory glance at indicators of wage and consumption levels reveals at once that the country of the "economic miracle" is not at all a front runner among West European nations. A recent survey of coal miners' and steel workers' real wages between 1954 and 1960 in the countries of the European Coal and Steel Community showed German coal miners' earnings in 1960 next to the lowest and as much as 10 to 15 per cent below those of their colleagues in the Netherlands and France, and German steel workers' wages to be as much as 20 to 25 per cent below the front-running Belgian and Luxembourg steel workers. These low 1960 figures represented the outcome of years of militant wage demands in Germany, during which the coal miners and steel workers increased their wages by more than one-fourth of what they were in 1954, considerably more than the wage gains of any other Schuman Plan nation.

A comparison of car ownership in 1963 likewise shows the West Germans with a rate of 108 passenger cars per one thousand inhabitants trailing Sweden with a rate of 192, as well as Great Britain, Denmark, France, Switzerland, and the Benelux countries. To be sure, the West Germans have done a great amount of catching up in years past and are now quite close to most other European countries except for the three or four front runners. But the West German economy has lost the momentum of the earlier days, when there was a considerable backlog to fill. In the years from 1958 to 1963, for example, the growth of 35 per cent in Germany's gross national product was not much faster than that of the Netherlands with 34 per cent or of France with 29 per cent; while that of Italy, another country that has a long way to catch up with its European neighbors in the Common Market, grew at the record pace of 59 per cent. German *per capita* income in 1964 was $1255, about the same as that of France.

From a consideration of all this it would appear that speaking of an "economic miracle" is a rather extravagant use of language. There is no question that Western Germany is one of the larger countries of Europe, in fact as large in size and population as Great Britain, though not quite as developed. And from its size and location follows a certain economic power even though the German coal and steel industry has long been under the control of the Schuman Plan and the Common Market increasingly pits French, Dutch, Belgian, and Italian industrial combines of comparable size in competition against Germany's industrial giants. It is also true that West Germany has experienced a period of rapid economic growth which has helped it catch up economically with the field of some, though not all, other free nations of Europe. Such periods of rapid economic growth have occurred elsewhere as well, most recently in Japan and Italy. But there appears to be no reason to speak of a German "economic miracle" unless for the purpose of fashioning a political myth for obscure uses or abuses.

"Looking at the norms and actual behavior of the people in the Federal Republic today, one is amazed to see how they contradict nearly every stereotype of German character known to literature . . . Striving for personal success, an orientation toward the enjoyment of leisure and consumer goods, individualism, a rejection of all military discipline, objectivity and 'materialism' are the most visible signs of behavior today."

Ralf Dahrendorf, *Gesellschaft und Freiheit* (1961)

4

THE NEW SOCIETY OF WEST GERMANY

It cannot but strike an outside observer as odd that the West Germans — and many foreigners as well — should exhibit such an undignified fascination with the production and consumption figures of their "economic miracle." In fact so much so that in a recent cross-national opinion survey, which elicited from Americans, Englishmen, and Mexicans rhapsodies of pride in their respective countries and forms of government, a representative West German sample could muster spontaneous pride only in their economic achievements. The reason for all this excitement about gross economic success lies far deeper and cannot be understood without going back to the deep-seated social tensions and fissures in German society which made it ripe for catastrophe and thereby for Hitler.

The development of German society since the days of Bismarck was characterized, as Thorstein Veblen pointed out half a century ago, by industrialization without real Western-style capitalism and without a classical bourgeoisie such as had fought off the feudal aristocracy in England and France and given the world the rights of man, written constitutions, and democracy. Instead of this powerful and liberating social force based on the dynamics of capitalism, German industrialization was carried out under the control of the old feudal elite and under the tutelage of the *Kaiser*'s state. What little grand bourgeoisie there was in the closed oligarchic circle of industrial power slavishly imitated the feudal-military way of life or, in the southern states and the old Hanse cities where there had been more potential for Western-style development, was smothered under Prussian domination with feudal and state control. Instead of the emancipation of vast economic and social forces experienced elsewhere, German industrialization remained in the strait jacket of an outmoded social order and of a state paternalism which allowed for little competition, private initiative, or self-help. A preference for state intervention permeated even the labor movement and led conflicting groups and interests throughout society to expect state-imposed solutions instead of working out their own compromises. Thus was fashioned a large part of the fatal weakness of the Weimar Republic, under which at a critical juncture power slipped back into the hands of the crumbling state machinery and the disintegrating old social elite, who in turn passed it on to Hitler. The post-war development of East German society and economy, incidentally, still follows the same state-controlled pattern, now on totalitarian lines.

What the West Germans are experiencing with such exhilaration today are the dynamic forces of a free market economy which is changing their lives and the character of German society before their very eyes. Starting from rubble, though not from scratch, a dynamic capitalistic economy has recapitulated past stages of industrialization in West Germany and forged on to an advanced stage. It has spawned a new and this time independent entrepreneurial and managerial class with a vested interest in parliamentary democracy. It also shattered the last buttresses of the old rigid class structure and brought into being an open, pluralistic society whose chief motive force seems to be the desire of individuals to improve their lot. The once all-powerful state has receded into the background of the great pluralistic society and has become merely one among several great social forces, albeit a force with a guiding role. All this social and economic upheaval may not thrill Americans unimpressed by the productive forces unleashed by free enterprise and pre-occupied with the problems that arise after the arrival of economic abundance. To a German or, for that matter,

almost anyone outside of this country, however, the economic dynamics of capitalism and its revolutionary effect on society are heady
stuff. In fact, on second thought there may indeed be some justification for speaking of a miracle brought about by the economic forces
that have been at work, a "social miracle," which is visibly changing
the face of West German society. In this chapter, some light will be
thrown on the various features of this newly emerging society: its social structure, its new elites and other social strata, its changing values, and also its forgotten pockets of traditionalism, poverty, and neglected public tasks.

There is no better introduction to the changing social structure of
Germany than to observe the strange odyssey of the word *bürgerlich,*
or bourgeois, from the 1920's to this day. In the 'twenties this term,
and with it the genteel way of life of the propertied, educated German
middle class, had somehow become stuck with the burden of social
guilt and tension of the entire crumbling old social order, as *déclassés*
of all classes, together with the disillusioned millions of war veterans, despairing victims of economic dislocation, and a nemesis of
alienated intellectuals and juveniles raged at bourgeois morality,
property-consciousness, and concern for manners and appearances.
Legions of militant workers proudly proclaimed themselves the vanguard of a proletarian order of the future which would scorn such
silly bourgeois preoccupations as family life, private property, parliamentary democracy, clean shirt collars, and neckties. Americans, who
so lightly use the term social class, rarely quite understand — except
for those of colored skin — the deep wrath of German workers excluded for half a century from the promise of sharing in the economic and political advantages which industrialization holds out for
any man. Even the Nazi party, to whom the bourgeois voters in the
end surrendered their ballots and their self-respect by the millions,
made no secret of its utter contempt for such bourgeois scruples as
good faith, *Kultur,* or the sacredness of human life and of international peace.

Today, most Germans have only the haziest notion of the meaning,
social, moral, or political, of the word bourgeois. No longer an object
of spite and controversy, and hardly of any concrete content any
more, it has a vaguely positive connotation with which everybody including workers and Social Democrats likes to identify himself. It

Karl Marx on May Day, 1963: Not all wheels are grinding to a halt in celebration of the traditional Day of Labor

would be difficult to find a man in Western Germany who would proudly call himself a "proletarian," a word which has now become clearly derogatory, though again with hardly any concrete content. It appears that the festering social cleavage once denoted by bourgeois and proletarian has lost its significance. This is only one more sign of the erosion of the old class structure which began with the first industrialization and has finally given birth to the new society under the influence of the second, free industrial development.

The demise of the chief buttresses of the old society, the old elites of the Prussian army, of the bureaucracy, and of the owners of the industrial giants as well as of the status distinction based on birth or *Bildung und Besitz* (education and property), can be traced over the last fifty years. Starting with the war experience of World War I, the class society has experienced a long series of shattering blows. There is an equality of bravery and death in modern war which pays no heed to social rank and stereotyped class attitudes and tends to revolutionize social classes even after it has ended. World War I was followed by economic dislocations and the terrible inflation of 1923 which took their toll among the propertied classes. The Great Depression again mowed down the classes of *Bildung und Besitz,* magnifying the psychological effect of the preceding crises and mobilizing an army of frightened lower middle-class families. The Hitler movement, it will be recalled, had distinct overtones of a populistic egalitarianism which demoted both the aristocratic privileges and bourgeois status by implication. The Nazi take-over again involved a vast amount of social reshuffling in which old cultural elites were thrown out of leading positions in government and business, to be replaced by individuals rising from the lowest classes, and at times literally from the dregs of society. The destruction and economic dislocations of World War II and its immediate aftermath, especially the expulsion and flight of millions of Germans in the east and the division of Germany which cut off the *Junker* aristocracy east of the Elbe, further contributed to the demolition of family fortunes and traditional positions of privilege. Since the Nazi take-over was carried along on such a vast wave of opportunism and bandwagon-jumping, it made a clean sweep of the traditional elites, excepting, of course, those who co-operated with the Nazis. Many falling into this latter category, however, were cut down to size by Allied tribunals and denazification courts. Between these two millstones and under the impact of the various economic crises and, last but not least, the currency reform of 1948, old class distinctions were pulverized and the entire society "homogenized," so to speak. The immediate post-war era in Germany was characterized by a great deal of *de facto* equality at marginal levels of existence, involved with the vast welter of welfare claims, and utterly subject to rationing of consumer goods and governmental control over private property.

The impact of the decade and a half of the "economic miracle," then, resulted in something quite different from the old class society. Deeply ingrained class patterns require a succession of many generations of inequality and immobility to jell. To be sure, the beginnings of Erhard's new economic policy and the currency reform gave some people, such as merchants and black marketeers with hoarded stock, a head start. Its immediate effect, and also the rise of the many new faces of the Western German business world, tended at first to restore old pre-Nazi elites and their social and political attitudes, which some observers characterized deprecatingly as the "Hindenburg Germans." In the long run, however, the head starts of some people were lost and the newcomers, including refugees with government credit, came to determine the character of the great economic upheaval. Fifteen years of competition in a relatively free market economy finally completed the transformation and brought about the new society of Western Germany.

Naturally, there are many gradations of income and standards of living from the top to the bottom of the new society. Sociologists are still arguing whether to speak of it as one great middle-class society of many gradations but no real barriers (Helmut Schelsky), or whether there are still states of mind and of social status roughly comparable to the old society, such as a small heterogeneous upper stratum, the old and new urban middle classes, the farmers and farm workers, and, most numerous of them all, the working class, using the word "class" loosely (Ralf Dahrendorf). Studies have indeed been made of the attitudes of workers in Germany and in other European countries which show that a great many of them, especially the older workers, still think of society in terms of a division into "them" and "us." But among the younger workers already, attitudes prevail that are not much different from those of the salaried middle class, the white-collar employees of government and business. Neither are the members of the top stratum of West German society very assertive about their status. When the American sociologist Morris Janowitz conducted a survey of West German social structure and asked his respondents to classify themselves as upper, middle, or lower class, less than 2 per cent of his sample indicated they regarded themselves as "upper class," and one-half of those claimants had to be rejected as scurrilous. The other four-fifths of what Janowitz considered the upper stratum classified themselves as "middle class" and some even as "lower" or "working class." Needless to say, this increasing absence of class-consciousness both at the top and the bottom is a far cry from German society of a mere thirty years ago. More and more, the new German society is coming to look like the American consumer society, though social mobility may still be hampered by the newness of the opportunities for advancement and by the German educational system, which is the last holdout of class distinction and privilege. But there is the same quest for status symbols at all levels, most notably the acquisition of a television set and of a car, or a fancy vacation trip abroad, or, of course, also the different sizes and price levels of cars and other status symbols. There are the same frantic efforts to keep up with the Schmidts or Muellers next door. There is the same emphasis on conspicuous consumption on many levels.

A subject of particular interest, both for the gossip columns of newspapers and for sociologists, is the nature of the new upper stratum. Dahrendorf lays great emphasis on its pluralistic composition of at least seven distinct elites: (1) the leaders of big business, (2) the political leadership of parties, parliament, and the executive branch, (3) the university professors and top educational administrators, (4) the church leaders of the different religions and regions, (5) the notables of stage and motion pictures, the mass media, and sports, (6) the military top brass of the "new army," and (7) the top of the legal profession. Every one of these components of the new upper stratum constitutes the pinnacle of a separate pyramid of achievement which largely precludes, for example, a movie star or business tycoon from changing from one elite into another. Even their social contacts among each other, save in small towns, are very limited. In view of the German past, not only the fading of the old aristocratic, land-owning, and military elites deserves particular attention, but also the emergence of new elites and notables of substantially civilian, middle-class outlook and habits of mind, far from the authoritarianism and military cast of mind of the past.

The most conspicuous among the competing groups of the new upper stratum are the new tycoons and top-drawer executives, a leisure class true to Thorstein Veblen's description and the object of as much deserved as undeserved criticism from all quarters. The new fortunes of West Germany, including a handful of the older business families, are not as substantially founded as were their predecessors of the "good old times" before 1914, when more than fifteen thousand gold-mark millionaires could be found in the German Empire, and Prussia alone had more than five thousand persons with annual incomes exceeding 100,000 gold marks. In 1957, economists counted

3500 millionaires of the new currency and almost five hundred persons with annual incomes over one million. In the 1961 elections, the opposition parties even spoke of "ten thousand" millionaires. But the shift from the solid substance of the gilded age to the tinsel of the affluent consumers' society of the present day is as obvious as the change from the days when the wealthy affected a feudal, aristocratic style of life and, as reserve officers of the Imperial Army, absorbed the military authoritarianism they then sought to introduce into industrial relations, the government bureaucracy, and middle-class family life. While there are still duelling fraternities at German universities and saber scars have not lost all their social prestige, the new leisure class has other, more harmless preoccupations and generally lacks an aristocracy above it from which it could learn all the wrong things. One can see the *nouveaux riches* in droves on the inner lanes of the *Autobahn* driving a black (or yellow for the *crème de la crème*) Mercedes, the status symbol of having arrived, and impatiently blinking their headlights at the lowly Volkswagens or Opels that dare to block their path. They own Chris-Craft cruisers and summer residences in fashionable resorts such as Lake Lugano in Switzerland or the Costa Brava in Spain and spend much of their time in search of vacation spots all over the world that are not yet overrun by their own kind. At home, they live in sumptuous mansions with swimming pools, small parks, and servants. They are rather unsure of themselves and exhibit many of the mannerisms of the newly rich which have delighted cartoonists and comedians of all ages and countries. Since American civilization is an object of great admiration and eager imitation to affluent West Germans, for example, they insist on using English words for their "swimming pool," "weekend," "bungalow" (a modern one-story house) or "living hall" (a hall for receiving visitors), instead of the accepted German words.

The life of affluence in Western Germany also has its psychological weak spots, a soft underbelly of insecurity and vulnerability, which is only in small part due to the passing nature of individual affluence. On the one hand, German folkways have always associated wealth and high status with uninhibited indulgence in the pleasures of *Wein, Weib und Gesang* (wine, women, and song). The West German "high society" has had more than its share of lurid scandals, involving prostitution, call-girl rings, spectacular bankruptcies, and horrible

crimes motivated by excessive greed or an enormous lust for high living. In the mid-'fifties, public opinion was rocked by the case of
Rosemarie N., a girl who had made a fortune ministering to the
mental and physical relaxation of middle-aged business tycoons and
was found strangled one fine day. On the other hand, the life of a self-
appointed member of this "high society" involves both deliberate
publicity-seeking and an insatiable need for social recognition which
can give rise to curious forms of exhibitionism. Most new tycoons or
stars of the entertainment world tend to encourage around them a
flock of hangers-on, parasites, and self-appointed publicity specialists
who will satisfy their ego for a price. These "new socialites" also seek
each other's company, vying for the recognition of what they imagine
to be the peer group of their highest social aspirations. In 1958, to
give a typical example, the editor of a fashionable magazine founded
the Madame Club in which new tycoons, old and new movie stars,
and other publicity-conscious people from Gina Lollobrigida to
ex-heavyweight champion Max Schmeling can enjoy an opportunity to display themselves and indulge in *la dolce vita*. In addition to
lavish summer festivals in Lugano and trips to New York, the
Madame Club has held forth in many of the localities discovered by
those prominent a generation ago, such as at the Bavarian town
Tegernsee, once popularly called "lago di bonzo" because of the large
number of Nazi dignitaries who had mansions there; the old Austrian
castle, Schloss Fuschl, which used to be the lair of the Nazi Foreign
Minister von Ribbentrop; or the Café Carlton in Munich, where in
the roaring 'twenties middle-aged ladies used to entertain their gigolos
and Hitler used to go for afternoon tea. Whatever people may say
about the high society sets of different German eras, they have always
demonstrated an unfailing sense for the best locations for the pursuit
of *Wein, Weib und Gesang*.

At the same time that this new "money aristocracy" is monopoliz-
ing the social columns, the scions of the old hereditary aristocracy
have in considerable numbers taken on bourgeois occupations in the
professions and in business. With many of the old estates in Russian
or Polish hands or redistributed by East German land reforms, many
titled persons appeared in the West without a penny to their name.
Some have been conspicuously successful in academic or journalistic
careers, belying their traditional reputation for stupidity. Others have
joined the publicity-hunt of the "money aristocracy." In Southern

Germany, where aristocratic circles had never been as exclusive and contemptuous toward the bourgeoisie as in Prussia and where many of the old estates are still intact, the old and the new elites have joined. The effect of such a social merger on the good taste shown by the new leisure class, which is rather abominable elsewhere, is quite noticeable. Even politically, the scions of the hereditary aristocracy are with rare exceptions perfectly reconciled with the Second German Republic. There is no "cabinet of barons," no aristocratic conspiracy plotting for the return of the monarchy, nor are the tycoons and the managerial elite of the business world looking for a Hitler to help them subdue organized labor and overthrow parliamentary democracy as in the Weimar days. The entire upper stratum has a vested interest in the political and economic *status quo* and has lent its support either to Adenauer's Christian Democrats or to the Free Democrats (FDP).

If the upper stratum is happy with the political and economic circumstances of the Federal Republic, this is no less true of the other components of West German society. The downward spread of unprecedented, if modest, affluence has also engaged the loyalties of the "old middle class" of independent small businessmen, artisans, and farmers, especially after the economic fate of the latter received a big financial and moral boost under the Green Plan for agricultural reform and similar support for small business and handicrafts. The "new middle class" of white-collar employees in government and business has also benefited from the "economic miracle," although perhaps not as much as the preceding categories. But they are well on their way from the bottom rungs of the ladder of affluence.

The same can be said, and with greater social significance, of the once so lowly German working class. The economic well-being of these latter two classes, and hence of the bulk of West Germans, has a natural, reinforcing effect on their political loyalties. They have been about evenly split between the Christian Democrats and the "loyal opposition," the Social Democrats (SPD), and so have supported the existing political and economic system. Very few, in fact no more than 1 per cent of the West German electorate, has felt any inclination during the last dozen years to vote for the "disloyal opposition" of the radical right or left, or by implication for a basic change of the existing system.

The drastic changes which make up the new society in West Germany and elsewhere in the New Europe could hardly have taken place without corresponding changes in values and attitudes. These are particularly strong among the young generation, but they also color the thought of their protesting elders. Depending on the prejudice or intent of the observer, the new values have been variously called materialism, selfishness, or the pursuit of happiness. Basic to the new attitudes is a turning away from such values as national grandeur or the well-being of the group or community and a new stress on individual effort and rewards. Instead of the identification with the fate of the nation, the pride in the collectivity, the self-denial of the individual for the sake of the group, and all the mystical nonsense about the special qualities of the German people which the Nazis and a generation of nationalistic historians and writers had taught, today's West Germans have discovered the challenge, the opportunities, and the satisfactions of individual existence.

In a low key, and still barely discernible against a tradition of German idealism, the ethics of self-interest, which for centuries have constituted the basis for economic and political individualism in other Western countries, have arrived in Germany. In post-war Germany, self-interest got its clandestine start in the last months of the collapsing Nazi empire when it was "every man for himself" for many a soldier or civilian. The collapse of the nationalistic dream, reinforced by the disclosure of the misdeeds of the Third Reich helped the development along. The ubiquitous black market of the occupation years, when almost every person was involved in a little illegal transaction here and there, from buying a few cigarettes or greasing the palms of a craftsman to sizable racket operations, subtly knocked the rest of the stuffing out of the ethics of romantic idealism. By the time of the currency reform of 1948, most West Germans were ready for the great scramble of self-interest which led them where they stand today, when progress is definitely considered a private affair, or at least as nothing more than the sum of many private advances to individual happiness.

One illustration of the changed attitude is provided by the business ethics of Western Germany, where the tolerance toward more or less illegal operations is now a good deal higher than it used to be and, in fact, where there is a grudging admiration for the man who manages to "beat the game" without getting caught. Considerable ingenuity is displayed, for example, in dealings with government red tape or with inspection on all levels. A notable instance is the thriving semi-illegal trade across the borders and through the hands of suspicious customs officials: although the Federal Republic maintains a Customs Crimes Institute with files on some 75,000 big-time smugglers, shipping agents, and trucking firms, this has not prevented an annual loss of around fifteen million marks in uncollected duties due to forged certificates, falsely declared shipments, and a "third country of origin" dodge used especially for the importation of merchandise from behind the Iron Curtain. Like many other police agencies in West Germany today, the Institute is evidently unable to keep up with the more extreme manifestations of naked "self-interest."

Another aspect is the great interest now displayed by white-collar employees and blue-collar workers in *Freizeit,* or leisure-time activities, in contrast to their previous willingness to work hard and to postpone rewards, an attitude generally acknowledged to have played a major role in the earlier phases of the "economic miracle." For the man of the salaried middle class and even more for the blue-collar worker, the hobbies and recreation activities of *Freizeit* are one of the most important outlets in life for getting the satisfactions which his job denies him. They are a significant part of his pursuit of individual happiness, along with the status symbols he can now afford. But there are also complaints that all this concentration on *Freizeit* has affected his famous working morale. There are even some who claim that all this prosperity and the critical labor shortage have gone to his head.

To give an illustration, the interviews of many a local newspaper-man with the foreign workers that are now in Western Germany could be cited. Following the usual questions about a foreign workman's family at home and how he likes working in Germany, there comes the standard query about what he does not like. The standard answer: "The German fellow-workers. *Troppo dolce far niente,* absenteeism, drinking on the job." Naturally, the foreign worker is anxious to earn within a short period of time as much money as possible in order to take it home to Turkey, or Greece, or Sicily. His German fellow-worker may frustrate him by his unwillingness to work overtime or on weekends. Coming from the poorer areas of Southern Europe, the foreign worker may be offended by the spendthrift attitude and conspicuous consumption of the affluent Germans, who appear to squander on frills and frolics what to him is a means for lifting up his family from the abject depths of poverty.

Nor is this just a matter of subjective impressions on the part of outsiders. An editorial in a large South German newspaper claimed that it is not uncommon in the land of the "economic miracle" for construction workers to start a noisy and alcoholic celebration at noon on a workday, say Thursday, and to take off the following afternoon or a whole day on full pay. Their boss cannot afford to punish or fire them for fear of losing irreplaceable skilled helpers. Some of these men very likely can be found "moonlighting," working on a highly-paid second job during these stolen hours. One-third of the entire working force of Western Germany has been estimated to have more than one job, with the likely result that the "moonlighters" may not give any of their employers their pay's worth of work. One out of ten changes to another company every year in quest of better pay. The German Institute of Industry recently computed that the year 1964 had only 237 working days per employee, after discounting all the long weekends, paid vacations, and holidays, of which Germany has a generous share. With an average of twenty-four further days lost on sickness and for other causes, this amounts to no more than 213 eight-hour days. Thus, German workers only put in the equivalent of 43 forty-hour weeks a year, even though in many industries they have not yet adopted the forty-hour week.

The labor shortage has also made small repairs a costly and time-consuming affair for private households and small businesses. For many service occupations the supply of new personnel has reached a critical impasse. Waiters and waitresses are so scarce that a tourist may find signs in some restaurants imploring the patrons to be kind to the service personnel: "Patrons come every day. But if you make my waitress quit, I'll never find another." Needless to add, the shortage of waitresses affects the quality of the service. Domestic servants, once the hallmark of the households of the upper bourgeoisie, are also in such short supply that they need to be coddled with many inducements, from higher pay and lighter workloads to television sets in the maid's room. At the same time, curious forms of psychological compensation express the less obvious improvement of status which has resulted from the shortage: a *Putzfrau* (cleaning woman) now wishes to be known as a *Raumpflegerin* (room attendant), and a "maid" would never dream of scrubbing the floor. Of course, there is a danger in generalizing from the more glaring examples. The majority of German workmen and service personnel have probably not abandoned to any noticeable extent their hard-working and conscientious ways. Yet these examples would seem to point up unmistakable trends which may be too subtle to appear in the statistics: vast numbers of Germans who for generations toiled faithfully but submerged in "the lower classes" are feeling the heady wind of a new freedom which comes with higher living standards and the great demand for their services. They may not always make the best of their rise from the submerged past, at least not at first. There may also be some undesirable side-effects accompanying their emancipation, such as inflation, critical manpower shortages, and a drop in working morale and standards of craftsmanship. But there is no mistaking the final collapse of the old class system: although the newly rich may strive to re-establish the upper end of a system of social classes, the people at its lower end will never go back where they came from. They have broken the mental chains which once kept them from desiring "what is not for the likes of us."

From another angle, it should also be stressed that a lowering of the working morale in Western Germany is not synonymous with actually working less or with a lowering of consumer demand. Quite the contrary. Their first taste of affluence has given West Germans an insatiable appetite for more. The annual automobile fairs which exhibit the new models often stir up an excitement in the public that many a newspaper editorial has likened to the biblical dance around the golden calf. Motorcycles as mass motor vehicles are disappearing fast from the highways. The recent trend with cars, the foremost status symbol, has shifted from the tiny Isettas and Goggomobiles through the small Fords, DKWs, Opels, and Volkswagens to a mass demand for a *Mittelklasse* of 1500 cc automobiles. Even the Mercedes manufacturers are getting ready for the top of the mass demand. As cars become more ostentatious and motors more powerful from year to year, a cynic might predict the appearance of tailfins by the second half of the 1960's. With television, the West German public is still in the first rapture of abandoned viewing which has brought about the closing down of scores of motion picture theaters in the big cities.

There are other side-effects of high demand. The great demand for cars, television sets, and kitchen appliances has not all come from the rise of wages. In a great many West German families, the only way of keeping up with the Schmidts next door has been to tear the wife of the household from her presumably sacred place with children, home, and hearth and to put her to work. Her salary together with his overtime and "moonlighting" pay, and perhaps the income of a teen-age child, may finally put the family's income into harmony with its desires. Once the family becomes accustomed to the higher level of consumption, of course, just keeping it there requires considerable and unflagging efforts from all the members.

A good illustration of West German eagerness to earn additional income was also provided by a traffic tie-up caused by a snowstorm in the city of Munich in January 1962. The city government issued the customary call for volunteers to shovel away the snow. Attracted by the doubled rate of pay — it was on a holiday — almost twice the number needed applied. The scramble for the available tools and po-sitions was so violent that police were called in to discourage some of the volunteers. Among the eager snow-shovellers were many white-collar employees, civil servants, and university students who a gen-eration ago would have considered such manual labor degrading.

While West Germans are generally happy about their prosperity, it would be unfair not to mention that they also worry about the effect of affluence on their moral fibre. Many thoughtful Germans have misgiv-ings about the crass materialism, envy, and greed evident everywhere. Every Christmas season a heated debate occurs over whether the giv-ing of expensive presents is killing the spirit of Christmas. Older Ger-mans look with dismay at the children of the newly rich who never knew hard times and look down upon the common man. Some Ger-mans wistfully remember the immediate post-war period as one in which there was still a sense of community and brotherhood amidst scarcity and ruins. They take a dim view of the egotistic pursuits of the *Wohlstandsbuerger,* the affluent citizen. There is also some feeling of discomfort about the direction in which affluence is taking West Ger-man society: the new affluence is unlike the solid prosperity of the "good old days" of the gold mark before 1914, when taxes were low and one gold mark corresponded to about three and a half of the pres-ent *Deutsche Mark.* Today's prosperity is more a matter of playing the role of a manipulable consumer unit in a highly productive and highly consumptive economic mechanism which depends heavily on advertising and on the precautions and safeguards of the welfare state. It is characterized both by the disappearance of truly independent wealth and by the man with a high income who has no qualms about availing himself of the state health insurance (*Allgemeine Ortskrankenkasse*). The modestly affluent man in the street is driven by the demands which advertising, his wife and children, and the Schmidts next door constantly create in him to embark on an unceasing and aimless quest for more and more. Volatile fashions in clothes, appliances, and even in furnishings take the place of planned obsolescence in Western Germany and produce the same net result of creating periodic new demands and encouraging installment buying. Hand in hand with the consumer-oriented society go conformity of taste and a declining appreciation for such old-time values as pride of craftmanship, creative endeavor, and conscientiousness. Young people no longer care to enter service occupations, which still bear the stigma of menial work from the days of the old class society. They also spurn jobs in which they could get their hands dirty, as long as they can find a white-collar job. In many cases they shy away from the commitment to years of apprenticeship and training required by most crafts and choose instead unskilled positions which offer immediate rewards but can promise no future.

Some Germans interpret many of these manifestations of an advanced industrial society characterized by high levels of mass consumption as "Americanization." Their misgivings about the replacement of the old-time values of thrift and conscientiousness by the ceaseless quest after ever higher living standards then appear to them as the reaction of the tortured German soul to this Americanization. "We are living like Americans, but cannot help feeling like Germans," an editorial writer of the *Sueddeutsche Zeitung* expressed his discomfort, disclaiming at the same time the nationalistic overtones his statement appeared to exhibit. There has certainly been a considerable amount of Americanization in Western Germany, a point which will be discussed in greater detail later. However, most of the changes described here have very little to do with Americanization, but are rather a consequence of the incisive impact of mass consumption on the older ways of German society.

Some of the discomfort caused by the "economic miracle" is due to side-effects which go far beyond the realm of economic attitudes and activities. This is particularly noticeable in the changing role of women and children in West German society. There has been an increase of almost 50 per cent in the number of women employed in the West German economy in the last decade. By all odds, this increase reflects a growing pattern of feminine independence from husband or family. This trend was already evident in the large number of business and career women during and after the Second World War who often came upon this new state of independence as a matter of necessity, their husbands or fathers being away at war or in prisoner-of-war camps. It was also laid down in the form of equal rights (*Gleichberechtigung*) in the law. By American standards, the public role of German women is still very negligible. Nevertheless, the loneliness and uncertainty between conflicting roles known to American women are not unknown in Germany. They are increased by the relatively low rate of marriages and by the large number of single women, as well as by the fact that Germans have very little of the gregariousness common in America. Needless to say, these developments signify a drastic departure from the traditional role of women in Germany. They also imply a corresponding change in the image of husbands and fathers. The once so prevalent "pasha" type, the overly domineering male, has practically disappeared and, except for the very young, women are generally rather disenchanted with love and marriage.

Even more significant trends have appeared in the relationship between parents and children, which was once at least as authoritarian as that between man and wife. In its subtler forms, the trend is in the direction of permissiveness toward children and the emancipation of teenagers as in the United States. The preoccupation of the parents with the pursuit of profit and pleasure and the free spending of the teenagers have probably had more to do with this trend than educational theories. Its crudest manifestations are, perhaps, the many-faceted problems of juvenile delinquency. West German cities have their *Halbstarke,* the German equivalent of the young toughs, and their street gangs which make some parts of Hamburg or Frankfurt no safer to walk through at night than Central Park in New York. To be sure, the disrupted families of wartime experience or refugee camps created a post-war legacy of juvenile delinquency as early as

1945. But the present-day *Halbstarke* grow from a different setting, best characterized with the phenomenon of the *Schluesselkind,* the "key child": both parents are at work all day, leaving him the key to their apartment and a great deal of free time in which to seek companions for his loneliness and boredom. By the time the neglected child has reached his teens, he is as fully aware of the desires for high living and social prestige of the adult world as any adult. Starved for parental attention and still without the stabilizing roles supplied by employment or family responsibilities, his craving for thrills and status leads him from joy-riding in stolen cars to the more serious and often violent kinds of juvenile crime, burglaries, armed robbery, muggings, and prostitution. The non-delinquent youth is no less addicted to the pursuit of happiness, although it limits its pursuits to the familiar patterns of teenage fads and idols and social merriment. There is also now a new pattern of early marriages which every August—the German equivalent of June — exceed in proportion to the population even the marriage rate of the United States.

There arc two more questions which need to be asked and answered in order to complete this survey of Western Germany's affluent society: First, is there no poverty left amid the affluence? Second, what about the important public tasks, such as hospitals, roads, and education? Are they taken care of in a manner commensurate with the high level of private consumption?

The answer to the first question is a qualified no. Western Germany is a well-functioning welfare state whose increased wealth has also found its way into state pensions for the old and disabled and into welfare services of every description. However — and this is a big limitation — there are also flaws in this system which can only occur in such a welfare state. There is, for example, the vast and ambitious effort of the Equalization of Burdens (*Lastenausgleich*) between persons who have saved their assets through the vicissitudes of war and post-war times and those who have suffered great material losses as a result of expulsion, flight, or other effects of the war. In the years 1949 to 1959, more than thirty billion marks were paid out of this equalization fund. Yet every year, about 100,000 of the claimants die whose claims have not yet been processed. By 1979, when the Equalization of Burdens is expected to complete its work, very few of the original claimants will still be alive and, in many cases, the equalization office may be concluding its negotiations with their grand-children.

Furthermore, the public welfare activities in Western Germany, while striving to establish a minimal living standard below which nobody is permitted to drop, naturally set a very modest level: in 1961, a single old man, for example, was entitled to a monthly pension of between 110 and 120 marks in addition to his rent and medical expenses. Even beyond welfare cases, there is ample room for hardship owing to various circumstances. Large families, bad luck with jobs, or a lack of initiative in pursuing available opportunities can put a person in an income category little removed from the welfare level. In some east Bavarian towns in 1961, for instance, unemployment rates of 10 to 15 per cent occurred while twenty-five thousand jobs were vacant in the Bavarian state capital. And then there is the vast number of customers of the lower world of big city night quarters, drifters, hoboes, and persons whose vices or crimes inhibit their return to full membership in society. These are cases that do not lend themselves to publicized charity since the affluent German of today tends to be as committed to Victorian notions of "worthy paupers only" as his grandfather was. Particularly offensive to him are the alcoholics, addicts, and voluntary slum dwellers (the so-called asocial elements) who prefer to live in barracks such as the Camp Frauenholz near Munich, where the city authorities had to provide parking for cars and supervise the erection of television antennas but also must use the services of a bailiff for the collection of the few marks of rent. On the other hand, some enlightened city administrations have taken great pride in the establishment of model homes for the aged in which old people of independent means and state pensioners share all the relative luxuries in perfect equality.

In the matter of attention devoted to important public tasks, in contrast to the high levels of private consumption, the story is one of gross neglect. In 1961, the news-magazine *Der Spiegel* ran an article series with the tell-tale title "The Federal Republic — an Underdeveloped Country" in which the sad state of hospitals, roads, schools, and universities was amply documented with figures and examples: there is in Western Germany a catastrophic shortage of hospitals, especially in the big cities, which in 1961 would have required the establishment of about 160 new modern hospitals of six hundred beds each in order to satisfy properly the present demand. The prevailing situation is characterized by unhygienic and undignified conditions with extreme overcrowding, poor organization and location, a severe shortage of personnel and laboratory facilities, and, in some cases, exceedingly primitive temporary quarters. The shortage of hospital beds was further aggravated by the increasing dependence of old people on hospital care rather than on staying at home, where neither medical attention nor the loving care of relatives are as easily available as they were a dozen years ago.

The state of public roads and highways in Western Germany was in no better condition than the hospitals. Although Hitler built the *Autobahn* for strategic and propaganda purposes in the 1930's, he failed to do anything to improve the deplorable state of the vast network of other highways and secondary roads. Today, more than twenty-five years and a vastly greater volume of traffic later, not enough has been done to keep up the over-all system of roads and even less to adapt it to the increased demands. The chief shortcomings appear to be the bottleneck passages of highways in small towns and villages and the conditions in and around the metropolitan centers, where most of the new car owners dwell. The big cities have not only a catastrophic shortage of parking space but are quite poorly equipped for handling the rush hour flow or the weekend exodus and return of vehicles. The resulting traffic jams and accidents rise in number and severity from year to year. The index of fatal West German traffic accidents per motor vehicle in 1960 was two to four times as high as in England, France, Sweden, and the United States, although these countries all exceed the *per capita* number of motor vehicles of the Federal Republic. Experts have expressed the opinion that this staggering accident rate might drop 25 or 30 per cent if the critical traffic conditions were substantially improved. There is a certain irony about the self-strangulation of German cities by all the new passenger cars which are at the same time the great pride of their newly affluent citizens. German cities, like other European cities, have excellent public transportation which could at least take people painlessly to and from their job. But when a man for the first time in his life has been able to afford an automobile, a status symbol of the first order in his society, he can hardly be expected to go back to riding a streetcar or bus. Meanwhile a further difficulty of the passenger car explosion has arisen. The competition for new car sales has made "trade-ins" a regular feature of 80 per cent of all new car sales, with the result that West German car dealers end up with about one million second-hand cars a year for which there seems to be no demand, except from behind the Iron Curtain and from the developing countries.

The physical state of German education is also in such a condition that a Danish university professor is said to have remarked: "In comparison to the Central European average, German schools and universities are in such a desolate state that one has to call the Federal Republic in this respect underdeveloped." The Permanent Conference of *Laender* Ministers of Culture and Education has indicated the need for more primary and secondary school classrooms at fifty thousand just to overcome the most glaring examples of overcrowding, inappropriate quarters, education in two daily shifts, and poor location of schools. One out of every six city schoolchildren has to put up with instruction in two shifts. There is also a critical lack of special facilities and of teaching personnel, not to mention the lack of student transportation and the poor physical environment of many urban schools. In rural areas, ancient school buildings in poor repair and one- or two-room schools with simultaneous instruction for several classes abound. Industry spokesmen and educational administrators claim that these shortcomings have caused a considerable drop in educational performance and that the current graduates of German primary and secondary schools are generally less well prepared in most subjects than their predecessors were before World War II. The answer to the question "why Hans can't read" or spell adequately is exceedingly complex and perhaps similar to that in the United States, regardless of the differences in teaching methods. However, German school administrators generally lack the sociological background even to recognize what the basic problems are. German higher education likewise suffers from a deplorable lack of funds commensurate with private affluence. With rare exceptions this shortage of funds has kept German universities unreasonably overcrowded and understaffed. There are also critical shortages in equipment and facilities, not to mention student housing, which at some universities is in such short supply that thousands of students have to seek places elsewhere. It seems unlikely that the quality of the instruction offered will be unaffected by these shortages.

The poignancy of these disparities in the fulfillment of private and public needs may not seem extraordinary in a country such as the United States, where private desires are always put ahead of public functions and where only a few grudging steps toward redressing the balance have been taken since the 1930's. In Germany, however, tradition has always put the public sector before the private, which makes it all the more noteworthy that this should no longer be so and that, at least for the moment, private progress has so considerably outpaced public progress. Yet this is a typical manifestation of the coming of what we call the new society in Western Germany.

5

AMERICANIZATION APACE

From the first two chapters one might gain the impression that Germans, as a people, are particularly inclined toward nationalistic narrowness and are lacking in empathy toward other cultures. In spite of the intense national egotism of the Hitler years and much of the preceding era, nothing could be further from the truth. Germans avidly adopted foreign cultures long before their greatest poet, Johann Wolfgang Goethe, coined the beautiful phrase that he who learns a foreign tongue gains another soul in addition to his own. Throughout the many centuries that Germany was little more than a geographical expression, a bundle of princedoms and duchies loosely held together by an archaic federal monarchy, each region of "the Germanies," or at least its upper classes, used to have close contact with the culture of neighboring countries. Artists, writers, and composers learned from each other across what are now presumed to be everlasting national boundaries, an international aristocracy used to intermarry, and wandering journeymen saw little difference between crossing the border from the Grand Duchy of Hesse into the German Palatinate and entering the Kingdom of France. To this day, Germans of all classes are avid travelers and more willing to learn and use a foreign tongue than, say, the French or the English. And for every noisily German tourist one may meet abroad, there are usually two whom one does not recognize as Germans because they are half acculturated to the country of their sojourn.

Even before nationalism belatedly arrived in Germany, there were successive waves of foreign fads or of acculturation that swept large regions or the whole geographical complex of Germany. It would be difficult to understand the peculiarities of what used to be Prussia and is largely now Communist Germany without some awareness of the Russian and Slavic influences, and perhaps also the proximity of Scandinavia. The Hanseatic harbor cities of Lübeck, Hamburg, and Bremen were fashioned by a maritime culture shared with English, Dutch, and Scandinavian traders, while traces of Italianate style, Austrian culture, and Swiss mores are common to the south and southwest of Germany. One of the longest and most thorough waves of acculturation was French. It began in the great age of French cultural hegemony in the seventeenth century and has never completely ended. Of profound influence also, at least for the educated classes of Germany, has been the influence of ancient Greece, or rather of the German interpretation of Greek antiquity, which is different from that of other Western countries. We shall return to these Platonic fixations of Germany's intellectual elite later.

These waves of acculturation and the seeming plasticity with which Germans have adapted themselves to other cultures reveal the agonizing search for a sense of identity that has characterized the evolution of modern Germany. "Who are we and what is our mission in the world?" the Germans have been asking themselves for at least three hundred years. The determined bid of the Germany of Kaiser Wilhelm's day for the status of a world power and the anti-Western stance of the years before 1945 were political manifestations of this search for identity. When the bid was defeated in World War I, moreover, the result was a decade and a half of a severe "identity crisis" during which the Germans of the Weimar Republic adopted in rapid succession a number of mutually exclusive regimes, such as Western democracy, right-wing liberalism, conservative reaction, and a kind of military collectivism, until Adolf Hitler succeeded in foisting his "national rebirth" as a new identity upon the disoriented German public. The dictatorial nature of the regime then stopped the search for about a decade, only to encourage its resumption in 1945 with redoubled effort.

When the Nazi empire collapsed in utter defeat and discredit and the emerging post-war leaders of Western Germany set their sights firmly on the democratization of Germany, they naturally looked around for suitable models to follow. Among the different Western democracies, France seemed a little too unruly, the small countries from Switzerland to Scandinavia too small for comparison, and the British mixture of tradition and democracy impossible to emulate, although there was no lack of South German admirers of Switzerland, Rhenish Francophiles, and North German Anglophiles. American democracy, somehow, seemed beyond flaw and criticism despite, or perhaps because of, its geographic distance from and previous relative non-involvement in German affairs. The American occupation authorities were probably the most popular and were least suspected of self-interested manipulations in the name of democratic re-education and reconstruction. The Americans had brought along as military advisers a number of American social science professors and historians with a life-long interest in and familiarity with German affairs; they were most effective in helping the German politicians to set their house in order. The American occupation also came closest by far to the realization — so difficult for a military mind to grasp — that only genuine persuasion stands any chance of surviving the few years of the military occupation of a vanquished country, and even that only if serious efforts are made to keep the inevitable resentment of foreign occupation to a minimum.

There is a danger here of overstating the influence of the foreign example, for there existed a definite German inclination in the same direction. Yet in those formative years of reconstruction, it can be said, the West German advocates of resurrecting the old German tradition of federalism received much moral and indirect support from the American example, even though the institutional arrangement of German federalism deviates very drastically from that of the United States. A strong basis was established by the reconstruction of viable state governments still under the tutelage of the occupation, and federalism finally became once more one of the leading principles of the 1949 Constitution hammered out for the new West German state. Another feature of that Constitution which may owe something to American inspiration is the strong position of the courts and in particular of the Federal Constitutional Court, although again we have to bear in mind that there were many other reasons that could suggest a strengthening of the judiciary. Finally, there is the conference committee, which has the function of settling legislative disagreements between the two houses of the federal Parliament, and which may have been inspired by the example of the conference committee of the American Congress.

The dangers of simple-minded generalization, which loom very large in attempts to trace the derivation of institutional design, are less present when it comes to policies and attitudes. In this connection, Adenauer's foreign and defense policy might be mentioned; for the first five years of the Federal Republic, i.e. before Western Germany received her sovereignty and was integrated into Western defense, he sought to gain West German freedom and equality of partnership by offering every co-operation with American foreign and defense policy interests in Europe. Against a vigorous chorus of criticism at home but with the assistance of close personal rapport at first with the American High Commissioner John McCloy and then with the Secretary of State of the Eisenhower administration, John Foster Dulles, Adenauer never flinched in his close adherence to the policies which he felt would give Washington a stake in the strength and security of Western Germany and Berlin. He finally succeeded both in winning the 1953 election on the strength of his foreign policies and in making West Germany a junior partner to the Western alliance, rather than the bargaining object of the East-West negotiations. Such a consistent course of orientation could hardly help leading to a far-reaching wave of pro-American and quasi-American attitudes both among the policymakers in government, legislature, and major parties and among a large part of the political commentators of press, radio, and television. Politically aware Germans simply learned to see world affairs with American eyes and took over the Dulles-Adenauer line, from the "roll-back" of Communist control to the policy of strength. This Americanization of their political outlook actually ignored some obvious differences of national interest, but it was of vital importance in overcoming the popular reluctance of West Germans to rearm and to take on a militantly anti-Communist stance. Since German rearma-

ment within the Western alliance was Western Germany's biggest bargaining point in return for American assurances and commitments,
the evolving defense administration of the Federal Republic tended
to be especially open to American influence and ways of organizing
and thinking. The strange career of Franz Josef Strauss from being
the champion of German demilitarization and neutrality to the position of Minister of Defense is a case in point. Once he was Defense
Minister, he took visible delight in his contacts with the Pentagon and
increasingly assumed the habits of thinking fitting for the military
super-power of our age. Finally, the sense of power emanating from
modern weapons seems to have led him along the path to demanding nuclear weapons for Germany, until his high-handed conduct toward the press fortunately brought about his downfall. The
militantly anti-Soviet and pro-American attitude fostered by continual crises and harassment in many West Berliners is another case in
point. Another avenue for the promotion of pro-American and quasi-
American thinking was the carefully promoted visits of leading German personnel to the United States, including the ambitious student
exchanges and the "foreign leaders" program, which by stays and
tours of from a few months to a year awakened appreciation for the
United States in tens of thousands of influential Germans.

Acculturation has been prominent and obvious in many areas of
German life, particularly in advertising, marketing, or social life
where a kind of learning process is taking place. A recent example
will illustrate the extension of these patterns even to matters of practical politics and campaign management. West Germany's major parties have long learned to make use of public opinion polls and surveys
for *das politische Marketing* of their candidates. The well-financed
Christian Democrats (CDU) have also employed professional advertising techniques for years, and more recently so have the Social
Democrats (SPD). Particularly in the 1961 election campaign for the
Bundestag — the Chancellor is not directly elected — Willy Brandt,
the leading SPD candidate, felt there would be so many parallels with
the American presidential election campaign of 1960 and the British
general elections of 1959 that he dispatched his campaign manager,
Klaus Schuetz, to these countries to observe what might help him in
1961. From a position of hindsight, it appears there were indeed numerous parallel aspects of the persons, issues, and situations between

Western Germany and these two Western democracies during their respective election years.

The similarities began with the fact that in each country relatively conservative administrations would be challenged after a long term in office by an opposition not too different in views and policies. In both the United States and Germany, the comparison went even farther: there was the venerable father-image of the incumbents, President Eisenhower and Adenauer, which the opposition was well-advised not to attack directly. There was also the issue of the contrast in age between the octogenarian Adenauer and the 47-year-old Willy Brandt. To be sure, Adenauer, unlike Eisenhower, was still in the running, but many voters expected him to retire soon in favor of a younger man, such as Economics Minister Erhard or *Bundestag* President Gerstenmaier. There was even an equivalent to the myth of the "old Nixon" who would throw off his mask once he was elected — Defense Minister Strauss (CSU), whom the SPD credited with eventually inheriting the reins of government from the aging Adenauer. Without much stretch of the imagination, Schuetz could see parallels and act accordingly.

There were also some parallels in the issues that moved the electorate in both countries. Not unlike Kennedy, Brandt accused the previous administration of having done nothing for many kinds of underdogs while a small segment of people profited disproportionately from the "economic miracle" of the Federal Republic. The SPD view was supported by public opinion polls which indicated that about three-fifths of the voting public felt that the benefits of the "economic miracle" were unjustly distributed. The optimism of the bread-and-butter elections of 1957, in which Adenauer had received a safe majority for his economic policy, had given way to widespread disillusionment. And so the SPD chose as one of its poster slogans, "Wealth Should Be Within the Reach of Everybody," and added numerous references to economic injustice throughout other advertising media.

Again like the Democratic platform of 1960, the SPD accused the previous administration of having neglected important public tasks such as school construction, higher education, hospitals, the alleviation of the housing shortage and of the chaotic traffic conditions in German cities, and the conservation of water, air, and other resources. The SPD claimed also that certain friends of the previous administration had derived great profits from this neglect, citing as instances the benefits to the real estate and construction interests of the continuing shortage of housing, and also Adenauer's costly and unconstitutional experiment with a federal television program.

Finally, and again not unlike the trend of sentiment in the 1960 American election, there had been growing dissatisfaction with the success of the foreign policy of the Adenauer administration. As in the United States, the man in the street found it difficult to put his finger on exactly what was wrong with the old policy. But he had become increasingly aware of the mounting difficulties abroad and vaguely felt that what was needed was perhaps "a fresh approach." The SPD was quick to seize upon this opportunity and to offer, in place of Adenauer's "sterile policy of strength, European commitments and pro-American sentiment," a new policy of strength together with a new commitment to European unity and to American support. The public image of Brandt made this new SPD policy plausible to the voters.

All of these similarities between the American electoral situation in 1960 and that anticipated the following year in Germany led Schuetz to suggest a number of significant innovations in the traditional manner of SPD campaigning to his party leadership. According to an article which appeared in *Der Spiegel* two weeks before the elections, many of his new measures were conscious adaptations of American practices which he had observed in 1960.

The Brandt campaign had to accomplish three goals in order to be successful: to break through the isolation which surrounds the German voter and to seek a more direct confrontation with him; to remain as aloof as possible from the SPD and its public image, at least at the outset; and to concentrate on the undecided few rather than on the many voters who are already committed to one of the major parties. The undecided voter was known to have made up his mind in the 1957 elections only during the last two weeks of the campaign. According to polls, moreover, there were about eight million undecided out of a total of 37.1 million eligible voters, a margin so large that it might well spell victory or defeat. In these three goals of the Brandt campaign, we again discover close parallels to the Kennedy campaign, where it was also considered important to remain somewhat aloof from the public image of the Democratic party and to concentrate on the undecided vote rather than on the bulk of steady Democratic voters. Kennedy needed a confrontation with the voters mainly because he was not as well known as his opponent. He achieved much of his national stature in the now famous television debates. Willy Brandt likewise proposed to debate Adenauer on television, expecting apparently to bring to bear on his opponent his easy charm and quick wit. The encounter would probably not only have pinned down Adenauer programmatically but also have brought out his increasing awkwardness and lack of preparation, which had become evident on other occasions. Such a debate in any case tends to create a semblance of equality between the contestants, and Adenauer was not prepared to forego the advantages of the long-time incumbent over the challenger. He turned down the proposal, probably aware of its significance in the Kennedy-Nixon campaign. He also turned down a suggestion by the German press to submit to an American-style press conference with the lame excuse that a man in his position could not just let himself be cross-examined.

To break through the traditional isolation of the German voter, campaign manager Schuetz also thought up a skillful adaptation of the American whistle-stop campaign to the German scene. Starting in May, Brandt and Schuetz undertook an ambitious automotive trip of some 20,000 miles through the towns and villages of Germany. For about three months they toured Germany in a cream-colored Mercedes convertible decked out with flowers. Several weeks ahead of them, an SPD functionary traveled along the same route to announce their arrival to the local government officials and the local party organs which would suggest the exact schedule that they were to follow. The mayor or city council, often CDU in partisanship, was told that the Lord Mayor of Berlin was coming in his official capacity to bring the greetings of his city. This was usually enough to gain an official reception and even where there was no official welcome, Brandt's visit stirred up enough publicity to keep the provincial newspapers busy for weeks. The campaign manager did his best not to leave out any local celebrations or festivities and to schedule visits to local sight-seeing attractions whenever possible.

A schedule was worked out which determined in great detail the length and number of speeches for each day, the exact route to be followed, where to stop and where to go slow. Schuetz had evidently been impressed by the flexibility of Kennedy's campaign schedule as compared to that of Nixon. He wanted to make it possible to improvise and to meet all opportunities of social contact with local friends and admirers. To compensate for the inevitable daily retardations in the schedule, a humorous variety program was provided to entertain the waiting crowds until Brandt could appear. His arrival in each town was heralded days before by posters, "Willy Brandt is coming," and by loudspeaker vans. An hour before his arrival, another loud speaker van would announce that Brandt was about to come down this particular street and would invite everyone to participate in his reception. Little flags with the coat of arms of Berlin and similar display objects were handed out to the children in the streets.

The crowds always responded very warmly to Brandt's appearance, charm, and personal magnetism. Appropriate little speeches were coined to flatter the audience and also to remind them of the meaning of Berlin as a symbol. Enthusiastic women and autograph-seekers were as common a sight as on the campaign trails of Nixon and Kennedy in 1960. This kind of a whistle-stop campaign was quite unprecedented in German politics and drew much comment in the press and among the politicians. The people in the small towns and in the country were flattered by this attention. Other politicians were impressed and awed by so much effort, since German candidates for public office rarely work this hard for their votes.

To achieve the second objective, namely to keep himself aloof from his party and its record, Brandt avoided the display of party labels during his entire whistle-stop tour. The posters and little flags never mentioned the SPD and he always spoke of himself as the Mayor of Berlin rather than as a candidate for Chancellor. Quite unlike the previous practices of SPD leaders during the campaign, he also refrained, with rare exceptions, from taking issue with the program and statements of his opponents while advocating points of the SPD program. He succeeded so well in separating his public image as a most attractive figure from that of his party that the CDU propaganda occasionally hinted that he was just a dummy that the SPD would discard as soon as the election was over.

To concentrate on the undecided few, finally, the party turned all of its appeals in such manner as to please voters who had never found the SPD or socialism particularly attractive. Election promises were expressed in the most concrete form possible and timed to correspond to what the average voter might be thinking about at a particular time. Since many of the undecided voters were young people and often new voters, the SPD also tried to appeal to their sense of modernity and marketed itself, like a popular soft-drink advertisement, as the thing for the people of today. The campaign management also planned Brandt's great tour through Western Germany to concentrate on those areas which in past elections had shown an increasing tendency to vote for the SPD. The campaign manager likened this decision to Kennedy's strategy of concentration on the big cities of the United States. The party felt justified in its emphasis on winning a large share of the pivotal group of undecided voters by public opinion data which disclosed that Adenauer had lost much of his earlier popularity with this group in 1957, whereas Brandt appeared to rate high.

Since proven ability to maintain good relations with the United States had emerged as an important virtue of Adenauer in the eyes of the voters, the managers of the Brandt campaign made a point of emphasizing the pro-American attitude of their party and candidate. Among the diverse and voluminous printed materials distributed, one illustrated election magazine showed no less than three pictures of Brandt together with President Kennedy. Manager Schuetz even proposed to put the two on an election poster. There was also about the Brandt campaign a deliberately fostered aura of fairness and appeals to decency which, instead of trying to outdo the dirty undercurrent of the CDU campaign,* made it backfire on its originators. It is not unlikely that this moral emphasis in campaigning, which helps to exalt democratic practices and flatters the voters, was also learned in England and the United States. Continental European election campaigns are rarely distinguished by moralism or great awareness of procedural niceties.

The touch of the professional advertisers and the sharpened sense of the party leaders for the desire of the "political consumer" were evident in many ways. One small leaflet showed how the high

---

* Among other attractions, the CDU campaign featured lurid campaign movies about the past score of the SPD and a book of fact and fiction about the love life of Willy Brandt. The circumstances of his illegitimate birth and his exile during the war, allegedly fighting the German army in Scandinavia, were favorite targets of personal attacks.

excise taxes on tea and coffee forced the average German to work many more minutes for a pound of coffee than the average Frenchman, Englishman, Scandinavian, or American. Large newspaper and magazine advertisements showed Brandt climbing into a tank of the new German army — in line with the changed attitude of the party toward German rearmament — or down a coal mine shaft. Election posters with the face of a pipe-smoking old man proclaimed that "old age pensions are no alms" and promised the old people free television sets, the foremost status symbol of the new society. Others announced the party's intention to increase the minimum paid vacation to four weeks; in fact one poster gave statistics about the six out of ten whose health and presumable lack of adequate vacations forces them to retire long before they reach the customary retirement age. Another vacation poster in gay colors appeared at the beginning of the summer and made its "four weeks' vacation" pitch under the message "happy holidays," adorned with a walking stick, a bunch of flowers, and a singing bird.

The professionals were also aware of the pitfalls of presenting their candidate too much in the role of the young hero in which his youth, vigor, and Berlin background had cast him. Adenauer's headstart in age and experience precluded any attempt at presenting Brandt as a father figure. Public opinion pollsters had also cautioned the SPD against overstressing Brandt's image as the "fighting mayor of West Berlin," lest the public perceive him as a "Crisis Willy," a harbinger of painful interruptions in their pursuit of happiness. Hence the party decided to soft-pedal Brandt's Berlin background until the building of the Berlin Wall five weeks before the elections forced their hand. To counteract the impression that their candidate was too youthful and inexperienced to inspire the confidence of the electorate, they had also prepared a set of campaign pictures of a statesmanlike "Serious Willy." By that time, the arduous campaign and the renewed Berlin crisis had also contributed to a change in his real appearance which matched the serious image. Only in the early stages of the campaign, when Mayor Brandt's efforts were devoted to a strategy of "embracing the public," did the SPD use the posters with the pictures of the youthful, friendly hero. This image of "Smiling Willy" also fitted the chief slogan of the SPD in 1961, *Voran* (Forward), which appeared on most posters along with the picture of Willy Brandt or the name of the party. *Voran* was a word of many meanings. First of all, it might remind old Social Democrats of the idea of progress which had once occupied such a central position in their creed and had lent itself also as the name of the party periodical *Vorwaerts,* later called *Neuer Vorwaerts.* At the same time, *Voran* was a subtle appeal to the economic ambitions of the West German voters among whom pessimism about the continuation of their economic boom is widespread. In this sense it was meant in particular for the individual who felt dissatisfied with his share in the "economic miracle" and was inclined to blame the old administration for the concentration of most new wealth in a few hands. For him, *Voran* signified a new deal in economic and social policy which would distribute the growing wealth with greater equity. To the millions suffering from inadequate provisions for traffic, hospitals, and schools, *Voran* was a promise of prompt action for these conditions. Finally, *Voran* also denoted a certain aggressiveness and timeliness, a new style in foreign and domestic policy, an updating of supposedly lagging conceptions, an appeal for confidence, and a faith in the future. It was the style of an ambitious new generation not unlike the slogan of the Kennedy campaign: Let's get this country moving again! As Brandt put it at Bonn: "The important thing for our people is that we must not stand still. It is because of the future, because of life, that our people must move on."

And what about the CDU campaign? While there may not have been such obvious parallels with the American scene in 1960 as the SPD had shown, their efforts likewise bore the hallmark of American-style professional advertising campaign management, as in previous elections. Where the SPD called for a change, the CDU understandably defended its record and admonished the voters to undertake "no experiments." The chief CDU slogans, which had been "unity, freedom, and peace" in 1957, were now "peace, freedom, and security," with a noticeable undertone of "let's not rock the boat." The public opinion pollsters had advised the party of the absorption of West Germans in their pursuit of happiness, and the CDU leadership had hopes of taking advantage of this, in their opinion, "unpolitical" attitude for its own continuation in office. The erection of the Berlin Wall rudely interrupted some of their campaign plans by awakening the electorate to the precariousness of their happy tranquility.

The CDU campaign also placed great emphases on its tried and true leadership figures headed by Adenauer, the "grandfather image," which had been so carefully cultivated by previous election campaigns. Since public opinion polls had indicated that two-thirds of the West German electorate considered the octogenarian ready for retirement from the office of Chancellor, however, the party made a point of playing up the presence of alternative CDU leaders, such as Erhard, *Bundestag* President Eugen Gerstenmaier, and the majority leader Heinrich Krone. These men were "the team," and their slogan, "success and experience," recurred throughout the campaign literature of the CDU. While *der Alte* himself was usually associated with the achievement of international status and the maintenance of West German freedom, Erhard figured prominently in all campaign material relating to prosperity, and also in pitches for the women's vote which made up a substantial majority of the electorate in 1961. Especially during the early stages of the campaign — the CDU had planned a "sympathy campaign" comparable to the SPD early campaign phase of "embracing the public" — a German housewife's job of balancing the family budget was often compared to the role of the Economics Minister. These "sympathy" advertisements in magazines were among the slickest Madison Avenue products used in the entire election campaign. Their purpose was generally to deliver a political message about the record of the Adenauer administration under the guise of an unusual picture, such as of a little boy on a chamber pot or a kissing bridal couple, with a teasing caption that would attract enough attention to get the readers to read the message as well.

There were also other touches of an expertise coming close to political motivation research. One advertisement of the "Experienced and successful leaders," for example, showed Erhard and two business executives striding imperiously across a factory yard amid seemingly awe-struck workers. Other recurring appeals aimed at the hidden streak of stubbornness in many Germans by linking the almost untranslatable formula *"jetzt erst recht"* (now more than ever) to a variety of last-minute appeals. Another pitch aimed at the peculiarly German pride of knowledge or expertise with various formulas all containing the words "you know," as in "now you know," "everybody must know," "what you ought to know," and so forth. Finally, there was the usual appeal to West German anti-Communism:

"Khrushchev commands that Adenauer be overthrown. Let us rally to our Chancellor *jetzt erst recht.*" This device had been used twice before, since the Soviet premier always obliged with threatening statements whenever there were *Bundestag* elections in the Federal Republic.

On balance, one feels tempted to say that *das politische Marketing,* the Madison Avenue approach to election campaigns, is actually more pronounced in Western Germany than in the United States, where such motivational research in politics is still left to the crafty politicians in their proverbial smoke-filled rooms. The reason for this seeming paradox appears to lie in the uneven development of politics and society in Western Germany, where economic advertisement and consumer mentality have evidently outpaced the development of practical politics and civic participation. Precisely because of this uneven development, the non-political areas of German life often show Americanization in even more apparent ways which the language faithfully reflects.

The German language has always mirrored the mixture of elements in an amorphous and, in some respects, still rather pre-modern culture. To begin with, there are the extraordinary differences in regional dialect, manner of speaking, names, customs, and even *cuisine.* Then there is the archaic complexity of the grammar which enabled, for instance, the early nineteenth-century poets Schlegel and Tieck to translate Shakespearean plays of the sixteenth century word for word into beautiful nineteenth-century German without missing an image or an inflection. It is also a medium of extraordinary plasticity and has none of the Latin strictures of syntax or of the English passion for plainness and simplicity, which has allowed it to appear with the abstruse pregnancy of Hegelian philosophy as well as with the Latin clarity of a Friedrich Nietzsche, who was one of the last writers to elicit real sparkle, elegance, and power from the reluctant medium.

There is also another aspect of the German language which has characterized, since the days of French acculturation, its receptiveness toward foreign words. Looking through contemporary West German newspapers and magazines one can surmise the extent of the newest wave of acculturation that has West Germany in its grip — Americanization. And by this word one should not imply the universal patterns of an advanced industrial society described in the preceding chapter, although the borderline may not always be easy to draw. There are plenty of other phenomena paying without any inner necessity the biggest compliment which one nation can give another, that of imitation. At the same time, however, a word of caution may be in order regarding some of the aspects of American culture which Germans have come to admire since the early days of the occupation: when nations like each other, no less than when they hate each other, their images of one another tend to be little more than a caricature of reality. Nazi war propaganda painted an extremely contemptible picture of Americans as a nation wallowing in debilitating vices, including (shudder) jazz, lipstick, and cigarettes. Some of these old hate images, indestructible as hate propaganda tends to be, are still around, but have strangely acquired likeable features. Besides, whether the attributes chosen for admiration are true or not, Americans are quite likely to find themselves admired for peculiarities of the American scene that they may consider neither typical nor praiseworthy, while their nobler traits may be ignored. Yet there is no mistaking the good will and the positive attitude behind these patterns of admiration and imitation amidst the prevailing misunderstandings. After all, friendship between nations is almost always based on mutual misunderstanding and, if misunderstand we must, it is undoubtedly better to love than to hate for the wrong reasons.

It will be remembered how West Germany's newly rich affect English names for such super-status symbols as their "swimming pool" or "living hall." The American fad is even stronger among the young and in such professions as advertising, certain branches of the armed forces, or in the social sciences, where American techniques play a great role in the training of personnel. In recent years, as we have seen, even the field of practical politics saw some attempts at imitation which were on balance, perhaps, more flattering to the United States than helpful to the politicians who used them.

The word "teenager" has long arrived in Western Germany, replacing older German words such as *Jugendliche* which used to refer to the same age group. With it have come blue jeans, also named *Nietenhosen,* and clothing such as sweatshirts and sneakers. West German teenagers also engage in activities their parents would never have dreamed of at the same age. They go *twisten* or *"zum* dancing"

or "bowling," words for which the German language has always had
satisfactory equivalents in *tanzen* and *kegeln*. The twist, in particular,
encouraged teenage fashions to emphasize bulky petticoats along with
the already unusually short skirts and peppermint stripes. West German teenagers have their own quickly changing fashions and produce,
from among their number, teenage bands and idolized singers. Most
of the songs and musical styles, however, are imported from the
United States or are at least under the pronounced influence of
American styles, such as rock-and-roll. The current hits are often
identical on both sides of the Atlantic and are bought on the familiar
45 RPM records.

For the twenty- to thirty-year-old group, West Germans have invented the name *Twens,* evidently derived from the English word
"twenty," but hardly known outside of Germany. Since 1959, West
Germany's *Twens* even have their own magazine, "twen," with a cir-
culation of over 100,000, whose style and content tell much about
the interests and the breathless pace of life of young men and women
in their twenties. To listen to its most scathing critics, the spokesmen
for the official youth co-ordinating agencies (*Jugendring*), it preaches
a super-individualism beyond the commitments and conventions of
society, with emphasis on sex, alcohol, cars, and a one-sided consumer mentality. There is indeed a world of difference between the
guitar-strumming hikers, the youth hostels, and the sexless blond
braids of German youth organizations from the turn of the century to
this day and the magazine "twen," whose romanticism has turned
from the fairy tales about castles on the Rhine to accounts of hot-rod
tests, cocktail recipes, reader surveys about pre-marital pregnancy,
and pictures of embracing couples in cars, on the beach, on park
benches, and in bed. And yet, "twen" is by no means lowbrow in its
literary offerings and occasional poetry. As notable as the content are
the aggressive style of writing and the deliberate absence of the cir-
cumlocutions about the facts of life that used to distinguish pre-war
German writing, for example, from that of France. West Germany's
young generation, if teenager or *twen,* evidently lives a rather different way of life compared to preceding generations. Even their collo-
quial language is so much unlike the language of their parents, both
in structure and in the number of slang expressions and words that no
dictionary can explain, that the usual difficulties of communication

between the generations are aggravated to the point of breakdown. Some of the change may be due to the rising individualism and consumer mentality which the young set experiences much more radically than their parents. But much of it hinges upon the flood of English words and American expressions which constitute such a large part of the youthful vocabulary, such as "last but not least," "take it easy," "first class," "fair play," "tops," "playboy," and "doll."

A large part of the Americanization of West Germany probably comes from American movies, the chief weapon of the American cultural offensive from which foreign nations derive their exaggerated notions about the cowboy and crime background of America and the glamor, hysteria, and bossiness of American women. West Germans are kept surprisingly well-informed about American movie stars, or at least about their publicity releases, by their numerous slick magazines which the average German receives in large quantities by subscription and reads far more avidly than the newspaper. Another part of the patterns of acculturation comes from personal contacts with American troops, tourists, and exchange students. American food and other products also occupy a great deal of space in advertisements and on the shelves of supermarkets. The markets themselves, along with trading stamps, antedate the wave of Americanization, but they have greatly increased their numbers in recent years and probably benefited from some of the merchandising practices observed in the United States. In 1963, two-thirds of the German housewives bought things in self-service stores. But there are many American products, such as Colgate, Scotch, or Kleenex, which have become household words. Other popular items are tomato catsup and instant or frozen foods, the use of which implies cooking and eating habits not previously associated with German homes. Then there are the English product names substituted for existing German words, as in "shaving soap," "after-shave lotion," or mixtures like *der Haarspray* (pronounced "spry") or Mercedes Sport ("shport") for a sportscar which, perhaps, betray the underlying acculturation in the clearest manner. For there is no functional reason discernible why Germans should now be eating "sandwiches," instead of *belegte Brötchen,* in a *Lunchstube,* instead of an *Imbissstube,* or why they should be spending "weekends" or buying "jumpers" or "slacks" in their favorite department store.

German business has known such Anglicisms as *der Manager, der Boss,* or *bluffen* at least since the 1920's. Now they have learned a great many new concepts and along with it the inevitable labels: *das Marketing, der Plan of Management,* and the quasi-military language of salesmanship courses which makes selling into a kind of lifemanship, the *Sich Verkaufen* (selling oneself). Especially in some accessory occupations to the business world, such as industrial psychology, the American influence is pervasive and has introduced numerous concepts simply by literal translation from the English which makes "human relations" into *menschliche* or *zwischenmenschliche Beziehungen.* Newspaper German has long popularized *Eierkopf* (egghead), *Beiprodukt* (by-product), *Herzattacke* (heart attack), *brandneu* (brand new), or *im gleichen Boot sitzen* (being in the same boat) in a similar manner. Unassimilable English words are simply adopted, as were "call-girl," "trend," "baby-sitter," "beatnik," or "stripper." Since the German language has long used many French words in Germanized form, there are also additional channels available for the assimilation of new words and meanings, such as those which are particularly popular with sociologists and psychologists, another important group whose training and professional pursuits are likely to include a good deal of exposure to American materials and methods. And the Germanized Latin formulas allow the formation of an -ism and -isation (*-ismus, -isierung*), a verb with *-ieren,* or an adjective of almost any foreign word. A related example is also the peculiar mixture of English and German used by the West German air force. Trained by Americans and on American planes, the German pilots simply tie together such English words and phrases as "parade formation," "landing gear," "airborne," and "down-wind" with German small talk and American expletives.

An unusual mixture of the ways of acculturation is presented by the advertising business, which occupies a key position both with regard to an economy oriented toward mass consumption and in relation to the status-seeking and social climbing instincts in people at large. Not only can the advertisers make attractive to the general public the things they have no need for, but they also train the public to respond to whatever cues of status and sophistication advertising can dream up. West German advertisers have long recognized the Americanization fad, as well as the snob appeal of things British, and they have probably contributed to their wide currency and influence. Especially with the ever-popular American cigarettes and Scotch whiskey, which have become status symbols throughout Continental Europe, Germans were long accustomed to find whole English phrases in the advertisements such as *"der* men of distinction Whisky" or encouraging customers to enjoy their beverage *"mit* Soda" or *"als* short drink on the rocks," or offering "king-size *Zigaretten mit* Filters." Clothing advertisements followed soon which praised *"den* good taste" or *"den* sincere look" of their men's suits or *"den* kitten finish" of their "self-conforming" hats or gloves. A person familiar with the German scene will also be amazed to find department stores advertising *"Rock 'n Bluse"* (skirt 'n blouse) or "twin sets."

Acculturation by advertising becomes even more of a complex process when one notes that no fewer than five subsidiaries of leading American agencies have established themselves in the land of the "economic miracle" and promptly proceeded to introduce the sophistication and drive of Madison Avenue into what used to be a rather stolid business. Their extraordinary success immediately aroused not only the resentful envy of their German colleagues but also a wave of imitation which went beyond the methods of presenting the advertisement message to include the entire organization and procedure of the agencies themselves. Now the West German agencies also have their task forces of specialists for each major account, including market research in depth. Among the specialists are *der Layouter, der Texter,* and *der Media-Mann* who work out *die Marketing Proposition.* After some *explorieren* and *vortesten* with the help of *ein Consumer Panel* have established the use of "glamour," "human interest," or *"ein guter* Slogan," they prepare either an advertisement for *die Massenmedien,* or for some "TV spots," or a "direct mail *Kampagne"* in the hope the client will be impressed by *"das* know-how" of his advertising agency.

Finally, acculturation sometimes assumes the appearance of shadow boxing, as when Germans voice their bewilderment at the "materialism" and individualism of an advanced industrial society by engaging in polemics against "Americanization," which is also blamed for the insolence of the young and even their delinquency. American political phenomena such as McCarthyism or crude anti-

Communism, and influential writings such as David Riesman's *Lonely Crowd* or the books by Vance Packard, are not only well-known but frequently discussed. Such discussions often involve a criticism of tendencies in German society by way of a critical echo of Riesman's or Packard's comments on American society, somewhat similar to the manner in which Khrushchev attacked the hard-liners in his own country and in Red China by way of an attack on Albania. In so doing, these German social critics are not at all discouraged by their obvious lack of insight into the nature of American society or even into the nature of Riesman's or Packard's comments on it.

Some readers may wonder what could be the point of considering at such length the patterns of acculturation, and especially of Americanization, in Germany. Does this not open a Pandora's box of likely misunderstandings by Americans and of German embarrassment and denials? It probably does. And yet there lies behind these seemingly random phenomena a deep significance. Unlike most modern nations, the Germans have faced enormous obstacles, geographic and otherwise, in developing a sense of national identity. There is a telling parallel between the "identity crisis" that can drive city youth to delinquency and the desperate quest for a "German race" of a Hitler and the uprooted German masses of the 1930's. For centuries, thoughtful Germans have immersed themselves in the study of Greek antiquity, of French culture, or of early Germanic history, searching for their own identity in the distinguishable features of others. If today masses of Germans think of themselves as "Europeans" or, with the help of shreds of American civilization, as quasi-Americans, it is a sign that the German search for identity is still going on. In contrast to what they have identified themselves with during the years from Bismarck to Hitler, moreover, their present understanding of themselves is distinctly Western and democratic.

About Dr. Globke, Adenauer's State Secretary until 1963:
"The political past of Dr. Globke has been examined in minutious detail by the Allies. No German agency needs to be any more minutious than the occupying powers."

Konrad Adenauer in 1950

"Globke once had the most idiotic hopes of helping somebody with some subordinate clause [Dr. Globke has also claimed to have brought about a delay of eighteen months in some of the Nuremberg legislation]. He was among our enormous number of simpletons in the civil service."

Prof. Franz Boehm, *Bundestag* deputy in 1961

"It is quite new to us that any legal commentaries to the Nuremberg Race Laws should ever have saved Jewish lives. What we do know is that these laws led to the criminal murder of six million men, women and children whose only crime in the eyes of the National Socialist regime was that they had been born as Jews."

Berliner Allgemeine, German Jewish newspaper, 1951

"In our opinion not a single affair of this kind could have happened [the Globke affair and that of ex-Nazi officials in the Foreign Office] if one had proceeded from the start according to a simple principle: to distinguish between person and function. A man might be beyond reproach or not, an accomplice or secret enemy of the Nazis; alone the fact that he had occupied a certain position or carried out a certain function under the Nazis should have precluded him from responsible positions in the higher administration."

Alfred Grosser, *La Démocratie de Bonn*, 1958

6

A MAN NAMED GRUBER

Joachim Kahler looked up from his Christian trade union journal, as Kurt, the Social Democrat, pulled up a chair to join him.

"You're early," said Kurt. "Did I tell you that Kenneth has already returned to England?" Before Jochen could answer, the door of the *Bierstube* opened wide and in limped Bernie on two crutches with his right leg in an enormous white cast extending from the toes to his knee. The two young men rose from their chairs and Jochen helped Bernie to sit down and lean his crutches against the nearest table. The *Bierstube* was almost empty.

"How did this happen?" asked Jochen.

"Automobile accident," growled Bernie. "Your countrymen are the worst drivers I ever encountered anywhere. There are just two kinds of German drivers, those who go too fast, too aggressive, and those who go too slow. And they constantly get in each other's way. The fellow who hit me, incidentally, was a Social Democratic city councilman, Kurt." Kurt's ears reddened and he looked as if he was personally responsible. Bernie went on. "I thought I could escape the

The Chancellor's right hand

law of averages, traveling around in your traffic jungle for a mere two months. One more week and I would have made it. My first thought on being rammed by that driver was that he must be one of the old Nazis and the crash a kind of poetic punishment for snooping around here. But he was very apologetic."

"Every time a foreign visitor gets a few favorable impressions here, the traffic rowdies spoil it all in a few minutes," Kurt said, still looking guilty.

"What makes you think you could recognize an old Nazi when you see one?" Jochen asked. "They look exactly like you and me and Kurt here. In fact, the better you get to know them, the more you recognize yourself with all your human frailties in them. Did you think they have horns and claws?"

"There but for the grace of God . . ." Bernie began, but Jochen pressed on: "I also don't like the phrase 'the old Nazis.' It's a propaganda phrase which deliberately glosses over the important distinction between an ex-Nazi who may have changed his mind completely and a neo-Nazi who holds Nazi views today. After all, it's been nearly twenty years since the end of the war and thirty years since the time when joining the Nazi party meant anything in the way of a commitment. Don't you think people have a right to change their minds in such a long period of time?"

Bernie looked a little flustered in reaction to this verbal *blitzkrieg*. Jochen added: "I bristle at the statement that 'once a Nazi, always a Nazi.' If you are going to adopt this point of view, it's no different from Senator Joseph McCarthy calling everybody an 'old Communist' for having attended a meeting back in the 1930's and at the age of fifteen."

"Look, Jochen," Bernie replied calmly, looking him straight in the eye, "this time you are not going to put any words in my mouth. This time you will wait until I have made some statements of my own choosing. Then you can launch your attack."

Kurt began to laugh: "Oh, don't mind him, Bernie. He has probably been rehearsing this little speech all night, getting hotter under the collar every time about what he thought you might say. But he is right about this 'old Nazi' phrase. Twenty, thirty years is a long time. In fact, most ex-Nazis who have not yet reached retirement age by today were in their twenties in 1935. If you take into account the peculiar character of devoted young Nazis, or for that matter of young Communists, you could say they got mixed up with it as a consequence of their youth and rebelliousness and may well have grown out of it by now."

"What do you mean by their character?" Bernie inquired.

"Well, you see, a very high percentage of the members of the Nazi and the Communist parties, and especially of their para-military organizations in the days of the Weimar Republic were in the age group

between 18 and 25," Kurt answered. "And so it seems likely that
their chief motivation was a matter of personality trouble, difficulties
of growing into adulthood, feelings of sexual inadequacy, rebellion
against parents and other legitimate authority, a desire to believe and
to belong. Some boys and girls react by becoming delinquents, joining
gangs, and committing crimes and anti-social acts. Others join the
storm-troopers and the Red Front. But some day, they may grow out
of this phase and become squares like the rest of us."

Bernie raised his bushy eyebrows: "You psychologists take all the
fun out of politics. Do you suppose the occupation authorities should
have set up psychiatric couches instead of denazification tribunals?"

Now it was Jochen's turn to grin while Kurt took Bernie's remark
good-naturedly. Jochen took up the cudgels and said:

"Far be it from me to defend the ex-Nazis as a group or any individual Nazi after all that has happened in our name. Although I was
too young at the time to have become involved in anything myself, I
feel as guilty and ashamed as any real Nazi criminal could feel." He
added as an afterthought: "Perhaps far more so, because I *know* how
utterly wrong their actions were, while many Nazi criminals may have
been deluded about the nature of their deeds."

"Amen," said Kurt.

"I understand," Bernie interjected. "The nice guys who would not
have committed the crime in the first place always blame themselves
far more than the nut who did it. I once heard a bank robber who had
shot and killed a teller and a guard in the bank during his hold-up
attempt tell the police: 'They asked for it. The teller would not give
me the money and the guard tried to stop me from getting away.' Or
the marriage swindler who cheated fifteen girls out of considerable
sums of money by promising to marry them. When the court asked
him, if he didn't think it wrong to propose marriage to fifteen different women, he replied: 'But they loved it.' "

"This is only half the story, Bernie," Kurt cautioned him. "I think
that most of the neo-Nazis and vocal anti-semites of today have enormous guilt feelings about the past. But they react to them not only by
persisting in their hate philosophy, but by defending the misdeeds of
the Nazis and publicly calling for more. Or take the juvenile delinquents who smeared swastikas on synagogue walls in the winter of
1959–60. I am convinced that many of them acted out of deep feel-

ings of unworthiness for which they wanted to settle accounts with society. You might say, they made themselves a perverse expression of the guilt feelings of us all."

"My God, this sounds sick, very sick," Bernie said with a sense of alarm.

"Of course, it is," Kurt nodded, "and we have to be positively aware of it because this tendency of some to want to be the delinquents of society corresponds to the tendency of society to make them so. It is so easy to beat one's breast and point to the criminals, or the juvenile delinquents, or to the Nazi leaders."

"Or to the Jews," Bernie interjected with furrowed brow. "What are you driving at?"

"I think I know what he means," Jochen opined. "I have been involved in many discussions, both with Germans and with members of various foreign nations, and it is always the same story. Nobody wants to bear even a part of the enormous mountain of guilt. The Germans want to blame it all on Hitler and a handful of Nazi henchmen, whom they call 'our misfortune' just as they used to call the Jews in Hitler's day. And our neighbor nations are anxious to unload it all on 'the Germans.' At the beginning of the controversy over the play *The Deputy* by Rolf Hochhuth I used to be naïve enough to try and answer the questions of foreigners about what I, as a German Catholic, thought of it. Then, inevitably, they'd say that I was just trying to pass on the German burden of guilt to someone else." And he added with a bitter smile: "As if there wasn't enough guilt to go around."

"But, look," said Bernie after pondering these thoughts for a while, "there must be some objective measure of guilt, independent of your subjective feelings of collective shame or co-responsibility, some way of determining in each individual case exactly how culpable a man is judging from the circumstances and from specific acts of commission or omission. After all, that's how law courts have run society from time immemorial."

"That is true," Kurt nodded gravely. "However, there are two major difficulties here which have never to my knowledge been satisfactorily overcome. One is the lack of adequate knowledge about what went on before and during the war. The Allied governments who possess the vast documentary materials about the Second World

War, including the documents captured in Germany, have by and large not made them available to researchers or even for prosecution purposes, with the exception of a few isolated war crimes trials, such as those of Nuremberg. The Israeli court which tried Adolf Eichmann, the shipping clerk of death, was content with a mere sketching of the 'final solution.' The concentration camp trials conducted by West German courts during the last ten years were largely dependent on surviving witnesses who accidentally met and identified their former tormentors. How many of those are likely to turn up?"

"What about the incriminating material that East Germany and some of the East European satellites have produced and offered?" Bernie inquired.

"That's mainly propaganda put out to defame the West German government," Jochen said with a derisive hand motion.

"Oh, now, I wouldn't be so sure of that," Kurt quickly intervened. "The material they had on people like Refugee Minister Oberlaender, or Adenauer's State Secretary Globke, or on Erhard's body-guard, the one who committed suicide, was certainly incriminating enough to dismiss them from office. If only Adenauer had not been so stubborn about considering that evidence . . ."

Jochen interrupted him: "Don't you think it strange that these Communist governments come up with this evidence only when it serves the purpose of defaming the Bonn government? If they were sincere about pointing out men with a record of Nazi crimes, they ought to do it for a street-cleaner just as much as for a Minister of Refugees. And did you know that the East German Communists approved no less than 42 former Nazis as candidates for their Parliament? Have you ever seen the Report of the Committee of Free Jurists in West Berlin with the names of hundreds of old Nazis who today are among the leading politicians, judges, army officers, and educators of the so-called German Democratic Republic?"

"Hold it, hold it there," cried Bernie laughing. "There are the 'old Nazis' again. You two are a living demonstration of what the principles of competition and free exchange of information can do for a country, whether it be between the government party, Jochen's Christian Democrats, and Kurt's Social Democratic opposition, or between Bonn and Pankow."

Jochen sputtered and Kurt mumbled something about unpacking

his information, when Bernie spoke again: "Kurt, you were about to name a second reason why it is so difficult to determine the objective measure of guilt in every case, when I interrupted you before."

"Oh yes," Kurt obliged. "My second reason is the dilemma of the shifting standards. I feel that from a psychological point of view any reasonable system of punishment must presume the existence of unchanging and generally known standards of conduct. I am not talking about legal criteria such as *ex post facto* legislation; I have learned to distrust all this formalistic legalism which has disguised political ineptitude, and worse, in Germany from the rotten judges of the Weimar Republic to some of our present laws. Neither am I denying the common sense justice of punishing the volunteer executioners and sadists of the Nazi death machine. The dilemma that troubles me is how to determine objectively the guilt of the hundreds of thousands of little wheels in the German administration and police, the millions of Nazi members, the Nazi voters of 1933, the conservative helpmates of Hitler, the enthusiastic crowds at his rallies."

"You can't punish people for political stupidity," Bernie said reluctantly, scratching the skin of his knee under the cast.

"But they all contributed to the end result," Kurt insisted. "Without the voters, the enthusiastic crowds, and the helpmates to power, there would not have been the legitimate authority to establish a police state and to pass the Nuremberg laws and other racist statutes. Once legitimate authority stood behind all kinds of small measures that added up to tyranny, how can you blame the little civil servant or soldier with a wife and four kids for carrying out his orders faithfully, or even for grasping for a promotion from this legitimate authority? And once all the little wheels of the powerful state machinery dutifully turned, the big bosses had the necessary precondition for using it for injustice, war, and genocide. There is a mountain of objective guilt here. But how are you going to determine it in each case, with standards changing from year to year, in a framework of moral ambiguity, and with few reasonable choices with regard to any particular act by any particular person?"

Jochen had followed this argument with increasing restlessness and looked ill at ease. Now he burst out: "This line of thought will get us nowhere. You have to draw a line somewhere under all that has come to pass in this merry-go-round where one thing led to another.

"When you started to talk about shifting standards I thought you were going to discuss the unequal standards of the justice meted out by the various tribunals of denazification."

"That just shows how you think," said Kurt acidly. "But history did not start in 1945. There are still some unpaid invoices from before that date."

"What about denazification?" Bernie asked in a tone of conciliation. "Don't you think it filled a necessary purpose? Or do you feel it was not administered right?"

"Badly administered," Jochen replied. "It was basically a good idea and served, among other things, to drive home the point that horrible things had been done for which many people would personally have to atone. But there were enormous obstacles to overcome in carrying it out, and this is where it was badly botched.

"To begin with, there was the problem of numbers. In the American zone, for example, occupation law demanded that all Germans over eighteen fill out a long denazification questionnaire, which resulted in a flood of over thirteen million questionnaires, including three and a half million from persons who had been members of a Nazi organization. I need not tell you that the checking of the truthfulness of the other ten million was done in the most perfunctory manner. The three and a half million members were then supposed to be classified by German denazification tribunals into five categories, namely," and he counted them off on the fingers of his left hand, "one, the major offenders and members of the key organizations; two, the activists, racists, and militarists; three, the profiteers and opportunists; four, the purely nominal members; and five, Nazis who had exonerated themselves by conduct hostile to the party.

"The enormous number of cases naturally tied up the tribunals for many years while the Cold War broke out, amnesties were passed, and the standards of punishment changed quite noticeably. The documentation of the tribunals was pitiful, and courts had to rely mainly on local witnesses and information volunteered by the accused. All a died-in-the-wool Nazi or even concentration camp mass murderer had to do was to go to another town where nobody knew him or to change his name and to claim he was a refugee from somewhere in the East. West Germany today is full of these fugitives from justice who are officially reported as dead or missing and are relatively safe as long as the devil within them does not give them away. And some of them have fled abroad, to Latin America or Egypt, where they sometimes work for the government."

"Some of them are in West German governmental posts, both large and small, or in lucrative positions in business," Kurt remarked bitterly.

"But, fortunately, this is often the point where pride or sheer nerve goeth before a fall, and they are recognized and exposed," Jochen nodded.

"Do you feel the same way about denazification, Kurt?" Bernie inquired.

"Yes and no," came the reply. "As I pointed out before, there is an enormous mountain of objective guilt that we should at least try to tackle. The Western occupation powers tried the maximal solution, a kind of dragnet approach with their questionnaires, though I admit that the numerical, administrative, and documentary problems made the success of such an all-encompassing approach doubtful. And I also have my doubts about the use of some of the presumably objective criteria, such as some of the categories used. Whenever I hear about the last category of 'exonerated Nazis,' I think of Hjalmar Schacht, who was classified that way. And I think of many a clever bloodhound of the innermost organization who, after contributing significantly to the mass murder of the Jews, decided to insure himself against a change of regime by helping one or two Jews to escape, on condition that they certify his good character. The escapees usually did so, of course, under an implied threat of death. On the other hand, people have been classified as major offenders by the mere fact of membership in certain organizations." He shook his head. "But then, some of these 'exonerated Nazis' may have been true converts, truly repentant, even before it began to be obvious that the war was lost. Who can really tell?" He mumbled something about never having been able to understand why a lifelong but repentant sinner should get a better break in heaven than a man who had always been good. Then he added aloud: "That's why I keep saying that a man's guilt or innocence is so extremely difficult to assess even under the most favorable circumstances of competent judges and a complete set of witnesses and documents, such as were rarely present in these cases."

"Anyway," Bernie interrupted his discursion, "the maximal approach toward denazification, as you call it, is not what the West Germans have been doing with their ex-Nazis since the establishment of the Bonn Republic, and it has not been used by the East German regime either."

"The Communists over there never carried out a real denazification at all," Jochen interjected, seemingly proud for a moment that there had been such a purge in the West. "They just equated Nazis and capitalists and invited many ex-Nazis to join their ranks as early as 1946."

"The West German courts," Kurt said without paying any attention to Jochen, "have been following a kind of minimal approach by trying Nazi criminals on the basis of violations of existing laws against murder, manslaughter, assault, and so forth. There have been tens of thousands of such cases which were either missed entirely by the Allied dragnet or got off too easily. These include some of the concentration camp cases about which you have been reading in the newspapers and also some of the last-minute executions of citizens, subordinates in the army, foreign workers, or prisoners by some officious person clothed in a little brief authority at the end of the war, as well as any other acts of unauthorized violence. I will admit that this approach has been surprisingly effective in flushing many of the big culprits out of hiding and showing to the general public what a monstrous collection of men it had tolerated. In fact, it is amazing how each of these cases seems to touch off a dozen new ones. Still, much as judges and the government have stated their moral disgust, this method fails to pillory the injustice of the regime itself and the horrors perpetrated with the backing of legitimate authority."

"Don't forget the political angle," Jochen implored him. "Crime and punishment can backfire if you don't make sure that no more than a small number of criminals are confronted with a vast majority of those who condemn their crimes. How could you get the vast majority of post-war Germans to condemn Nazism if you put all of them under suspicion and made them fill out questionnaires? Don't you run the danger of creating a feeling of solidarity among ex-Nazis, big and small, if you make all of them, more than one fourth of the adult population, go through court procedures in which they bear the burden of proof? Don't you run the risk of solidifying their Nazi views of

yesterday at a time when the legions of little ex-Nazis are all too willing to cast away their old delusions as criminal and mistaken?" He
turned to Kurt who was frowning deeply: "This was the upshot of
your maximal approach to denazification, Kurt. It led to a *renazifica-
tion* of vast numbers of people. And after the occupation had started
us on this dangerous course, then, of all things, they turned the reins
over from the authoritarian occupation regime to democratic elections by the people, a quarter of whom had just been renazified."

"You're exaggerating," Kurt interrupted him.

"Am I really?" Jochen said. "Can you deny that the problem of
how to tame the former Nazis and to commit them to the new Bonn
Republic was one of the biggest legacies of the occupation regime?"

"All right," Bernie intervened, "so there was a reaction among the
little Nazis against being held responsible, while some of the big fish
got away."

"I think Jochen has a point," Kurt conceded. "We have to be real-
istic about just how much of a change of mind could be expected of a
people vanquished from without. This is not just a question of right
or wrong, but also of the identification of a people through war and
defeat with their government and its deeds and misdeeds. It is hard
enough for an adult to admit he was wrong in small matters. What
can one expect of a whole people that is being forced to purge itself
by its former enemies? Can you think of a single nation in history
which was willing to take the word of its conquerors and occupiers
that it had been wrong? Or that it should put its own alleged wrong-
doers on trial?"

"Just think of the American South after the Civil War, Bernie,"
Jochen eagerly chimed in. "Suppose the victorious Northern forces
had expected Southerners to do penance for slavery and to put slave-
holders and other leaders of that evil cause on trial for their crimes
against humanity. How much co-operation, do you suppose, would
you have received from Southerners in general? Would they not have
shown more solidarity and been more defensive the more pressure
was applied to make them feel guilty? Well, you know what
happened."

Bernie had followed Kurt's and Jochen's argument with increasing
anger until he could contain himself no longer: "I'd like to know
what you are driving at."

"I don't know about Jochen," Kurt said in a conciliatory tone of voice, "but all I am trying to say is that most foreigners tend to look at West Germany's treatment of its ex-Nazis with wildly unrealistic expectations. They expect the West Germans to have acted as nobody else ever has. And by measuring their performance against this improbable yardstick, they fail to appreciate that there really has been a voluntary change of mind among the West Germans, a series of efforts rising against considerable resistance over a period of time.

"To be sure, it has been a story of fits and starts, of bureaucratic tangles and notable lapses, of unnecessary compromises, especially by the Adenauer administration," he threw a sidelong glance at Jochen and quickly went on, "but a story of dogged persistence in pursuing the goal. There were ups and downs, but there was also a continuing trend that in retrospect shows purpose in the hodgepodge of moves and countermoves."

Bernie lowered his skeptically raised eyebrows. He inquired: "Would you care to describe these ups and downs in more detail?"

"I can try," Kurt obliged. "At the very beginning, under the occupation regime, I believe, there was a real willingness among the West German officeholders, politicians, and the public opinion media to punish the guilty and to expose their crimes. It is true that these Germans had been screened under the licensing procedures of the occupation authorities, but they were largely the same groups and persons who are dominant in politics today. There was also mild criticism of some of the sweeping measures of dismissal, categorization, and imprisonment for years without a trial, but it usually came from such unimpeachable sources as the churches.

"Then, when the Federal Republic was established in 1949 and the new German government took over the basic policy toward the ex-Nazis, the situation changed substantially. I grant you, Jochen," he added with another glance at the protesting young Christian Democrat, "that it makes all the difference in the world when the power no longer comes from the anti-Nazi occupation but from the electorate of whom one fourth were ex-Nazis of various shades of contrition. I'll concede that it was wise of Adenauer to try to win over as many of them as he could so that they would not become a powerful bloc of opposition and obstruction when the Bonn government had plenty of other problems to deal with, such as economic crises, unemployment, and millions of restless refugees."

Jochen looked mollified and Kurt proceeded, after drawing a deep breath: "Still, this meant passing the 131 law * which reinstated most ex-Nazi public employees or granted them and their heirs whopping pensions, unless they had been classified as major offenders or activists by the denazification boards."

"That law, my dear Kurt," Jochen interrupted him, "was passed by the *Bundestag* against only two no-votes, in other words, with the heartfelt support of the SPD and even the dozen or so Communist deputies who were still there in 1951."

"Well, anyway, we know now that this law went too far," Kurt said. "As a consequence, we have now these embarrassing cases where some retired high officials of Nazi vintage, or their widows, receive huge back payments and monthly pensions that are two or three times the amount granted to German resistance fighters or survivors of concentration camps or their surviving families. And even worse, this is how many judges and civil servants both high and low who held office under the Nazis got back in."

"But you must not imagine that every reinstated ex-Nazi holds Nazi views today," Jochen said, "or that he would in any way be prepared to assist a reappearing Nazi-type revolt. There are a few exceptions, and every now and then a man like that is fired or tried for a violation of some of the anti-defamation laws we have.

"It is very difficult to make any modifications in the 131 law now for the simple reason that the public in general has accepted it, feeling that you have to give the little ex-Nazi another chance as long as you cannot prove him guilty of specific criminal acts. And since we accord these men all the freedoms of a democracy, they have votes, they can speak out, they form pressure groups, and they can go to court if they feel injured in their legal rights. The Nazis left out in the cold by the 131 law unsuccessfully sued before the Federal Constitutional Court. And the civil service lobby, which is one of the most powerful in this country, would rather tolerate a few scandalous cases than allow anyone to dilute their iron-clad tenure rights with what they consider 'political considerations.' Still, I would say with confidence that at least 90 per cent of these little ex-Nazis are today reliable, loyal servants of the new democratic regime. Don't you agree, Kurt?"

* Named after Art. 131 of the Bonn Constitution.

"I suppose you are right," came the reply after some hesitation, "I grant you that they are really not much different from the other typical little civil servants at the local level, narrow-minded, conformist, conservative, and pedantic, lacking in generosity and imagination. There have been complaints about the lack of zeal, if not silent resistance, of some police administrators and even local restitution offices regarding the ferreting out of Nazi criminals in hiding or action on claims for restitution by concentration camp victims or their families. I have always suspected, however, that this resistance comes equally from the little ex-Nazis and from narrow-minded officials with the same traits but no Nazi background. They are both defensive about these reminders of a past with which both cannot help identifying even though they may have no love today for a Hitler or for neo-Nazi groups. They are simply too petty to be able to forgive themselves or anybody else and thus become unwitting accessories to a kind of repetition of the crime they feel guilty about. I am afraid there is no way of making them grow up. Perhaps, their present place is still one where they can do the least wrong."

"But do you really need these people so badly that you have to reward them with the prestige and salary of a *Beamter,* a professional civil servant?" Bernie asked with a frown.

"Did you say reward?" Kurt turned to him. "If you compared the salary and pension of a small civil servant with the wages and old-age income of a skilled worker or a white-collar employee in private industry today, you would say that they are not very exciting. And public prestige? Pshaw! That time is past."

"I think you're exaggerating just because they won't join a labor union and refuse to vote SPD," Jochen interjected. "Let me tell you of a very typical example, Bernie, of an ex-Nazi of the more obdurate sort who works with my sister in a state police administration office. This is a real case and very typical and totally different from the stereotype of the 'old Nazi' which certain people in the United States and in Britain have invented to suit their own political purposes. Listen to his life story.

"This man — let's call him Johannes Gruber — was born and raised in the Bavarian Woods, a poor rural region of great beauty near the Czech and Austrian border which is today considered a chronically depressed area. As a young man in the late 1920's — he is in his mid-fifties today — he moved to the city of Regensburg, where he joined the police force. He still speaks in glowing terms of his days at Regensburg, his first urban home, although he won't tell you whether or how much he got involved with the Nazi movement, which had just come to power in Germany. He also won't tell you anything more than the fact that he transferred from the police to the Gestapo in the early years of World War II.

"The American occupation forces promptly put him into a labor camp for three years, although, as he claims today, 'he did not do anything.' He also complains that they 'slapped him around,' and he still feels intensely sorry for himself for those camp days. During his imprisonment also, his wife left him for another man, which confirmed his already rather negative opinion of the other sex. His denazification board must have been very gentle with him, for under the 131 law he qualified for reinstatement, from which former Gestapo members had been categorically barred. However, he was reinstated at a lower level and, as it turns out, his superiors will not promote him, either because of his background or because of his present obstreperousness. Johannes is very bitter about this. He looks with disapproval upon the increasing affluence of West German society and loses no opportunity to prophesy the end of the 'economic miracle.' Not to stand aside, however, he bought a taxi cab, which he drives in his free hours or allows another driver to use for a cut of the earnings. He has also married again, this time for money, or so he says, but seems to get along well with his wife and with his mother-in-law, with whom they live.

"What kind of man is this Gruber? He is a rather handsome, big fellow of well-groomed, if conservative appearance and ramrod-stiff bearing. He has very conventional views about women, what they should wear and how they should adorn themselves. His biggest chagrin is about his grown son, who has taken up with a young divorcee. He grew up a Catholic but no longer goes to church, because the Church 'betrayed' him when he was imprisoned and his wife left him.

"Johannes is a tightwad who would never dream of buying a female fellow-employee favors at office parties at the *Oktoberfest*, nor would he ever think of making a compliment or even talking pleasantly to the girls in his office. In spite of his lowly position, in fact, he is a holy terror to his fellow-employees. He has needled certain men or some older women so constantly and mercilessly about their real or alleged weaknesses that many have resigned or asked for a transfer. He is so compulsive about this that his needling often does not even imply a dislike for the victim. And he can be genuinely sorry when the victimized person is in tears or is ready to quit or transfer. I should mention that he does have his generous moments when he feels someone needs his helping hand, provided it doesn't cost any money.

"His relationship to his superiors is very poor, for he resents them and often gets into violent arguments with fellow employees which disrupt the activities of his office. His superiors dislike and dread Johannes Gruber and often punish him in small ways, to which he reacts with weeks of sulking. But they cannot get rid of him under the civil service regulations as long as he avoids open insubordination."

Bernie had followed this description with rapt attention: "And that is a typical ex-Nazi, you say? What about his political views? What are these loud arguments about?"

"Typical of unreconstructed ex-Nazis rather than of the little guy whose membership was merely nominal to begin with, I would say. The latter type is pretty much committed to parliamentary democracy today," Kurt interjected with an amused smile.

"Not as unreconstructed as you might think, though perhaps more obnoxious and belligerent than most of them," Jochen hastened to add. "I was going to talk about the subjects of his arguments in a minute. I hesitate to call them political, though, even if they often have political overtones. His politics seems to be little more than a reflection of his hostility toward everything and everybody. He is actually not at all well-informed and tends to think in clichés and along circular lines. Of course, the less he knows about something the louder he shouts. Let me try to give you a list of the groups of people that he hates and despises categorically and without leaving, as we say in German, 'a single good hair' on them.

"On the top of Johannes Gruber's hate list are Americans, the people who put him into the labor camp and 'slapped him around.' He never misses an opportunity to vent his vitriolic wrath on America and all it stands for. He will argue with you for hours, at the top of his voice, that there is no higher education, no art and culture, no refinement of any kind in the United States, where he, of course, has never set foot. West German juvenile delinquency and organized crime, in case you did not know it, Bernie, were also brought here by the Americans, who are corrupting the whole German way of life. Johannes gloats over America's failures with Castro's Cuba and over every fizzling rocket at Cape Kennedy. On the other hand, he makes no secret of his admiration for the monolithic power and ideological force of Communism and parades his contempt for Western material-ism and 'softness.' His instinctive admiration for Communism and the Soviet Union goes together in the typical pattern of the extreme right with a virulent anti-Communism and a strong dislike for labor unions and the Social Democrats.

"His second great hate is the people who used to be the chief de-votees of German *Kultur,* the educated and refined, along with former military officers, intellectual eggheads, and every species of social ex-cellence. He got to know their servility and treacherous character in the labor camp, he claims. Johannes has no taste for anything cul-tural, although he will unfailingly cite German *Kultur* in his diatribes against foreigners, learning foreign languages, using foreign words, and even against foreign travel. 'Why don't you go and see the Bavar-ian Woods first,' he scolds his colleagues when they tell of trips to Venice or Paris.

"One of his chief subjects of heated discussion, in fact, is the 'for-eigner' and the Second World War. The different kinds of foreigners, including former Nazi allies such as the Italians, but not the Japa-nese, are invariably cast in very unfavorable stereotypes, although he has never been abroad nor known any Frenchmen, Englishmen, or Poles personally. He has not seen active service either, the member-ship in the Gestapo being a convenient draft dodge. But he picks with considerable venom on war veterans in his office, belittling their war experiences and personal dangers. At the same time, he has some very definite and altogether favorable ideas of what 'the German sol-dier' would do and what he wouldn't do in occupied countries.

"I hope I am not boring you with this description. His next object of contempt is the 'city-slicker' who doesn't know how to distin-guish different kinds of grain or how to milk a cow. He hates big city life in Munich, comparing it to a cancerous growth. Raised as a farm boy, he apparently used up his ability to adapt himself in getting used to Regensburg, a city of less than 150,000, and he could not digest metropolitan Munich, which is not even very much like a big city. He is also a physical culturist who is very much preoccupied with his robust health and often assails young men as unathletic weaklings.

"I am probably forgetting some more objects of his hatred. But let me conclude with the group he calls 'old women.' They are one of his favorite targets. He actually tells some of the office girls who are about the same age as he that they are bound to get more untidy, unclean, and repulsive every day. Again he has very definite views about the inevitability of old age and about the proper clothes and conduct of that age group, at least for 'old women.' "

"What about his political activities today?" Bernie inquired. "Do you happen to know how he votes or if he works for any political party?"

"Well, that is the interesting part of it," Jochen replied. "In spite of what you might expect, Johannes Gruber has nothing but contempt now for the neo-Nazi lunatic fringe. He does not even recognize those points in their propaganda which are identical with some of his own rantings. For him, the Hitler regime is a bad memory, perhaps not so much because of its crimes — although the concentration camp trials bother him very much, and he wishes there would finally be an end to all the public waving of the bloody shirts of the Nazi era — but because it messed up his own petty life. Today Gruber hates Hitler.

"I cannot tell you how he voted at the first *Bundestag* elections in 1949, but in 1953 and 1957 he voted for Adenauer. He identifies vaguely with the CDU, partly because of his rural Catholic background, partly because of the new stature of the Federal Republic in international politics, and perhaps also out of dislike for the SPD. He used to eulogize Adenauer in extravagant language that sounded very strange coming from a former partisan of Hitler. But then in 1961, all of a sudden, he became a vitriolic critic of the Old Man, using language just as irrational to condemn him as he had used to praise him. In the elections of that year, he voted for the third party, the Free Democrats (FDP), who had made a big pitch for disaffected CDU voters. But, you see, he has as yet to vote for an extremist party, in spite of his views. Well, somehow, a glimmer of light penetrated even the thick skull of obnoxious, impossible Johannes Gruber and made him realize that you cannot solve political problems by voting for a Hitler, or his contemporary equivalent."

A silence settled upon the little group while each of the three pondered the difficult road to political maturity of the Grubers of this world.

Finally Kurt said: "One good thing about even the most incorrigible of the ex-Nazis is that they are getting older all the time. I would assume, for example, that anyone who by his state of mind contributed to the great fever of the 1930's and thereby brought the Nazis to power, must have been, say, eighteen years old in 1933. Well, those men and women would have been at least fifty in 1965. What is more, they only make up about one-fourth of the present West German population, one-third of them being persons past retirement age. Of course, most of the people of that generation neither voted for Hitler nor joined his bandwagon anyway. Still, you can see how some of this unstable element is slowly but surely disappearing as a function of the change of generations."

"This reminds me of one of our favorite political parlor games, Bernie," Jochen chuckled. "In its most popular form it goes like this: The generation that has run the West German economy and state so far was born about in the 1890's — except for Adenauer whose birthday goes back to 1876 — and has reached retirement age some time during the last ten years. The second generation, that of Johannes Gruber, was born between about 1910 and 1920, so its character was formed at least in part by the Weimar crisis years and the heyday of Nazi triumphs. And as the Cassandras of doom have it they are about to inherit all the leading positions. The formative period of the third generation was the years of defeat and painful reconstruction, and they are reliable pillars of the second German republic. But the rigid age stratification of German society will not admit them to the gates of power for at least another decade." He chortled and turned to Kurt. "After us come the babies who were born after 1940 and are pure products of the affluent society. Having had no bitter experiences, they did not learn anything very profound.

"Well, anyway, I am rather skeptical about this generational determinism. Surely, there must be innumerable exceptions to every category. And if age really has so much to do with who holds the power in this country, then let's change the rules. I for one suspect that the problem of fighting off Nazi tendencies and unreconstructed ex-Nazis is a continuing struggle which is going to have to be fought again and again, year after year. I place much more faith in some of the public opinion polls on what West Germans think about Hitler than in the change of generations. According to the polls of public opinion institutes, the percentage of West Germans in favor of Hitler or somebody like him has fallen from as high as 15 per cent in the early 'fifties to a mere 3 per cent in 1962, while the percentage against him has risen from 67 per cent of the population to over 80 per cent. At the same time, a breakdown by age groups shows this anti-Hitler sentiment to be rather uniform for all ages over 25. Under 25, strangely enough, the percentages for and against are not quite so favorable — with 5 per cent for and 78 per cent against. Evidently, we need to worry less about the older generation and more about the youngsters we are raising now, for whom the Nazi era is really a piece of distant history."

"I have seen those polls, too," Kurt said. "And I think that perhaps one should emphasize that percentages of 12 to 15 of definitely pro-Nazi sentiments were present pretty uniformly from the earliest polls conducted by the occupation until about 1957. From that year on they have dipped decisively. You might almost say that it took twelve years to live down the spell of the twelve years of the Hitler regime."

"It would make more sense," Jochen objected, "to link the change of mind to the economic recovery. By 1957, the West German public began to feel that they had succeeded in climbing out of the economic hole and saw themselves within reach of consumer goods on a mass basis. Contrary to the popular myths about the corrupting influence of affluence, I suspect that the feeling of having satisfied his basic economic needs gave the average West German his first chance to pause and reflect upon his state of mind and his conscience."

"Maybe so," Kurt conceded. "Of course, that was also the beginning of a barrage of soul-searching offerings throughout the public opinion media. The newspapers took a second look at some of the trials of Nazi criminals that had been going on all along. The East German Communists and other satellites began to publish specific incriminating information about particular officials in Bonn, which, of course, they should have done long before that time. Movie producers came out with documentary accounts of the Third Reich, there were showings of *The Diary of Anne Frank* and of other such plays on the stage, the new television program went to work enlightening its eager new viewers about their own past, and even the illustrated magazines, I thought, took a noticeable turn away from the peephole stories of the 'I was Hitler's valet' type and the romantic war experience tale to more serious and often accusing accounts. The bookstore windows seemed all of a sudden full of shelf after shelf of devastating and often scholarly accounts of Nazi crimes against the Jews and in occupied countries, including translations of Leon Poliakov's *Harvest of Hate* and other works, Shirer's *Rise and Fall of the Third Reich,* Hilberg's *Destruction of European Jews,* and innumerable German studies of particular aspects of the Nazi regime."

"I have noticed much of this literature," Bernie nodded; "and it seems to sell well. I was under the impression that it is downright fashionable among the affluent set to put these tomes on the coffee table in the living room or to display them prominently on book shelves." Noticing the frowns on Kurt's and Jochen's faces, Bernie added: "Oh, don't be dismayed. This is a good sign. If we must have fads, let's have sensible ones like this."

Jochen grinned and said: "You are right. These years since 1957 were also the time when the special prosecutors' office was established in Ludwigsburg near Stuttgart as a central co-ordinating center to prepare cases against the rest of the more noteworthy Nazi criminals before the statute of limitations on murder and manslaughter ran out. That was in 1958. Since that time, the skeletons have tumbled out of closets, sadistic criminals in hiding were exposed and brought to justice, and scores committed suicide or hightailed it to Nazi colonies abroad, only to be faced then by attempts of the West German government to get them extradited. They claim there were about one thousand specialists of mass murder and they have seized them all, at least those who are known to be still alive. The Ludwigsburg office has also raised the rafters on repeated occasions by accusing some state and local police administrations of being unco-operative and by digging up documents incriminating certain police adminstrators and judges who deceived the denazification tribunals about their past deeds."

Kurt nodded eagerly: "The disclosures in a case in 1959 even prompted the *Bundestag* to ask all judges who had any reason to fear new disclosures about their past to retire immediately. This is a real dilemma. On the one hand, you want to make sure there will be no

political influence on the judges. On the other hand, the denazification records were so incomplete and the 131 law so sweeping that
some of the blood judges and prosecutors of Hitler are back on the
bench and in office. And most of them are the kind that would never
admit they are guilty and won't resign even while a case is being prepared against them. They may also relish the thought that their case
with all its publicity will embarrass their own hostile government."

Bernie inquired: "What about the Eichmann trial? Didn't that also
help to trigger an honest reappraisal of the past?"

Jochen had to think for a while before answering: "Well, it did not
trigger so much as reinforce what was already getting to be a major
wave of anger and impatience directed at the remaining evil-doers in
our midst: anger at lenient judgments, impatience with some of the
more obvious excuses such as that there were considerable numbers
of Ukrainians, Hungarians, Austrians, and other non-Germans among
the killer units in Eastern Europe, or that Germans had suffered too.
Of course, the Eichmann trial was only in 1961, but it received ample
attention and coverage in the press, in editorials, and in the readers'
letters."

"This is largely a matter of how people look at the evidence and
whether they choose to face it or to play it down or ignore it," Kurt
interjected. "The individual guilt feelings or the collective shame is
not in the evidence so much as it is in the heart of the man or woman
who looks at it unflinchingly. I cannot even recall hearing the phrase
of the 'undigested past' before the period we have been talking about.

"Speaking of triggering the reappraisal, I think the rash of swastika incidents in the winter of 1959–60 did more than any other
single event. It may be true that anti-semitism is a phenomenon in
many countries and that there were such incidents elsewhere too. But
that they should happen here in Germany, at the scene of the most
senseless genocide of all times, raised the hair on the necks of all of
us. As you know, I am a psychologist and ought to know better than
to feel unreasoning hatred toward juvenile delinquents, for that is
what most of them were, even though they may have chosen Hitler
and his troopers as their heroes instead of some big gangster or a
neighborhood gang. But I have never felt such mortification and utter
despair about the abject depths of insanity in and around us everywhere, threatening to engulf us the moment our guard is down. Soci-

ety can still manage to cope with a handful of seriously disturbed people, but not if they become so numerous and well-organized that they take over politics."

Bernie looked at him with a thoughtful expression on his face, evidently pondering experiences he did not care to share. Finally Jochen broke the silence and asked him: "Aren't you going to ask us how much anti-semitism there still is in Germany?" Bernie made an encouraging gesture with his hand and Jochen began: "It has declined even more than pro-Nazi sentiment. Even Johannes Gruber, with all his prejudices and hatreds, never once mentions the Jews or attempts to defend the genocide of the Nazis. It is true that the restitution payments to Israel, the trials, and swastika incidents also produced some stridently anti-semitic voices. But these voices belong to a tiny minority among the neo-Nazis and outright psychopaths. A case in Landshut, Bavaria, found its way into the papers a few years ago. It was about a local butcher who kept urging several Jewish businessmen to do something about swastikas that appeared again and again on the doors of their stores. When the businessmen did nothing except tell the police, the butcher approached the Jewish community in Munich and finally wrote a long letter to the biggest Jewish newspaper in Western Germany. Meanwhile, the Landshut police succeeded in catching the culprit in the act. And guess who it was? The butcher himself, who had even claimed he was Jewish. As it developed he had a grudge against the city government and wanted to pillory the whole town. He also had a criminal record including theft, rape, slander, and several cases of fraud. Just think how much damage a single psychopath like that can do."

"What sentence did they give him?" Bernie wanted to know.

"Seven months," was the reply. "What can you do with a man like that?"

"I think you are much too optimistic about anti-semitism in Western Germany," Kurt spoke up. "I disagree with you and the official opinions of the West German government and other public agencies. You seem to think that all you have to worry about are overt attacks and incidents. And if you have done enough outlawing and jailing and recompensating you can rest on your laurels. The real problems go much farther. There are, first of all, the generations that were evidently anti-semitic enough to help Hitler to power."

"But you just told us how they are dying out," Jochen objected.

"Now, in retrospect, we can see that they were never much of a threat. But for a while there, people tended to overrate them and were particularly worried about the ten million refugees who looked to anyone familiar with European history like a dynamite keg of potential irredentism. Then there are various neo-Nazi youth organizations which are composed mostly of the children of the neo-Nazis. The only real menace among them, the National Student Association (NSB), which spread neo-Nazi propaganda among university students, was outlawed in 1960. Finally, there are the numerous veterans' organizations most of which are interested chiefly in bread-and-butter issues. As in the case of the refugees, this has greatly facilitated dealing with them. At one point, to be sure, the Association of German Soldiers, in which the different veterans' groups are represented, was beginning to steer too far to the right and had to be threatened by a united front of the three major parties in the *Bundestag.* Then there was the *Stahlhelm,* the old fighters of both world wars whose old-style militarism struck fear into many hearts and called out a trade-union demonstration of major proportions in 1955. By now, hardly anyone takes this little band of ancient diehards seriously. The last on this list of paper tigers is HIAG, an aggressive mutual aid society of former members of the *Waffen-SS* (SS army shock troops). After a decade of organized demands for pension rights under the 131 law they got them in 1961. Now, if they persist in their agitation, they will be outlawed, too."

"How much did these groups and former Nazi generals have to do with West German rearmament?" Bernie asked with the undertone of a cross-examining district attorney.

To his surprise, the two young men violently shook their heads and Kurt, the Social Democrat, spoke up: "Uh, uh. I am glad you asked. This sounds like a wild propaganda story, spread by the East. No, the neo-Nazi groups and the politically active former Nazi generals such as Guderian, Rudel, or Ramcke have fought West German rearmament tooth and nail from the beginning. Some HIAG leaders still consider it dishonorable for one of their boys to serve in the West German *Bundeswehr* (Federal Army).

"The backers of West German rearmament within the Federal Republic were from the start a widening segment of middle-of-the-roaders around Adenauer and his party, and later also the FDP and

SPD, but all reliable democrats, the pillars of the Second German Republic. Its opponents were initially from many quarters, including large sections of the SPD, some representatives of the churches, the youth organizations, the trade unions, and also both Communists and neo-Nazis. According to public opinion polls, the public also took a long time in coming around to supporting it. From less than 50 per cent in the early 'fifties, its support slowly rose to over 70 per cent by 1960, while its opponents dropped from about one-fourth of the population to 15 per cent. I guess the occupying powers 'demilitarized and reeducated' us very effectively."

"The lunatic fringe on the right is nationalistic in the sense of neutralism, Bernie," Jochen said. "While it may be hazardous to generalize among so many small groups from the monarchistic right to Otto Strasser's national bolshevism, they are all rather favorably inclined toward Communism and the Soviet Union and believe the Germans should make a deal with the East. Some of these organizations and a few periodicals are openly financed from East Germany. None of them likes the Western democracies, and they positively hate America and all the 'un-German' attitudes that they claim have been introduced from there."

"If this is so," Bernie continued to cross-examine, "then how come you have those two old Nazi generals, Speidel and Heusinger, again occupying prominent positions in your 'new army'?"

"Watch out, Jochen, there are those 'old Nazis' again," Kurt joked.

Jochen answered very seriously: "These two men played only a minor role in Hitler's army and were associated with the resistance to Hitler, though I won't assert that they played a major role there either. But this is not really the point. The objective of the Adenauer administration was to create a new, democratic army which would depart radically from the goose-step tradition that had been entrenched for centuries in Prussia. For such a task we needed specialists who could be trusted in every way to carry out this mandate. Speidel and Heusinger were associated with Adenauer's Defense Commissioner Theodor Blank for five years as civilians before they even got their commissions. These two generals, incidentally, have always enjoyed the confidence of the SPD as well as of the governing coalition.

"The government parties were fully aware of the necessity of handpicking the brass of the new army with extreme care. They set up a Personnel Advisory Board, made up of reliable persons of established democratic character and, in some cases, those with first-hand experience with the resistance movement and concentration camps, to screen the officer candidates from the rank of colonel on up according to their human and professional qualities. Care was also taken to insure civilian control over the military and to democratize the relations between superiors and subordinates."

"You forgot to mention the official efforts of the Adenauer regime and its grassroots organization," Kurt exclaimed with a mocking smile, "to spread a spirit of Cold War consciousness and anti-Communism among the people. Evidently the Old Man feared that all his draftees were going to be conscientious objectors."

"You know," Bernie said, "I had an opportunity to go to a big meeting of what they call the 'returnees,' prisoners of war whom the Russians kept for years after 1945. I rather expected a real earful of aggressive saber-rattling talk. To my surprise, the chairman announced that they had laid a memorial wreath at the site of Dachau concentration camp. There was a lot of talk about the 'irresponsibility of war' and 'never again.' The phrase that received the longest applause was something to the effect that 'the gratitude of the fatherland' was for the birds. They also introduced representatives of foreign veterans' organizations."

"Not all of these organizations sound quite that harmless," Kurt asserted. "But Jochen is right in saying that they either have proven to be paper tigers or backed down when threatened by a united front of the three major parties. In a sense, these new right-wing formations, as well as the ghosts of the German past, are a continual, healthy challenge to the political alertness and readiness of the democratic forces of the Federal Republic. In a free society, they are going to be around for a long time, a constant irritant, a reminder, and again and again a goad to democratic action. If all goes well, and our chances are promising, perhaps this will be the recurring challenge our society needs to develop a strong, liberal camp. The public opinion media and the three major parties have responded very well to the challenge. Now, if we could only get our university students out of their medieval fencing corporations and into the world of the political issues of today."

"You know, having been in World War II and having been very much aware of what Germany has meant to the Western democracies for as long as I can remember," Bernie said pensively, "it is so easy for me and many of my friends to see something threatening in much of what the Adenauer administration has done. German rearmament in itself raises so many bitter memories. Every time NATO quarters German army units somewhere in France or in England, I cannot help sympathizing with the uneasiness of some people there. Now they even have rockets and tactical nuclear weapons, though without nuclear warheads. I suppose it is not very likely that West Germany would ever use these forces to attack her Western neighbors again, after getting all tied up with the European Coal and Steel Community and the Common Market. Still, just the possibility that she might use all this rebuilt military power for a unilateral strike at the East, involving us and NATO in a third world war, is absolutely frightening. The relations between the West and the Soviet Union have already been strained to the breaking point for so many years, and now the thought . . ."

"But, Bernie," Jochen interrupted him, "these possibilities have all been carefully forestalled by contractual and institutional fetters, unlikely as they are in my opinion. Hostilities among the Western countries are unthinkable. That kind of anti-Western German nationalism is dead, buried, *fini*. The last hold-outs of anti-Westernism, the neo-Nazi fringe, has not polled more than 1 per cent of the national vote since 1953. West German youth has grown up in a world of youth exchange, intimate contact with the youth of other European countries, and in the great flush of excitement about building a united Europe.

"And regarding unilateral action against the East, I am sure you are aware of the repeated solemn pledge of the Adenauer government never to use force to achieve reunification or to regain any former German territories in the East. Surely you also know of the arms control provisions of Western European Union, the successor of the still-born European Defense Community. And you must be familiar with the organization of NATO, which has complete control over all units of the German *Bundeswehr*. We have no national army, nor did we withhold divisions as the French and British and, of course, you Americans have done. Before West Germany could undertake any

Nikita, the poacher, to JFK: "Say, your watchdog is poaching!"

such unilateral action, for which we have never, and I mean never, shown any inclination, we would have to withdraw our units from NATO, which is extremely complicated and would arouse a great deal of unfavorable attention. We would be immediately isolated and face hostility from all sides."

At this point Kurt could contain himself no longer and broke into the conversation: "Are you aware of the fact that Western Germany is one of the most pacifist nations today? That according to recent public opinion polls, 70 to 80 per cent of West Germans favor a nuclear test ban and are against atomic bombs ever being dropped on enemy cities, against nuclear armaments for the *Bundeswehr,* and against atomic bombs being stationed on German soil? Far more than among the British, Bernie. And as recently as 1961 a similar percentage of Germans was polled as favoring general and complete disarmament, while only 43 per cent of the British expressed this sentiment. Why pick on us?"

Bernie listened with evident surprise. But before he could reply, Jochen had resumed the center of the stage again: "Without the support of NATO, we are a small power and not at all militarily self-sufficient. Our geographic position lays us wide open to Communist pressure. A withdrawal from NATO would destroy our own security and the whole position that we have worked so hard to gain. It would also ruin our economy by destroying our links with the Common Market and other Western countries.

"Really, Bernie, unilateral action by Western Germany would be so mad and suicidal — even if you don't consider the nuclear might of the Soviet Union, which has threatened to turn us into a 'veritable cemetery' just for being in NATO — that it is completely out of the question. And, frankly, I cannot take seriously the expressions of fear of West German aggression by the Kremlin, which strikes me a little like Mussolini voicing fear of Abyssinia. How many Soviet megaton bombs does it take to wipe the densely settled areas of Western Germany off the face of the earth? Two or three? And the Communist leaders of the satellites also know that the Soviet Union would protect them against any German attack."

"Let me add my bit to this, Bernie," Kurt said with an undertone of bitterness. "I speak as a Social Democratic student who spent week after week demonstrating against German remilitarization in the 'fifties. I have made my peace with it since, but don't blame me for being cynical, because I feel I have seen it all. I saw the devastation and organized brutality of the war and experienced the demilitarization and re-education against militarism by the occupation. That was not the smallest reason that motivated me and the *Ohne mich* (count me out) generation to fight rearmament every step of the way from the battle over the European Defense Community Treaty until 1958.

"There is, to my mind, an ironical poignancy to your crying on our shoulders about West German rearmament. Anything the Adenauer government did to promote this course of policy was always to please Washington. There would be absolutely no West German army today if it were not for American approval, encouragement, and assistance. Rearmament is your creature. And if your generals should decide tomorrow to give nuclear warheads to the *Bundeswehr* and the new German Minister of Defense again catches a bad case of Pentagonitis, recognizable by delusions of military grandeur and a pyrotechnical glint in his eye, don't take your complaints to me. This is the wrong address."

Kurt looked pale and drawn, his pointed nose sticking out under his glasses. Bernie was at first offended by Kurt's tone of voice. Then a fleeting smile crossed his face and he asked: "May I ask what made you change your mind about German rearmament? How come the SPD is now supporting the new German army?"

Kurt hesitated a while, reluctant to abandon his erstwhile argument. Finally, he said: "Oh, well, we lost the fight. That is a good enough reason not to say no forever. Besides, the whole international situation had changed in the meantime. By 1958, it was becoming crystal clear that the American superiority over the Soviet Union had been lost and that there would never be a 'roll-back' of Communist control over the Eastern satellite countries, as Eisenhower and Dulles had said. In fact, the Americans were not even prepared to bail out Hungary in 1956, not to mention the Sputnik, the ominous symbol of Soviet advance in military technology. We began to realize that we really could not even be sure of holding West Berlin against the unrelenting pressure of the East. And Khrushchev became so menacing in his threats and his hate propaganda against the Federal Republic that we began to feel we had to dig in and consolidate our ties to NATO and the West.

"More recently, our earlier impressions were confirmed by the seeming readiness of the Kennedy Administration to make a deal with the Soviets at our expense. We had the distinct feeling that there was an enormous bill coming up for payment, one which we had avoided paying ten years earlier due to some lucky circumstances. So, naturally, we stiffened our backs and got ready to hold the line as best we could. And the more we got ourselves entangled in the Western alliance, the harder it would be for the West to throw us to the wolves."

"He is just about paraphrasing Adenauer, Bernie," Jochen chuckled. "And then the SPD claims it did not reject its erroneous notions of the past decade in exchange for those of the Adenauer government."

Bernie looked at his watch and said: "Just one more question, before I have to return to the hotel and pack. Tell me, both of you, why is the West German government so tough and unbending on such matters as the recognition of the East German government or of the Oder-Neisse line as the permanent German-Polish border? Until very recently, you even refused diplomatic relations with anyone who did recognize East Germany. You could so easily relax world tensions, if you gave in. Why are you so wary of negotiations between the United States and the Soviet Union? Your obstruction and objections are the biggest obstacles to world peace."

"Bernie!" Jochen and Kurt exclaimed simultaneously. Jochen went on: "We have no objections to your friendship for the Soviets. We ourselves used to get along well with the Russians for centuries, whenever our interests coincided. We don't hate them. We don't even hate Communism, although we know it too well from the Soviet Zone to want it established here. But you are asking us to be on the menu for your friendship banquet with the Soviet Union. How can you possibly expect us to co-operate with our own weakening and destruction?"

Kurt broke into the conversation to say: "What makes you think recognition of East Germany would relax world tensions? It would only contribute to making the reunification of West and East Germany even more unlikely."

"Reunification is unlikely anyway," Bernie continued to prod. "Why do you want it so stubbornly, if not to assemble enough strength to be once more a world power? No one else seems very anxious to see German reunification."

"Really, Bernie," protested Kurt, "what a thing to say! We want reunification, because these are our people over there. I have relatives in East Germany. And you don't need to be a rabid anti-Communist to abhor a foreign occupation that has oppressed the East German population now for twenty years with the help of its Stalinist puppets and Soviet tanks. We simply cannot sell them down the river, even if our government has been only lukewarm in its support of reunification.

"Besides, German reunification would solve the Berlin problem permanently, that monument which your military geniuses erected themselves at the end of World War II. No other solution would be both permanent and fair to the Berliners. But maybe you are one of those people who think the Berlin crises are caused by the West. Did you by any chance get to Berlin on your trip and see the Wall?

Magician Khrushchev: "German reunification is purely an internal affair of the Germans."

"Let me remind you also that the United States, Great Britain, and France are on record with pledges regarding peaceful German reunification as the basic goal of their German policy."

"What about the recognition of the Oder-Neisse line?" Bernie queried, looking once more at his watch and getting ready to pay for his glass of beer.

"The Oder-Neisse line is a historical question of enormous complexity," Jochen answered, "and it could only be settled in a peace conference considering all the frontiers of a reunified Germany. It is hardly a subject for unilateral action either by the Soviets or Poles, or by the Federal Republic, which does not even border on it. Here, too, the United States, Great Britain, and France have not accepted the present solution as final until such a conference. The immediate origin of the Oder-Neisse line, as I am sure you know, was the Soviet refusal to return that eastern half of Poland to the Poles, which the former had seized under the Nazi-Soviet Pact of 1939. So they simply reimbursed them with East German territory. But nationality problems in Eastern Europe being what they are, the question of just where to draw a national boundary has never been very clear. And the Poles moved all the remaining German population out of the area beyond the line. After proposing that the disputed area be administered jointly or put under international control, Adenauer was immediately under violent attack both from the Poles and from German refugees who came from there. You can't reason with these nationalistic hotheads. We young Christian Democrats feel so tired of these pointless border squabbles. As far as I am concerned, these areas would make a nice bargaining point at the final settlement, but of course not without a *quid pro quo.*"

Bernie had risen and was already saying goodbye as he limped to the door. Jochen offered to walk him to his hotel in order to tell him the rest of what was on his mind. As they walked, he had to raise his voice above the din of the traffic on the street and the bustle of pedestrians: "I suppose you must feel very tempted after all that has happened in the past to be impatient with us. And it's true that we are only one of the many political problems you have all around the world and that we keep getting in the way of a Cold War settlement between the United States and the Soviet Union. But put yourself into our shoes. Look at our exposed geographical position, divided and right at the edge of the huge Eurasian Communist bloc. We cannot stand by ourselves."

He startled a well-dressed young lady coming toward them with a sweeping gesture of his hand and barely missed colliding with her.

"We were half-dead back in the late 'forties when you helped us raise ourselves from the rubble. Today, we are back on our feet and dearly love our new life and growth and health." They were passing a row of food stores and a bakery. "That is no aggression, no menace to anyone. Naturally, we hang on to our security, our acquired positions on the edge of the Iron Curtain, because they guarantee our life. We tremble that the *status quo* might be upset in our disfavor; that the rug might be pulled from under all we have rebuilt since the war. We want to hang on to the West, for that is where life is."

How he pleads with me, thought Bernie, as if I was about to become President of the United States and he had to save Germany all over again by convincing me that it was worth it. They had arrived at the hotel lobby and Bernie entered the elevator, with Jochen still pumping his right hand: *"Auf Wiedersehen."*

"From the chaos of guilt and shame, into which the idolization of a criminal adventurer threw us, an order of democratic freedom can grow only if we return to the cultural, moral and intellectual forces of Christianity and open up this source of strength more and more for our people . . .

Great is the guilt of wide circles of our people who lowered themselves all too willingly to being the tools and help-mates of Hitler. All guilt calls for atonement . . . Fighters of truly democratic faith, Protestant and Catholic Christians, countless Jewish fellow-citizens, men and women from all classes of the people suffered and died. In the spirit of their legacy, united by the same love of our people, we recognize our duty of going with this people the way of atonement, the way of re-birth . . ."

From the *Appeal of the Christian Democratic Union*, Berlin, June 1945

"As the most immediate goals of our difficult and long task we recognize: External and inner liberation of the German people from the shame and scandal of National Socialism. Punishment of all those who during the war and before committed crimes against the law and against humanity, as well as against those who bore the political responsibility for the tyranny of National Socialism since 1933. Respect for human dignity without regard to race, class, age and sex . . . Reconstruction of German community life on a truly democratic basis with the aim of political, economic, social and cultural justice . . ."

From the *Appeal of the Liberal Democratic Party*, Berlin, July 1945

"The German Social Democratic Party rejects with determination any relapse into totalitarian thinking and action. In this spirit it will carry on a policy of independence and autonomy toward all forces of domestic politics and foreign powers and also toward other parties . . ."

From the *Political Principles of the SPD*, Hannover, May 1946

7

THE POST-WAR METAMORPHOSIS
OF GERMAN POLITICS

From all that has been said about the undigested past, the erroneous impression might arise that moral indigestion is a condition characteristic of all post-war Germans. Such an impression would hardly do justice to the significant numbers of men and women who participated actively in the resistance against Hitler, those who suffered persecution ranging from dismissal from office to years in the jails and concentration camps of the Third Reich, or those who sat out the years in bitter exile, in hiding, or in voluntary retirement. These anti-

Nazi elements spent their time largely in thinking and rethinking the fateful course of the German past and evolved several distinctive theories of what went wrong and how their country might attain to the right path in the future. Many sought refuge in one of the oldest solvents of guilt and error in Western civilization — their religion.

The victors and occupying powers gave these oppositional elements the chance to solicit political support from the electorate and, when elected, to take over the reins of government. From this background emerged the political leadership which has conducted the affairs of the Bonn Republic during the first decade and a half of its existence. The leadership is still substantially the same today as in the occupation years except for a limited number of newcomers and those who have been in the "loyal opposition." And if some of its original thinking is no longer as prominent today as it was in 1945 or 1946, the reason lies as much in the fulfillment of some of its primary goals as in the appearance of new problems.

The Post-war Setting

The initial setting for the rise of the new Germany was the utter prostration of catastrophic defeat, a defeat all the more catastrophic because German power fell within less than one year and a half from the highest point of its military expansion. Now the country was conquered from without, its armed forces decimated and in captivity, and its civilian population under foreign military occupation. The victorious powers immediately proceeded to round up and intern thousands of Nazis and to extract reparations in kind. In the East, moreover, vast areas of what used to be German territory under the Treaty of Versailles were turned over to the Soviet Union and Poland. The expulsion of their population further contributed to the stream of millions of refugees and expellees who trekked into Western Germany.

The occupying powers divided the country into four occupation zones, intending at first to administer it jointly. French and Russian obstruction and the force of circumstances, however, frustrated these plans at an early stage. Hence the four occupation zones for several years were each administered as if they were separate countries.

The devastated and desolate state of Germany in 1945–46 has

been hinted at in a previous chapter. Victor Gollancz in his book, *In Darkest Germany,* and the official reports of the American, British, and French military administrations paint a grim picture of hunger, misery, and despair, far worse than the conditions of 1918–19 or 1932. Under these conditions, the masses of Germans were so intensely preoccupied with the daily necessity of staying alive that they had no thought for politics. When people are reduced to subsistence level, they seem to lack the strength to rebel, to be obstinate, or to be ambitious. The millions of refugees and expellees, who had ended up in the Western zones in a state of utter exhaustion and destitution, showed little inclination toward nationalistic irredentism and acquiesced in the occupation measure forbidding them to organize for political purposes. The millions of little ex-Nazis who found themselves caught in the dragnet of denazification were content with a little grumbling. The millions of war veterans returning from prisoner-of-war camps, sometimes many years after the armistice, quietly joined the rest of the population, although the situation in which they found themselves was surely worse than the one which had driven the veterans of World War I to form and join para-military organizations of all kinds, from the *Stahlhelm* and Hitler's storm-troopers to the Communist Red Front. The population at large, finally, showed little nationalistic resentment toward the occupation by foreign troops. The relationship between the occupiers and the occupied, in fact, was often cordial, and there was little animosity among Germans toward the "collaborators" — including what the French during their occupation by Nazi troops used to call the "horizontal collaborators" — in their midst.

The absolute collapse of the country after total war led many a German observer to speak of it as "point zero" in the historical continuity of German affairs, a break so complete that they compared it to the ravages of the Thirty Years War of 1618–48. The implication was that 1945 might constitute a decisive turning-point, a breaking of the disastrous spell on the development of seventy-five years of German history, and an opportunity for a new beginning. This attitude was prevalent among the small minority of anti-Nazi leaders into whose hands the direction of German affairs gravitated naturally, as the masses of Germans reacted to the catastrophic defeat with stunned silence and by turning from politics to the daily struggle for food and shelter. The desire to liquidate the German past and to lay the foundation for a new beginning was at least as great among Allied occupation forces as among the new German leadership, although there were differing opinions among the occupying powers regarding the direction the future Germany ought to take.

In the Western zones, the reckoning with the past took the form of denazification, demilitarization, and decartelization. The reconstruction began with a carefully considered system of licensing newspapers and political parties, which automatically served to give a political and press monopoly to the minority of new democratic leaders we referred to above. Since democratic reconstruction in the Western zones began at the grass roots and, due to zonal boundaries, with the re-establishment of state governments and constitutions long before a national government, the rebuilding of German democracy received a healthy regional foundation under Allied tutelage before a more encompassing level of government was made responsible for Germany's democratic future. Thus the new German democracy was based from the start upon a federal system whose *Laender* (states) politics was as democratically sound and about as stable as the Bonn government has turned out to be. In fact, looking back upon the good political record of each of the West German *Laender* today, one cannot help noting the number of *Land* Minister Presidents, other important ministers, and legislative and party leaders who have held office there almost continuously since the early days of the occupation. The democratic *Laender,* of course, also constitute a training ground and reservoir of new democratic leadership for the national government.

In the Russian zone of occupation, the political development followed somewhat different lines. The Soviets were not particularly interested in the persecution of Nazis, except for war criminals who had been guilty of atrocities in the East. They placed great emphasis on reparations and on the revival of political life, which led to the readmission of various political parties earlier than anywhere else in occupied Germany. After one year, however, the Soviet military administration carried out a cold seizure of power by the Communist Party (KPD) by such means as forcing the East German SPD to merge with the Communists and transforming the other political parties into willing tools of Communist manipulation. The new puppet government of East Germany then carried out all the economic and agricultural reforms that seemed necessary in order to transform the Russian zone into a Communist state. While the Western zones subsequently advanced, step by step, toward self-determination via the formation of a West German State, the Federal Republic, the Russian zone of occupation remained completely under the control of the Soviet Union. To be sure, the Communist government of Wilhelm Pieck, Otto Grotewohl, and Walter Ulbricht went through all the motions of drawing up a constitution, establishing the German Democratic Republic, and being formally granted full sovereignty by the countries of the Soviet orbit. But there has never been a free election since the KPD-SPD merger party, the Socialist Unity Party (SED), failed to receive a majority from the East German electorate. The puppet regime faithfully follows the line laid down by its superiors in Moscow. Only once, except for the stream of refugees that has come to West Berlin over the years, have the East Germans managed to express themselves freely: in the uprising of June 17, 1953, where the rebellious workers were joined by the defecting "people's police." But Russian tanks appeared shortly and suppressed the uprising, demonstrating clearly in whose hands the power of Eastern Germany lies.

The New Political Leadership

Since the occupation in the Western zones could not and did not last for more than a few years, the most revealing questions about the starting point of Adenauer's Germany concern the nature and the views of the new democratic leadership of Western Germany. Who were the men and women who founded new parties and revived old ones during 1945 and 1946; who were licensed to publish newspapers and run radio stations; and who were entrusted with governmental authority by the Allied occupation? Where had they been during the Nazi years? What were their views regarding the German past? And how did they envisage the German future?

The men and women who took to political action and monopolized the mass media when everybody else was apolitical were an extraordinary assortment of old and new political elites. There were, for example, the members of an older generation, now in their fifties and sixties, who had played an important role in the democratic parties of the Weimar Republic. Many of them had belonged to the Catholic

Center Party or its Bavarian offshoot, the Bavarian People's Party (BVP). Others had been with left-wing Liberals (DDP) or right-wing Liberals (DVP), or even conservative German Nationalists (DNVP), whose chief geographic base was now behind the Iron Curtain. The occupation authorities made sure that no persons with Nazi backgrounds could become leaders of the new parties, which began to form spontaneously in many places just as soon as the SPD and the KPD had risen again in all their Weimar splendor. The groups to the right of the SPD attempted to rally together under the new banner of the Christian Democratic Union, a mass party composed of old members of the old Catholic parties, of Protestant Conservatives in the north and political Protestantism (CSVD) in the southwest, and of former liberals of various descriptions. Other liberals insisted on forming their own party, the FDP, DVP, or LDP. The founders and leaders of these new or revived parties had with rare exceptions not occupied key positions in their parties under the Weimar Republic for the simple reason that they had been too young in a country that emphasizes seniority. They had belonged to the second string in the Weimar gerontocracy. During the twelve Nazi years, many of them had been in concentration camps, in hiding, or in exile from which they now returned, eager to serve the democratic reconstruction. Yet others, though not too many, had been active in the resistance movement against Hitler. There might have been many more, had not the Nazi purge after the attempt on Hitler's life of July 20, 1944, made such a clean sweep of real and suspected enemies of the regime. A large number of post-war leaders had been active democratic politicians or journalists in the Weimar years and had weathered the storm in retirement or "inner emigration," which meant a withdrawal from political involvement behind the guise of social welfare work for the churches, a law practice, or purely commercial activities.

In addition to the democratic continuity represented by Weimar leaders there were also hundreds of men and women who had discovered the need for political participation and democratic reconstruction in personal encounters with Nazi tyranny. Among them were intellectuals, university professors, scientists, artists, clergymen, professional military men, civil servants, and many others who in the traditional German scheme had never before thought of their role in society as having anything to do with politics. There are many personal testi-

monies to the sudden awakening of a feeling of political responsibility
in academic ivory towers, monastic cloisters, or in the amoral havens
of expertise which Germans have always known how to create. One
of the most moving accounts comes from Professor Carlo Schmid,
who emerged as one of the new SPD leaders after the war:

> Until the end of the Second World War, I myself failed to act.
> I also thought: "My God, political life is horrible and parties
> are really dirty. What business of yours is it? Read good
> books, write a few books yourself, and cultivate your friend-
> ships. That is much more beautiful and dignified." But during
> the time of the Third Reich I asked myself, "Is it not your
> fault, as well, that this beast has come to govern Germany? If
> you had not felt so comfortable in your beautiful garden in
> Tuebingen, if you had entered the market square and others
> with you, then perhaps he would not have succeeded. And be-
> cause you did not do it, you, too, are guilty, perhaps more so
> than some stupid Stormtrooper, who did not know any better."

The Religious Revival

What were the political views of the new political leadership who
took on the difficult task of rebuilding a society ravaged by totalitarianism? What were their attitudes toward the fateful developments of
the German past, which appeared to have led in an unbroken line
from Bismarck to Hitler? What popular currents of opinion colored
their vision? How did they envisage the reconstruction of their society
and state which would be necessary for a brighter future?

With the spectacular collapse of the enormous Nazi empire and the
nationalistic ideology and vision it had engendered, there was an
enormous vacuum of moral values and political ideas. While the
masses of West Germans fell silent, preoccupied with the daily struggle for food, fuel, and shelter, the minority we have described as the
new anti-Nazi leadership was almost infinitely receptive to the various
political and religious ideas which began to flow into the vacuum left
by totalitarianism. The spirit of founding a new society upon ideals of
justice, brotherhood, and democracy pervaded everything written during the first two years after the war. Ideas like the sanctity of human
dignity, Christian charity, and the natural rights of man were experi-

enced afresh as perhaps never before and again. A naïve, democratic fundamentalism and the reintroduction of religion into politics were propounded with a spiritual fervor that seemed to thrive on the same economic misery which turned other people away from politics. Since totalitarian ideologies have a narcotic effect on the human mind, followed by mental agonies upon their withdrawal, nothing seemed more natural than to seek comfort with religion. The religious revival in post-war Germany runs like a scarlet thread through most of the distinctive phenomena of the intellectual and political scene: the spontaneous foundation, in many places at once, of a great "Christian" party encompassing both major faiths, the new appreciation for democracy and the dignity of the individual, the anti-Bismarckian reappraisal of German history, the return to federalism within and hope for federal union with other European countries, and the high prestige of the churches which more than any other German institution had emerged relatively untarnished from the Nazi era.

The word "Christian" in Christian Democratic Union, or Christian Social Union (CSU), as the new party was called in Bavaria, has none of the right-wing overtones in Germany or in the many other European countries with a corresponding movement that it would have if applied to an American political party. In the post-war context, the emphasis was not even so much on its anti-Communist connotations as on the positive message of Christian Socialism, the gospel of practical Christianity, brotherhood among all groups, and altruistic works for the building of a good society. The fervor of the religious revival was mirrored in the rallies of CDU and CSU at which speakers would address the crowds on such topics as "the duty of a Christian in politics," "politics conducted from faith," "Germany's longing for eternal peace," or "the obligations of Christian moral law." Some prominent politicians would carry the word from rally to rally like roving evangelists. Christian brotherhood was to heal the wounds of society, reconcile the classes and antagonistic groups and nations, and blaze a trail into a future of reason and cooperation under God. The waves of religious inspiration went far beyond the CDU/CSU into the Liberal camp and into the SPD, where active religious circles were founded. As rumor had it, the SPD leader, Kurt Schumacher, was even contemplating a splitting of his own party which would have shaken off its anti-clerical extreme left wing so that the bulk of the party could form a kind of British-style Labour Party with the support of the Christian Socialists.

Democracy and Social Reconstruction

At the same time, the concept of democracy held by many of the influential post-war leaders and publicists differed somewhat from that commonly held in the Western democracies. Rather than sharing the radical individualism of Hobbes and Locke or of the French Revolution, post-war sentiment tended to take what they considered a Christian view of democracy. The deep inhumanity of the Nazi period, especially of its propaganda and concentration camps, for instance, led now to a particular emphasis on human dignity. It was generally recognized that the totalitarian regime had corroded the substance of human integrity itself and that a new body politic could not be founded upon a society of cheap opportunists, informers, sadistic degenerates, and petty tyrants. The spokesmen of a better future were gripped by the same excitement and holy fervor of founding a new and more just political community that had distinguished the democratic revolutions of the late eighteenth and early nineteenth centuries. Instead of the anti-religious attitudes of the French Revolution, however, many of the opinion leaders of the day equated the totalitarian aberration with what they called the "great defection" from European universality, Christian faith, and charity. The rise of the Age of Enlightenment or, if you will, the victory of nominalism over realism in the Middle Ages was regarded as the beginning of the inexorable decline of modern man, who became less free the more he broke the bonds of spiritual and secular authority. This was the same argument as that of the Austrian poet Franz Grillparzer, who had warned his contemporaries in the nineteenth century that their worship of "humanity" might lead them to the worship of "nationality" and, finally, of "bestiality."

This Christian conservative turn of opinion had been long in coming. It was not incompatible with democratic theory and practice, although it strove to replace the radical individualism of the French Revolution with a deep sense of social obligation and brotherhood. Social philosophers spoke of the "end of the Modern Age" and its arrogant humanism and the beginning of a socially minded era, a kind of Christian collectivism. Democracy was conceived of mainly in grass-roots terms, and a host of works extolling the educational virtues of local self-government found avid readers. In southern and southwestern Germany, this trend received much inspiration from the example and encouragement offered by Switzerland. To members of the petit-bourgeois society, the relationship between mass democracy and the Caesarism of the Nazi era was obvious. Democracy seemed meaningful only in the form of small communities linked together in a federal manner. Switzerland with its federal system, and, in a remoter sense, the United States also, seemed admirable examples of "organic democracy." In the west and northwest, by the same token, the conception of a viable form of democracy was less petit-bourgeois and more attuned to the higher stage of urbanization and industrialization of those areas. Great Britain under the Labour regime seemed to many to represent the ideal. Democratic freedoms were seen more in the sense of industrial democracy and the power of organized labor, while social obligation was understood to mean the enlightened welfare orientation of the governments of large cities and industrial concentrations.

Thus the frail young sprout of German democracy grew along its own characteristic lines in spite of the presence of the Western occupying powers, who gave what encouragement they could. It was rather different from Weimar conceptions of democracy too, although it subsumed in a way much of the anti-democratic criticisms of the last years of the Weimar Republic (although there has not been any respectable criticism of democracy in Germany since 1945). On the one hand, the preaching of democracy from academic chairs and pulpits and in the discussion circles which sprouted everywhere indulged the need for a naïve democratic fundamentalism. It emphasized the values and principles of democracy, including pluralism, without going into the characteristic group processes and the play of interests that had been the chief butt of criticism in the declining years of the First German Republic. On the other hand, opinion leaders were perfectly aware of the fact that Hitler's rise to power had reflected popular preferences and followed the rules of the "most democratic constitution" of that age. Consequently, the vocal minority felt a deep distrust of the masses and their sudden passions, and blamed "mass democracy" for the catastrophe. The two obvious remedies for mass

GERMANY: YESTERDAY AND TOMORROW

democracy were "organic democracy" and the institutional contrivances of constitutional government which might restrain the excesses of the popular will. The Swiss economist Wilhelm Roepke expressed the attitude of many Germans when he suggested reversing the progress of industrialization, urbanization, and Caesaristic mass democracy: craftsmen in place of proletarians, village communities in place of metropolitian areas, and the "organic democracy" of federalism in place of the mass democracy of large-scale unitarism seemed to offer a more wholesome and meaningful existence to rootless modern man. While it was hardly practical for industrialization and urbanization actually to be reversed, the introduction of federalism and constitutional government would not be difficult. And even beyond that there might be further ways of breaking up the excessively large industrial and functional groupings of society by various devices.

The Return to Federalism

The religious revival and the impulses toward democracy and federalism are inextricably interwoven. Before 1933, Germany had possessed a distinctive tradition of federal organization dating back to the Middle Ages. A number of characteristic differences distinguished German federalism from its American counterpart, most of them related to the role of monarchic institutions in Germany. There was no particular reason, then, why the Germans should look to the occupying powers to lead them back to their federal traditions. For the last 150 years, however, constitutional changes had consistently moved toward greater centralization, until, finally, the Nazi regime transformed Germany into a unitary state. The drastic reversal of this development in 1945 would seem to call for an explanation.

The breakdown of the intense nationalism of the war years and the collapse of anything larger than local and regional communications under the occupation might have been reason enough for a return to regionalism in post-war Germany. Democratic reconstruction of the government from the bottom up to the level of the *Laender* may also have invested these constituent bodies of a larger federation with greater importance and legitimacy in the scheme of things than they seem to deserve. But the wellsprings of federalism went much deeper, as can be seen from even a cursory survey of the political literature of the years between 1945 and 1948. Dating back, in fact, to the writings of many German expatriates and Swiss, American, and French friends of Germany during the Hitler years, this literature shows an astonishing consensus on the desirability of Germany's return to federalism. What is more, all the post-war democratic parties endorsed a federal form of government for Germany; they only differed on the degree of decentralization which was desirable. The concept of the Bavaria Party (BP) and of the German Party (DP) harked back to the states' rights of the early days of the Empire under Bismark. The CDU made federal government one of its chief planks, and its Bavarian affiliate, the CSU, was not far from the particularism of the Bavaria Party. The small, revived Center Party endorsed the federalistic theories suggested by Catholic social philosophy. Even the FDP and the SPD, who represented what were once the chief forces for unitary government, were for a modicum of federalism, or, as Dr. Kurt Schumacher put it: "As federalistic as possible, as unitary as necessary."

Catholics active in the Center Party, in the new Christian Democratic movement, or in the field of letters, as well as some Protestants, considered federalism and the reorientation of life according to Christian principles as part of the same mission. As one of the founders of the CDU wrote later:

> Any serious Christian will have to understand the deepest roots of the German and Central European catastrophe in this fateful process of intellectually going astray . . . the "great defection" . . . the secularization of the public and thereby of political life which replaced God with public idols and finally banned all morality, all social ethics from its thinking in order to replace it with a relativizing reason and, consequently, the adoration of materialism.

Only an extensive reform of society and its institutions could overcome the depersonalization and mechanization which had been the result of the application of rationalistic natural law to society and the state over the past 150 years. Among the evil influences which had been most responsible for bringing about Nazi totalitarianism were the "atomization of society" by liberalism, the centralism of the absolutistic state, Marxian socialism, and Rousseauean nationalism.

Hence, the CDU/CSU and large parts of the uncommitted intelligentsia were very receptive to the principles of subsidiarity and solidarity which Pope Pius XI had advocated in his encyclical *Quadragesimo Anno* (1931) to overcome the crisis of state, society, and the economy.

Subsidiarity refers to the rights of the responsible human being toward whom the social group has only subsidiary rights and duties. "Subsidiary" in this connection means to help him regain his powers in a crisis which is beyond his responsibility and capacity. In the same manner, the larger community and especially the state should only be of a subsidiary character and must not take away what functions the social group can fulfill:

> because on account of the evil of "individualism," as we call it, things have come to such a pass that the highly developed social life, which once flourished in a variety of prosperous institutions organically linked with each other, has been damaged and all but ruined, leaving thus virtually only individuals and the State. Social life lost entirely its organic form. The State, which now was encumbered with all the burdens once borne by associations rendered extinct by it, was in consequence submerged and overwhelmed by an infinity of affairs and duties.
>
> It is, indeed, true, as history clearly proves, that owing to the change in social conditions, much that was formerly done by small bodies can nowadays be accomplished only by large corporations. None the less, just as it is wrong to withdraw from the individual and commit to the community at large what private enterprise and industry can accomplish, so too it is an injustice, a grave evil and a disturbance of right order for a larger and higher organization to arrogate to itself functions which can be performed efficiently by smaller and lower bodies. This is *a fundamental principle of social philosophy, unshaken and unchangeable* and it retains its full truth today. Of its very nature *the true aim of all social activity should be to help individual members of the social body,* but never to destroy or absorb them. The State should leave to these smaller groups the settlement of business of minor importance. It will thus carry out with greater freedom, power and success the tasks belonging to it, because it alone can effec-

tively accomplish these, directing, watching, stimulating and restraining, as circumstances suggest or necessity demands. Let those in power, therefore, be convinced that the more faithfully this principle be followed, and *a graded hierarchical order exist between the various subsidiary organizations,* the more excellent will be both, the authority and the efficiency of the social organization as a whole and the happier and more prosperous the condition of the State. [Italics added]

This is a part of the encyclical dealing with the problems of capital and labor, but the sweeping generality of the statement appeared to justify its application to the problems of federalism as well. In order to insure that the principle of subsidiarity would not lead to excesses of particularism and separatism in the regional sense or in that of individual or group egotism, Catholic social theory uses the principle of solidarity to balance it with the requirements of the common good.

Germany and Europe

Much of this great reappraisal, together with the return of German politics to regional bases, really amounted to a conscious rejection of Bismarck's attempt to establish a powerful German nation-state in the center of Europe. The return to federalism was a return to the elements extant before national unification, and the Christian reorientation of politics and society was meant as a corrective to Bismarck's *Machtstaat,* the power-oriented state and its militarized society. It is also no coincidence that the great emphasis on the papal encyclical *Quadragesimo Anno* should coincide with the thinking of Constantin Frantz, the nineteenth-century philosopher who advocated federalism as a principle of social organization and who was a little known, but articulate antagonist of Bismarck and his policy of national unification. Like his Christian Democratic successors of 1945, Frantz criticized classical liberalism for its one-sided emphasis on the individual and Marxian socialism for its exclusive concern with the common good. A healthy balance and mutual relationship between the two concerns might well produce a reasonably harmonious "solidarity" among the interests of the whole and the parts. In this manner individual and group interests would be limited by the demands of the common good, while the common good likewise would be dependent upon the satisfaction of individual and group interests. The Catholic opposition to Bismarck during the early years of his rule thought along substantially the same lines.

This pattern of thinking, of course, did little to persuade the Liberals of the FDP to abandon their liberal principles, which in those days of scarcity and rationing could only apply to cultural policy. Nor did it carry a great deal of weight with organized labor and the Social Democrats, who had little to feel guilty about and who actually became considerably more nationalistic than they had been in the Weimar days. But the Christian Democratic movement happened to hold the cards for the immediate future of the country. And though its ideas on the German situation may have an unreal, medieval ring to Western ears, they were supremely well-suited to the task of bringing about the extraordinary metamorphosis of the educated middle class that occurred in these difficult years. No one can claim to understand the character of Adenauer's Germany unless he is willing to consider this metamorphosis in the terms in which the German contemporaries understood themselves at the time.

This great philosophical reappraisal of the German past was also supported by a number of German historians, who undertook to revise past views on such topics as the significance of Bismarck's policy for national unification, the alternatives to his course of action, and the merits of different conceptions of a German national purpose both in internal policy and in its relations to the rest of Europe. Their historical reappraisal produced a far more unfavorable image of Bismarck than had ever appeared before in German historiography. It also served as the basis for a complex theory which claimed that the foundation of a powerful German nation-state had indeed been the first step on the slippery road to World War II. This reappraisal thus represented both a final departure from German nationalism and a step toward European unification.

The relation between the geopolitical situation of a state and its internal organization is rather generally recognized today, although it becomes a subject of controversy once it goes past a few simple assumptions. Most historians will agree, for example, that strong, centralized government often emerges in response to constant threats from without, or that the decentralized form of government of the nineteenth-century United States was practical only because of the splendid isolation of the New World from Europe. Beyond this few are willing to go for fear of being considered geographical determinists. In post-war Germany, however, many leaders of opinion came around to a far more complex hypothesis linking geography and politics. Their interpretation of the German mission in Europe was not original but followed the thinking of Constantin Frantz and the German pacifist Friedrich Wilhelm Foerster.

For centuries before Bismarck, geography had imposed a peculiar role upon Germany or, as she was long called, the Germanies. Her central location and the common borders she shared with most of the new nation-states evolving around the rim of Europe made her a kind of buffer-state among these neighbors. Often fought over and always entangled in the international relationships of Europe, she could absorb the ebb and flow of the internal consolidation and occasional external aggression of the nation-states around her only because of her peculiar inner structure. She was a loose conglomeration of fairly independent states held together in a quasi-federal manner by the Imperial crown of the Hapsburgs, poorly organized for purposes of aggression and yet large enough and strong enough to survive. As the "federal core" of Europe, she was in a perfect position to mitigate the conflicts among her neighbors. Her major regions were oriented mainly toward neighboring foreign territories, the west and southwest toward France, the southeast toward Austria, the east toward Poland and other Slavic peoples, the northeast toward Russia, and the north and northwest toward Scandinavia and England. She was also a convenient basis for a treaty system pacifying Europe, such as the one promulgated by the Congress of Vienna. Her happy reconciliation of unity and diversity, combined with the universal spirit of the old Hapsburg Empire, symbolized not only a past where there had been friendship and unity within the European family of nations but also a future where there would be an end to the wars and the struggles for hegemony which then existed among the nations of the continent.

Under these circumstances, the application of the principle of nationality to Germany could only be a capital mistake which would bring disaster to Germany and to Europe as a whole. Nationality, with its emphasis on man's physical characteristics, might seem an un-Christian principle upon which to construct a nation-state, but it was a relatively innocuous principle when applied to fairly distinct and

homogeneous nations like England, France, and Spain, whose geographic location provided them with no such mission of mediation.
The Germans, however, were neither distinct nor homogeneous, but
were rather composed of a number of ethnic groups who were united
only by a common language and could just as well be a part of a
neighboring country as of Germany. The borders of this German nation were in fact so indeterminable that any delimitation of a German
nation-state was bound to stir up a hornets' nest of border disputes
with the Danes, the Dutch and Belgians, the French and Swiss, the
Italians and the Austro-Hungarian Empire, and last but not least with
the Poles and the many other groups of multi-national Eastern Europe. Germans who lived in the border areas and were minorities
deep in the territories of other ethnic groups got along fairly well with
other groups until they became obsessed with nationality. The very
absence of distinct borders and the scattering of German minorities in
neighboring countries was an open invitation to German national
ambitions. It seemed easy enough to include the Alsatians, the German Swiss, the South Tyroleans, and the German minority areas in
the east and north in the projected German nation-state. This indis-
tinct, indeterminate, and heterogeneous nationality may well have led
nationalistic zealots to think in terms of a master race.

The political consequences of applying the principle of nationality
to Germany followed with the inexorability of an avalanche.
Schleswig-Holstein is a good example of an area inhabited by Germans and non-Germans under a political arrangement linking the two
halves federally to Denmark and Germany, respectively, and also to
one another. The national movements in both countries insisted on
imposing an abrupt national frontier in place of the amicable federal
relationship. This produced minority frictions, war, conquest, and an
abiding distrust between the two nations in place of the previous
friendship and good ethnic relations.

Since Germany's major regions, moreover, were oriented toward
their respective neighboring countries rather than toward any central
point or area within Germany, the German national movement felt
compelled to sense, for example, that any Francophile manifestation
in the Rhineland represented a move toward treasonable secession
and that every Bavarian quest for regional autonomy represented sep-

aratism. Finally, the trend toward governmental centralization, the wars and border disputes, and the unlimited territorial aspirations of German nationalists had their inevitable effect on the relations of the new nation-state with its European neighbors. In place of a non-aggressive, buffer-state federation in the heart of Europe, there was now a powerful nation-state demanding a "place in the sun." Instead of the universal orientation which had the interests of the European family at heart, there was now a narrow nationalism with hegemonial appetites and a mystic faith in German "racial" superiority.

This line of reasoning cast a particularly strong spell over the new Christian Democratic movement, various states' rights parties, and many intellectuals. The collapse of national pride and glory in 1945 led with compelling logic to a belief in European universality and unity, which was always envisaged as a federal union. The vogue of federalism was so great that even world federation became a prevalent idea at the time.

Many leading federalists in the CDU were in contact with the *Union Européenne des Fédéralistes.* Others were convinced that only the utmost decentralization of Germany as a confederation could overcome French fears and gain entry for Germany into a European federation. Their belief in the principle of solidarity also made them anxious to work for the adjustment of national claims within the common good of more inclusive communities such as Europe or the world as a whole. Germans were quite aware of the discredit and distrust with which their European neighbors regarded them for recent hegemonial conquests, and they were anxious to demonstrate their change of heart so they would be accepted again. There was also a feeling that German reunification might be facilitated if Western Germany was a loose federation of autonomous *Laender* to which East Germany could be joined. Finally, the problem of social reform, as we have seen, was considered a European question and had already led to the creation of parallel Christian movements in Italy, France, Luxembourg, and Belgium, so that the path to European integration was already prepared. Hence, federalism as a universal principle of German and European political organization was a natural choice for the various Christian Democratic or Christian Social parties and their European organization, the *Nouvelles Equipes Internationales.*

The Realization of the Goals

Looking back upon the immediate post-war period with the cynicism of the new affluence and the benefit of hindsight, many a German has wondered aloud what happened to all that holy fervor. Some intellectuals have also suggested that in the rush toward economic recovery and rearmament many a beautiful dream of future social justice and international understanding was stifled, and many an opportunity for a new beginning lost, never to return again. It would seem, however, that both the cynic and the nostalgic intellectual make their choice too easy. It is hardly reasonable to interpret a set of goals in such an ideal, literal, or final manner that they are turned into an unattainable utopia, a heaven on earth. Nor is it reasonable to expect the simultaneous realization of mutually exclusive goals. A modest and practical set of expectations is more likely to be met in this world.

Actually the Christian Democratic movement has continued to stress a Christian approach to politics, as in its early days, despite its inevitable concern as the governing party with the various economic interests of the country. In fact, public opinion polls taken of CDU/CSU members show this "Christian" emphasis as the most characteristic attitude. There has also been no lessening in the post-war fervor for Christian social policy; nor have the Christian trade unions, and the numerous Catholic and Protestant lay organizations, and in particular the Social Policy Committees (*Sozialausschüsse*), lost much of their previous weight. Unquestionably West German Protestant and Catholic churches wield more social and political influence today than at any time during the last century, if not since the French Revolution. With religious forces of society in such a strong position, there are naturally cries of clericalism from those opposed to these tendencies, as well as expressions of fear that religious intolerance may be injected into political or cultural issues. But at least no one can say that the religious revival of the post-war period has disappeared without a trace.

There has also been no lack of attempts to make concrete applications of Catholic social philosophy and related theories of "social federalism," although the results achieved and the methods employed may be open to criticism. To begin with, there is a long record of efforts to reconcile conflicting groups, classes, and nations, ranging from reparations to the state of Israel and the co-operation between the two major Christian churches to the policy of establishing friendship with France and other former enemy countries. On a broader level, the policies and programs of the CDU/CSU and of the Center Party also aimed at, and may have contributed to, the waning of the ideological and class antagonisms in Germany that were once so crippling to the politics of the Weimar Republic. And they have also deliberately wooed many a potentially dissident group — from refugees, veterans, and little ex-Nazis to the farmers and German handicraft and small business. But here lies a difficulty of interpretation: it is impossible to separate Christian brotherhood and a desire to reconcile disaffected groups from plain good political sense, and the additional fact that most of the relevant legislation was endorsed by the Social Democratic opposition as well.

Secondly, there are the measures of social and economic policy which made a point of the subsidiary role of the state toward the existing autonomous units of society. The institutions of "social self-government" were reintroduced, including "labor co-determination" by paritatically constituted works councils in industry and "personnel representation" in the public service; management and labor have been represented likewise on the labor courts and social security boards, not to mention the restoration of the autonomy of collective bargaining — social functions which the ubiquitous state had had in its clutches, at least since 1933. Although they have no basis in Marxism, most of these measures were in principle, if not in detail, as welcome to organized labor and the SPD as to the disciples of *Quadragesimo Anno*. Then there was Erhard's "social market economics," which at first glance had been understood to imply pure market economics, or laissez-faire capitalism. Yet it also had its social policy aspects, such as encouraging an independent entrepreneurial class, instituting anti-trust action, and conducting "property policies," which attempted to spread the ownership of private property as widely as possible by issuing "people's stock" certificates of denationalized enterprises, granting savings premiums to people of limited income, and, most recently, giving workers a share in their company by means of "investive wages." Finally, the controversial Family and Youth Ministry sought to strengthen the institution of the family by such measures as childrens' allowances, tax breaks, special savings premiums for young couples, and other protective legislation. All of these policies tended to encourage or strengthen the pluralism of the "individual members of the social body," in Pope Pius XI's words, in accord with the philosophy of social reconstruction espoused in the first postwar years.

The checks and balances of constitutional government and federalism had been designated as a third goal by the early Christian Democratic movement, which hoped thereby to establish "organic democracy" and restrain the sudden passions of the multitude. When the German political leadership of the Western zones was allowed to draw up a provisional constitution in 1948–49, the Basic Law, they chose not only to make it a federal constitution — in accord with their own desires and Allied instructions — but to go considerably beyond the degree of decentralization contained in the Weimar Constitution. They did so although most of the *Laender,* on which the West German federal system is based, had been delimited in a rather accidental way, and some of them are uncertain about their territorial status to this very day. To be sure, there has been some centralizaton in the West German federal system since 1949, as could be expected, since the whole country is no larger than the state of Oregon. But at the same time, the present *Laender* governments have proven as viable and useful as they could ever be. Even the SPD, which gave federalism only lukewarm support in the beginning, has discovered its great virtues: the presence of *Laender* governments offers the party out of power at the federal level a splendid opportunity to exercise authority and to take on the governmental responsibility denied to it for so long in Bonn. The only issue that still engenders serious criticism of the federal system in the Federal Republic today is education and cultural policy, a field of *Land* jurisdiction; the regional differences in educational policy and institutions are the butt of endless and generally well-founded criticisms. However, there can be hardly any doubt about the contribution of federalism to the political stability of the Federal Republic.

The restoration and deepening of constitutional government in the Bonn Republic form another aspect of the same point and are similarly connected with the *Laender* constitutions and the new Basic

Law. Here, too, there remained a continued emphasis on well-designed institutional structures and constitutional law relationships even after the Basic Law had been produced. As a matter of fact, the politicians of the Federal Republic have by and large adhered closely to the constitutional system of the Basic Law and the *Laender* constitutions; for they take matters of legality far more seriously than their Weimar predecessors who had a disturbing habit of abiding by petty details while ignoring essentials of constitutional government. A special role in the new constitutional system has fallen to the Federal Constitutional Court, whose sweeping powers to outlaw subversive movements, to guard civil rights, and to oversee the constitutional relationships between the different organs and levels of government exceed even those of the United States Supreme Court. The *élan* for constitutionalizing political relationships of the post-war leadership may have gone too far in this instance; it seems to have ignored the fact that the proper places in a free society for resolving political conflicts should be the ballot box, the floor of the legislature, the editorial page, or any other forum where political issues are debated and decided.

Perhaps the most characteristic goal of the Christian Democrats has been European union. The contacts of members of the CDU/CSU with other Christian Democratic parties and with the *Union Européenne des Fédéralistes* and the *Nouvelles Equipes Internationales* antedate the establishment of the Federal Republic. The Basic Law of 1948–49 specifically provided for the transfer of sovereign rights to an international body. Within a year after the Basic Law had taken effect, negotiations had begun to place the German coal and steel industry, along with that of France, Italy, and the Benelux countries, under the High Authority of the Schuman Plan. Two years later, the still-born European Defense Community Treaty would have provided the proper European framework for West German rearmament, had not the French seen fit to veto the plan. In 1954, the Federal Republic was integrated into NATO and the Western alliance and only thereupon given her external sovereignty, though still subject to Allied rights relating to the conclusion of the final peace treaty. Attaining sovereignty by no means dampened the European fervor of the Christian Democratic government, which promptly "relaunched" the movement for European unification at Messina and Rome, the conferences which led to the launching of the Common Market and the European Atomic Community.

There is poetic justice, perhaps, in the fact that the three Christian Democratic leaders who stood at this threshold of European union were Robert Schuman, Alcide de Gasperi, and Konrad Adenauer. Each of the three came from a border area that had long been in dispute between their neighboring countries — Alsace, South Tyrol, and the Rhineland. It was almost as if the border populations themselves had grown so tired of being a bone of contention that they sent spokesmen to plead for making their areas a link between two cultures rather than a boundary, a bridge between two nations rather than a trench, an open door rather than a wall.

8

DUMMKOPF, VOTE FOR ADENAUER

In Lower Saxony they tell the story of an old, belligerent farm organization leader who had just been released from internment for his involvement with the Nazis when the neo-Nazi Socialist *Reich* Party (SRP) began to make headway among Lower Saxonian voters in 1950. The gnarled old man who used to spend his days on a bench behind the house brooding over his fate and muttering incomprehensible phrases behind his cold pipe was a curiosity to the local teenagers. They sensed his humiliation and bafflement, and with the cruelty of youth persuaded the old man's nephew to ask his advice on the approaching state elections, which featured not only the demagogues of the SRP and other parties, but also the German Party (DP), a regional conservative party that had always been dear to the hearts of Lower Saxonian farmers. While the other boys huddled behind a stack of wood in anticipation of a wild neo-Nazi harangue or some such explosion of sentiment, the youth approached his uncle and popped the question. The old man took his pipe from his mouth and his pale eyes transfixed his nephew: "Who you should vote for, lad? For Adenauer, *Dummkopf,* vote for Adenauer. Vote for the CDU. No question about it. None at all."

The story may be apocryphal, but it demonstrates well the extraordinary ability of politics to bring together the most disparate elements, to bridge the deepest gaps, and somehow to enable a people to live on despite deep and unresolved problems and permanent threats to its very existence. Post-war Germany was hardly in a better position to cope with the basic cleavages of German society and the additional problems resulting from defeat and division than was the luckless Weimar Republic. Yet there was present after 1945 a far stronger will to keep the elements together and to succeed in forming the odd collection of persons and families, of localities and economic enterprises that is West Germany into a functioning body politic capable of determining its own affairs in a rational manner. This political consolidation and resulting stability have been the chief characteristics of Adenauer's Germany. As German critics of the thesis of an "economic miracle" have pointed out, the political stability and steadiness are far more surprising than the indices of industrial production, if we recall the chaotic multi-party system of Weimar and its vacillations and evasions in the face of the fundamental challenges which surrounded the government of Weimar on all sides. Konrad Adenauer's role in the political consolidation of the Federal Republic is considerable, although one should give due weight to the many other forces that contributed to the ultimate success of his enterprise.

Adenauer's Background

Who was the man whom the public associates more than anyone else with the rise of Western Germany after the war? Which of the many faces of historic Germany does he represent? Born in 1876, only five years after the national unification of Germany, his life seems to bridge the enormous social and political upheavals, the wars, and the changes of mind which we have tried to chart in the early chapters of this book. His age alone is a fit subject for reflection, for he was already too old for military service in World War I. When the Nazis drove him out of office as Lord Mayor of Cologne in 1933, he could almost regard it as an early retirement at 57. And when his spectacular post-war career began in 1945, he was nearly 70, an age at which even the more tenacious political leaders of the Western democracies are about ready to retire.

Konrad Adenauer's background and what he represents and has represented in the past are often misinterpreted, not so much because of prejudice but because people are not properly aware of the complexities of the German past and because some of them have an exceedingly short memory which makes them think in black and white terms quite devoid of meaning. A sketch of his background should contain the following chief elements, though not necessarily in this order. First, he grew up and came to maturity in an environment as settled and well-ordered as any that nineteenth-century German novels of bourgeois life have depicted. Far from the stresses and strains of urbanization and industrialization, Adenauer was raised in a stable, if penurious lower-middle-class family, within the well-ordered community life and social structure of the Rhineland city of Cologne. He aspired to a career in the law and married into one of the patrician families of the city. Hard work, ability, and ambition soon led him into the city government and finally to the very top of this small and well-settled world, with moderate wealth, the Lord Mayoralty, and a position in the upper house of Prussia, the Council of State. Within this world of certainties and known standards, the ambitious young man evidently never had a moment's hesitation or doubt about himself or his goal in life. What a world of contrast existed in the first quarter of this century between this uncomplicated life and the nation's self-tortured intellectual and artistic life, which followed strange and esoteric paths and broke forth in avant-garde brilliance! What a contrast also to the apocalyptic broodings of the European underground, the anarchists, revolutionary Socialists, and the hundreds of diminutive, secretive cults including the perverse romanticism of young Hitler! It may well have been his well-settled, orderly background which gave him the equally well-settled frame of mind toward such symptoms of the great sickness of twentieth-century Germany as anti-semitism or the militant ideological movements of the right and left. As Lord Mayor of Cologne, he preferred to play the political game for such concrete stakes as votes for parks and municipal projects, not visionary millennia. Adolf Hitler was to him, as he once put it, "an actor" whose emotional histrionics he detested.

Adenauer, moreover, is a Prussian, though from one of the most liberal parts of that kingdom. His father fought the Austrians at Königgraetz in 1866, a circumstance as revealing as an American civil war record, and later became a minor Prussian civil servant. Konrad Adenauer himself occupied a high position in the Prussian state machinery as a member and President of the Council of State. There can be little doubt that he liked the Prussian system of government, a preference which brought him into conflict with South German proponents of federalism and states' rights after 1945. It is also likely that he fully identified with the patriotism of the *Kaiser*'s Germany before and during the First World War and had little sympathy for the revolution or for the coming of the First German Republic, although he adjusted admirably afterwards. At the same time, Konrad Adenauer also harbored the resentment of the liberal, urbane Rhinelander against the military caste and the *Junkers* who dominated Prussia. His anti-Prussian bias became particularly evident in 1919 when he was temporarily involved in an attempt to create a powerful new Rhenish Republic inside the German federation by separating the Ruhr and the Rhineland from Prussia and joining it with the Palatinate. If successful, this plan would have weakened Prussia, pleased the Western allies, and forced a pro-Western course upon the Weimar Republic rather than the neutralist *Schaukelpolitik* (see-saw policy) between East and West of Gustav Stresemann — and, before Weimar, of Bismarck — of which Adenauer took a dim view. This incident anticipated in many ways Adenauer's post-1945 foreign policy course. After the dissolution of Prussia in 1947, his anti-Prussian attitude took the form of a hearty dislike for Berlin and the East German successors to the old Prussian ruling class and strong objections to their readiness to sacrifice the rights of the individual to the demands of the state.

Furthermore, Adenauer represents Catholic Germany and the traditions of the Center Party of the Empire and the Weimar Republic. Being a Catholic under Bismarck meant being bitter about his "blood and iron" policy, designed to bring about national unification under a Prussian-dominated "Little Germany," with a Protestant King of Prussia and German *Kaiser* and excluding Catholic Austria. As a result, Adenauer and Catholics like him befriended the Poles and Alsatians, who unwillingly found themselves inside Bismarck's

new nation-state, and sympathized with the apprehensive French and
the defeated Austrians. They were also put on the receiving end of
the *Kulturkampf* which practiced official chicanery against their
church and baited them with frequent jibes of "ultra-montanism" and
"unpatriotic motives." Adenauer probably learned this lesson of political minority status early and inevitably inherited the political attitude of German Catholicism as he rose in the hierarchy of the Center
Party. It is also true that Konrad Adenauer has been a devoutly religious man all his life, although in the tradition of the light-hearted,
liberal Rhineland this has never made him particularly obsequious
toward the Church or its high officials. Fellow Rhinelanders chuckle
over the fact that he never greets the Cardinal of Cologne in any
other way except "Good day, Mr. Frings," or that, by his own admission, he never kisses the ring of any cardinal. While ties of close personal friendship and even of family may connect him to many a
highly placed clergyman, Adenauer has seemingly refused to accept
the dignitaries of his Church on any other level than that of a social
equal.

Adenauer's curiously ambiguous attitude toward social issues also
deserves some attention. On the one hand, he seems to be a bourgeois
at heart, with the healthy respect for wealth and status of a man who
was not born with a silver spoon in his mouth, but had to earn his own
status the hard way. His marriage into the Cologne patriciate and rise
to high office soon opened the doors of the wealthy Rhineland
oligarchy to him. Consequently, he was known as a conservative in
the Weimar Center Party and showed an unconcealed dislike for the
Christian Socialist overtones in the programs of the Christian Democratic movement immediately after World War II. His rise to power
within the CDU, therefore, was accompanied by a deliberate effort to
bring more business elements into the party, especially from among
Protestants, and to weaken the influence of the labor wing and its
economic and social policies. On the other hand, Adenauer always
paid homage to the Center Party philosophy of reconciling the social
classes and their antagonisms and of including the faithful of all
classes equally in the concerns of the party. He fully appreciated the
first great papal encyclical on the social question, *Rerum Novarum*
(1891), and was very moved by *Quadragesimo Anno* (1931), which
he read some years later while hiding in a monastery from the Nazis.

It was while there that he had the chance to ponder what had gone wrong and how his country could be reconstructed, if ever the day would come. His commitment to Catholic social philosophy gave him the incentive to play the role of broker among the different groups and interests of his movement rather than attach himself to any particular group or any special economic and social doctrine. Such a role better suited his political instincts, for he soon turned his main energies toward foreign relations and the international position of Western Germany. The domestic policies of the Adenauer administration simply became a function of its foreign policy, beginning, of course, with its overriding desire to keep together the different social groups and to get them to support his foreign policies.

The Ascent to Power, 1945–50

The Christian Democratic movement had emerged at almost the same time in several different geographic centers. Divided by occupation zones and *Laender* boundaries, it failed signally to achieve organizational unity during the first four or five years of its existence. There were noticeable differences between the Christian Socialist views of the Frankfurt and Cologne circles and the more conservative views of Christian Democrats in Schleswig-Holstein and Munich. The consolidation of these diverse and decentralized elements into a nation-wide party was most likely to produce rivalries between different regional leaders and different viewpoints.

Adenauer as seen by (1) his own party, (2) the opposition, (3) Walter Ulbricht,

Konrad Adenauer had been reinstated as Lord Mayor of Cologne by American troops in May 1945. A few months later and for reasons that still remain obscure, the British dismissed him summarily and even forbade him for a while to take part in any political activity. Oddly enough, this humiliating dismissal started him on the road to national leadership. As soon as the ban on his political activity was lifted, he threw himself into the task of renewing old political contacts and preparing the ground for his rise to leadership within the party. Still in 1945, when the Christian Democrats of the Western zones were organizationally barely off the ground, a formidable bid for leadership came from Berlin. Andreas Hermes, a former Minister of Agriculture of the Center Party under the Weimar Republic, took advantage of the decision by the Soviet military administration to allow political activity in the Soviet zone by establishing an imposing CDU organization there. By the end of 1945 he announced his claim to the national leadership of the new movement from the old capital. But the Soviets abruptly ended his meteoric post-war career by ordering him to give up his party offices before the year was out.

Adenauer, meanwhile, built up his own organization within the party. At a first zonal meeting of the British zone CDU in late January 1946, at Herford, he was still only one of five delegates of the *Land* CDU of Rhineland. Another serious contender for zonal leadership, Hans Schlange-Schoeningen, a Protestant conservative who had been influential in the German Nationalist Party (DNVP) of the Weimar Republic, had almost attracted enough following before the

(4) the anti-clerical camp, (5) the Chancellery officials, and
(6) everybody — a hard nut to crack

meeting at Herford, but hoped to win the zonal chairmanship there. Quickly spotting his chance as the meeting began, Adenauer strode boldly to the empty chairman's seat, sat down, and announced to the surprised gathering that, being the oldest man present, he might as well preside over the meeting. Hermes and several companions who had appeared uninvited were told to wait outside the door, and they soon left in anger. Before the meeting was over, Adenauer was elected chairman of the British zone CDU. The *Land* CDU of Rhineland subsequently made him their chairman as well. A second zonal conference at Neheim-Huesten a month later confirmed Adenauer's coup and drew up a new party program which clearly bore his mark, stressing the vital role of the individual and de-emphasizing the nationalization of parts of the economy.

Once elected to zonal leadership, Adenauer soon silenced his critics within the CDU by a creditable effort at consolidating and unifying the party organization throughout the British zone. Membership figures rose prodigiously and local and county organizations were strengthened or established where non-existent. Conservative Protestants in the north and in the large harbor cities were brought in to make the CDU a true union of both Christian faiths and, of course, also to create a balance between conservatives, and the Christian Socialists among the founders, and the Catholic elements coming from the Weimar Center Party. The consolidation of the British zone CDU is also significant because it enabled Adenauer to frustrate one more attempt of the CDU "national headquarters" in Berlin, this time under the Christian trade unionist Jakob Kaiser, to assert its leadership over the nation-wide movement in 1946. Having made certain that the South German CDU/CSU organizations were no more willing to recognize Berlin leadership than he was, Adenauer simply notified the Berlin office that it could communicate with the individual *Land* parties in the British zone only through the zonal party organization. The CDU Zonal Council even rejected offers of financial support from Berlin. The standard excuse was that it was not in the interest of the nation-wide movement nor particularly safe for it to have headquarters behind the Iron Curtain, not even in West Berlin.

Zonal boundaries and the extreme sensitivity of the states'-rights-minded South German Christian Democrats prevented Adenauer from spreading his power into the south. But they could not stop him from skillfully exploiting South Germany's dislike for Berlin and Jakob Kaiser's pretensions to national leadership. He also flattered the Hessians by emphasizing again and again that Frankfurt and not Berlin should become the new German capital, a ruse which also pleased other South Germans far more than would the thought of Bonn or Cologne as capital. In this atmosphere of bitter animosity between the British zone CDU and Kaiser's East German CDU, and with the South Germans suspicious of any kind of centralized authority, the organizational consolidation of the Christian Democratic movement was unlikely to advance. This was a serious weakness in view of increasing competition from the SPD. The Social Democrats of the Western zones had meanwhile rallied around the leadership of Kurt Schumacher in response to the forced merger of SPD and Communists in the Soviet zone in 1946 and re-established their pre-1933 apparatus. The Christian Democrats, by contrast, set up a powerless Co-Ordinating Office (*Arbeitsgemeinschaft*) in Frankfurt early in 1947, which received no transfer of authority from any zonal or *Land* party. Then the advocates of decentralized federal government in the American zone CDU/CSU, mostly important figures in the various *Laender* governments and *Land* parties, founded the Ellwangen Circle. The purpose of this regional group, which soon extended to the French zone CDU as well, was to agree on a draft of a federal constitution in anticipation of the day when the Allied occupying powers would permit the Germans to establish democratic government on a nation-wide level. Since the Co-Ordinating Committee in Frankfurt had already been charged with the drafting of a federal constitution, it was quite evident that the South German federalists were intent upon securing more states' rights.

Late in 1946, the occupying powers in the West started on an era of governmental reorganization which aimed at the establishment of German interzonal administrations in the fields of food and agriculture, economics, transport, and finance. The Soviets had demonstrated their unwillingness to co-operate, and the French, until 1949, also kept their zone out of the administrative merger, which was, therefore, at first limited to the British and American zones. These bizonal institutions were continually reorganized to create greater central authority and to increase, step by step, the geographical area over which the German government, under Allied tutelage, would have control. This situation afforded Adenauer the opportunity to expand his power by using his slim majority to give him control over an ever-widening area of authority. His British zone CDU chairmanship not only established him in the Rhineland CDU but also in the new *Land* North Rhine Westphalia, whose fourteen million inhabitants and concentration of two-thirds of German heavy industry immediately made it the most powerful *Land* of the Western zones and the dominant section of the British zone. With this consolidation of his hold over the British zone CDU, Adenauer equally stood to gain from a bizonal merger, for the British zone CDU was both larger and better organized than the autonomy-oriented *Land* parties of the American zone CDU and the Bavarian CSU. Adenauer himself, as well as his emerging Social Democratic rival Schumacher, stayed away from the bizonal administrations and the Economic Council at Frankfurt, where a coalition "government" of the CDU/CSU, FDP, and German Party (DP) representatives enjoyed a narrow majority over an "opposition" composed of Social Democrats and Communists. But being the chief party in the "government" provided a powerful stimulus for the CDU/CSU of both zones to stick together, despite the acrimonious squabbles that developed between South German agricultural interests and the CDU Food Director Schlange-Schoeningen and Economics Director Erhard. And within the CDU/CSU delegation in the Economic Council, the British zone delegates were predominant. Adenauer and Schumacher contented themselves with using their influence behind the scenes and so avoided the inevitable antagonisms which finally brought Schlange-Schoeningen's career to an end.

By the middle of 1948, Adenauer had clearly emerged as the unchallenged leader of the CDU/CSU. Jakob Kaiser's position in the East German CDU had been completely undermined by Soviet manipulations which had turned that party into a satellite of the SED (Socialist Unity Party). His championship of German unity began to ring hollow as his base shrank to the size of West Berlin and as Germany itself visibly broke asunder into East and West. Finally, Kaiser submitted to Adenauer's leadership and became the chairman of the exile CDU, a collection of East German CDU members who had fled to the West rather than remain with the satellite CDU of Communist

Germany. The South German *Land* parties were barely beginning to realize that Adenauer's ambition might be a danger to their autonomy. The *Land* parties of the French CDU had not yet been allowed to establish organizational links beyond the *Land* level, and they came into the game too late to join forces with the South German federalists. Adenauer's Francophile background also endeared him to a significant section of the Christian Democrats in the French zone. These were the circumstances under which he became the President and acknowledged CDU/CSU leader of the Parliamentary Council, the constituent assembly called in September 1948 to draw up the Basic Law of the Federal Republic.

There still was no organizational unification of the CDU/CSU outside the Parliamentary Council; but two political developments that occurred during the eight months that the Parliamentary Council was working on the Bonn Constitution served to push Adenauer even more to the forefront of the Christian Democratic movement in the Western zones. First, the clash between the two major parties, each of whom had the same number of seats in the Parliamentary Council, as they had before in the Economic Council, became increasingly bitter. Even though the parties had a basic desire to co-operate in writing the Constitution, so that a broadly based popular document could be produced, in contrast to the unpopular Weimar Constitution, rivalry between Adenauer and Schumacher broke out again and again and even took the form of personal insults.

At the same time, there was a strong movement to bring about a united front for as long as Germany remained occupied. Both Christian trade unionists in the CDU/CSU and *Laender* chiefs in both parties hoped for a "great coalition" of the two major parties in the future federal government, such as had already been in existence in all *Laender* governments since their establishment. But each party's leaders were confident that they would have a plurality when the first federal elections were held, so their attitude toward long-term co-operation was irreconcilable and intractable. Disagreement over the economic policies of Ludwig Erhard, who had begun lifting government controls from production after 1948, further added fuel to the partisan fire. Since the labor wing of the CDU/CSU also was highly skeptical of Erhard's policies, the Christian Democratic movement might have seemed in real danger of splintering, had it not been for the personal animosities between the party leaders and for the necessity for the CDU/CSU to cultivate the FDP as an ally. Erhard had been brought forward in the first instance when the FDP insisted on a Bizonal Economics Director to its liking. With the benefit of hindsight, we can easily see how things could have developed quite differently. What did eventually happen, however, not only proved to Adenauer's liking and helped his ascent to power, but also demonstrated his political skill, for he was able to prevent the labor wing from leaving his party for the SPD.

Equally important in advancing Adenauer's cause was the bitter struggle that took place over how much decentralization should occur in the federal system as determined by the Basic Law. Here too, Adenauer and the British zone delegation had definite preferences, patterned somewhat after the Prussian constitutional tradition of unitary government with decentralized administration or at least after the rather centralized federal system of the Weimar Republic, and the SPD shared their views. The CDU/CSU delegates of the French and American zones, on the other hand, favored strong state governments and a second chamber in the form of the traditional *Bundesrat*. But the real disturbance came from the Bavarian CSU, anxious to retain its autonomy and its own name but plagued by four separate factions fighting each other with reckless fury. One of these factions even left the CSU and established itself as an exceedingly successful nativist movement under the name Bavaria Party (BP), with an almost separatist program that also advocated restoration of the Bavarian monarchy. Thus Adenauer was hindered in his efforts to bring about a compromise between the differing conceptions of federalism, for he was constantly forced to deal with extreme demands from CSU delegates and the CSU government of Bavaria, who in turn were fearful of losing all their voting support to the BP. The CSU tried everything to advance states' rights, including a "deal" with the SPD to put over the *Bundesrat* idea, and they hoped that the occupying powers would write greater fiscal autonomy for the *Laender* into the Basic Law. Adenauer dug deeply into his rich collection of diplomatic skills, but he ended up by agreeing to most of the demands of the states' righters. Yet he kept the channels of communication open and managed to avoid creating hard feelings; in the end he was in a position to put the Bavarian CSU in his debt by holding out vast promises of patronage.

The Bavaria Party still stole most of the CSU vote in the federal elections, and the Bavarian *Landtag* (parliament) refused moreover to ratify the Basic Law (since it knew full well that this would become binding upon ratification by the other *Landtage*). But once the new federal government was ready to be formed, the CSU was as well prepared to accept Adenauer's leadership and the spoils of office as any other group in his coalition.

The first federal election in 1949 was a well-calculated gamble. The CDU/CSU campaigned largely on the basis of Erhard's economic policies, which constituted a large part of the party program, the Duesseldorf Principles. But at this point, after years of rationing, Erhard's free enterprise policies had mostly benefited a numerically small segment of aggressive new entrepreneurs, who had thrown hoarded goods on the market and taken advantage of the opportunity for new production. Some real fortunes were made, and commercial empires were created out of practically nothing. But unemployment had also increased sharply, and had reached nearly two million by the end of 1949. And the inflated prices which Erhard had said would gradually drop and return to a reasonable level had not yet shown much inclination to do so. Could the voters be made to believe the optimistic forecasts of the Christian Democrats? Would they not be more likely to agree with the Social Democrats, who were heaping scorn upon the sudden switch to neo-liberalism of a party that in the British zone had endorsed the nationalization of large sectors of industry as recently as the Ahlen Program of 1947? The CDU/CSU and SPD results in preceding *Landtag* elections were an unreliable basis for forecasting the election, since they indicated only that the CDU/CSU held the narrowest of margins over the SPD. When the final results were in, the CDU/CSU had polled 31 per cent of the popular vote, as compared to 29.2 for the SPD. Six other parties shared the rest of the seats, ranging from FDP, with 11.9 per cent, to a Bavarian middle-class party, the Economic Reconstruction Union (WAV), with 2.9 per cent. The distribution of seats in the new *Bundestag* slightly inflated the percentages of the three larger parties.

The election results handed the initiative to Adenauer. The labor wing of his party and the *Laender* chiefs all expected him to approach the SPD to form a "great coalition" government. The Social Democrats, however, showed little eagerness to come to terms, and there was reason to think that they would exact a very high price for their co-operation. Taking advantage of the fact that there was still no recognized party organ of the CDU/CSU that could have made a binding decision and that the Christian Democratic caucus of the new *Bundestag* had not yet met, Adenauer invited some twenty-five CDU/CSU leaders to a little social gathering at his house at Rhoendorf near Bonn one week after the election. The men assembled were not exactly a representative group, and some were not even quite aware of the significance of the meeting, when Adenauer and a few of the initiated proceeded to broach the subject of a government coalition with the Free Democrats and the conservative German Party (DP) instead of with the SPD. There was considerable resistance to this idea at the meeting, and even more afterwards from CDU leaders who had not been invited there. Nevertheless, a communiqué was issued to the press which spoke of an election mandate — evidently the 1.8 per cent margin over the SPD vote — to continue the economic policies begun by Erhard in the Economic Council. A week later the CDU caucus met and endorsed Adenauer's plan.

The new coalition numbered 208 out of the 402 members of the new *Bundestag*. When the time came for the *Bundestag* to vote on a Chancellor for the new federal government, Adenauer was elected by a majority of one vote — his own. At least five members of the coalition voted against him. Adenauer's coalition plan at Rhoendorf had sought to attract the FDP by assuring it of the federal presidency, a largely honorific office, for its chairman, Professor Theodor Heuss. To the objection that Heuss was too outspokenly anticlerical, Adenauer replied: "But he has a pious wife. That's enough." However, Heuss still had to be elected by an electoral college made up of the *Bundestag* deputies and an equivalent number of delegates from the *Landtage*. The new coalition controlled only 395 of the 804 and lost 18 of its own members on the first ballot. Fortunately, small party support materialized on the second ballot, and Heuss was elected. Adenauer had also promised the *Bundesrat* presidency to the Bavarian CSU, but here the opposition within his own party finally won out and elected instead Adenauer's rival, Karl Arnold of the CDU labor wing, Minister President of North Rhine Westphalia. Adenauer had to indemnify the Bavarians with a disproportionate number of cabinet posts, including those of the powerful Finance Ministry, the Agriculture Ministry, to keep the Bavarian farmers happy, and the Postal Ministry. This was quite a haul for a mere 24 *Bundestag* deputies of the CSU, while the 115 CDU deputies only received five cabinet posts in addition to that of Chancellor. The 52 FDP deputies were given three, aside from the federal presidency, and the 17 DP deputies two.

With the federal governmental authority safely under his control and at the head of a party coalition whose left wing, the Christian trade unionists, he could play off against the right wing, the FDP and DP, Adenauer was safely ensconced in power. He could afford to postpone the organizational consolidation of the extra-parliamentary CDU/CSU for yet another year, during which time the British zone CDU office would still remain the most effective party agency. Since his internal opposition had not yet calmed down, he may actually have prevented a split in the party by his delaying tactics. Late in 1949 he rejected a plan for the establishment of a national party executive because he feared he would supply a forum to his enemies' advantage. In the meantime, elements friendly to Adenauer went to work in each *Land* to undercut the regional CDU leadership and its "great coalition" with the SPD. This course of action effectively weakened the last dissident *Land* leaders of the CDU/CSU and brought them round. By the spring of 1950, finally, Adenauer considered the time ripe for extra-parliamentary organization and permitted preparations for a CDU party convention to get under way. By this time the Bavarian CSU had decided to remain an autonomous party, linked with the CDU only in the *Bundestag* in a common caucus. The CDU convention met in October at Goslar and elected Adenauer party chairman; Kaiser of the exile CDU and Holzapfel of the Westphalian CDU became vice chairmen. The chairmen of the *Land* parties entrenched themselves in the Federal Committee of the CDU, from which they fought further efforts at centralizing power within the party. Adenauer subsequently used the extra-parliamentary party organization only sporadically and centered his power instead in the Chancellor's office at Bonn. There, in the provisional capital which lay at the doorstep of his house at Rhoendorf, he could oversee the evolving politics of the new state, much as a patriarch surveys the daily life of his own family.

The Adenauer Elections

One of the greatest handicaps of the transition from monarchy to popular sovereignty under the Weimar Republic was the manifold social cleavages and divisions inherited from the old society. These traditional groupings were in essence states of mind that rigidly determined how a civil servant, an aristocrat, a professional officer, an artisan, a shopkeeper, or an artist ought to think of himself and how he ought to act. Applied to politics at a time of great crisis and rapid change, these built-in divisions of opinion resulted in a nightmare of criss-crossing disagreements and a general inability to evolve any kind of public consensus on the form of government and on the policies it should adopt. Each little group tended to form its own militant discussion club, pressure group, or political party, where it evolved an elaborate ideology built around its particular prejudices or interests and then threw itself into the political arena with all the means available, from the ballot box and lobbying to propaganda campaigns and para-military organizations. The number of political parties in the Weimar *Reichstag,* not counting the legions of other more or less political organizations, rose at one time to more than thirty and never declined to less than eight permanent groups of clearly definable membership. There were the Communists, representing deeply disaffected working class elements; the Social Democrats, a *bona fide* Socialist workers' party; the Catholic Center Party and its rural-conservative Bavarian offshoot; the Bavarian People's Party (BVP); the left-wing liberal Democrats (DDP) and the right-wing liberal German People's Party (DVP), who represented different layers and regional segments of the middle class; the German Nationalists (DNVP), a collection of landed aristocrats and other conservative elements of northern Germany; and finally the motley collection of racist and right-wing extremist groups from among whom the Nazi movement sprang.

In this period, too, people were appalled at the chaos of struggling groups and blamed it on the unfamiliar machinations of parliamentary democracy, from which they sought to escape, either back into the womb of the monarchic-authoritarian state or forward into a conflict-free Communist future or ill-defined nationalist utopia. They failed to see their way into a democratic society where social conflicts are carefully managed within a framework of generally accepted rules. The system whereby each adult citizen, whether a university professor or merely a day laborer, takes an equal part in the making of political decisions by his own vote remained as much of a mystery as did the gentle sway public opinion can hold through the consensus of the majority. In these circumstances the Germans stumbled into the trap of National Socialism.

In contrast to these rigidities and failures of the Weimar Republic, the political developments in the new Bonn Republic are noteworthy in several respects: there is, for example, the emergence of what we have earlier called the "new society," whose disappearing social cleavages helped facilitate the formation of popular majorities and of a consensus of public opinion far better than Weimar society ever could. Then there is the development of electoral majorities for Adenauer and his Christian Democrats, a phenomenon quite unprecedented in the brief history of German electoral politics from Bismarck to Bonn. Finally, there is the slow rise of popular appreciation for the institutions and principles of democracy which on a mass level came only after Adenauer had proved to his fellow citizens beyond reasonable doubt that democracy can be just as successful and rewarding as any dictatorial regime, if not more so.

The direct predecessor of the Christian Democrats, the Center Party of the Empire and the Weimar Republic, was distinguished from all the other important German parties by the fact that it united members and voters from all social classes and ways of life; this made it unusually responsive to the shifts of public opinion. Nevertheless, there was still an important limitation: it was confined to Catholics in a country with a Protestant majority. Even though occasional attempts were made to lead the party out of this "tower" of religous confinement, it was prevented by this rigidity from ever polling more than 20 per cent of the popular vote. The founders of the CDU/CSU, on the other hand, placed great emphasis on overcoming the religious division from the very beginning. Favored by the post-war climate and their conciliatory attitude toward all groups, except for outright Nazi criminals, the Christian Democrats garnered on the average between 30 and 35 per cent of the vote in the *Land* elections under the Allied occupation. In the first federal elections, as mentioned above, they polled 31 per cent, a narrow plurality among the eight parties that won representation in the *Bundestag*. In the 1953 elections, after four years of the Adenauer administration, the CDU/CSU won 45.2 per cent of the vote, which gave it a bare majority of the seats in the *Bundestag,* the first real sign that a significant political consolidation had occurred. Only four other parties were still represented in the *Bundestag:* the SPD, with 28.8 per cent, the FDP, with 9.5, the new Refugee Party (BHE), with 5.9, and the DP, with 3.2. Among the four small parties which no longer qualified were the revived Center Party and the Communists, who had polled 5.9 per cent in 1949; and neo-Nazi groups also failed again as they had in 1949. In the 1957 elections, the CDU/CSU won 50.2 per cent of the vote, giving them a comfortable majority; the SPD followed with 31.8 per cent and the FDP with an alarmingly low 7.7 per cent, just barely above the 5 per cent clause of the electoral law. The Refugee Party lost, as did the extremists of right and left, and the DP managed to hang on only by virtue of its close association with the CDU, which allowed it to win direct mandates. Finally, in the 1961 elections, the DP also failed to win representation, which left three survivors — the CDU/CSU, with 45.3 per cent, the SPD, with 36.3, and the FDP, with 12.7. Adenauer lost his majority of the seats, although the Christian Democratic vote still demonstrated the stability of this political consolidation.

The rallying of voters in support of the Adenauer administration raises many interesting questions regarding, for example, the voting behavior of the various social groups and the role played by the policies of the federal government and of the CDU/CSU in attracting majority support. At the risk of overgeneralization, we can say now that in elections since 1953 the Christian Democratic voters have been far more representative of the different groups in West German Society than those of any other party. As the emerging "new society" increased the homogeneity of German society and obscured the old social cleavages, the CDU/CSU was able to attract large numbers of workers as well as businessmen and professional people, white-collar employees as well as civil servants, city folk and farmers alike, Protestants as well as Catholics, and refugees as well as native West Germans. The CDU/CSU voters would come quite close to being a cross section of the West German population except for three deviations which still retain to a certain extent the divisions of traditional German society. There are a disproportionate number of Catholics — a ratio of about five Catholics to four Protestants, although Protestants make up slightly more than half of the population — of farmers, and of women. This highlights some of the party's parochial overtones and, of course, its origins, although it should not obscure the fact that two-thirds of the Christian Democratic voters were either workers — equal to about three-fourths of the number of workers voting for the SPD — or white-collar employees in government and industry. The latter are especially concentrated in better paying positions and were probably attracted principally by the economic success of the government policies and by effective campaign management. It would seem obvious, then, that the CDU/CSU cannot be called a bourgeois party, even though most of its financial support has come from business and industry. Instead, it should be called a party of "democratic integration" — to use the phrase of the late Sigmund Neumann — because of its basic tendency to bring together all groups of society under the flexible banner of "Christian politics."

The elaborate structure of functional committees in the CDU/CSU also furthers this effort at social integration. In these committees the party calls on the organized groups of society to present wishes for specific ideas and what policies the party should adopt. Among these committees are the Social Policy Committees for labor policy, the Economic Committees for business policy, the Young Union for the Christian youth organizations, and similar committees for women, agriculture, refugees, local government associations and other organizations. This committee structure is the direct link between the various organized interests of society and the party, which in turn integrates these varying and at times conflicting demands into its public policies as harmoniously as it can.

What were the issues and policies which Adenauer's party used to rally the voters in such numbers? In 1949, the emphasis had been on Erhard's economic policies, which at that time seemed to hold, at best, a dubious promise for the future. But in 1953, the electoral program of the CDU could already claim that under Adenauer's leadership the party had led the people "from hunger, misery and deadly isolation." After the initial economic reverses of 1950 and 1951, the economic recovery had moved into high gear, and SPD claims to the contrary met disbelief from increasing numbers of workers and salaried employees, as well as businessmen and professional people. Naturally, the Christian Democrats promised more of the same, directing their pitch in particular to the refugees, to the farmers, to the lower income groups, and to small business and handicraft groups who were beginning to worry about their position among the giants of economic competition. This economic program undoubtedly played a major role in producing the peak of the electoral surge for Adenauer's party in 1957, just as West German society entered the stage of mass consumption.

But the chief emphasis of 1953 was on foreign policy, the area in which Adenauer was performing his extraordinary feat of rehabilitating and integrating Western Germany within the Western family of nations. Among the most attractive aspects of his policies were his emphasis on Franco-German friendship and on European integration, which enjoyed the support of 75 to 85 per cent of the electorate, including that of SPD and FDP adherents, and were actually opposed by only some 10 per cent of the people. Close to three-fourths of the West German electorate, also, was consistently in favor of cooperation with the United States. The prestige stemming from Germany's becoming once more a respected partner in the councils of European states probably played an important role in popular support of Adenauer's pro-European and pro-Western policies. German rearmament within the framework of Western European defense, on the other hand, proved far more controversial. Even as late as 1955, after the decision to rearm was already being implemented, a slim majority of the German people was still against disarmament. In 1956, however, at the time of the Hungarian revolution and the Western failure to intervene, the West Germans dramatically changed their minds about the need for a German army and came to appreciate it as a guarantee of their security against Soviet aggression. By the early 'sixties, the opposition to West German participation in the Western alliance had shrunk to 10 or 15 per cent, while over 70 per cent of the population supported it. In the long run, it would appear, the objections to German rearmament faded before the force of circumstances, as did the opposition to Erhard's economic policies. Finally, one should not overlook the effectiveness of the well-financed and professionally managed election campaigns of the CDU/CSU.

Beginning in the 1953 campaign, the Christian Democrats employed sophisticated advertising techniques. Indeed, their campaign was based to such an extent on "marketing" the personal image of Adenauer that the leadership of the old Center Party of the Weimar Republic would have been highly embarrassed if they had seen it. Right after the 1953 election, for example, public opinion pollsters learned that more than half of the people polled considered the CDU/CSU propaganda campaign the best and the biggest put forth by any of the parties.

During the period of 1949 to 1961, the CDU/CSU was also successful in attracting the floating vote, or, for that matter, any voter who was not already firmly committed to another party. In Germany, as in the United States and Great Britain, between two-thirds and three-fourths of the voters are steady partisans of a particular party. The SPD, for example, is reputed to have the largest percentage of faithful adherents, followed at some distance by the CDU/CSU. The smaller parties, on the other hand, have a fickle clientele. There can be little doubt that at least one half of Adenauer's newly won supporters were taken from among former voters of the Bavaria Party, the Center Party, the German Party, the Refugee Party, a collection of less familiar groups, and even from the FDP, which, however, took revenge in 1961 by appealing to CDU/CSU voters who were tired of Adenauer. The other half of Adenauer's new supporters evidently came from among the non-voters of 1949, some nine million new voters, over three million East German refugees, and the voters of the Saar after the plebiscite, a total turnover of more than 40 per cent since 1949. Young voters in particular turned out in force for the CDU/CSU in 1953, although more recently they have tended to favor the SPD, a significant portent of the future. Adenauer's election campaigns have also exhibited an uncanny knack for attracting the voters who could not make up their minds until the last minute. There was an additional 10 per cent voting in federal elections compared with *Land* elections, and of these the CDU/CSU has always claimed the lion's share.

Finally, there is evidence of the voters' growing attachment to the democratic institutions of the Federal Republic. This increasing acceptance of their own form of government is reflected in, first, the rejection, and, later, the approval of the black, red, and gold of the

Bonn flag in place of the black, white, and red of the former Empire
and the Third Reich. It is also expressed in the gradual spread of understanding about such complex institutions as the West German
electoral law, which allows the voter to cast one vote for a representative for his district and a second vote for a party list. From 1951,
when only one-third of the voters understood that they had a representative for their district, the number grew to three out of five by
1956, though even then less than a fourth were able to name this representative. While the level of political information rose noticeably
with every election campaign, it still remained woefully inadequate
among some groups, especially the women. The most revealing feature, perhaps, is that the West German electorate is taking an increasingly positive and self-confident attitude toward the procedures and
processes by which a democracy makes its decisions, such as the elections, conflicts between two or more political parties, or squabbles in
the *Bundestag*. Separate opinion polls in 1950 and 1956 which asked
the public to evaluate the work of the *Bundestag* and the qualities
necessary for a *Bundestag* deputy indicated, for example, a noticeable
switch from a negative to a positive opinion, even though the *Bundestag* actually declined in importance during the second legislative term.
During the same six years, the democratic party system, as contrasted
to government without parties or a one-party state, likewise grew in
public acceptance, from a two-to-one majority to a six-to-one majority. At the same time, three-fourths of the electorate were firmly
committed to parliamentary democracy, the system which the Germans of 1933 gladly exchanged for a dictatorship.

Public opinion polls have also been heartening in what they reveal
about the gradual disappearance of the legacy of fear and mutual distrust from totalitarian times. For instance, there has been a sizable
increase in the number of West Germans who feel they can freely
speak their minds on the subject of politics — from less than half in
1950 to three-fourths of the people polled in 1955. Last but not least,
these polls have revealed a startling change in attitude toward what
form of government Germans consider best for themselves. Supporters of monarchy, for instance, have dwindled from one-third of the
public in 1951 to a mere 5 per cent in 1960, mainly old-timers and
farmers. Those favoring authoritarian forms of government decreased
from one out of twelve in 1953 to one of fifty in 1960. And all the

while there has been a marked increase in identification with the Second German Republic, Germany's second try at democracy — from a bare majority to three-fourths of the West German public. To have rallied these popular majorities to support of democratic government, which at the outset had only been championed by a crusading antifascist minority, surely ranks as the most significant by-product of Adenauer's election campaigns.

The Rise of Chancellor Democracy

Given his initial position as West German Chancellor and party chairman of the CDU, and the electoral landslide of 1953, Konrad Adenauer soon became the pivot in the developing political system of the Federal Republic. Political commentators and critics in press and radio coined the word *Kanzlerdemokratie* to denote what they considered to be an authoritarian, plebiscitarian departure from their own conceptions of democracy. Even members of his own governing coalition began to complain about his evident disregard for their wishes.

As with other fashionable phrases, "Chancellor Democracy" should not be accepted without a careful definition of terms. This is particularly important in this case because many sweeping slogans have been applied to the politics of the Federal Republic: conservative constitutional lawyers still assail the Bonn system as a *Parteienstaat,* a state ruled by political parties; political scientists complain about the *Herrschaft der Verbaende,* the domination by interest groups who are said to control the executive branch and the *Bundestag* alike; some observers claim to perceive a restoration of the "old Nazis" to power; and others insist that Adenauer is the tool either of the churches or of Washington. When all these slogans are taken into account, Chancellor Democracy can hardly be more than a partial explanation of the complex, pluralistic system of political forces that emerged under Adenauer. What the phrase does do is to focus attention on the crafty empire-builder who knew how to pull together all the pluralistic forces into a stable system during a crucial decade of reconstruction. No lesser authority than Winston Churchill has compared Adenauer to Bismarck, another master-builder who managed against improbable odds to bring off German national unifica-

tion, to consolidate the new state by tying its disparate elements together in an ingenious structure, and to prop up his artificial creation
in the international world by a no less ingenious treaty system and by
his skillful diplomacy, the "game of the rolling balls." Adenauer's
Chancellor Democracy should likewise be considered first of all as a
political edifice instead of a deviation from ideal democratic politics
which Germany has never known and certainly never could have
achieved in the early years of the Federal Republic. Defined in this
manner, then, the term Chancellor Democracy becomes politically
neutral and merely describes the complex system of relationships
which Adenauer established and sought to exploit for the purpose of
consolidating the exceedingly weak and unstable body politic. The extent to which he succeeded and the extent to which bad precedents
and undesirable side-effects occurred during this undertaking should
become clear by the end of this chapter.

This consideration begins with Adenauer's foreign policy, which
had importance in his entire post-war career second only to a desire
to consolidate and bring under his political control that accidental
piece of German geography and provisional creation of constitutional
law which was the Federal Republic of 1949. As he confided to a
British journalist in the early 'fifties, he was mortally afraid of a revival of German nationalism, and evidently he felt that a neutral Germany between East and West would always be tempted toward nationalism and power politics. West Germany was set on its present

The voters' image of the Chancellor: Is it to be conservative (Frederick the
Great of Prussia), nationalistic (Bismarck), monarchic (the *Kaiser*),

course by its situation as a divided nation due to the outbreak of the Cold War, and by the strong desire of its Chancellor to see it integrated with other Western European states. The attack of North Korean forces upon South Korea, together with East German rearmament and the presence of Soviet striking forces in Eastern Germany, provided the setting for the agreement between the United States and Adenauer on West German rearmament within the NATO framework. One of the most important "rolling balls" of his entire system was his close relationship to the Eisenhower administration and to the late John Foster Dulles, which he played off against the background of the East-West conflict. He never hesitated to use it as a weapon against critics and opponents at home. When finally the American ball threatened to slip from his hands, he turned to De Gaulle for new reassurances and nearly succeeded in splitting his party into a Gaullist and an Atlanticist faction. All the while, his foreign policy served as the loyalty test and political whip held over the heads of all members of his party and the government coalition, a stifling condition for an intelligent exchange of opinion on foreign policy and, in particular, on approaches and explorations regarding the touchy issue of German reunification.

The second pillar of Chancellor Democracy was the mass of voters who turned out in the elections of 1953 and 1957, as if in plebiscites, to ratify the policies on which Adenauer had embarked and who

authoritarian (Hitler), awe-inspiring (De Gaulle), or youthful and urbane (Kennedy)?

thereby gave him the authority to face down any opposition he might encounter in his party or in the government. Thus, during the 1959 crisis over whether or not he should run for the office of Federal President, he could remind his party in the *Bundestag* that he owed his position to a popular mandate and not to their support. The fact that the national elections became popular votes of confidence for or against Adenauer also did much to sterilize political life by stifling the small parties and attaching to the great opposition party the label of "the eternal nay-sayers." It would be hard to imagine a more effective way of spreading political obscurantism. The landslide elections also produced another unhealthy side-effect, for they brought increased influence to back-benchers who had been elected to office by hanging onto Adenauer's coat-tails and who condoned his arrogant treatment of his own cabinet ministers and other Christian Democratic leaders.

His overwhelming election victories also made it possible for him to put his smaller coalition partners into a crushing embrace. After the 1953 elections, he still took the Refugee Party, the FDP, and the DP into his governing coalition, although the CDU/CSU already commanded a majority of the *Bundestag* seats. For a while, he actually needed the additional votes in order to muster the two-thirds majority necessary for revising the Bonn Constitution. No sooner had the revisions been accomplished than complaints were heard from the Refugee Party and the FDP about his high-handed treatment. A coalition crisis was first precipitated regarding the Refugee Party, then by the FDP, and four years later with regard to the DP, each time with the same result: the small party would be split, its cabinet ministers and their friends persuaded to stay with Adenauer — only to sink into oblivion after the next election — and the rest of the party pushed into opposition.

The FDP is the only party that survived this treatment. In the 1961 elections it inflicted an electoral defeat upon the Old Man, although it failed in its avowed objective of forcing him to retire. Since he had lost his *Bundestag* majority, however, Adenauer was forced to enter another coalition with the FDP and had to accept a coalition contract which obliged him to retire well before the 1965 elections. The FDP used its pivotal position resolutely in the scandal involving the news magazine *Der Spiegel* late in 1962 when it withdrew all of its ministers from the coalition cabinet and threatened to topple the Adenauer government by forming a new coalition with the SPD. When Adenauer finally agreed to drop Defense Minister Strauss (CSU), the instigator of the raid on *Der Spiegel,* another large crack had appeared in the solid edifice of Chancellor Democracy.

A third important element in the structure of Adenauer's power was the constitutional position of his office *vis à vis* the other organs of the government. The framers of the Basic Law had agonized over how relationships among the Chancellor, the cabinet, the Federal President, the *Bundestag,* and the *Bundesrat* could be established so that possible crises, imaginable or otherwise, could be successfully met by the new government. They finally decided on a figurehead President, but they set up a strong Chancellor who would be superior to his ministers and would enjoy special safeguards against the momentary whims or obstructionist coalitions of a *Bundestag* which might reflect the despair and confusion of the masses, as had the *Reichstag* of the early 'thirties. The orthodox parliamentary relationship between *Bundestag* and Chancellor was modified by the famous Article 67, according to which the legislature can overthrow a Chancellor only by a "constructive no-confidence vote," i.e. by mustering a majority for the investiture of his successor. The framers also thought of further provisions that would check the legislative authority of the *Bundestag* with that of the *Bundesrat,* the chamber representing the *Laender* governments, and could even transfer the legislative authority of the directly elected *Bundestag* for an emergency period to the *Bundesrat,* whose *Laender* bureaucrats were believed immune to the passions of the untrustworthy masses and their totalitarian movements. No one could have imagined, with all this carefully considered handiwork of the finest legal minds of post-war Germany, that within four years after the ratification of the Basic Law a crafty master-politician in their midst would use the constitution they had built as a nearly invincible fortress from which to control the executive branch and a majority of the *Bundestag* seats.

Adenauer immediately proceeded to reduce the power of the federal presidency, despite its eminently popular incumbent, Theodor Heuss (FDP), to an absolute minimum and to use the *Land* elections as a vise to put partisan pressure on the guardians of bureaucratic federalism in the *Bundesrat.* The *Bundestag* majority of his own coalition — indeed, the body as a whole — found itself relegated to a rather minor position. It was starved of vital information and hardly allowed to make or even debate important political decisions. It was not surprising that its work increasingly shifted to the committees, where expertise was appreciated and the representatives of interest groups could take a hand in the fashioning of legislative details. Even here the Chancellor increasingly preferred to negotiate directly with organized interests themselves. The provisions of Article 67, together with Adenauer's insistence on party unity and his hostility toward the SPD, put too high a price on any insurrection against his policies. The fawning conduct of the back-benchers who had risen with Adenauer and the long tenure of the Old Man himself also created a sizable bloc of faithful followers who supported practically every move of their idol.

Adenauer's relations to his cabinet ministers, finally, were seemingly patterned on the old city charter of Cologne, which also placed the Lord Mayor above the councillors of the different areas of municipal activity and accorded the latter merely an advisory capacity. Adenauer had no compunction about running the Federal Republic in as authoritarian a manner as he had run the city of Cologne. As soon as he had overcome the considerable resistance of his ministers, he imposed his discipline upon them and used partisan channels to dissuade them from making their own "Sunday speeches" without consulting him. Having broken them of this habit, which is so deeply ingrained in American cabinet officers, he was not prepared to accord them the collective responsibility customary in British cabinet government. In fact, he even took over such cabinet functions as deciding disputes between ministries, which the Basic Law had clearly reserved to the cabinet as a body. Moreover, he employed the State Secretaries of his Chancellery to go over the heads of individual ministers in order to obtain information and to make decisions. In the field of foreign policy, there was such frequent interference with departmental procedures that the Federal Republic could often be said to have more than one foreign policy. Once Adenauer had brought the cabinet under his control, and began to reward obsequious ministers with long tenure, he also tended to enlarge their number considerably so that he could pay off and manipulate the various personalities and factions of his coalition in the *Bundestag*. One of the most telling accounts of the life of a prominent and successful cabinet minister under Adenauer is the fate of Ludwig Erhard, who endured slights and humiliation from the Chancellor for close to a dozen years, ranging from being overruled and not even notified of such actions, or having functions of his ministry carved off and transferred to other ministries, to highhanded arrogance and humiliation in public. Adenauer repeatedly asserted that Erhard lacked the stature and ability to succeed him. Erhard in vain attempted rebellion on several occasions but did not resign nor was he dismissed. In the end, and in spite of everything, he succeeded to the chancellorship for which he had been so patiently waiting.

The last and perhaps most important pillar of Chancellor Democracy was Adenauer's control over his party. It will be remembered that Adenauer never quite subdued the autonomy-minded chiefs of the *Land* parties of the CDU/CSU and that he preferred to center his power on the Chancellor's office instead. On repeated occasions, to be sure, he turned to the party organs for help to enforce his discipline over his ministers or over dissident individuals. He also needed the party to persuade the electorate of the desirability of his policies. But he proved unable to stop changes in the composition of the federal party organs, and found himself faced with a regular coalition of *Land* party chiefs in 1956 which, under the leadership of Joseph Hermann Dufhues of Westphalia, imposed two more unwanted vice-chairmen upon him, *Bundestag* President Eugen Gerstenmaier, and his old labor-wing rival Karl Arnold, who had just lost office as Minister President of North Rhine Westphalia. During the succession crisis of 1959, when Adenauer changed his mind about becoming Federal President upon learning that Erhard would succeed him, the Old Man staved off trouble from the party only by refusing to call the usual quarterly meetings of the Federal Committee of the CDU for a whole year.

The developments in the *Bundestag* CDU/CSU were no less symptomatic of the wax and wane of Adenauer's control over his party. During the first four years of the *Bundestag*, party discipline was quite low and erratic, except on the issues of foreign policy and rearmament, which came to be the battleground of partisan controversy between government and opposition. The wave of new backbenchers swept into the *Bundestag* in 1953 signaled the high point of

Chancellor Democracy, momentarily prolonged by the smaller wave of 1957. By 1958, however, Adenauer's neglect and highhandedness toward his parliamentary party had led to so much restiveness and resentment that bitter clashes began to occur between parliamentary leaders and their Chancellor. As early as 1956, public opinion polls had already shown that a majority of those expressing an opinion would have liked to see Adenauer retire in favor of a younger man after the 1957 elections. Even among Christian Democratic voters one out of four felt this way. When the succession crisis of 1959 broke, majorities of two to one welcomed the Old Man's original decision to become Federal President in the general public as well as among voters of the CDU/CSU. Pluralities of two-fifths of both groups expressed a preference for Erhard as the new Chancellor.

Adenauer's Decline

The parliamentary CDU/CSU took the initiative in the succession crisis, when news leaked out that Adenauer had successfully persuaded Erhard to run for the federal presidency and thus to eliminate himself from the competition for the chancellorship. At this point, the party reacted against the years of humiliation it had suffered at the hands of the 83-year-old Chancellor, who had tenaciously held office with an almost unchanged cabinet. This was first reflected in a strong protest by the *Bundestag* CDU/CSU, which was soon echoed by local party units throughout the land. Erhard withdrew his candidacy for Federal President, and an intensive campaign began throughout the party to persuade Adenauer himself to run for President. The most persuasive argument used for this purpose was that he could continue to direct foreign policy from that vantage point. Adenauer evidently came to accept this line of reasoning and even thought he would be able to nominate his own successor when he announced his candidacy for President in April 1959. The press and the SPD were quick to point out, however, that such changes would do violence to the Bonn Constitution and that they slighted the current Federal President, Theodor Heuss. Some even suggested that Adenauer was trying to imitate the authoritarian De Gaulle Constitution, which had just gone into effect. A bitter internecine struggle ensued between the numerous supporters of Erhard on the one hand and Adenauer, who was trying to promote his Finance Minister Etzel for the chancellorship while at the same time he was increasingly pre-occupied with the critical international developments, mainly the Geneva conference and the new Berlin crisis. The *Bundestag* CDU/CSU was far more worried about the next elections, and the press had all but written off the Old Man. When Adenauer realized in June that he could not stop the parliamentary CDU/CSU from nominating Erhard as Chancellor, he suddenly withdrew his candidacy for Federal President and announced that he would remain Chancellor until further notice. In the resulting uproar in the *Bundestag* CDU/CSU, Adenauer calmly suggested that his critics try to remove him from office with a "constructive no-confidence" vote. They shied away from that step but were more resentful than ever. So, Heinrich Luebke (CDU) was eventually elected Federal President.

Chancellor Democracy had held fast once more, thought it was a Pyrrhic victory. Public opinion polls showed the reaction of the public to this amazing turn-about. Two of every three persons polled thought Adenauer's change of mind a bad decision, including one out of three Christian Democratic voters; half of the latter and three-fourths of the general public expressing an opinion felt it did not reflect well on him. Worst of all, four people out of every seven thought the CDU should have removed him, and four out of five refused to accept his contention that Erhard lacked experience in foreign policy and did not have the qualities for leadership.

And thus Chancellor Democracy drifted toward an inevitable end, though four years more were to go by before its final collapse. The bitterness of 1959 lingered on in the CDU/CSU, where an internal opposition, the *fronde*, formed around Erhard, Gerstenmaier, and the Hamburg deputies Blumenfeld and Buccrius, the publisher of the prestigious weekly *Die Zeit*. At the height of the 1961 election campaign, when the Old Man appeared to falter, the *fronde* openly attacked him and began to campaign for Erhard, with the support of many a *Land* party chief, who felt the electoral majorities of the CDU/CSU slipping away. Franz Josef Strauss, the chairman of the Bavarian CSU, threw his energies into the advancement of Erhard in the hope, as the newspapers claimed, of succeeding him eventually in the chancellorship. Erich Mende, the chairman of the FDP, campaigned on the slogan "no more monopoly" of Adenauer and his

The little domestic tyrant: "I don't wanta go to bed yet!"

CDU, and he had a secret understanding with the Erhard camp that the FDP would do what no one else cared to do: play Brutus to the aging Caesar.

When the 85-year-old Chancellor faced his Party Executive Board in 1961 two days after his party had lost its electoral majority, the end seemed to be near. Yet before the week was over, gasps of uncomprehending protest could be heard throughout the editorial offices of the German press. Cartoons appeared depicting Adenauer as a naughty child who refuses to go to bed. Newspaper editors wrote the letter of resignation he should have written, and *Der Spiegel* sighed editorially: "Why won't he quit while we still respect him?" But it was to no avail — six weeks later, Adenauer had once more been elected

Chancellor by the *Bundestag* for at least two more years. To understand this startling turn of events, we have to examine two further aspects of the edifice of Chancellor Democracy. For they allowed its
architect to stave off his final demise.

To explain the collapse of FDP opposition to Adenauer, one has to
be aware of the basic constellation of organized interests which developed under the Adenauer administration: Western Germany today,
after years of intensive development, is a small and economically and
socially unified country whose "new society" facilitated the rise of a
great combine of interest groups with access to the governing coalition. The bulk of these groups — industry, big and small business,
and agriculture — has traditionally supported the FDP only on condition that it remain with the CDU/CSU. In the 1957 elections, when
the FDP asserted its independence and availability for a coalition
with the SPD, it was brought to the edge of financial and electoral
ruin. In the post-election struggle of 1961, Adenauer only had to hint
at a coalition of CDU/CSU and SPD if the FDP insisted on holding
out against him, and Mende's resistance yielded.

As for Adenauer's victory over the *fronde* within his party, one
needs to recall the pluralistic structure of the CDU/CSU, which is
composed not only of *Land* parties but also of fairly cohesive functional groups such as the labor-oriented Social Policy Committees,
the agricultural, small business, handicraft, industry, refugee, youth,
and other organizations within the party. In the critical moments after
the 1961 elections, Adenauer managed to mobilize the entire labor
wing against Erhard's candidacy as a threat to Christian social policy.
The protectionistic interests of West German big business and the
farm, handicraft, and small business interests always had misgivings
about Erhard's championing of anti-cartel measures and "excessive"
economic competition. The Old Man also conjured up once more the
specter of an impending foreign policy crisis, presumably an understanding between the United States and the Soviet Union at Germany's expense. As a result of these group pressures, Strauss proved
unable to deliver the votes of the CSU deputies in the *Bundestag* to
Erhard's cause. Sensing a similar loss of support everywhere, Erhard
once more decided to wait. The frustration inside of the CDU/CSU
and the FDP was reflected by the number of coalition members who
voted against Adenauer or abstained from voting when he was finally
installed for a fourth term. He received a *Bundestag* majority of only

eight votes. Forty-nine deputies, roughly divided in equal numbers between the CDU, the CSU, and the FDP, broke party discipline and
failed to support him — the largest opposition ever from within the
coalition to his leadership.

In joining the coalition, the FDP at least scored what appeared at
the time to be a paper victory: a coalition contract was drawn up and
signed by the two parties which specified that the Old Man would
step down in time to give his successor a chance to establish himself

The West German government — still going strong

in office before the 1965 elections. It also contained a clause barring
any part of the coalition parties from voting with the opposition, as
the FDP feared the CDU/CSU labor wing might do. There was no
lack of derisive comments about reliance on "a scrap of paper," and
by March 1963, *Der Spiegel* counted no less than eleven instances
within eighteen months when either the FDP or the CDU/CSU had

indeed bolted the coalition and voted or negotiated with the SPD.

But while the coalition contract might lack the power to compel, the FDP was in a key position to enforce its will upon the CDU/ CSU. Its best opportunity to assert itself arose during the *Der Spiegel* affair late in 1962, when Defense Minister Strauss ordered a raid on the magazine and the arrest of its editors on charges of obtaining and publishing classified defense material. Joining the uproar in the German press and in opposition circles, the FDP threatened to topple the government by withdrawing its support unless Strauss was dismissed and Adenauer reaffirmed his pledge to step down in another year. The SPD added its voice to the demand for ousting Strauss. When the FDP turned out to be stubborn in the face of various diversionary maneuvers, including a threat to form an SPD-CDU/CSU coalition and to change the electoral law to ruin the FDP, the entire cabinet finally resigned and was reconstituted without Strauss and a few other ministers. There could be little doubt that the FDP was able and willing to accord the same treatment to Adenauer himself should occasion demand it. In anticipation of a final showdown, the Old Man began to court the friendship of the SPD, but the *Spiegel* affair had already convinced a great many more of his own party members of the fact that his own refusal to resign was becoming more of a liability every day.

The first sign of the final decline of the 87-year-old Chancellor was his inability to stop his Foreign Minister Gerhard Schroeder and a substantial faction within the CDU/CSU from pursuing their own foreign policy. Faced with President De Gaulle's surprise move to shut out Great Britain from membership in the Common Market, Adenauer had seen the edifice of his international grand strategy beginning to crumble. Never particularly fond of the British and suspicious of American agreement with the Soviet Union, he moved to shore up his disintegrating system with a reaffirmation of Franco-German friendship in a declaratory treaty. But his magic spell over the CDU/CSU no longer worked. The CDU caucus chairman of the *Bundestag,* von Brentano, whose career as Foreign Minister Adenauer had practically stifled, now strove to pick out a course which would spare West Germany the need to choose between France and the United States. While Adenauer was away on vacation, he added a pro-American preamble to the laws implementing the Franco-

German treaty. Foreign Minister Schroeder, who had studied at the University of Edinburgh and emulates in his conduct and dress the model of the British "gentleman-politician," proceeded to chart what is likely to be the future foreign policy course of the Federal Republic: toning down the Gaullist orientation in favor of co-operation with Great Britain and the United States; reaching an agreement with the Eastern European countries about the price for the final cession of the areas beyond the Oder-Neisse Line; and taking part in the relaxation of tensions between East and West. The old Chancellor, who had once used his foreign policy line as a loyalty test for and whip over his own party, stood by in impotent anger, unable to prevent the "softening" of his hard line.

The final showdown came in March and April of 1963, amid continued press hostility and rumors of an attempt by an SPD-FDP coalition to replace Adenauer with the Anglophile Erhard. Adenauer's friends still carried out diversionary maneuvers, such as a plan to postpone the Old Man's resignation until the fall of 1964, by which time the federal presidency would have become available once more for Erhard, and Schroeder could be Chancellor with von Brentano as his Foreign Minister. The Chancellor's State Secretary Hans Globke, of all people, proposed a plan to keep Erhard under control, if it should be impossible to block him from the Chancellor's office: he should be made to agree not to succeed himself after the 1965 election, leave his ministerial staff advisers behind in the Economics Ministry, and give the cabinet control over determining the guidelines of his governmental policy, despite the fact that the Bonn Constitution expressly grants this privilege to the Chancellor. Adenauer himself continued his efforts to embarrass Erhard and to mobilize opposition to him. At one point he spread the rumor that Erhard was about to become President of the Common Market Commission in Brussels. He also produced medical reports on his own excellent state of health, and confided to reporters that, if only there were an election held now, he would show his mettle to his own party. Ironically, it was precisely the threat of elections which prompted the CDU/CSU to force the final showdown.

The 1962 *Land* elections of Hesse already indicated the public reaction to the *Spiegel* affair: cover pictures of the news-magazine's issue on Strauss were found pasted over CDU election posters, and the hostile press reports and the questions at political rallies seemed never ending. Early in 1963, the *Land* elections in West Berlin and in the Rhineland Palatinate proved to be severe setbacks to the CDU, and the *Land* parties of these states immediately attributed this to the unresolved leadership crisis in Bonn. The *Land* party of Lower Saxony and its representatives in Bonn trembled at the thought of what might happen at the impending May elections, if Adenauer had not resigned by then in favor of Erhard. As pressure within the party began to build up, *Bundestag* President Gerstenmaier successfully moved a resolution in the CDU/CSU caucus which laid down (1) that Adenauer would resign by the fall of 1963; (2) that it was up to the caucus and its chairman von Brentano to select the new Chancellor; and (3) that the chosen candidate should be presented to the public before the summer recess. Von Brentano also enjoined Adenauer from attacking and intriguing against Erhard, who was known to be favored by 40 to 50 per cent of the electorate, ahead of Schroeder, with about 12 to 15 per cent. Schroeder was content with awaiting his chance later, and even Adenauer's long-time trusted ally Heinrich Krone began to urge the Old Man to see the light. Now Joseph Dufhues, the executive director of the extra-parliamentary party, canvassed all the *Land* parties except the Rhineland CDU and ascertained their support for an immediate decision in favor of Erhard; the Rhineland CDU still had hopes for Schroeder. Then Dufhues, von Brentano, and Kurt Schmuecker, the spokesman for the jittery Lower Saxonians, confronted Adenauer in a three-hour session of the executive board of the CDU/CSU caucus in the *Bundestag* and demanded the immediate choice of a successor. They left no doubt as to who that should be. For the first time in his long political career, the octogenarian did not have the strength to "out-sit" or out-talk his opponents. The following day before the entire caucus meeting, he tried to fight back once more. But the CDU/CSU caucus went ahead and elected Erhard as his successor for the following October with a vote of 159 against 47 and 19 abstentions. Thus Chancellor Democracy was dead, never to rise again.

The months until his final retirement passed slowly for the Old Man. He still went to Lower Saxony for the election campaign, where he carefully avoided appearing together with his successor and where he displayed ill humor toward well-wishers. Lonesome at party

gatherings, he watched the haggling over positions in Erhard's cabinet, and with sadness saw the never-ending stream of visitors to Erhard's summer home on the Tegernsee — as they had once come to
his own vacation retreat at Cadenabbia on Lake Como. Yet it was
unlikely that Konrad Adenauer would sulk for very long. By September he had already become reconciled enough to the new Chancellor,
against whom he had fought for so long, to caution him against
premature commitments to office seekers or to the demands of
organized interests. On October 15 he tendered his resignation. When
Erhard was installed as the new Chancellor, with 279 votes and 24
abstentions out of 499, Adenauer made a point of voting for him and
proclaiming himself a friend of Erhard. Even in private, he was said
to show no signs of bitterness or ridicule toward his successor.

There had been speculation in the press and among Christian
Democrats as early as 1961 and especially in the months before Adenauer's downfall as to what he might do after his resignation. Should
he become a federal minister without portfolio, a parliamentary
party leader, or an obnoxious back-bencher venting his spleen on his
successor, or should he turn his energy and abilities to renovating the
extra-parliamentary party organization whose chairman he still was?
There was hardly a chance of his being included in the Erhard cabinet or of being elected caucus chairman after he fought so long and
so hard against his own demise. But he has become an influential
spokesman of the Gaullist wing of his party on the floor of the
Bundestag and has acted as elder statesman and oracle at official
party gatherings.

More significant is Adenauer's interest in the party organization.
To the dismay of Dufhues, who passed up a cabinet post in order to
become executive director and reorganizer of the CDU, Adenauer
showed increasing interest in party reform at the same time that he
reconciled himself to losing the chancellorship. At first his critical attacks on Dufhues were rejected by a unanimous Party Executive
Board, which pointed out to the Old Man that the poor state of the
party organization was due to a dozen years of neglect by the party
chairman himself — Konrad Adenauer. But soon Adenauer's acceptance of Erhard improved his position in party councils, and Dufhues,
who would really have preferred to keep government and party separate, began to promote Erhard as the new party chairman. Erhard,

however, showed no interest in becoming party leader, and Dufhues himself stood little chance of beating Adenauer, who evidently wished to be re-elected for an eighth term as party chairman. Adenauer's chief motive for seeking this new career at the age of 88 appeared to be his desire to advance a Gaullist foreign policy. Dufhues had disappointed some of his supporters when he proved unable to centralize the party organization against the stubborn resistance of autonomy-conscious *Land,* and even county, organizations within the party, but also because of the recurrent crises over the succession to the chancellorship. Now that he was finally making headway on a membership drive planned since 1961 and on other party reforms, he could not but blanch at the thought of the Old Man's comeback.

In March 1964, the CDU convention at Hannover re-elected Adenauer party chairman with a handsome majority, though not without some challenge from Gerstenmaier and many lesser lights. And while the press watched in amazement and speculated whether the Old Man would ever find time for his memoirs, tempers flared between two of the members of the troika now guiding the CDU/CSU: Adenauer refused to accept the congratulations offered by Dufhues, who vowed in turn to conduct the election campaign of 1965 without the Old Man. The assertion of leadership over the party by the third member of the uneasy troika, Erhard, is contingent on his winning a resounding victory in the 1965 elections. However, it may yet be some time before the Old Man says goodbye to politics.

Erhard, Adenauer, and German Democracy

No sooner had Ludwig Erhard received the endorsement of the CDU/CSU *Bundestag* than he flung himself into activities designed to project his image as the next West German Chancellor, although his installment in office was still half a year away. He set forth three principal guidelines of his policy which were evidently a reaction to public criticisms of Adenauer. First and foremost, he would democratize the chancellorship by putting an end to "lonely decisions" and recriminations against rivals and opponents. This desire to act by the rules of constitutional democracy is held deeply and genuinely by Erhard and his followers, who regard the *Spiegel* affair with a righteous anger which promises scrupulous observance of democratic methods in the future. He also promised to pay more attention to domestic affairs, and, thirdly, vowed to place as much or more stress on the Anglo-American ties of the Federal Republic as on those with France.

The public reaction to Erhard's final ascent to power casts an illuminating light on the forces he represents. Back in the years from 1951 to 1956 he rose in public acceptance from one out of four persons polled who expressed an opinion to five out of six. His growth in favor did not fully coincide with the greater acceptance of free enterprise over economic planning, for it only changed from three out of seven in 1951 to somewhat better than two out of three in 1963. Three-fifths of the public preferred him now as Chancellor, but they were split right down the middle on the question of whether or not he should continue Adenauer's policies. CDU/CSU supporters felt by margins of four to one that he should; FDP adherents split; while those identifying with the SPD preferred by three to one that he should not. More specifically, Erhard's stress on democratization enjoyed substantial support among the FDP and SPD supporters, but less among adherents of his own party. His pro-British policy enjoyed little support among CDU/CSU supporters and only a little more in the SPD and FDP electorate, whereas Schroeder's policy of a rapprochement with the Eastern European countries enjoyed very substantial backing in the CDU/CSU and majorities among SPD and FDP adherents. Finally, similarly strong hopes were expressed on all sides that under Erhard the two major parties would co-operate better.

Immediately after his endorsement, Erhard made three early triumphs in rapid succession: he plunged into the bitter labor dispute of the metal workers, gambling his reputation on his ability to settle a major strike, a risk that no other politician and least of all Adenauer would have taken. Erhard won his gamble and went on to score a minor triumph in the tariff negotiations of the General Agreement on Tariffs and Trade (GATT). Finally, he went to Lower Saxony to campaign with great zest in the *Land* elections. He succeeded in reversing the series of losses of the CDU/CSU. The party was delighted, and observers in the press reflected somewhat fatuously on the whirlwind of youth which the 67-year-old Erhard had introduced into a tired party led so far by an octogenarian.

Erhard's exuberant early start may well characterize the great difference in style and temperament between him and his predecessor. As short and rotund as the Old Man is tall and haggard, Ludwig Erhard loves action, drama, and resounding phrases. The sparse phrase, the calculation, and the peculiar technique of letting things develop before taking action which were so typical of Adenauer are alien to his successor. His boundless optimism in economics is based on a deep and somewhat romantic faith in a pre-established harmony of economic relationships, an economic *ordre naturel* of eighteenth-century vintage which may require guidance and occasional intervention but certainly not planning. Erhard has a similar faith in human nature. Were he an American, he would probably be a back-slapping glad-hander who likes everybody and is equally well-liked in return. Being a part of the German intellectual establishment, however, he appears to be naïve because of his democratic faith in people and his romantic tastes in music and things intellectual. Despite his own detachment from the world of German intellect, Adenauer clearly sensed this weakness in his rival and proceeded to puncture it with rapier-like tongue. His repeated argument that Erhard lacked political instinct and a feeling for the machinations of international power politics could not but impress a sophisticated audience. When asked whether they considered it to his credit that Adenauer always got his way, majorities of West Germans said yes. A substantial segment of German intellectuals used to despise Adenauer as "an intellectual primitive," but they increasingly admire his sense for the political jugular and for *Realpolitik,* in contrast to Erhard's abiding faith in the common man and dislike of cynicism and morbidity, which they do not share. Adenauer's treatment of Erhard undoubtedly contributed to the subtle undermining of the authority of the man who believed in fairness and in turning the other cheek. On the other hand, one should note that large numbers of West Germans who continued to support him through the early 'sixties motivated their preference by saying that he was "decent, *sympathisch,* and no pushy power type."

Born in 1897 in Fuerth, in the heart of Franconia, Ludwig Erhard is the son of a small textile merchant. Unlike Adenauer, who never wore a uniform in his life, Erhard was scarred by severe injuries in World War I, a bitter memento of Germany's violent past. But his career did not suffer, as he pursued a university education in Frankfurt and broke into print with articles about the economic background of the German right wing in the declining years of the Weimar Republic. Hitler's ascent to power made it impossible for Erhard to teach at a university, but it did not bar him from carrying on economic research and publishing a journal of market research. His present opponents have pored over back issues of this journal in an unsuccessful search for Nazi influences. In 1942, he was dismissed by the Nazis from his post at the Institute of Economic Studies in Nuremberg. Two years later he contributed a plan for the post-war economic reconstruction of Germany to the German resistance to Hitler. The plan was gratefully acknowledged, and Goerdeler, one of the resistance leaders who was jailed after the abortive attempt on Hitler's life on July 20, 1944, still smuggled a message to his friends outside before his execution, in which he urged them to seek Erhard's advice on economic matters. During the last year of the war Erhard continued to ponder post-war reconstruction with the Munich economist Adolf Weber and his friends. The American occupation also received a reconstruction plan from Erhard and probably regarded it as just as unrealistically "liberal" as had the cartel-minded economists of Weimar, the Nazis, and the SPD leader Kurt Schumacher, who called Erhard contemptuously "a propaganda balloon of German entrepreneurs inflated with the foul gases of decaying classical liberalism." But Erhard went on to become Bavarian Economics Minister, still without a party label, and then Economics Director of the Bizonal Administration. There he joined the CDU and began his great attempt to bring real capitalism to Germany, persuading the CDU/CSU too to gamble on what seemed at that moment an extremely risky policy.

In those early post-war years, the peculiar relationship of Professor Erhard to administrative work and to politics began to appear. Impatient with the slow processes of administration and uncomfortable with bureaucratic hierarchies, he is a very different man from Adenauer, the burgomaster, whose style of politics has often been called quasi-administrative or quasi-bureaucratic. Adenauer's manner of leadership would have to be depicted in the form of complex organizational diagrams. Erhard's approach, on the other hand, is rather that of the brilliant inventor or philosopher king who catches a glimpse of the real nature of things and then uses all his powers of persuasion in the market place to sway men's minds in the right direction. For a while he was even planning to set up a brain trust after the model of President Kennedy. Persuasion, or the authority of presenting the right solution to a problem, as Erhard has countered Adenauer's gibes, is of a higher order than political pressure or administrative compulsion: "Power is always barren, dangerous, brutal and, in the last analysis, stupid." There is in his attitude at least a hint of the old intellectual and liberal disdain for the *Machtstaat,* the state of power politics. Having created the right social and economic order and having called upon the civic consciousness (*Staatsgesinnung*) of "the German people," Chancellor Erhard feels he has laid the foundations for happiness within and for peaceful policies without.

In keeping with this approach to politics, Erhard has given a clear indication of how he intends to carry on his office. Unlike Adenauer, who never gave up his rather unsuccessful wooing of the party organization of the CDU/CSU, his successor turned down the opportunity to become party chairman from the beginning — although he did take the trouble to make an appeal for party unity to the Rhineland CDU after his inauguration. Never given much to political maneuvers or wire-pulling he seems to prefer to be a *Volkskanzler,* a "people's Chancellor" whose authority is derived chiefly from his popularity with the electorate. Unlike the all-embracing edifice of Chancellor Democracy, Erhard's design would stress the latent plebiscitary features of the American presidency in the Bonn Constitution rather than those of a British-style cabinet linked indissolubly with the majority party. The party or governing coalition in the *Bundestag* and outside would constitute the Congress-like sounding board and sooner or later an effective check on the power of the Chancellor. While it may still be too early to generalize, Erhard's first steps as the new West German Chancellor lend some credence to this view: despite early efforts to hem in his authority between the established positions of power held by the many ministers remaining from Adenauer's last cabinet, power immediately began to gravitate toward him. He took firm control, detaching himself equally from the CDU/CSU in the *Bundestag* and from the extra-parliamentary party, making it clear that he owed no debt nor was dependent on anyone. His relation to the restless partner of the coalition, the FDP, has been cordial but aloof. And he has gone out of his way to court the approval of the Social Democratic opposition, which cheered his inauguration and first declaration of policy as much as his own party did. There had already been a growing feeling of solidarity and fellowship between the SPD and the government parties since the succession crisis of 1959 and the SPD change of policy during the same year. Now that Erhard praised opposition leaders and paid tribute to the vital role of a "loyal opposition," it took little imagination to sense the possible emergence of a new political pattern, characterized, perhaps, by bipartisanship in foreign policy, defense, and certain other lines of policy, and by the entire *Bundestag* — CDU/CSU, SPD, and FDP — as a quasi-Congress facing the quasi-President, Ludwig Erhard, the steward of the German people. Less than fifty years ago, the famous sociologist Max Weber expressed the hope that a President fashioned after the American model would stabilize the new Weimar Republic. The theory behind this plebiscitary executive would be the precedent for what Chancellor Erhard appears to have in mind. Most prominent party politicians of the three major parties and opinion leaders in the press and the business world, however, take a dim view of Erhard's *Volkskanzler* idea. They prefer a British-style parliamentary executive wedded to the leadership of the majority party or coalition of parties.

This analysis of the practical import of the changing of the guard in the Chancellor's office must stand in the shadow of the question whether Erhard's leadership will mean a more democratic Germany. This question could easily be answered in the affirmative, but such an answer would cater to the overwhelming desire of many people to look for a rationalization of what they are already inclined to believe. Let us briefly examine the fourteen years of Adenauer's rule in the light of the criticisms advanced and make an attempt to reach a fair and balanced judgment about the man and his accomplishments.

It has been said of Bismarck, and now also of Adenauer, that they vitiated their great merits by failing to teach their people democracy. Needless to emphasize, it takes an astonishing depth of paternalistic conviction to expect the strong-willed East Elbian *Junker* to have had even the slightest desire to teach anyone democracy, considering that he did not believe in it himself. What emerges from history is that Bismarck satisfied the deep craving of the bourgeoisie for national unification at the same time that he erected an invincible fortress of privilege for the monarchs and aristocrats of Imperial Germany. The fault hardly lies with Bismarck, whose predilections were in accord with much of the sentiment of his age; rather, it should be sought with the popular forces and politicians succeeding him, who indulged in worshipping the Iron Chancellor and in their own militaristic and imperialistic fantasies, instead of devoting their energies to updating the increasingly anachronistic political system and its burgeoning social tensions. Measured by the shifting standard of timeliness, Bismarck's system was quite appropriate for, perhaps, the first fifteen years of his rule. After that and in the following thirty years, it turned more and more into a menace to Germany and to the rest of the world, a menace that was finally turned loose for the thirty years' war of 1914 to 1945.

Adenauer's task was somewhat different, though just as limited in its time as that of Bismarck: he had to breathe political life into the totally defeated and sequestered body politic which had just been torn into an eastern and a western half, with the latter in limbo between the attraction of reunification and the fear of a Communist take-over. He also had to crank up and keep going a democratic machine which had until 1949 derived its strength solely from Allied tutelage and a dedicated band of anti-fascist leaders such as himself. This involved his wrestling not only with economic misery, but with an electorate that was not much less obstreperous than that of the Weimar Republic. It included such menacing dragons as the ten million expellees and refugees, a potential hotbed of irredentism, several million resentful ex-Nazis and former military men, two million unemployed among the legions of social welfare claimants, businessmen, and farmers who had once set their bets on Hitler, and substantial numbers of convinced Communists and neo-Nazis, all of whom had to be bribed, cajoled, or out-maneuvered in order to consolidate the body politic into the reasonably happy, prosperous, and democratic state which the Federal Republic is today.

To appreciate the political vacuum of 1949, we must recall the choice of approach decided on by Kurt Schumacher and the SPD in those days. On the basis of the Weimar experience and of a well-considered analysis of the snake-pit of potentially undemocratic groups enumerated above, the Social Democratic leadership had de-

cided to place its emphasis on a nationalistic appeal. With all due respect to the staunch democratic sentiments that have always characterized the SPD, we must remain skeptical of what was likely to result
from adding the fuel of nationalism to the embers of ex-Nazi frustration and expellee bitterness. It did take considerable courage in the
early years of the Federal Republic to steer a pro-European and pro-
Western course, and in 1953 it was not at all a foregone conclusion
that voters could be successfully rallied to this policy. In fact, according to the public opinion polls, earlier in the same year the SPD
was actually ahead in the polls. Not of the least importance, of
course, were the diplomatic efforts of Adenauer to bring about European integration and to tie Western Germany to the Western alliance. These policies had strong popular backing and did as much as
any policies of the Federal Republic to break the fateful chain of
Western rejection and German nationalistic resentment which has led
modern Germany from disaster to disaster. Having moved his country out of the European dog-house, he also gave it back its self-
respect and greatly strengthened his image at home as a leader with
international prestige. This resurgence, as well as the rise of prosperity, were the very last thing Germans had expected to see such a short
time after their total defeat and devastation in 1945.

Viewing the task before Adenauer in the early years of the Federal
Republic, only an exceedingly biased observer can deny that it was
formidable and that the Old Man solved it beyond the wildest expectations. It is, of course, not impossible that someone else might have
succeeded as well, but none of the available leaders appears to have
been even close to possessing the necessary political and diplomatic
skill. Ludwig Erhard, in particular, who today may be the democratic
champion of the hour to a higher degree than his predecessor, would
not have been equal to the task of 1949 to 1953.

This brings us to the question of whether the creation of the powerful combine of Chancellor Democracy was detrimental to the development of West German democracy, as has often been claimed by
neutral observers as well as opponents. The seeds of Chancellor Democracy were sown in the early period of the Federal Republic with
the avowed aim of building an impenetrable fortress against the expected onslaught of undemocratic forces. As it developed, the building of the fort for the defense of democracy succeeded a little too

well. The hostile onslaught never materialized, and Adenauer suddenly found himself without a serious rival or force to challenge his enormous power. Whenever power is accumulated to such an extent and without any check, abuses develop. Chancellor Democracy at its crest was no exception, although too much is made, perhaps, both of Adenauer's autocratic streak and of the alleged personality cult of his supporters.

His personal authoritarian attitude, apart from what one would expect of a person born in the *Kaiser's* Germany *anno* 1876, has often been exaggerated. A true authoritarian personality could not operate effectively as a politician in securing the co-operation of his followers, unless, like Hitler, he was dealing with disturbed minds. It is true that Adenauer could be ruthless on occasion and that he asserted his power without hesitation once he had it in his control. It is also true that his Catholic background gave him a greater appreciation for the role of authority in society and more of an instinct for the realities of power than Ludwig Erhard, the Protestant, appears to possess. But these qualities were essential to Adenauer's success in the early years of the Federal Republic. They become obnoxious only when Chancellor Democracy turned out to have created a giant without a rival. There is, moreover, poetic justice in observing the recurrent clashes between the Gaullist wing, led by Franz Josef Strauss, and the Protestant phalanx of Schroeder, von Hassel, Gerstenmaier, and Erhard who are guiding the Federal Republic today. Strauss, who was re-elected chairman of the Bavarian CSU at the stormy, demagogic 1963 *Land* convention, presents a caricature of the very authoritarianism of Catholic countries of which Adenauer has, unjustly, been accused. The Protestant CDU leaders, on the other hand, represent a kind of democratic conscience of the party which has frequently protested against abuses of power and kept alive a spirit of decency and fairness. If it was typical of Chancellor Democracy that a Strauss could rise, it was also typical that it nurtured a democratic response in his party and in the public that finally overthrew him and caused Adenauer to step down.

As for Adenauer's alleged charismatic qualities or the cult of popular hero worship surrounding him, one can compare the political developments with the results of opinion polls which contradict the popular idea that Adenauer was just another "strong man" to the supposedly strongman-happy Germans. In fact, it would be more correct to say that Adenauer's political rise as a vote-getter and the rise of his image as a historical figure took place separately and even at different times. Although Adenauer has never been such a dynamic, eloquent speechmaker as his successor, his early rise was promoted greatly by the bitter public rivalry between him and Kurt Schumacher. Until the death of Schumacher in 1952, these two came to monopolize the attention of the political public to the exclusion of any other figure. At that time Adenauer was mentioned as the "most capable German politician today" by only a third of the public polled. During the CDU/CSU election campaign of 1953, the emphasis on the achievements of his administration and on his person helped to bolster his popularity to a clear majority of three-fifths, with men still outnumbering his numerous women supporters by a considerable margin. During the years 1953 to 1955, his supporters named in particular his part in the re-establishment of Germany's international reputation, his efforts to provide security against the East, and his economic policies as their reasons for supporting him. At the same time, there arose a chorus of criticism, namely that he was getting too autocratic or that he did not care enough for the economic interests of the man in the street. A large majority was against making him Commander-in-Chief of the armed forces. The public also thought it good that Adenauer and Schumacher's successor, Ollenhauer, almost always disagreed. Significant numbers said they would feel dislike for his face if they did not know who he was, and no more than one out of ten considered him kind-hearted or a genius. All this was hardly the language of hero worship.

Beginning late in 1955, his political popularity began to decline and fell below 50 per cent by election time of 1957, when his party won a majority of the popular vote for "Adenauer and the team." There were recurrent majority opinions voiced to the effect that he was getting too old and losing his grip on power. The public evidently hoped for another Chancellor after the 1957 elections. The succession crisis of 1959 finally made his popularity plunge to the 1951 level, where he was overtaken in turn by Theodor Heuss, Erhard, and Willy Brandt.

While majorities of West Germans were no longer willing to call Adenauer the "most capable German politician today," however, their esteem for the Old Man as a historical figure rose to remarkable heights. In 1952, when one-third of the respondents had named him the "most capable politician," only 3 per cent considered him "the great German who has done most for Germany." In the same poll, Hitler received three times as many votes and Bismarck twelve times as many as Adenauer. After the 1953 elections, he barely caught up with Hitler, but still received only one-fifth of his accolade as the "most capable politician" of the Federal Republic. Even at the height of his political popularity, in 1955, only one-fourth of his political admirers placed him on top as a historical figure and Bismarck still outpolled him two to one. It was not until 1958, after his political career had entered its decline, that one-fourth of his countrymen considered him the greatest historical figure, a few more than admired Bismarck most, and a majority considered him "one of the really great men of our century." By this time, the critics of the 82-year-old Adenauer had begun to refer to him in jest as "the monument." Their efforts during the following year to make Adenauer run for the figurehead presidency could be interpreted as an attempt to induce him to retire from his political career to the pedestal of his historical image.

Yet, to come back to our initial question, we still have not clarified Adenauer's contribution or lack of a contribution to Germany's education in democracy. Is it true, as Dean Acheson put it in a last tribute to the Old Man, that "the Adenauer years were years of education" that changed the German people? The answer would seem to hinge upon one's conception of how and whether democracy can actually be taught. German intellectuals criticize Adenauer for having been a bad schoolmaster who never bothered to explain anything and gave some notably bad examples to his rather dense schoolchildren. But the man in the street knows a different story. He measures a regime by its success, and in his understanding the Adenauer years demonstrated beyond a doubt that democracy can be eminently successful in every way. He also thinks of it in terms of how well off he is under it: two-thirds of the West German public say today that the country never had it better. And he learns democratic politics not from theoretical treatises, but by practical involvement. Every election campaign teaches him more about the process than all the civics courses in school were ever able to.

There can hardly be a more fitting tribute to what Adenauer has done for German democracy than the comments of the leaders of the Social Democratic opposition. "Adenauer contributed a good deal to the stabilization of our democratic system," Willy Brandt remarked on an American television program. Herbert Wehner, another prominent SPD leader, was more specific in an interview about the "craftiest, most unscrupulous politician of our time" with a reporter of *Der Spiegel*. Wehner felt that Adenauer's consolidation of West German politics was not a "restoration" of the old ruling circles. Adenauer and his great popular rally had done the SPD a great service by forcing it out of its working-class mold into a similar attempt at rallying support regardless of class lines and social divisions. The trouble with the Weimar Republic was the lack of a democratic society to go with the democratic Weimar Constitution. The feudal and authoritarian forces of Weimar society had been so strong that they had intensified the misery and hostility of the workers. But Adenauer's Federal Republic was different, and despite occasional disagreements the SPD was unflinchingly committed to its democratic framework and to the ground rules of political competition. After all, Wehner felt, *"Es haette viel schlimmer kommen koennen,"* things could have become so much worse than they were under Adenauer.

"Opposition, to quote my Italian friend Manzoni, is the art of sawing off the branch on which the government is sitting in such a way that you can sit on it yourself."

Fritz Erler (SPD) before the *Bundestag* in 1961

9

THE OPPOSITION IN THE WINGS

For a properly functioning constitutional democracy there must be not only capable and honest leadership but an equally capable and honest opposition which offers constructive criticism and alternatives to government policy and stands prepared to take over the reins of government. Yet there can be an excess of opposition, both in numbers and in degree. The Weimar Republic had a majority hostile to its democratic constitution almost from the beginning, and in July 1932 it faced a combined majority of Communist and Nazi voters which effectively frustrated the attempt to continue a democratic government. The Bonn Republic has been fortunate in not having to withstand a similar onslaught of either reactionary opponents of democracy or totalitarian fanatics bent on establishing a dictatorship. The Bonn Constitution and democratic government enjoy the support of all the major political and social forces, and there is no socially or intellectually respectable opposition to democracy as there was in Weimar days. While there is a "loyal opposition" embodied in several parties, the "disloyal opposition" of Weimar memory presents no threat.

In the early post-war period, however, this safety of a democratic consensus was by no means clear. The Communist Party (KPD) had been readmitted by the Allied occupation after the war and was polling 10 to 15 per cent of the vote as before 1933. Nazi sentiment and political activity seemed subdued mainly because of the presence of the Allies and their policy of denazification. The anti-fascist German post-war leadership had every reason to tremble before a possible resurgence of nationalism or totalitarian utopianism among the German masses, who for twelve years had been immersed in Nazi propaganda. The ten million eastern expellees and refugees, nearly one of every four West Germans, were regarded with particular suspicion, and, in fact, they were barred from political activity by the Allied occupation. What would happen to the frail sprout of German post-war democracy once the Allied occupation turned the government over to the Germans? Could the handful of democratic leaders maintain democracy during years of economic misery and unemployment?

The framers of the Bonn Constitution and of the electoral laws for the federal elections tried to anticipate some of the most obvious emergencies that might arise. They empowered the Federal Constitutional Court to outlaw subversive, anti-democratic parties and movements. The electoral law, moreover, set up special rules to discourage the formation of splinter groups in the hope, thereby, of consolidating the power of the large, established parties and to make the rise of new groups difficult. For this purpose, the electoral law of 1949 demanded that a party receive at least 5 per cent of the second ballots in one *Land* or a plurality of the first ballots in at least one electoral district before it could be represented in the *Bundestag*. In 1953, the electoral law demanded that the 5 per cent of second votes be received throughout the federation. In 1957, the number of electoral district pluralities required was raised to three. With every tightening of the rules, further small parties were disqualified from representation in the *Bundestag*, whereupon they disintegrated or had to limit their activity to a few *Laender* where their strength lay. And since 1957, there has been recurring talk between the two largest parties, the CDU/CSU and SPD, about further changes in the electoral law that might decree a similar fate for the last surviving small party, the FDP.

Late in 1951, at the height of the economic dislocations caused by

the Korean War and while unemployment stood at record levels, the
cabinet in Bonn became alarmed about a new neo-fascist party, the
Socialist *Reich* Party (SRP), which had polled 11 per cent of the
popular vote in Lower Saxony. A suit was filed with the Federal Constitutional Court in Karlsruhe, and this tribunal outlawed the SRP a
year later. Other, less strident, neo-fascist splinter groups were permitted to continue, but they have never since managed to poll more
than 1 per cent in a federal or 5 per cent in any *Land* election. In
1961, the largest of these groups, the German *Reich* Party (DRP),

---

The Trend Toward a Two-Party System

		Seats in the *Bundestag* by party		TOTAL
1949	139 CDU/CSU (incl. 24 CSU)	52 FDP, 17 DP, 17 BP, 10 Center, 14 KPD, 22 others	131 SPD	402
1953	243 CDU/CSU (incl. 52 CSU)	48 FDP, 15 DP, 27 BHE	151 SPD	487
1957	270 CDU/CSU (incl. 55 CSU)	41 FDP, 17 DP	169 SPD	497
1961	241 CDU/CSU (incl. 50 CSU)	66 FDP	190 SPD	497

---

again remained far below 1 per cent. Its election campaign stressed
"national opposition" to the "un-German" Western decadence and
the rampant individualism of the Bonn Republic. It conducted diatribes against the pro-Western foreign policy of Bonn and employed
the slogan of "a new Versailles," which referred to an imminent sell-
out of such vital German interests as Berlin and reunification by the
three leading parties in order to please the West. The foreign policy
advocated by the DRP is based on neutralism and disengagement,
with a strong undercurrent of admiration for the power and ideological force of the Communist colossus. At its election rallies, the German equivalent of little old ladies in tennis shoes can be observed
nodding eagerly whenever a DRP speaker explains the experiences of
recent German history by pointing out that this is a cruel world where
might makes right and eggs are broken for the making of omelets.
And militancy and covert militarism frequently appear behind these
neutralist slogans.

Since the Korean War and East German rearmament had raised the specter of a Communist coup against West Germany, the Adenauer cabinet also submitted a similar suit against the KPD within three days of the SRP action. The Federal Constitutional Court took a long time with this second suit while the Communists used legal delaying maneuvers and advanced many arguments to prove that their party had a democratic character. It took the Federal Constitutional Court until 1956 to pass judgment on the KPD. During this time the Communist vote had slipped from 1.8 million in the early state elections to 1.4 million in the federal elections of 1949 and to 0.6 million in 1953, which kept them out of the *Bundestag* after 1953. Meanwhile, West Germans had been changing their attitude toward the Communists, for they were acutely aware of what their friends and relatives had had to endure in the East under Communism. As a result, the KPD's political activity was effectively choked off. But even though the party has been outlawed and has encountered virulent opposition from the public at large, it has continued to work underground. No effort was made to prohibit later splinter groups who were known to have accepted financial support from the East.

Germany's post-war leaders have also been greatly concerned about the millions of expellees and refugees from the eastern territories, for the dramatic circumstances of their flight before the advancing Red Army has elicited much sympathy both within and without Germany. The established major parties, especially the SPD and CDU/CSU, made great efforts to attract refugee and expellee voters in the early years when the Allies still barred refugees from organizing political parties. They were fairly successful, but so was the Economic Reconstruction Union (WAV) of Alfred Loritz, a rabble-rousing attorney in Munich. And there were solid pockets of refugee discontent in the rural areas of Schleswig-Holstein, Lower Saxony, and Bavaria, where vast numbers of refugees and expellees had ended their exhausting trek just this side of the Iron Curtain, often outnumbering the unfriendly native population, with inadequate food and shelter, and little hope of employment or economic advancement. These victims of Hitler's folly stood as an open invitation for nationalistic demagogues and men on horseback to use their bitterness and anguish to advance their own interests.

No sooner was the Allied ban on political organization lifted than refugees founded the Union of the Expellees and Disowned (BHE) in 1950 in Schleswig-Holstein, where they won nearly one-fourth of the popular vote in the *Land* elections the same year. In the following years, the BHE organized in the other *Laender* as well and soon was admitted to the governing coalition of most *Laender* governments and, after 1953, to the federal government. Instead of indulging in nationalistic or irredentist demagoguery, however, the BHE concentrated at first on joining governments and influencing legislation favorable to refugees and other groups with welfare or restitution claims. In this it enjoyed the eager co-operation of the three largest parties and benefited from the favorable economic circumstances of the mid-'fifties, for economic expansion supplied jobs and opportunities and a new wave of urbanization encouraged the refugees and expellees stranded in rural backwaters to move to the cities.

The BHE and government efforts to integrate the millions of refugees into West German society soon proved so successful that the support for a special refugee party such as the BHE began to dwindle. The BHE leaders remembered too late the nationalistic angle of their position and began to assert claims to the Sudetenland and to the areas beyond the Oder-Neisse Line. Already in the opposition and separated from some of their leaders by Adenauer's crushing embrace, they saw their vote in the 1957 election fall short of the necessary 5 per cent by less than half a percentage point. Evidently neither enough of the refugees nor any other Germans were willing to support the foreign policies of the BHE over that of the major parties. Only in three of the original refugee *Laender* and in Hesse could the BHE still retain more than 5 per cent of the popular vote. Frantic, the BHE concluded a merger with the German Party (DP), a conservative regional party whose main strength lay in Lower Saxony and which had also lost out in the 1957 elections. Their new party was called the All-German Party (GDP), after the second title of All-German Bloc (GB/BHE) which the BHE had added to its name as early as 1952. The GDP suffered a crushing defeat in the 1961 elections when its electoral support, once at 8 per cent for both parties together, slipped below 3 per cent. At this, even some of the old party stalwarts of both parties, including the founder and guiding spirit of the DP, Heinrich Hellwege, left to join the major parties. The rest of the GDP went on with moderate nationalistic slogans of self-determination for the Germans in the German Democratic Republic (DDR), while there was no real hope for the party's future.

The FDP — The Party of Bildung und Besitz

When, in November 1948, the various Liberal *Land* parties formed the FDP/DVP (DVP, or Democratic People's Party, is its name in the southwest) of the three Western zones of occupation, this seemed at first a historic turning point in the history of German liberalism. For the first time in a hundred fateful years, German Liberals were united in one party. Yet the triumph was not permanent, nor did the new unity go very deep. In the nearly two decades of its existence this party has exhibited an inner unrest and aimlessness which reflect both its uneasy position between the two party giants of the SPD and CDU/CSU and its historic collapse before the appeals of National Socialism.

The two main branches of German liberalism date back to the days of the national revolution of 1848 and existed in similar form in the Empire and in the Weimar Republic. There were the left-wing Liberals, variously named Democrats or Progressives, whose roots lay in the early development of liberal democracy in the German south and in the great harbor cities of the north, who soon had substantial support throughout the commercial middle classes of imperial Germany. There were also the National Liberals, Bismarck's staunchest supporters, who represented the new "barons of industry" and were on the best of terms with the aristocratic ruling class, the *Junkers*. While the Progressives favored parliamentary democracy with all the individual liberties and political freedoms of classical liberalism, the National Liberals were satisfied with constitutional monarchy and favored economic protection and political authoritarianism. Together, they represented the pillars of bourgeois society, *Bildung* (education) and *Besitz* (property), a guarantee of political order and stability even after the days of the *Junkers*. Under the Weimar Republic, successor parties of both wings continued to battle each other until the Great Depression and the Nazi movement all but wiped out their voting support, which had stood at about 15 to 22 per cent of the popular vote until 1930. The economic and moral collapse of the Liberal voter masses was generally interpreted to mean that liberalism as a philosophy had become absurd and out of touch with the economic and political realities of the twentieth century. This was the legacy which the FDP inherited after the war, an obvious contrast to the unbroken strength and untarnished shields of the Social Democrats and the Catholic precursors of the CDU/CSU.

When the FDP was established in the various *Laender* after the Second World War, its founders became aware of the great exodus of former Liberals to the CDU/CSU and even to the SPD. The FDP only succeeded in retaining elements that were too anti-clerical to feel attracted by the cathartic religious revival of the Christian Democrats and too bourgeois or too individualistic to see salvation in socialism, which in those days was popular with all political parties except regional movements such as the Bavaria Party or the DP. Since these are traditional attachments, they imposed considerable limitations upon the growth potential of the FDP in a rapidly changing society. Two camps, furthermore, asserted themselves from the beginning. One was the southwestern group — true successors to the Progressives and Democrats — typified by leaders such as Theodor Heuss or the Minister President of Wuerttemberg-Baden, Reinhold Maier, and popular also in Bavaria and among the old patrician families of Hamburg and Bremen. The other were the nationalistic and rather conservative heirs of the National Liberal tradition in North Rhine Westphalia, Hesse, and Schleswig-Holstein, led by Adenauer's Vice Chancellor Franz Bluecher. The two factions found common ground in the economic individualism of its business and professional clientele and in the cultural and educational philosophy of the educated middle classes, the old establishment of *Bildung* and *Besitz*. Cultural liberalism is concerned with preserving and passing on a deep appreciation for the cultural values of occidental civilization, with special emphasis on humanistic education. Like the educated middle classes, the FDP abhors the "false doctrines of Marxist and of biological materialism" and values Christianity, without, however, favoring church influence in politics or education. There was also some common ground in a modicum of nationalism even among the southerners, which kept alive in them a nagging concern for German reunification. But on such questions as the reintroduction of the death penalty, which post-war Germans had abolished in revulsion from the bloodshed under the Nazis, the two camps are in sharp disagreement.

The evolution of West German economy and society in the early 'fifties brought further conflict into the FDP. The right-wing components of the FDP associated themselves with splinter groups of the far right and bitterly opposed the SPD regimes of Hesse and Lower Saxony and even the left-leaning CDU administration of Karl Arnold in North Rhine Westphalia. The southwestern FDP/DVP and its supporters elsewhere frequently entered government coalitions with the SPD and were positively appalled at the courting of lunatic fringe groups. They grew even more uneasy when they became aware of abortive plans by the North Rhine Westphalian and Hessian Liberals to transform the FDP, with the help of other right-wing groups, into a nationalistic mass movement. The dispute finally culminated in separate conferences for each wing in 1952. The right wing drew up a "German Program" in which the words "democratic" and "liberal" were conspicuous by their absence. The left wing retaliated with a "Liberal Manifesto."

The restlessness of the FDP also led to friction with Adenauer, whose coalition cabinet the party had joined. The same 1953 elections that put Adenauer at the pinnacle of power found the FDP leadership desperately trying to persuade the public of its own usefulness. The CDU/CSU was getting all the credit for the economic policies of Ludwig Erhard, whom the FDP had launched on his career as Bizonal Economics Director and considered "really a Liberal." The FDP went out of its way to attack the CDU/CSU as "church-dominated" and "too European," only to find itself under pressure from industrial and other special interest groups who represented the sources of its campaign funds. These groups had learned that they could control a small party far more easily than the powerful Christian Democrats, who could and eventually did procure campaign financing by allocating public funds to all the parties represented in the *Bundestag*. In 1953 the interest groups simply forbade the FDP to campaign against the CDU/CSU or lose their financial support. But how else could the FDP attract bourgeois voters?

The FDP lost some of its voting support in 1953, but, worst of all, Adenauer received a clear majority of *Bundestag* seats. The FDP was still taken into the government as a coalition partner. But the situation had changed; not only could the Chancellor exclude the Bavarian Liberal, Thomas Dehler, from reappointment to the cabinet, but he could afford to ignore the protests of his coalition partners on several vital issues and punish them severely for showing signs of rebellion.

The modicum of nationalism which united both factions of the FDP was also reflected in misgivings about Adenauer's foreign policies. The disagreements between the extra-parliamentary FDP under the leadership of Dehler and a ministerial faction loyal to Adenauer came to a head over a Christian Democratic proposal of electoral reform in 1955. The new electoral system bore the ominous name "ditch system" and was sure to cost the FDP about one-fourth of its seats, judging from the last election returns. The CDU/CSU finally withdrew its proposal, but by that time a revolt in the FDP had already been triggered. In February of 1956, the "Young Turks" of the North Rhine Westphalian FDP, in the largest *Land* of the Republic, decided to overthrow the CDU government of their *Land* by withdrawing from their coalition with the Christian Democrats and going over to the opposition SPD instead. Adenauer promptly retaliated for this revolt by sending the FDP in the *Bundestag* to the opposition benches. The ministerial faction, a third of the FDP deputies, left the party and stayed with the Old Man. Later they formed their own party with the name Free People's Party (FVP), which soon merged with the DP and was never heard from again.

The Young Turks of Duesseldorf were a group of angry young men who had come of age in World War II. They were very pro-American. Led by Wolfgang Doering, a former tank officer of the *Afrika Korps,* the group included Erich Mende, who had received one of the highest German war decorations, the *Ritterkreuz,* while an officer in the Second World War. Their political style was youthful, brisk, and radical and bore the marks of an officers' junta holding power behind the facade of one of the grand old men of the party, the old-style Liberal Reinhold Maier, who was elected party chairman early in 1957. Maier expressed with moderation and dignity what the Young Turks felt strongly about: namely, that Adenauer's policy of European integration and German inclusion in NATO was likely to block German reunification forever: "First Germany, then Europe." The cradle-to-grave security offered to West Germans by both CDU/CSU and SPD was unnecessary and wasteful: "Fewer laws, less bureaucracy and less taxation." Germans no longer needed a king, a *Kaiser,* or Adenauer. The FDP, Maier urged, could be the "third force" between the two major parties, whose co-operation would check the conduct of whichever party it joined in a government coalition.

By asserting its independence from the CDU/CSU, despite the wrath of the business and industrial pressure groups, the FDP hoped to gain vital breathing room. A big pitch was made to small party voters and, among others, to former Nazis. Unwittingly, the party also found itself in a silent oppositional alliance with the SPD against Adenauer. Both parties were vitally interested in seeing the FDP attract enough Christian Democratic voters to frustrate another *Bundestag* majority for Adenauer, and neither party expected to gain any voters at the expense of the other. There had been enough *Land* government coalitions of FDP and SPD, especially under Maier in Baden-Wuerttemberg, to make this a plausible possibility at the federal level. To its dismay, the FDP found out in the 1957 elections that many of its voters were not prepared to grant the party this much choice. While Adenauer rolled up the biggest majority ever — 50.2 per cent of the popular vote — the FDP vote had dwindled to 7.7 per cent from 9.5 in 1953 and 11.9 in 1949. The 5 per cent hurdle was menacingly close.

The great debacle of 1957 forced the party to reappraise its position, without, however, offering much of an alternative. The FDP leaders dimly realized that the fundamental economic and social changes of West German society were eroding the social distinctions of *Bildung* and *Besitz*. Instead of depending on the propertied and educated classes as of old, Western Germany was rapidly turning into an open society of few distinctions and maximum opportunities without regard to education, inherited social rank, or inherited wealth. Even the newly rich were shareholders of the gross national product rather than owners of independent wealth. And the cultural heritage of the West seemed all but buried in the new materialism. Replacing the dwindling core of old-style Liberals with unreconstructed ex-Nazis and the fickle clientele of other right-wing groups was a risky undertaking, to say the least. Nor did the cultivation of a neo-liberal ideology on the lines of the Viennese school of Friedrich von Hayek and others really offer much of a solution in an age characterized as post-Marxian or post-ideological.

Nevertheless, the flood of pamphlets, articles, and speeches at the *Land* and federal FDP conventions of the years following the 1957 elections focused again and again on the question of what liberalism was all about. A Friedrich Naumann Foundation for educational reform was set up and named after the great left-wing Liberal of the turn of the century, who had deeply influenced Theodor Heuss and had shown a way out of the Liberal dilemma by expressing great concern for the underdogs of society. A new quarterly with the name *liberal* was founded as a sounding board for the younger generation in particular to express its thoughts about the aims and philosophy of the party. The Young Democrats, an organization of some 20,000 Liberals under 35 years of age, went furthest in its reappraisal: disdaining the talk of the "end of ideology" and their elders' emphasis on the bread-and-butter issues of various middle-class groups, the Young Democrats regard liberalism as the one and only anti-ideology to Communist collectivism and take a dim view of the Social Democratic or Christian Democratic "compromises between liberalism and collectivism." To update liberalism and attune it to the realities of the modern industrial society, however, they consider it necessary to revise their traditional philosophy in three important respects. Personal freedom can be secured only with the co-operation of the state, rather than against it. Without adequate social security and state protection against totalitarian enemies, constitutional liberties are not much help to the freedom of the individual. Secondly, the anti-clerical effect of traditional liberalism should be overcome. And third, there is a sense of social responsibility. Social Democratic observers have noted gleefully that such a program brings the Young Democrats into the immediate neighborhood of the more progressive parts of the SPD, who also share an aversion to West German nuclear armaments with them. Instead of a desire to co-operate with the SPD, however, the Young Democrats prefer to think of it as the empty shell of an outdated philosophy and express the hope that a broadly based Liberal Party will some day succeed the SPD as the second major German party. Such extraordinary optimism would seem to call for an explanation. The cultural philosophy of the educated classes of *Bildung* and *Besitz* has always been anti-Marxist and anti-materialistic. It is also Hegelian in the sense of being overly concerned with the life of ideologies and too little aware of social needs and social realities.

While the Young Democrats may have been too idealistic in their hopeful flights of fancy, their elders in the FDP were all too willing to come to terms with the powers that be. To begin with, they only allowed the young dissidents to occupy the functionary positions in the party which no self-respecting old-style Liberal wanted. In this respect the FDP is still a rather different organization from the two major parties, with their concentration of functionaries in key party positions. The nominations to the *Land* diets and the *Bundestag* as well as the more representative party offices were reserved for the old notables. In 1959, the FDP also made its peace with the special interest groups in order to regain its chief source of campaign funds, although the Young Democrats viewed this relationship with suspicion. The party patched up its relations with the CDU/CSU and with Adenauer, against whom the Young Democrats had borne a deep grudge since 1956, and made a tentative offer to form a coalition with them after the 1961 elections. This time the FDP would not scare away its bourgeois voters by hinting that it was willing to form a government with the SPD. Again the Young Democrats would have preferred to leave this question open. At the same time, the FDP had put forth a well-considered scheme to break the control of the CDU/CSU: Erich Mende, who early in 1960 succeeded Maier as FDP party chairman, appealed to the voters in 1961 not only to end the "one-party monopoly" in Bonn, but also initiated the slogan "Never again Adenauer." This was a calculated pitch at those Christian Democratic voters who were exasperated by the tenacity of the Old Man. By voting FDP they could force his resignation and yet still vote for a coalition government led by the CDU/CSU, for the FDP had promised not to join the SPD. "People who think ahead vote FDP," said the little election plaques handed out by the party.

Mende's gamble with anti-Adenauer sentiment paid off very handsomely in gathering votes for the FDP: its percentage of the popular vote rose to 12.7, higher than it had ever been before. But despite assistance from the *fronde,* Mende proved unable to dislodge the octogenarian Chancellor for reasons already discussed. Instead, the party had to beat an embarrassing retreat marked by severe inner strains and dissensions. The FDP neither obtained Adenauer's immediate resignation nor even a definite time limit on his tenure. Its share of ministerial positions in Adenauer's new cabinet was minor, and it never received all the positions promised. The Christian Democrat's assurances on various economic and social policies were laid down sketchily in the coalition contract, and there was ample reason to doubt their willingness to abide by the provisions of what Adenauer contemptuously called "the FDP paper." Most notably, the FDP's bright hopes in foreign policy, which had played such a large role in its election program and pamphlets, were snuffed out. At its Frankfurt Convention of March 1961, the FDP had still come out for a policy of disengagement, for greater flexibility in negotiating for German reunification, and for replacing the NATO guarantee of German security after reunification with a European system of mutual guarantees. But Adenauer and his party insisted that the continuation of their old foreign policy was a minimal requirement for a coalition. Fearful of a "black-red" (CDU/CSU-SPD) coalition, the FDP accepted.

Mende himself had to bear the brunt of press ridicule for giving in to the durable Old Man. As the sharp tongues of his critics put it, "people who think ahead should have voted CDU to begin with." He finally decided to save face by not entering the new coalition cabinet until after Adenauer's resignation. Accusations by CDU/CSU leaders calling the FDP "unrealistic," "disloyal," and even "unworthy of confidence" hardly facilitated the painful compromise. Within the FDP, two camps had formed once more. One consisted of FDP politicians who remembered Adenauer's past treatment of the party all too well, Hamburg deputies who feared the wrath of the voters in the imminent *Land* elections there, Young Democrats who impatiently awaited the end of the Adenauer era, and right-wingers toying with the thought of playing the "national opposition" during the international trials and tribulations that lay ahead for West Germany, the "new Versailles" of the far right. The *Land* party chairmen of Hesse and the Saar actually resigned over the issue of Adenauer's continuation. On the other hand, the *Land* parties of North Rhine Westphalia and Baden-Wuerttemberg were for a federal coalition with the CDU/CSU which would facilitate similar coalition governments in their *Laender*. Faced with so much dissension, the FDP leaders in the *Bundestag* passed the decision on to the Main Committee of the extra-parliamentary party, and it endorsed a coalition with Adenauer. Nearly seven weeks after the election, the shotgun wedding was performed, and the FDP was once more a part of an Adenauer cabinet.

The frequent breakdowns in the stormy marriage have been mentioned in the preceding chapter. One of the highlights was the *Der Spiegel* affair; its publisher, Rudolf Augstein, is considered close to the FDP, especially on foreign policy issues, where he has always favored the legacy of *Schaukelpolitik* (see-saw politics) between East and West associated with the names of Gustav Stresemann and Bismarck. The FDP not only succeeded in imposing its will on Adenauer in regard to the removal of Strauss, but there were persistent rumors about a plot to overthrow the Old Man with a constructive no-confidence vote of the FDP and SPD which would have made Erhard Chancellor. This confused scheme was said to have foundered only on Erhard's unwillingness to be promoted in this fashion. By the time Adenauer's definite retirement was voted by the CDU/CSU caucus in the *Bundestag,* the FDP again tried to get into the act with a threat to publicize the secret coalition contract of 1961 and to vote him out of office.

Erhard was obviously more willing to deal fairly with the FDP as a coalition partner than was Adenauer or, for that matter, the CDU/CSU. The new Chancellor had to overcome considerable resistance in his own party in order to fulfill the demands of the FDP for cabinet posts in his new government. But even his tractability was not sufficient to bridge the frequent disagreements on personnel and policy. There have been repeated clashes between the coalition partners since 1962 on such questions as holiday passes to East Berlin, reforming the compulsory health insurance system, updating child allowances, on automobile customs duties, internal security, and trade with the East. And in early 1964 another issue arose when the FDP announced that it did not favor the re-election of Luebke as President of the republic. The disagreement, as in most of the other coalition crises, was hardly ideological, nor even a matter of concrete economic interest. Rather, the FDP viewed Luebke as an enemy who had repeatedly called for a "black-red" coalition as a way out of the difficulties of the CDU/CSU with the restless FDP. It is symptomatic of the tensions between the two parties that both immediately threaten to form a coalition with the all-too-willing SPD whenever they cannot reach a compromise.

Even when Erhard called on the coalition to stick together until the elections of 1965, one could hardly fail to notice the threatening un-

dertone in the appeal. For the pivotal position of the FDP as the bal-
ancer in the *Bundestag,* nay its very presence there, is as uncertain as
a tightrope act. The odds against its survival rise from one federal
election to the next. Its good showing in 1961 was based on the
promise of forcing Adenauer to resign. The FDP failed to make good
this promise, and now is not even in a position to repeat it in 1965.
As the sociological and public opinion studies of the 1961 elections
appear to indicate, the FDP vote of 12.7 per cent was composed of
three-fifths of voters who switched to the FDP, mostly from the
CDU/CSU, and promptly abandoned the party again in later *Land*
elections. Barring miracles, this state of affairs brings the party so
close to the 5 per cent hurdle that it can be only a question of when
the tightrope walker will stumble.

There are other indications of the erosion of the party's basis of
Bildung and *Besitz.* For one thing, the "rugged individualism" of
property ownership is gradually fading away for various reasons, not
the least of which is the CDU/CSU (and FDP) policy of broadening
ownership by people's stock and savings incentives. It is no secret
either that the privileges of the educated and the prestige of intellectuals are beginning to crumble. When the FDP balked at renomi-
nating Luebke for the federal presidency, it advanced a candidate
whose qualifications say much about the values of the FDP — the
famous physicist Friedrich von Weizsaecker. "Thank you, no Professor
Hindenburg," was the tell-tale reaction of the SPD, whose votes
would have been needed to elect him. The statement equated the
selection of an internationally respected representative of the intellectual world with the Weimar politicians' choice of General Hindenburg
for President of the Weimar Republic as the unpolitical symbol of
past greatness and authority. Professor von Weizsaecker, in fact,
exhibited a great deal more timeliness and acumen when he turned
down the offer and advised that they select a political figure instead.

West German intellectuals, artists, writers, and academicians, who
are about equally divided between supporters of the FDP and SPD
and those strongly opposed to all the major parties, have been among
the most irreconcilable critics of the politics of the Federal Republic.
They are as unhappy about West Germany's affluent society and its
preoccupations as American intellectuals were with "normalcy" in
the 1920's. Some think back nostalgically to the intellectual and artis-

tic glamor of the Weimar Republic. Some believe that the hopeful vi-
sions of social reconstruction and justice of the immediate post-war
period were lost in the gears of economic recovery, caught in the net
of the Western alliance against the East, or crushed in the construction of the edifice of Adenauer's Chancellor Democracy. Others again
rebel against the influence of the churches on cultural life, against the
shallow anti-Communism of West German society, and against the
present trend toward social conformism. All have been visibly nettled
by the pointed disdain of Adenauer for intellectuals and the anti-
intellectualism fashionable in the CDU/CSU and among influential
economic groups of Western Germany, who like to speak of them as
"uprooted," "homeless," and even "immature."

But there are deeper causes for the alienation of the intellectuals
from the economic, political, and social life of their country. One factor is that in their own traditional terms of reference, "civilization"
really won out over *Kultur*. Another is the fact that they are the products of a self-perpetuating educational system whose evolution
stopped in the nineteenth century, with the result that they are not at
all prepared to face the new society now evolving in Western Germany and tend to think along the same circular lines as before. Hence
they confuse, for example, pragmatism in society and politics with a
lack of ideas, and like to ideologize and think in terms of broad categories and grand alternatives about problems that rarely profit from
such treatment. Their alienation has also been caused by their loss of
a position of authority in society, especially on questions of culture
and values. German bourgeois society was always possessed of a
quasi-platonic cast of mind which placed supreme emphasis on expert
knowledge and accorded to the intellectual elite the role of a platonic
philosopher-king. These quasi-platonic features are such an intimate
part of German humanistic education that its best products automatically take on a paternalistic, if not condescending, schoolmasterly attitude toward the common people on all levels "below" them. Such
common people in the new society, however, refuse to listen, evidently preferring to make their own decisions about their lives and
votes. A public opinion research institute once asked West Germans to
name the persons of their personal acquaintance in whose political
judgment they had confidence. Nearly one-half the persons named
were in the manual trades and another third shopkeepers and white-

collar employees. Only one out of seven respondents named a person of higher education, such as a teacher or professional person. And no more than 2 per cent named a *Respektsperson* (person of authority), such as a burgomaster or clergyman. The spurned philosopher-kings of quasi-platonism react to such neglect as would any child denied attention: they sulk, rebel, or show hostility from the depth of their being. And the ironic aspect of their situation is that the affluent society which shows so little interest in their quasi-platonic, constructive advice will pay exceedingly well for their protests and even tantrums in print. Intellectuals thus find themselves at the same time not taken very seriously and yet bribed with membership in the affluent new society.

With the succession of Erhard to the chancellorship, even the CDU/CSU began to show some concern about the alienation and disaffection of German intellectuals from politics, especially since in 1961 a number of notable writers had composed a book with the title *Do we need a new government?* a question most contributors answered in the affirmative. Professor Erhard talked about a brain trust. Protestant CDU leaders have always been closer to the world of German intellect than Catholics such as Adenauer or the bogeyman of the intellectuals, Franz Josef Strauss. After the 1964 CDU convention, Gerstenmaier, a Protestant, even held a lengthy public discussion with university students and intellectuals about the present relationship between *Macht* (power) and *Geist* (intellect). On hearing about this meeting, Konrad Adenauer produced another of his famous aphorisms: "People aren't that interested in politics. They would rather watch television."

The Background of the German Social Democrats

If it is true that West German politics is moving toward a two-party system — and there can be little doubt about it — one of the foremost objects of curiosity is the other great party which may someday inherit power from the Christian Democrats. The Social Democratic Party recently celebrated its one-hundredth birthday, a century of party history from the day in 1863 when Ferdinand Lassalle founded the General German Workers Association. It is an inspiring story, spanning not only the whole era of German social transformation which we have tried to survey in the first two chapters, but also the progress of the German working men, who rose from the depths of an oppressive class society to some measure of freedom and dignity, and intermittently even to the exercise of power.

For the first eighty years of that long history, the fate of the SPD was characterized by two poles of feeling and attitude. One was the earnest desire of men like Lassalle, and many after him, to fit party and working class in a dignified and loyal manner into the existing state and society, reforming them perhaps from within, but only by means of the ballot and by state-sponsored undertakings to provide social security and economic stability. Lassalle himself had negotiated with Bismarck about such state action and regarded universal suffrage as the only means necessary to give working men a fair deal. The other pole was the revolutionary dogma of Karl Marx, whose followers disdained political accommodation, because they considered economic relationships the only social reality and were looking forward to the violent collapse of the whole economic and political system.

Behind the belligerent advocacy of "class struggle" and the "dictatorship of the proletariat" lay the deep alienation and disaffection from society and state of the men and women who found themselves discriminated against and excluded from everything from the day they were born. Americans have never known anything like the effect of class distinctions in pre-1914 Europe, unless, perhaps, they were born with colored skin. The German working man and woman stood outside the barrier erected by polite, bourgeois society, exploited for economic gain, and with their needs and rights unrecognized. Bourgeois employers were unwilling even to sit down at the same table to discuss wages and working conditions with their workers because this would have implied social equality between them. Bismarck's state outlawed and persecuted the SPD for twelve long years. It never allowed the party to participate in political responsibility and prohibited public employees from joining it until the end of World War I. Small wonder that the Social Democrats created a world of their own within this hostile society, complete with a web of auxiliary organizations for Socialist education, recreation, and a Socialist press numbering thirteen dailies and twenty-eight other periodicals as early as 1877, the year before they were outlawed. In this separate world of socialism they mulled over the bitter word that the bourgeois *Rechts-staat,* constitutional government, was really an *Unrechtsstaat,* a state of injustice; and that the famous civil rights and human freedoms were only bourgeois rights and freedoms.

Their best friends were the Socialist movements of other countries. Rejected each by the dominant elements of their own nation-states, they could dream together of an international utopia of brotherhood and justice that would rise after the rotten societies around them had collapsed through their own moral decay. There was one difference between German socialism and the Socialist movements of France and other European neighbors that is still important today. The SPD encountered sympathy and co-operation from the Catholic Center Party, which was similarly besieged by Bismarck and took a far more enlightened attitude toward labor problems than the liberal bourgeois establishment. From this circumstance stem the good relations between the labor wing of the CDU/CSU and the SPD and, perhaps also, the mildness of the secularism and anti-clericalism of the latter.

In spite of all persecution and discrimination, or perhaps partly because of them, the SPD emerged after the turn of the century as the most powerful party in the *Reichstag,* with about one-third of the popular vote. This did not assure political influence, so long as the *Reichstag* had no power over the executive and so long as Prussia, with its discriminatory three-class electoral law, dominated German government. At the same time, the Social Democrats had come a long way from the depths of disaffection, since legislation outlawing them had lapsed in 1890. The legalization of their work in trade unions, co-operative associations, and in the diets of state and federal governments had contributed greatly to moving the party toward accommodation. Especially outside of reactionary Prussia, and particularly in the south German states, where the social barrier between the classes had never been strong and liberal governments rarely indulged in the discriminatory practices common in the north, strong sentiment for democratic accommodation was matched by frequent co-operation between bourgeois parties and the SPD. These circumstances increasingly prompted the party to identify in practice, if not in theory, with the "evolutionary socialism" of Eduard Bernstein rather than with the revolutionary, chiliastic creed of Marx, who had believed in the automatic collapse of the capitalist state and society. As long as the

SPD remained in the opposition, however, there was little chance of resolving the irreconcilable contradiction of its two poles of orientation.

With the outbreak of World War I and its catalytic effect on the ruling classes of Germany, a series of events was set in motion which split the Social Democrats into warring camps. At first the hostilities muted the latent conflict between those who were anxious to prove that the German Socialists were not "fellows without a fatherland" and those whose pacifism and internationalism inclined them to cooperation with foreign Socialist parties against this "clash of the economic interests of the bourgeois classes of different nations." The SPD viewed the war as a defensive struggle of Germany and voted to support the war effort of the government, especially against the "fortress of reaction," Tsarist Russia. The Socialists of other Western countries, by the same token, were anxious to protect democracy and social progress against reactionary Germany. With the first German successes, it became evident that the leading circles of the *Kaiser's* Germany were not content with a "defensive war." And the first rumors of government plans for annexations induced the SPD to press for an early, conciliatory peace without annexations. By this time, a small minority of revolutionary Socialists had begun to gather around Rosa Luxemburg and Karl Liebknecht; in addition, militant, democratic followers of Bernstein had begun to see the war with different eyes and to dread an all-out German victory by the annexationistic clique of generals, industrialists, and Pan-Germans whose dictatorial propensities were becoming more evident every day.

From this time, then, the split took place that has since propagated itself in ever-changing forms and alignments. While the SPD struggled on in "loyal opposition" to the disastrous course of the *Kaiser's* government, a dissident group argued that the terrible world war was a product of the conflict of national imperialisms which represented the natural offspring of capitalism headed for its predicted collapse. Naturally, there was no point in workers sacrificing themselves on the altar of imperialism before the time was ripe to inherit the world. After the outbreak of the Russian revolution, this dissident group became associated with the Bolsheviks, whose leader had long indicated his willingness to accept national defeat as the price for the collapse of Russian autocratic government. A steadily growing minority among the SPD deputies in the *Reichstag,* moreover, refused to support revenue bills that would enable the government to prolong the war. In 1917 this second group split off from the SPD to form the Independent Social Democratic Party, a very sizable group which did not return to the fold until 1922. The absence of the Independents, who strove to bring about immediate socialist reforms in the economy, decisively weakened the SPD during the transition and the formative stages of the Weimar Republic, when their combined vote ran as high as 40 per cent. On the other hand, it has also been suggested that the SPD could have broken the power of the reactionary establishment once and for all, had it participated in a revolution of economy and society in 1918–19. The first-mentioned dissident group became the German Communist Party (KPD) in 1919, and it remained a powerful revolutionary force throughout the fourteen years of the Weimar Republic. The rise of the Communist vote to 12.6 per cent in 1924 and 16.7 in 1932 indicated the seriousness of the crises of the republic in these years.

After the collapse of the Empire, the SPD worked together with the Center Party and the left-wing Liberals, who had joined it in the famous peace resolution of 1917. There was not much inducement to revolution in the realization that the German workers would suffer most from the economic dislocations of defeat just as they had suffered most during the war. The revolutionary example of Russia on the one hand whetted the appetite of the dissident groups for immediate action. The resistance to even a modicum of constitutional reform by Prussian aristocrats and the annexationists, on the other, prepared the SPD for the double assault from both wings which it faced throughout the Weimar Republic. At the same time that the party took over governmental responsibility and strove to establish and fortify democratic institutions in Germany, revolutionary turmoil existed and efforts were made to set up Soviet regimes in some parts of Germany; these posed a real threat and had to be suppressed by force. At the same time, these revolutionary disturbances brought forth a vast anti-Communist reaction among the bourgeoisie, who encouraged the formation of an anti-democratic front reaching all the way from monarchistic and conservative groups to the storm-troopers of Hitler. Besieged from both sides, the SPD, together with the other defenders of the republic, attempted a holding operation for democracy, but it was finally overwhelmed by the Great Depression. The Communists, in contrast, made no effort to defend the democratic republic against the rising tide of Nazism and conservative reaction, but instead frittered away the strength of the left wing in unceasing and bitter attacks on the SPD, whom they called "social fascists."

It would be a misunderstanding, however, to think of Weimar Social Democrats and Communists in the black-and-white terms of loyal and subversive, constructive and obstructive, or sane and disturbed. The borderline between the two parties and their voters was always fluid, and large numbers of adherents and voters moved back and forth between them. The Weimar KPD, like the pre-war pole of extreme disaffection, represented for many only a state of mind, a symptom of times out of joint and an expression of deep anguish. Whereas the members and voters of the Weimar SPD were generally recruited from the more stable and settled strata of the laboring classes and were closely identified with trade union activity and the web of organizations concerned with workers' adult education and other self-improvement schemes, the KPD members and voters came from different groups, with the exception of a small number of prominent leaders and functionaries. Before the war, chicanery, exploitation, and oppression had aggravated the strains of urbanization and economic crises — producing much disaffection and utopian sentiment. The war heightened the feelings of abuse and exploitation and provided the worker with experiences of massive violence and destruction which made it doubly impossible for him to go back to his humdrum existence afterwards. Hence arose the revolutionary postwar period when the masses hoped to establish a mighty German Soviet Republic, a Bolshevik *Reich* of workers and soldiers. The youthful street fighters and members of this Red Front hardly differed from the Nazi storm-troopers. Likewise, in the last years of the Weimar Republic, the KPD was inundated with the radicalized masses of unemployed workers whose profound existential despair drove them to political militancy against the established order.

In the period in between, the KPD was chiefly a haven for people in a personal crisis of one kind or another, idealists in collision with social realities, uprooted farm boys, disaffected intellectuals and artists, young people in search of themselves, Russophiles, romantics, and missionaries in search of a mission. The rapid turnover of membership facilitated authoritarianism, centralized leadership, and control from Moscow. The steady stream of ex-Communists who had moved past this phase either disappeared without a trace in the unpolitical general public or joined one of the numerous groups and sects of dissidents. In the Weimar Republic there was also an easy transition from Communism to the revolutionary right wing, where the inner kinship, militancy, and common authoritarianism of Communists and Nazis or other "national Bolsheviks" were readily appreciated. Many ex-Communists, for example, the late Lord Mayor of Berlin, Ernst Reuter, found their way back to democratic parties and often made constructive contributions.

In the declining years of the Weimar Republic, from 1930 on, the SPD was once more shut out from power, though it was willing to support the measures of Heinrich Bruening, the first in a series of cabinets without a parliamentary majority. The Nazi landslide failed to make any significant inroads into the steady core of seven million SPD voters or the more than one million members of the party. As parliamentary activity seemed less and less designed to counter the threat in the streets, the SPD became the chief buttress of the *Reichsbanner* Black-Red-Gold, the para-military veterans' organization which the parties of the "Weimar coalition" — the SPD, the Center, and the left-wing Liberals (DDP) — had established as a counterweight to the right-wing para-military formations and the Red Front. Special shock troops, the "protective formations," were added in 1931. In the same year the Harzburg Front of the right wing was countered by the formation of an Iron Front of SPD, trade unions, and workers' athletic organizations designed to demonstrate the readiness of republican forces to resist a Nazi *coup d'état*. Yet when in July 1932, Chancellor von Papen deposed the SPD-dominated *Land* government of Prussia by intervening unconstitutionally, the defenders of the republic failed to take action but relied instead on the imminent federal election, only to witness a second runaway Nazi landslide.

The fatal error of the SPD, the *Reichsbanner,* and the Iron Front in sticking to legal measures was promptly repeated when Hitler was appointed Chancellor. Somehow the SPD leaders were too organization-bound to seize the initiative, too rational in their thinking to grasp the demonic nature of the forces before them, and too optimistic to imagine that nearly a century of progress against considerable odds could end with such a complete lapse into atavistic barbarism. In the last *Reichstag* elections of March 1933, the SPD already found itself harassed by storm-troopers and its election rallies cancelled by Nazi-dominated authorities. It had one last great moment when, alone in the *Reichstag,* it voted against the infamous Enabling Act which suspended the last checks on Hitler's dictatorial power. In June 1933, the SPD was outlawed, and there began the bitter road of tens of thousands of Social Democrats into exile, into the jails and concentration camps of Nazi tyranny, and into the underground resistance movement where many found a violent death, especially after the abortive attempt on Hitler's life of July 20, 1944.

The organizational core of the exile SPD at first established headquarters in Prague and retreated before the advancing German armies from there to Paris and finally to London. They tried to maintain contact with all opposition elements within Germany, for they knew that only the combined efforts of all parties and individuals, and especially of conspirators in the officers corps with their access to the means of violence, stood a remote chance of defeating the well-guarded system of totalitarian control that had settled over their native land. Resistance of this kind at last created a feeling of common interest among the many different groups and elements that had never existed before. There was, moreover, a self-searching mood of reappraisal in resistance and exile which led to important long-range developments in the SPD's philosophy and approach to politics. One important school of thought, typified by the historian Arthur Rosenberg, concluded from the debacle of Weimar that the SPD should immediately have broken the backbone of reaction by fundamental administrative, social, and economic reforms in the 1918–19 period. Consequently, the party envisaged a post-totalitarian Germany characterized by the socialization of monopolistic industries and a strong representation of organized labor in all decision-making bodies of state and economy. Another large group felt that the party had failed to appeal to the nationalistic passions of the masses in the way the Nazis had so successfully done. This view was especially held by the younger generation of SPD leaders, including Dr. Kurt Schumacher, who felt that anti-nationalism, the public image of Socialist collaboration with the victors of World War I, and the prominent identification of the SPD with international socialism had been disastrous to the party. The obviously popular nationalistic frenzy in Nazi Germany and the hostility of foreign governments and peoples, who were rarely willing to distinguish between what a Frenchman once called *"les boches et les allemands,"* or the bad and the good Germans, may have contributed to this turn of opinion among both underground and exile Social Democrats. So did harsh criticism from the extreme left-wing of the SPD, which called on the party to return to the rigorous principles of revolutionary Marxism, and even more the efforts of the Moscow-dominated KPD to take over the SPD while professing a newly-discovered friendship for the "social fascists" of yesterday. The Social Democrats of national persuasion also felt that the SPD should not have limited itself to the working-class, but should have offered its hand to all classes and especially to the millions of victims of the Great Depression who flocked to Hitler in their confusion and despair. This group regarded with admiration such foreign models as the British Labour Party and the great Scandinavian Socialist parties — a preference for Western-style democracy over the authoritarian, chiliastic socialism of Moscow. The exile SPD also voiced its unwavering commitment to democracy in several documents. Thus, long before the end of the war, the second major party of post-war Germany had begun to explore ways of breaking out of the traditional limitations of ideology and social class.

The SPD in the Schumacher Era

In the first months that followed World War II, the SPD made a determined effort to reject a bid to easternize the party. At first antifascist committees composed of Social Democrats and Communists who had survived the end of the Nazi regime in Germany, to bring camps appeared all over the Soviet zone of occupation, where political parties were encouraged to operate as early as June 1945. There was a considerable movement among the Social Democratic leaders, who had survived the end of the Nazi regime in Germany, to bring about a fusion of SPD and KPD. Fortunately, the KPD, which had largely spent the war years in the Soviet Union and returned full of ambition, had other plans for its eventual coming to power. The Soviet military administration encouraged both parties, as well as the

CDU and a Liberal party (LDP), to reorganize in a highly centralized fashion from the top down, but clearly favored the KPD in any
way it could. Otto Grotewohl, a former *Reichstag* deputy, became the
head of the "unity-minded" central committee of the East German
SPD, which had built up a membership of several hundred thousand
by the time the Western allies even permitted partisan activity to
begin in their zones of occupation. Yet the exile SPD executive in
London refused to turn over to Grotewohl's committee in Berlin the
mandate of representing the whole party, which it had received from
the last national SPD conference before 1933, until the party could
be re-established from the grass roots up throughout Germany. Resistance to the claims of the Berlin leadership, as well as to its plans
of fusion with the KPD, finally centered upon Kurt Schumacher, who
had built up a network of party channels and communications from
Hannover right after the war.

In October 1945, Schumacher called a conference at Wennigsen
near Hannover, and there representatives of the Soviet, British, and
American zone SPD discussed post-war plans. Among the subjects
covered were economic policies and plans for socializing mining,
heavy industry, power, transport, insurance, and banking. Schumacher dominated the meeting. The new emphasis on the national point
of view made itself felt in his words:

> We German Social Democrats are not British and not Rus-
> sian, not American and not French. We are the representatives
> of the German working people and hence of the German na-
> tion.

The conference also expressed its opposition to the idea of a German
"collective guilt" for Nazi crimes, a slogan which the KPD, among
others, had found useful to justify Soviet tutelage for the "immature
German people." It protested as well against Allied attempts to strip
Germany of industrial equipment and to turn her into an agricultural
country. Social Democrats were to stand up to the occupying powers
in defense of the interests of the civilian population. This truculent
nationalism, above all a reflection of the good conscience of the SPD
about the past, was perfectly compatible with the Social Democratic
disavowal of Bismarck's anti-liberal and anti-Western nation-state
and of the right-wing nationalism of the Empire and Weimar Repub-

lic. The SPD strongly supported a drastic program of denazification and demilitarization and saw itself as the chief supporting force of the Second German Republic of the future. A truly democratic society and state, it was argued, would automatically assure socialist brotherhood and guarantee the working man a fair deal. The meeting at Wennigsen succeeded in postponing the designation of a center or leadership group until such time as the local and regional organizations of the party were fully re-established and could elect delegates to a regular party convention. It also rejected a compromise solution of the Berlin central committee to form a provisional party executive, including Erich Ollenhauer as a representative of the London exile executive and Schumacher and others for the Western zones. In the meantime, a call was issued to Social Democratic exiles scattered all over the world to return and to join those who had never left the country in reviving the great party.

By scrupulous observance of democratic principles the SPD was saved from injurious entanglement when the Soviet military administration and the East German KPD suddenly changed their course in the months that followed. The chaotic conditions of post-war Germany, the misery, hunger, and hopelessness of millions of natives and refugees, appeared to offer the Communists a unique opportunity to attract the masses of voters. In the Russian zone, moreover, the occupation quickly launched an agrarian reform aimed at pleasing the small farmers and farm laborers in a manner reminiscent of Lenin's program of 1917. But post-totalitarian Germany was different from post-Tsarist Russia. By January 1946, the Communists had suffered several humiliating electoral defeats and quickly turned from the ballot box to more promising approaches. Taking up the idea of a fusion of SPD and KPD again, they soon began to make the appropriate steps. While the SPD in the Western zones declared fusion to be a matter for a duly elected national convention to decide, the Soviet military administration began to harass and imprison East German SPD members who were against the merger and to suppress all mention of unfavorable local party resolutions, such as those that originated in Leipzig and Rostock. Only in Berlin, where by this time all four occupying powers had established themselves, were the Soviets powerless to stop a vote of all SPD party members, which came out against fusion. Nevertheless, the merger of the East German SPD and

KPD into the Socialist Unity Party (SED) became a fact in April 1946. And in an amazingly short period of time, the new party had reshuffled and purged its internal leadership in such a fashion that the unquestioned control of such Moscow-trained Communists as Wilhelm Pieck and Walter Ulbricht was complete.

The SPD of the Western zones and of Berlin was deeply shocked by this demonstration of the Communist approach to democratic politics. The forced merger in the Russian zone brought about a complete split with the rump SPD — symptomatic of the German division to come. Communist high-handedness also caused a sharp dissociation of Western from Eastern-oriented German socialism. Meeting three weeks after the merger in Hannover, the first post-war convention of the rump SPD elected Kurt Schumacher chairman and placed itself once more firmly on the ground of Western-style democracy. Firmly anti-Communist long before such an orientation became fashionable in Western capitals, the party convention also pointed out that the emphasis on economic planning did not imply "enforced uniformity or lack of economic freedom, nor collectivization or a regimented garrison socialism." Above all, the SPD firmly emphasized its task as the chief supporting party of the new German democratic state, and it set itself on guard against designs on the territorial status and economic assets of Germany. It was critical of the continuing division of Germany into occupation zones and of the Allied reluctance to restore power to the Germans so they could go ahead with the construction of the Second German Republic.

While the party participated with the CDU/CSU and other West German parties in all the *Laender* governments, it frequently took upon itself to lecture them on democracy and on what was good for their country. The SPD yearbooks are also full of accounts of the exceedingly critical attitude of the SPD toward occupation policies and measures that the stalwart patriots of the left regarded as short-sighted or selfish. Despite the loss of the Russian zone, where the SPD could have expected broad electoral support, and the formal dissolution of Prussia, the old SPD stronghold before 1932, the party had attracted some seven million voters in the Western zones and was confident of becoming the strongest party in the new state. The trade union movement, split into many ideological factions before Hitler, had been re-established in the form of a single, powerful organization capable of

mobilizing tens of millions if ever the need arose. Forgotten were labor's demoralization and the scattering of its organized might in the
early 'thirties. Once more there was the feeling of power, of solidarity, of pride in the discipline and organization of the working masses
that had given Social Democrats and trade unionists an unshakable
faith in the survival and ultimate triumph of their cause through the
trials and persecution of the Empire and the Weimar Republic. And
now they also had a brilliant leader, a man of vision and of will
power, whose charismatic appeal could cast a spell even over the
skeptical Germans.

Kurt Schumacher was born in 1895 in Kulm on the Vistula, a
mixed German-Polish community in West Prussia, far beyond the
Oder-Neisse line, and even beyond the German borders determined at
Versailles. His father was a well-to-do merchant and local government official, a Liberal, who raised him in a strict, Protestant household. As the story goes, his family lived on a street leading from a
military garrison to a Catholic high school, which gave him an early
impulse to become a Social Democrat. Decorated in World War I and
severely wounded, he lost his right arm. While studying law and economics at the university, Schumacher wrote a dissertation on "The
Struggle for the Idea of a German State in German Socialism," in
which he already showed a lively appreciation for the Lassallean tradition which later, after 1945, would earn him the epithet "the Red
Prussian." He began his political career in the Social Democratic
party press in Wuerttemberg, where he also emerged as a well-known
speaker, editorial writer, and deputy in the *Landtag* and *Reichstag*.
Still suffering from his severe injuries, he acquired a reputation for his
brilliance, political insight, and polemical gifts. In the early years of
revolutionary preparations by Nazis and Communists, Schumacher
also developed effective ways of discovering and exposing their arms
caches and subversive activities, but the national party and the authorities showed little appreciation for his services. His brief *Reichstag* career in the crisis years of 1930–33 further endeared the acid-
tongued young war veteran to the Nazis, whose uncouth verbal sallies
he was quite prepared to match. Unlike most of his older, tradition-
minded party friends, Kurt Schumacher clearly foresaw the awful
future, the terror, and the preparation for aggressive war. He also
knew his prominent place on the list of revenge of the Nazis. Yet he

did not flee the country, despite the pleas of his family in Hannover, financially dependent on him since Kulm was turned over to Poland by the Treaty of Versailles. He said to friends that the SPD would need men who stuck it out once the Nazi dictatorship collapsed of its own weight. But he could hardly have been unaware that he was likely to experience violent death at the hands of his enraged enemies whom he knew lacked all scruples. Unlike the aging leadership of the various republican parties, he shared the agony, belligerence, and frustration of a generation scarred by World War I, the feelings that had provided the fuel for the lawlessness of Nazis and Communists. In his deep attachment to his own people, perhaps, he felt ready to go to the very limit to endure their sickness, even if it meant losing his life. Instead, however, he somehow survived ten years of Nazi concentration camps and mistreatment, although his frail health was so far endangered that he was finally turned over to his sister as a hopeless invalid. He was arrested once more after the abortive assassination of Hitler, but eluded the Nazi executioners.

Once the war was over, Schumacher quickly emerged as the most likely man to lead the party. Unlike the exile Social Democrats, against whom there was some latent resentment, he had stuck it out under the heel of Nazi jackboots. He went to work immediately — despite Allied prohibition of political activity — re-establishing connection with his few party friends in the Western zones who had somehow survived amid the awesome swath Nazi tyranny had cut through their rows. The party's early statements on program and strategy bore the mark of his thinking. He warned the party not to commit itself to a fully-developed program until the Allied powers had decided on the limitations within which German economic and political life would be allowed to develop. All the elements of early post-war policy of the SPD can be found in Schumacher's notes of the fall of 1945: the pro-Western, though critical, attitude toward the United States and Great Britain; the deep concern about such threats to the territorial integrity of Germany as separatist movements, zonal boundaries, and the separation of the territories beyond the Oder-Neisse line; and the hearty dislike for the German Communists, who simultaneously were the most vociferous German super-patriots and yet the most prepared to sell out German vital interests to the Russians.

Schumacher also had very definite ideas about the political party system of post-war Germany. He was willing to see the SPD enter coalitions with the CDU/CSU, but had his doubts about the democratic character of that party, which was far too clerical for his taste. "The fifth occupying power is the Vatican," he once remarked. He doubted, in particular, that the CDU/CSU as the successor of the Catholic Center Party would ever be able to overcome the religious division of Germany. He could see no democratic future for Germany, or even for Europe, unless a socialistic state and society were realized. A two-party system for Germany seemed unlikely, even undesirable. Schumacher also expected the SPD to inherit the allegiance of the intellectual and cultural elites of Germany. But the chief goal was the winning of the support of the old and new middle classes so as to preempt the middle ground between the CDU/CSU and the KPD. Thus his desire to expand SPD support right across old class lines clearly complemented Adenauer's attempt to walk down the middle of the road with his shoulders squared.

Schumacher's frank criticism of Allied policies soon made him known abroad, where political leaders and the press reacted with surprise, and often dismay, at finding a fearless and articulate spokesman of German national interests so soon after the utter defeat of Nazi Germany. As early as November 1946, moreover, he was invited to visit the British Labour Party, which earned him — for he had not been abroad during the Nazi era — the first glimpse of an international reputation long before most people had even heard of Adenauer. Half a year later, he had the task of persuading a conference (COMISCO) of the Second Socialist International to admit the German SPD. The proposal narrowly failed to be carried, although almost all Western Socialist parties supported it. Invitations by American trade unions and Scandinavian Socialist parties soon followed; everywhere he left a favorable personal impression and gave rise to speculations about his future career in a democratic post-war Germany. As later with Adenauer, his foreign critics fell chiefly into two categories: those who thought they heard a frightening echo in his more nationalistic remarks and Communist spokesmen who claimed he was selling the country to Western "capitalism and imperialism." But there can be little question that his influence did as much as any event to convince Western observers that there were reliable democratic forces alive in Germany.

His active participation in regional election campaigns and in the organization work of the SPD confirmed his hold over his party at home. A spellbinding orator with persuasive clarity of thought, he seemed to rise in indomitable will power as his health failed, for finally one of his legs had to be amputated. His refusal to engage in national self-pity or self-hatred, coupled with his unquestionable antifascism, gained him the confidence of the voters. His approach to denazification similarly struck a statesmanlike note: like De Gaulle, who on his return to France generously proclaimed that all Frenchmen had always been for him and not for Vichy, Schumacher took a dim view of the systematic prosecution of millions of small Nazis, for it extended over too many persons and too long a period to be very effective. The big Nazis should be punished, the former concentration camp inmate felt, but everybody else, and especially those thirty years old or younger, should re-examine their consciences and should make a genuine attempt to return to decency, rather than be faced by a sentence imposed by society. He also had misgivings about the Allied zeal for re-educating Germans for democracy, which he apparently considered ill-advised — democracy being based on the free decision of individuals — and, perhaps also, unfair competition for the most democratic of German parties, the SPD.

The SPD had been quite successful in attracting new voters and members from 1945 to 1948, presumably from such groups as the refugees and the many people whose bourgeois occupation or business had disappeared in the economic dislocations of that period. The party polled overall an average of 35 per cent of the popular vote, and over 40 per cent in Hesse, Lower Saxony, and Schleswig-Holstein, and as a result it held a leading position in the all-party coalitions customary in most *Laender* governments at that time. Five of the eleven *Land* Ministers Presidents, eight of the Economics Ministers, and eight of the Ministers of the Interior were members of the party early in 1947. The SPD had built up solid strength in many regional centers where such leaders as Max Brauer in Hamburg, Wilhelm Kaisen in Bremen, Hinrich Kopf in Lower Saxony, or Wilhelm Hoegner in Bavaria enjoyed genuine popularity. But when the Allied occupation encouraged the Germans to form bizonal institutions, the SPD almost imperceptibly slipped into the opposition. Partly because it lacked a majority of the seats in the Bizonal Economic Council and partly because it continued to be serious about the socialization of the basic industries — which the occupying powers would not permit to be carried out anyway — the SPD chose to remain in opposition to the crystallizing bourgeois coalition of CDU/CSU, FDP, and DP. One by one, the members of this coalition dropped their earlier programs favoring socialization, and, finally, by the middle of 1948, had adopted Erhard's controversial plan of economic liberalization. From that time on, the SPD steadily lost members, losses which the party said resulted from the currency reform, unemployment, and other financial strains that followed from the new economic policies. In the year 1949 alone, more than 100,000 members, almost one out of every seven, left the party. This was bitter medicine for the party which above all others was dedicated to relieving the post-war economic misery in German society.

SPD deputies in the Parliamentary Council, which drafted the Bonn Constitution in the months between Sepember 1948 and May 1949, co-operated closely with the other parties in fashioning the framework of the future West German government. The SPD delegation had contributed its own constitutional draft, which resembled the structure of the Weimar Republic. Its draft reflected the post-war revival of federalism, for it disagreed with the CDU/CSU only in particulars and in the degree of decentralization it considered desirable. Since Schumacher was in the hospital because of his leg amputation, the delegation was led by the mild-mannered Carlo Schmid, a university professor from the southwest and one of the many German intellectuals who had joined the party after 1945. Although there was little friction between the parties in the Council, it existed outside between the SPD leadership on the one hand and the CDU/CSU and the Allied military governors on the other.

Near the end of the Council's work a great clash occurred, which clearly showed the difference in political manner between Schumacher and Adenauer. With doubtful wisdom, the military governors had repeatedly intervened in the constitutional debates. They now made their final approval contingent on a number of changes in the constitutional draft which would make for a greater degree of governmental decentralization than the German parties had agreed on in the Parliamentary Council. The proposed changes did not accord with Adenauer's views, though they may have pleased some of the states' righters in the CDU/CSU. But he was not going to let such details spoil his scheme, which would bring the West Germans substantially closer to complete self-government. But Schumacher, who had faced so many crises of life and death, chose to make this issue a showdown between good and evil, between those tampering with the sacred processes of constitution-making and those defending them. He became so bitter over the issue that even some of his friends in the party came to lose confidence in his leadership.

If the SPD had expected that opposition to the Allies or its resistance to Erhard's policies would impress the voters, it must have found the first federal elections of 1949 a great disappointment. It received 29.2 per cent of the popular vote, which did not represent an actual loss of voters but did mean that it had failed to attract a proportionate share of the new voters and previous non-voters. The only consolation was that the CDU/CSU did not fare much better, though it did well enough to allow Adenauer to form a government along the same lines as his CDU/CSU-FDP-DP coalition in the Economic Council. There has been some controversy over the question of whom to blame for the fact that the two great democratic parties, the CDU/CSU and the SPD, did not form a "great coalition." But it was rather obvious that neither Adenauer nor Schumacher demonstrated any particular eagerness to start negotiating to bring this about. In addition, the two men differed sharply on social and economic policy and had a long history of personal antagonism.

The SPD, then, gathered around Kurt Schumacher and engaged in what they preferred to call "constructive opposition." Actually, they co-operated a good deal with the ruling coalition in domestic affairs, but were irreconcilably opposed to its foreign policy and its approach to European integration. Again, there has been considerable controversy over whether the SPD lost ground because Schumacher conducted too aggressive verbal attacks on the government, or because its policy alternatives did not impress the German people, who turned instead to support the evidently successful policies of Adenauer and Erhard. It is never pleasant to be in opposition to a government that is conspicuously successful. As a result, the party's loss of the 1953 elections led to a great deal of self-searching. On balance, Schumacher's acid tongue — he once called Adenauer "the Chancellor of the Allies" — may have helped the party more than it harmed it, even though public opinion polls have shown that Germans prefer a consensual pattern of politics, where all parties co-operate, to clashes between the parties. It is only recently that the German voters have begun to have an appreciation for this important facet of democratic politics, a development which represents a major contribution that Schumacher and the SPD have made to German democracy.

A better explanation of why the opposition was so ineffective was that their criticisms were unnecessarily subtle. A prime example was Schumacher's showdown with the military governors, as small a molehill as was ever made into a mountain. Other examples were the SPD's critique of Adenauer's conciliatory attitude toward the French over the Saar and his policy of European integration. Here Schumacher countered the charge that the SPD was nationalistic by pointing out that the party was already internationalist in the days of the Weimar Republic, for it had called for a United States of Europe in 1925. The SPD leader insisted that a truly European policy would have to include the nations outside of Little Europe as well. And when the *Bundestag* became concerned with German rearmament within the Western alliance late in 1950, Schumacher once more did not endorse neutralism or even oppose German rearmament as such — although he would have been supported by broad segments of the public and his own party if he had. Instead he insisted mainly on better guarantees for German security and criticized Adenauer for having taken the initiative by offering German rearmament to the Allies instead of waiting to be asked by them for a German military contribution. All these issues lacked the drama or plausibility which would attract broad masses of voters.

The most decisive reason why the SPD made such a poor showing, however, was the success of Adenauer's and Erhard's policies. In 1949 Schumacher had presented cogent reasons why Erhard's policies would never produce economic recovery and bring about jobs and prosperity, so when these policies were successful the SPD could not help but look foolish. And no matter how appropriate Schumacher's defiant "no" to unequal treatment for Germany might have been for the century after 1848, it little served the nation's purpose after 1949. Once Adenauer had skillfully used Germany's assets and international events to make the nation a respected partner in the

Western alliance, the SPD could only appear as "eternal nay-sayers." No opposition party could possibly have used these developments to its advantage.

The tragedy of the SPD went even deeper. In August 1952, Kurt Schumacher died. His loss was the severest blow the party had sustained since 1945. Schumacher had been nearly as widely known and as popular as Adenauer, and he seemed to possess all the dynamic and persuasive powers which his close friend and successor Erich Ollenhauer lacked. At the same time, the party had been buoyed up by a series of conspicuous gains in the *Land* elections of the two preceding years, when increased unemployment and adverse reaction to Adenauer's rearmament plans had greatly increased the opposition vote and had caused the SPD leaders to call for new elections in the *Bundestag*. At the time of Schumacher's death, the party was also preparing a Program of Action, which was subsequently adopted by the party convention at Dortmund. This program advocated German reunification by means of free elections and called for a larger European union, both juxtaposed to Adenauer's "conservative-clerical-capitalist" Little Europe. However, it devoted a great deal more space to domestic than to foreign policy. It advocated the promotion of economic democracy by means of labor codetermination similar to the arrangement introduced into the coal and steel industry in 1951; a "libertarian socialism" designed to bring about greater individual freedom by means of higher living standards, consumer sovereignty, and structural improvements in the national economy; a mixture of free competition and "as much planning as necessary"; the socialization of basic industries in order to undo Allied decartelization measures and to assure supplies basic to the whole economy; tax reform and special programs for the benefit of farmers, artisans, refugees, and German youth. As Schumacher wrote in his preface to the program, the post-war policies of the SPD were directed toward the creation of a socialistic society which would make a repetition of the German past impossible and would facilitate international co-operation and understanding on a basis of equality.

During the election year of 1953, the SPD engaged in a determined fight to halt ratification of the European Defense Community Treaty both in the *Bundestag* and before the Federal Constitutional Court and echoed Schumacher's ringing denunciation: "Any man who supports the EDC ceases to be a German." Neither the uprising of East German workers against their Communist puppet government nor the persistent taunts of the CDU/CSU, which associated the anti-Communist, pro-Western SPD with Moscow and the Communists, seemed able to shake their confidence in this issue. The voters, however, handed down a shattering verdict when they gave Adenauer and his CDU/CSU five million votes more than in 1949. The SPD, to be sure, also gained one million, but its percentage of the popular vote dropped to 28.8, while the CDU/CSU received 45.2 per cent and a majority of the seats of the *Bundestag*. To add insult to injury, moreover, public opinion studies ascertained that one-fourth of the SPD voters actually agreed with Adenauer's policies and only a little more than one-third opposed them. And while the CDU/CSU voters, as mentioned above, came close to being a socio-economically representative cross-section of the whole population, more than two-thirds of the SPD voters of 1953 were composed of blue-collar workers, just as two-thirds of the FDP voters were made up of the educated upper middle class. It was clearly evident that the SPD under Schumacher had failed substantially to widen its traditional base as a working-class party.

The SPD on the Way to Success

The 1953 elections led to an extraordinary amount of self-criticism and mutual recriminations within the SPD. It was only then that some party members became aware that Schumacher had been an autocrat who suffered little contradiction and had, by his very intransigence, increased the dominance of the party apparatus by full-time functionaries. His continued belligerence and his bitter polemics likewise may have fit an age when the SPD was facing "class enemies," "clerical-fascist reaction," or life-and-death struggles for national survival, but it hardly fitted into the politics of the Federal Republic, domestic or foreign. The policy alternatives presented by Schumacher also came under strong fire. But change and reform were not so easy to achieve.

The biggest obstacle to reform, as people slowly began to recognize, was the whole complex of forces making for continuity in the SPD. More than 90 per cent of the early post-war membership of the party were estimated to have been active members before 1933. Four-

fifths of its leadership had suffered persecution and exile during the
Nazi years. Two-fifths of the SPD voters could even claim that their
fathers and grandfathers belonged to the party. It could well be said
that the post-war SPD was practically identical with the pre-1933
party, only older. It was imbued with a spirit of solidarity and group
discipline that can hardly be grasped by an outsider. Much of the rigidity resulted from the dominant role played by the party apparatus,
the magnificent organization built by August Bebel more than half a
century before to withstand all adversity and persecution. The functionaries of this apparatus, particularly the numerous unpaid district
officials rather than the full-time staff at the national level, were the
main props of the organization's conservatism. Equally important
was the attitude of the membership, which had become so used to ignoring public criticism and viewing outsiders with suspicion that it
found it difficult to respond to changing public sentiment. Without
such responsiveness, however, a major democratic party cannot adapt
itself to changing conditions, appeal to the uncommitted voter — the
"floating vote" — or capture an electoral majority.

Following the debacle of the 1953 elections, the SPD was racked
by factional struggles. A right wing within the party, largely composed of younger men and women between 35 and 50 years of age,
demanded that the whole ideological orientation of the SPD be re-
vamped, the Marxist overtones of "class struggle" and "class enemy"
dropped, and the style, organization, and leadership of the party drastically changed. They also insisted that the struggle against the European Defense Community Treaty and the demand for socializing
basic industries should be abandoned and the program adapted to the
problems and popular inclinations of the mid-'fifties. The right-wing
reformers hoped thereby to remold the SPD from a doctrinaire workers' party into a broadly responsive *Volkspartei,* a people's party capable of winning majority support from all segments of German society. The wave of right-wing criticism was violent and beat against the
ramparts of the apparatus in many localities at once. But it lacked
national co-ordination and soon began to ebb, after it had provoked a
reaction from the left wing and from the apparatus. These groups
promptly tried to exclude such bright new talents as Willy Brandt and
Fritz Erler, as well as the unorthodox and popular regional leaders,
from positions of influence in the national party.

No sooner was the right wing of the SPD beaten off than the left wing rode to the attack on party policies and leadership. Composed mainly of old Social Democrats, who were still imbued with quasi-religious expectations of salvation through a socialist society, as well as intellectuals and university students whose quasi-platonic education led them to search for an ideology like Marxism which can explain everything, the left wing of the SPD also represented a militant pacifism. This wing was particularly in evidence at the 1954 party convention in Berlin, where its representatives reflected an outdated, dichotomous view of "capitalist society" and called for a determined campaign against German rearmament and involvement with the West and for the neutralization and reunification of Germany at any price. The party apparatus under Ollenhauer's leadership was saved from having to undertake any real reform by the feuding of the two wings of the party.

Despite their strong position between these antagonistic wings of the party, Ollenhauer and the party apparatus were forced by the debacle of 1953 to recognize the drift of the times. Between the Berlin convention, when the 1952 Program of Action was readopted with few changes, and the 1956 party convention in Munich, important changes took place. The EDC Treaty was finally rejected by the French National Assembly and promptly replaced by the Paris Treaties, under which the long-opposed German army became a reality. Since it was no longer able to stop Adenauer, who since 1953 controlled a two-thirds majority in the *Bundestag,* the SPD now participated actively in amending the Bonn Constitution and later in shaping the civil-military relations so that it would be impossible for a powerful, self-sufficient military establishment to form a state within the state as it had in the Weimar Republic. Schumacher might have done the same. But the left wing of the party grew understandably alarmed, especially since the leadership also failed to express strong opposition to the plans for the establishment of a European Common Market and a European Atomic Community. Actually for a while in 1955 the left wing, joined by the trade unions, the Protestant churches, youth groups, and the academic community, conducted such determined agitation against rearmament that it created the false impression that the whole party was against any German contribution to Western defense. At Munich in 1956, however, the party presented a different face to the public: two key speeches by Carlo Schmid and Leo Brandt explored the implications of automation, the "second industrial revolution," for society and economy. Ollenhauer himself, in the keynote address, argued that the SPD had no intention of tearing up treaties that the Federal Republic had duly ratified, despite SPD opposition, nor of passing up the chance to improve laws whose passage it could not prevent. In this fashion, the party leadership skillfully pursued a middle course increasingly directed toward the future rather than the past. The party responded to this appeal with gratifying unity.

Ollenhauer's keynote address bore the optimistic title, "At the Turning Point of German Politics." The SPD was indeed confident of victory after closing the gap in a series of *Land* elections and trouncing the CDU/CSU decisively in the local elections of North Rhine Westphalia, Hesse, Lower Saxony, and Baden-Wuerttemberg. In North Rhine Westphalia, for example, 19 of the 23 cities over 100,000 inhabitants had elected Social Democratic mayors. The public opinion polls in the winter of 1956-57 showed the party in the lead with as much as 45 per cent of the vote, and the "loyal opposition" had ready-made issues in public concern over rising prices and the possibility that German NATO units might be equipped with tactical nuclear arms. The party's platform put particular stress on the need for German reunification but did not explain in any great detail how this might be achieved. It came out against general conscription and against a "policy of atom bombs," and suggested that an all-encompassing European system of collective security and disarmament take the place of NATO and the Warsaw Pact. In their election program the party also demanded a stop to price increases and free, competitive enterprise — the anti-cartel bill of Ludwig Erhard had been passed only with the assistance of the SPD, since protectionistic interests in the CDU/CSU were not prepared to vote for it. The program also included planks dealing with social and cultural policy and warned that another majority for Adenauer would endanger German democracy. Conspicuously missing from the program were the usual pleas advocating socialism and socialization, an attitude which Carlo Schmid had called one of the "infantile disorders" of SPD history. Instead, the program proclaimed:

> We Social Democrats demand a free economic development, free competition and private property conscious of its responsibilities to the general good.

Needless to say, Adenauer and the CDU/CSU did what they could to remind the electorate of the past commitments of the SPD. The Old Man even went so far as to tell a Bamberg audience that the choice before the voters was between Christianity and Communism.

The 1957 elections ended with another demoralizing defeat for the SPD. It still remains to be explained why the popularity of the SPD always dips so drastically at election time. Public opinion studies have pointed to the voters' cautious, conservative frame of mind and to their overriding preoccupation with their private lives, and these same studies inspired the CDU/CSU to adopt "No Experiments" as their slogan and the SPD "Security for All." In the last months before the election, the CDU/CSU once more aroused an extra margin of millions of undecided voters and rolled up an absolute majority of 50.2 per cent of the popular vote. The SPD polled 31.8 per cent, with an increase of a million and a half votes over 1953. Their gains came chiefly from former KPD voters, young people and city-dwellers, while their number of supporters in rural areas declined. The SPD could also take pride in having made greater inroads among white-collar employees and civil servants than ever before. In the fleeting moment during the winter of 1956–57 when its popularity was highest, the party had done even better among the "new middle class" of white-collar and civil service and had also attracted large numbers of independent businessmen and professional people, in addition to numbers of workers who abandoned it again before election day.

As soon as the 1957 elections were over, the critical mood within the party came to the fore again. This time, however, both wings turned upon Ollenhauer and the party apparatus. Against Ollenhauer's resistance, three party vice-chairmanships were created. One of his old vice chairmen resigned, the other was voted out of office. In their place came three new men, who now constituted the real power behind Ollenhauer's throne: one was Carlo Schmid, who represents the anti-Marxist humanism of the German intellectual world, with strong Western overtones; another was Fritz Erler, the defense expert of the SPD, a relatively young Wuerttemberger of 44 who spent the Nazi years in various prisons; the third was the left-winger Herbert Wehner, a shoemaker's son from Dresden and an ex-Communist who had become a great admirer of Kurt Schumacher as well as his protégé. These three very different men became the troika of the SPD on the way to a brighter future. At about the same time also, Willy Brandt moved into the limelight as the new Lord Mayor of Berlin, where he had presided over the City Assembly. Furthermore, measures were bring considered to reduce the political power of the party apparatus, either by the establishment of a party advisory council composed of the many able mayors and regional leaders the SPD maintained throughout this period, or by a more direct election of the delegates to the party convention.

Once the ramparts of the establishment within the SPD had been won by the insurgents, the party proceeded to chart its future course in a manner characteristic of the German Social Democratic Party. It drew up a new "program of principles," the first such undertaking since 1925, which represented a considerable departure from the programmatic tradition of nearly a hundred years of Social Democracy. The party may have been encouraged to do so by the example of the Austrian Social Democrats, who had arrived at a similar reappraisal about the same time. Apart from a few formulas that had already appeared in the Program of Action of 1952, the new program exhibited a new pragmatic spirit. It redefined the party's goals and abandoned, at long last, the quasi-religious Marxist utopia that it had promised the depressed working classes in the past and that had represented its chief hold on them. This program was first presented in draft form to the Stuttgart convention of the party in 1958 and was adopted in final form one year later at Bad Godesberg, and henceforth it was known as the Godesberg Program of 1959.

The new program put its main emphasis on democracy, "which must become the general order of state and life, because it alone expresses respect for the dignity and responsibility of man." In practice the SPD leaders, of course, had aimed at and defended democracy since 1918, if not before, but their programmatic theory had never considered democracy more than a means to the final end — socialism. And the theory used to be as pivotal to an understanding of the party as it is in analyzing Soviet policies today. The Godesberg Program also made it very clear that democratic socialism was not a substitute religion and that it had no desire to proclaim any final truths. It was derived "from Christian ethics, humanism and classical philosophy" and named as its present goals personal freedom, democracy, solidarity, and social justice. Instead of being concerned with what Karl Marx called the "self-alienation" of the exploited workers, the party would now be mainly concerned with higher living standards, free consumer choice, and free choice of a place of work. Instead of the "class struggle" between "capitalists" and "proletarians" — a word of little meaning to German workers today — there would now be a mild concern about what big business, monopolies, and the profit motive might do to democracy, social security, and individual freedom. The Godesberg Program proposed that the problem be solved by subjecting all concentrations of economic or political power to democratic and public control and by promoting competitive enterprise as opposed to monopolies and cartels. The remaining class resentments would be over the class distinctions and privileges fostered by and resulting from the German educational system. Thus there no longer exists any conflict between the orthodox Marxism of some SPD diehards and the preference of the trade unions for labor codetermination in industry.

The economics of the Godesberg Program, finally, rested firmly on the basis of a mixed economy which allocates equal purpose and function to private, co-operative, and public enterprises. "Competition and the freedom of initiative of the entrepreneur are important elements of SPD economic policy." Instead of economic planning, which presumes a stable demand, there is now the principle of guidance which seeks to adjust the economy to the dynamic changes of economic growth aiming at "doubling living standards in a single generation." Alongside many of the goals and means of Erhard's economic policy, there is the total input-output analysis (National budget), which constitutes the chief device for gauging and guiding dynamic change. The SPD Hannover convention one year later added to this a plan for a German "people's stock certificate" through which the public and small and medium-sized enterprises could acquire a significant share of the profits of big business, large inheritances, and real estate speculations. This program was to be based on legislation and administered by a Deutsche Nationalstiftung, a kind of missing link between government bond issues and a mutual investment fund. This remains one of the few differences between the two parties on economic policy, for Erhard's "people's stock" is issued by denationalized individual enterprises and hence likely to fluctuate. The SPD and the German trade unions still call the CDU/CSU policy of furthering property ownership among the masses a dubious device, which may be intended to divert attention from the lucrative manipulations of big business. They do, however, approve of savings premiums and of "investive wages," or profit sharing. The SPD now expressly called itself a broad people's party rather than a workers' party. Social Democrats wanted it known that this program represented its true intentions — not principles adopted by the party sixty or a hundred years ago — and should be used as the basis for criticizing them.

In addition to this New Dealish social and economic program, the SPD made a significant change in its foreign and defense policy. Early in 1959, the Party Executive Board had still approved the *Deutschlandplan,* a proposal for German reunification, by way of disengagement along the lines suggested by George F. Kennan and Adam Rapacki, the Polish Foreign Minister. But in June 1960, a month after the summit meeting in Paris broke down, Herbert Wehner, the architect of the Godesberg Program, launched the new foreign and defense policy in a speech before the *Bundestag.* Later in the same year, at the party convention at Hannover, the party adopted the new policy, and also nominated a "government team" headed by Willy Brandt and including such SPD notables as Carlo Schmid, Fritz Erler, economics expert Heinrich Deist, and regional leaders Brauer (Hamburg), Zinn (Hesse), and Steinhoff (North Rhine Westphalia). The new policy declared that the changed international situation and increasing pressure from Soviet Communism made necessary bipartisanship in foreign policy and defense. This implied, among other things, a firm commitment to NATO, to the economic and political unification of Little Europe, and to German defense, though not to providing the German army with atomic weapons. The party had no objections to nuclear arms for NATO as long as the Warsaw Pact possessed similar armaments. At the same time, the SPD once more confirmed its strong support for controlled, step-by-step disarmament and, first and foremost, nuclear disarmament.

Adoption of these new policies by the SPD signified that the old establishment had finally collapsed and had been replaced by younger elements, especially the popular and successful regional and local leaders and, above all, the new candidate for Chancellor, Willy Brandt, the fighting Lord Mayor of West Berlin who had long held views similar to the new policies. At the same time the party changed its attitude toward conducting politics. It showed a new appreciation for attractive personalities, whereas in the past it had tended to over-emphasize ideas and policies and shy away from personalities. In its 1961 campaign, the SPD also made much use of the pragmatic approaches it had observed in the preceding British and American election campaigns. In addition to features we have described, this new style took the form of a "government program" presented at a dramatic SPD convention at Bonn in the middle of the election campaign. This program very skillfully turned the Christian Democratic characterization of the opposition as "eternal nay-sayers" back onto the government spokesmen and accused them of having failed to bring together all the democratic forces behind a common policy. It likewise accused the Adenauer administration of treating pressure groups with weakness and opportunism, of undemocratic and even unconstitutional shenanigans, of unwise saber-rattling and unco-operative attitudes abroad, and of glaring neglect in furthering education, science, and the welfare of the broad masses. More specifically, the "government program" as well as SPD posters and handbills proposed to lengthen the legal minimum of paid annual vacations to three, and then to four weeks, and to improve the medical services and hospitals as well as the public health insurance available. Pensioners were promised a better deal, including aid with the acquisition of a television set. One handbill also offered to lower the exorbitant excise taxes on coffee, tea, and cocoa. A pamphlet version of the "government program" of the SPD presented each point of the program sepa-rately in one column, and in the next column specified "what the CDU concocted," which in most cases was very vague or "nothing."

The new style of the SPD campaign, its attractive young candidate for Chancellor, and its changes in program began to pay off visibly in the 1961 elections. To be sure, the general shift of the party to the right cost about 5 per cent of its old voters who voted for the German Peace Union (DFU), a pacifist splinter party with enough Communist members and financial support to be called a front organization. The Adenauer government was perfectly aware of the nature of the DFU, but refrained from any steps that would prevent this fringe group from drawing away SPD votes. At the same time, the SPD gained about 20 per cent new voters, or two million, as compared to

1957. A large portion of its new supporters came from the middle classes, whereas some of its working-class supporters switched to the CDU/CSU. The final tally gave it 36.2 per cent of the popular vote, or even 38 per cent if we include the DFU voters who will sooner or later return to the fold. This is the highest vote the SPD ever received in a national election, and there is every reason to believe that the trend for greater gains will continue in future elections. According to public opinion studies since the early 'sixties, the rigid divisions of the German electorate have begun to dissolve, possibly as a result of the final arrival of mass consumption, of the "new society," on all levels. Increasing blocs of voters are fluctuating between the major parties. And while the German voters still cling to preconceived political loyalties and stereotyped images and are not easy to reach with the campaign message of a political party, persistent efforts on the part of the SPD cannot fail to make an impression in the long run. After all, in many electoral districts, all the SPD needs to do is to convince the voter to have as much confidence in its national leadership as he has long shown in regional and local SPD leaders. A good way of accomplishing this goal is to give these popular SPD mayors and *Land* Ministers President a prominent place among the party's national leaders. As we have seen, the SPD has already gone to some lengths in this direction, though with some timidity. After Willy Brandt had fought the 1961 election as SPD candidate for Chancellor, for example, he preferred going back to Berlin to becoming opposition leader in the *Bundestag.* Several SPD notables, among them Adolf Arndt and Karl Schiller, took positions in his city administration. By the time Lord Mayor Brandt appeared again on the national scene, when he was elected successor to party chairman Ollenhauer, who died in December 1963, rumors were already going around that the southwestern SPD was grooming Fritz Erler for this position. Brandt was elected chairman in 1964, but now he had to divide his party headquarters between an Executive Board office in Berlin and a Presidial Secretariat in Bonn which also includes the section for foreign affairs and the press office of the party.

The party's timidity was also at issue when the editor of "The Falcons," the SPD youth organization journal, raised questions about the party's decision to present Willy Brandt as a personable, attractive young man with a good-looking family rather than as an able political

leader in the 1961 campaign. The controversy was a reflection of previous feuds between the SPD and the frequently dissenting Falcons as
well as of an extended dispute over whether the "undecided voters"
are so unpolitical that they only react to non-political appeals. But
the point was well-taken, for it showed how uncertain the SPD is of
how to present its national leadership in the correct light. At the same
time, it should not be forgotten what a demoralizing effect twelve
years in opposition can have. Willy Brandt was by no means the first
SPD figure to prefer the satisfactions of *Land* politics to the frustrations of Bonn.

There is a law inherent in two-party systems which states that incumbents become fat and lazy, if not corrupt, after a succession of
terms in office, and a determined opposition sooner or later gets its
chance to show what it can do. But for this mechanism to function,
the opposing party must not be separated from the governing party by
insurmountable class lines, religious or geographic differences, or by
an irreconcilable ideology. And the opposition party must, of course,
try harder than those in power to adapt itself to the changing currents
of public opinion and to the unmet needs of evolving society. The
SPD has demonstrated its departure from the limitations of class and
ideology in the years since Schumacher's death. Its support for a
broad consensus on foreign, defense, and even basic economic policies between CDU/CSU and SPD since 1959 has been reaffirmed consistently in all particulars at party conventions, formal occasions, and
before the *Bundestag*. Its co-operation with leading Christian Democratic figures and with their measures and policies was particularly
evident when the pro-British and pro-American preamble was added
to the legislation implementing the Franco-German friendship treaty;
indeed, whenever the CDU/CSU had difficulties with its coalition
partner, the FDP, and more recently during the re-election of Federal
President Heinrich Luebke. The SPD policy of "embracing" the government, in other words, has helped to erode somewhat the dependence of government leaders like Ludwig Erhard, Gerhard Schroeder,
Kai-Uwe von Hassel, or Luebke on the support of such erratic allies
as Strauss's Gaullist faction or the FDP. It has also given the SPD an
opportunity to participate in the shaping of important policies and
has established the party leaders as able and reliable national policymakers. And even if Brandt's popularity should decline, the "shadow

cabinet" nominated at the 1964 convention in Karlsruhe includes many well-known figures.

One of the most interesting aspects of the "embracing" policy is the effort of the SPD to invade the innermost sanctum of Christian Democratic strength with invincible brotherly love. In spite of the evident good will of the post-war SPD toward the churches — there were even Christian Working Committees in the SPD immediately after 1945 — and the close relations prominent Protestant clergymen have had with the party, there has been a certain amount of Catholic "pulpit support" for the CDU/CSU during various elections. As late as the 1957 elections, a high Catholic dignitary in the Rhineland stated publicly that no truly faithful Catholic could feel loyal to the SPD. Since that day, however, there has been no lack of overtures for a rapprochement between the party and the Church. When the Godesberg Program appeared, Cardinal Frings of Cologne and many other prominent Church leaders expressed delight with the section on the churches and with what they perceived as a far-reaching agreement with Christian Socialist doctrines. In the years since 1960, moreover, there were overtures by prominent SPD members, most notably Gustav Heinemann, the one-time Minister of the Interior of Adenauer's first cabinet, signifying SPD approval for denominational primary schools (*Bekenntnisschulen*) and other facets of CDU educational policy, which had long been a bone of contention between their party and the Church. To the alarm of the CDU/CSU, a Monsignore Forster of Munich, who had for some time been a vocal supporter of better understanding, expressed the hope that future elections might leave Catholic voters a free choice, once the SPD had eliminated from among its membership the last traces of anti-clerical or anti-Catholic sentiment. At this point, to the relief of the Christian Democrats, this liberal point of view was refuted by the conservative *Osservatore Romano,* the Vatican's influential paper, and this article was picked up widely by the CDU/CSU party press. Yet the SPD was not to be denied. In April 1964, a delegation of Social Democratic leaders visited His Holiness, Paul VI, in the evident hope of surmounting even this last barrier. *Amor vincit omnia.*

It is still too early to tell when this policy of "embracing" all manner of enemies will lead to success and what this success will look like. Will it be a coalition government with the FDP, with whom the

SPD has also co-operated on occasion? Will it be a black-red coalition of CDU/CSU and SPD for which the SPD has shown its readiness since the debacle of 1953? Or is it going to be the all-party coalition for which Herbert Wehner has been pleading tirelessly up and down the country since 1960 and for which he has also been an inexhaustible powerhouse of "embracing" ideas and measures to overcome the resistance and prejudice of bourgeois, clerical, and anti-Marxist circles? A visitor to a Social Democratic election rally today will be hard-pressed to find proletarian dress or features anywhere in the audience. Everybody wears urban suits and white collars. At a meeting of party members he would find it not much different, except perhaps for the shirt-sleeved informality that reminds one more of a bowling club or of a guild meeting of artisans in pre-industrial times than of the "rising of ye wretched of the earth." They still insist on addressing each other with the democratic *Du* rather than with *Sie, Herr,* or a title. And they still call each other "comrade" (*Genosse*), though again with a flair that smacks more of a medieval guild or a co-operative (*Genossenschaft*) than of the dark conspiracy of "the prisoners of starvation" or the brotherly piety of a Messianic sect awaiting the day of deliverance. Young members say "comrade" with a slight curling of the upper lip and with the insolence of youth that has been spared the trials of their elders.

The SPD may find its triumph is a straight electoral victory. Kurt Schumacher used to spend sleepless hours toying with electoral statistics, examining past election returns district by district under the spell of the figures, but a premature death snatched him away long before the hour of triumph. The young Social Democrats who spent the years from his death to 1957 in violent rebellion against the rearmament policies of Adenauer now have not only accepted the Godesberg Program but have turned into sophisticated campaign managers, image molders, and campaign sloganeers easily rivaling the professional qualities of anyone ever hired by the CDU for "*das politische* Marketing" of candidate Adenauer. To be sure, it took a purge of the leftish Socialist Student Federation (SDS) and a handful of sympathetic university professors to unite all the young Social Democrats behind the new goals. Yet it is remarkable how thoroughly the young Socialists have exchanged their ideology for a rational and pragmatic common-sense approach, while at the same time the Young Union of the CDU/CSU and the Young Democrats of the FDP are retreating visibly into the ivory towers of ideological thinking.

Herbert Wehner's strategy of embrace, finally, is also aimed at electoral results. On his advice, the SPD not only intends to make it extremely difficult for the governing parties to reject its co-operation in the *Bundestag;* it also hopes to make a better showing in those electoral districts in the Lower Rhine area or in Lower Bavaria where Catholicism and bourgeois prejudice have so far kept the Social Democrats from gaining a foothold. Wehner has spurned no speaking engagement, whether in the smallest town or before the most insignificant local athletic club, which would allow him to spread the word about the new open-minded spirit of the SPD. Membership figures have taken the first strong upward turn since the decline of the late 'forties and early 'fifties. The new members may lack sectarian conviction and may not attend meetings faithfully, but at least the party has made an opening and has broken down the all too solid solidarity. Wehner also promotes meetings at which popular SPD mayors and county officials explain to their less successful colleagues how one goes about topping the 30 per cent barrier which is still stopping progress in many areas. Many reports show how these "embracing" contacts with various groups and agencies have been breaking the ice and have democratized the attitudes of the people toward their social and governmental authorities. There are some fascinating public opinion polls that show that SPD voters more often discuss politics than those of the CDU/CSU, but that they do their politicking only with fellow employees, and not with superiors. Perhaps now they will talk with the boss, too, and the boss with them.

"If we are smart and do not permit ourselves to lose our tempers, if nothing disturbs us too much and no effort is too great for us," Wehner has stated repeatedly, "then we shall win the confidence of the people and reach our goal." No incumbent party or elected official, no matter how reluctant to be embraced, is going to withstand this irresistible force for very long. One can only hope that the possession of power, so ardently yearned for, will not disappoint the Social Democrats once it is theirs. It will be a good experience and beneficial for the proper functioning of German democracy when the reins of government change hands from one major party to another. When the time comes, the SPD will have richly deserved it. For it will already have rendered German democracy an enormous service, an unenviable one perhaps, but beyond doubt a service which no other German party could have accomplished without casting away its brittle faith in democracy: it has remained in opposition for a very long time without losing its integrity or even its stamina to reform itself and to win out ultimately.

10

WHITHER, GERMAN DEMOCRACY?

With this survey of the evolving political parties of Western Germany, our journey through the political state of mind of post-war Germany has come to an end and we may stop to look back. The predominant theme of this book has been the evolution of the new politics of Western Germany, for the modern mind has difficulty grasping anything unless it develops from recognizable antecedents. More specifically, we used the phrase "digesting the undigested past" to draw these antecedents into the pale of the living. Unlike so many contemporary exposés by flashback, however, this account has not depicted German history as stages on the way toward the goal of Hitler's millennium nor has it seen the present as an outgrowth of the Third Reich, if not identical with it. This would have meant using history as a weapon rather than as a means for discovering the facts. Such an attitude would also presume an identity among the many generations of Germans, the many groups and individuals, their thought and their traditions, and their attitudes and feelings over a period of a hundred years or more which it would be extremely unlikely could ever have existed. Carried to its logical conclusion, any notion of an unchangeable national character or culture becomes the same as the questionable concept of "race."

Germany and Modernization

Instead of such an approach, this study has set the digesting of the past into the context of the process of modernization, that immense journey that all advanced industrial societies have slowly and painfully traversed during the last centuries on the way from traditional cultures to an urban-industrial way of life. The Anglo-American countries, including the older dominions, have enjoyed a headstart in this development, and this would seem to explain, better than any idea of innate qualities or mystical identities, why they have been "the envy of less happy lands" in their political, social, and economic adjustment. More recently, the Scandinavian and other continental European countries have begun to reach a similar stage of maturity. What we may call maturity today is, of course, again only an intermediate stage on the way to we know not what. At the same time, the colonial powers awakened scores of new nations from their traditional slumber and induced them to aim at catching up by the shortest possible route. In the most advanced among them — Russia, China, or Egypt — the force of this change has become the fuel for a powerful military machine which in turn has been directed against weaker and mostly less modernized nations. Russia, we hope, is about to outgrow this transitional phase and join the advanced countries of the West in concentrating her energies on her internal affairs. Thus it is not only the painful transitional phase through which countries go while becoming modernized, but also the gap between more modernized and more backward nations that has been a major cause of internal convulsions and dictatorships as well as of international wars and conquest in our time. This, in considerable simplification, also explains how the transitional growing pains turned Western nation-states into colonial empires through the conquest of weaker peoples who were still in the traditional frame of development. Today it explains the quest of Communist Russia and, increasingly, Communist China for control over the developing areas of the world, as well as the reason why Communist dictatorships arose in these two countries.

Where does the German past fit into this picture? To use a simile,

Germany has been the middle child between her more advanced brethren in the West and her more backward sisters in Eastern Europe, Germany's geographical equivalent to the overseas colonies of Western nations: too old to be treated with the indulgence and aid due to a nestling, but also too young and irresponsible to be accorded the recognition and freedom of development granted an older child. Her entire adolescence, so to speak, was spent in futile rebellion against her older brothers, against their dominant position and, in its wildest and wooliest manifestations, literally against growing to similar maturity herself. Thus the anti-Western and anti-modern stance found its backdrop in the preference for *Kultur* over "civilization," for childhood tradition over greater maturity. Whenever the courage of the rebellious adolescent to face his older brothers in the West flagged, he could regain it by comparing himself to the still much smaller children to the east and by considering plans to dominate them. What symbolic gratification in defeating the Polish cavalry in the *blitzkrieg* of 1939 and plunging deep into Russia two years later. In World War I, the young rebel was forcibly subdued and shaken up by his older brothers, and his sense of humiliation and lust for revenge burned like a raging fever until he was ready to surrender his ravaged mind and body to the great seducer, Hitler, the totalitarian dictator.

It is difficult to follow the course of the sickness and rebellion with any degree of certainty through the years of totalitarian dictatorship and total war, because there one can no longer tell to what extent the rebellious people are acting out their hostility and to what extent they are compelled by the will of the totalitarian movement and the momentum of all-out war. During the first years after our adolescent rebel's maniacal fling was over, there was also no way of telling what to expect next, for he was too preoccupied with his wounds from the last licking and was also once more under the complete control of his older brothers. In the intervening years, however, it has become abundantly clear that at some time between 1939 and 1949, possibly still while the totalitarian dictatorship of Germany was carrying out some of the most heinous crimes known in the history of the world, the adolescent finally reached maturity. Naturally, both older and younger brothers and sisters continued to watch him warily, and some of the younger children even discovered that cries of alarm about him were a good attention-getting device. But the truth of the matter is that the youthful rebel of yesterday has not engaged in any notable act of rebellion for twenty years but, on the contrary, has shown much evidence that he has been absorbed by the same kind of preoccupations that are typical of his mature brethren in the West. Such maturity or adulthood, of course, is no guarantee against adult failings or diseases, nor against crushing mediocrity or any manner of imperfections. But it is unlikely that Germany will ever be a flaming young rebel again.

So far the simile. While they may not prove anything by themselves, similes do lay down analogies and suggest a way of looking at the historical facts. While some people may have legitimate doubts about how far one can compare the process of modernization with the way in which a child matures, or the tensions arising from different stages in modernization with sibling rivalry and adolescent rebellion, there are other methods in vogue that would seem to be a great deal more ludicrous than this psychological analogy.

One is the ideological approach, which tries to reduce the pluralistic complexity of generations and social groups to one evolving *Nationalgeist* marching through German history from Luther to Hitler. The effort to combat National Socialism as a system of ideas and values is well-meant but about as ineffectual as combating the "ideology" of a juvenile delinquent by tracing it back to the writings, say, of the Marquis de Sade. At its worst this method has led to the denigration of certain historical figures, the expurgation of important philosophical thought, and the casting of simple-minded suspicions by well-meaning zealots on all kinds of social and political phenomena which are current in all countries at some time. To give examples, one can hardly suppress a smile today about the earnest proposal by some post-war thinkers to transform the big cities of the world again into village communities and big industry into village craft shops in order to combat the pernicious influence of "mass democracy" that is said to have led to the rise of Hitler. Likewise, it would be sophomoric to burn the beautiful poetry of German Romanticism, banish Kant and Hegel, exorcise Luther and parts of modern Protestant theology, and cast out Nietzsche and nihilistic turn-of-the-century poets.

To adopt a legalistic approach and try to determine the extent to which the rules of constitutional government were being broken long before 1933 and even before 1918 has some merit. But in the end it too fails to capture the essence of what went on, for rules are determined as much by the evolving cultural system as is their observance or non-observance. A moralistic approach stands no better chance of grasping the essence of what went wrong with Germany during the fateful three-quarters of a century for the simple reason that changing moral standards are a universal phenomenon of the modernization process. To return to our juvenile delinquent, it is fortunate that enlightened societies have learned not to try and cure his ailment with ideological remedies, with the rule book or moral preachings, but to go to the psychological and sociological roots of his wrong-headedness.

Psychology still may not be able to tell us the whole story; it can only furnish us with inferences from scattered personal statements that may or may not be representative — after all, there were no public opinion polls before our time. So our chief source of reliable information about the great transformation is sociology, the science which is often credited with being for our age what theology was for the Middle Ages and scientific philosophy for the rise of the Modern Age. According to sociological studies of the process of modernization, the immense journey is marked by such indications as the transformation of large masses of people from a traditional rural society to urbanization and industrialization with many "stages of economic growth" and of urban transformation; from localism to a national orientation, along with the corresponding development of transportation and communications; from a religiously defined cultural system to secularism and religious toleration; and from a traditional society full of carefully maintained divisions, hierarchies, and social classes to a relatively egalitarian, individualistic society in which each person, man or woman, has left the old collectivistic shell defining his or her place in the traditional society and strives to take care of himself by all means available for individual advancement, economic, social, and political. When the journey's end has been reached, this also constitutes the social basis for democracy, though not the only possible one.

Sociology can also tell us about the explosive tensions of the transition from traditional society to modernity. Urbanization has its maladjustments and its aches and pains in slum housing, employment, and effective self-government. Industrialization brings labor problems, technological and economic impasses, and some of the most devastating domestic crises since the Black Death. Nationalism can carry in its wake extreme xenophobia, violence, militarism, war, or perhaps a yearning for empire. As communications media have expanded, men have also abused their function by preaching prejudice, hatred, and violence. Loss of religious faith has helped produce mass anxieties, and it can give rise to fanatical ideological movements in quest of salvation and with an apocalyptic drive toward catastrophe and death. The breakdown of a hierarchic class society can be marked by the rise of class-consciousness, bitter class struggles either gradual or sudden, and social revolution. The fear of equality may lead the descending social strata into racial fantasies and fascist coups designed to arrest the advent of the egalitarian society. Once traditional collectivism wanes, the emancipated individual must take control of his life with decisiveness and an unlimited willingness to learn and to adjust himself to the changing conditions of his new life. He must also adapt the political, economic, and social institutions to their new functions. A failure to take control and to adjust brings about chaos, maladjustment, and, possibly, an escape from freedom into totalitarianism or its equivalents.

As we have seen, the German story fits this process of modernization quite faithfully with only a few complications. In fact, most of the so-called attributes of the German "national character," such as militarism, authoritarianism, hero worship, romanticism, or subjectivity are really universal attributes of societies in the throes of the transition to modernity. Modernization started in Germany considerably later than in the West, and the Napoleonic invasion created an anti-Western attitude by calling attention to the backwardness of society and by intensifying German nationalism. Then the national unification effected by Bismarck and the power of Prussia and its *Junkers* inhibited social revolution and eventually diverted it to imperialistic ambitions.

With defeat in World War I, finally, the stage was set for the endless list of troubles that doomed the Weimar Republic practically from the start. Every conceivable crisis of the transitional phase broke over the heads of the republican politicians as soon as sudden defeat had toppled the monarchy and stunned the nation: the urban troubles were augmented with a farm crisis, both contributing to the traditionalist revolt. Industrialization and the market economy did their worst, causing painful dislocations and two catastrophic collapses, the second one with deadly mass effect. Belated nationalism raged against the "dictate of Versailles," the "November traitors," and assorted separatist movements until it was assuaged in the "national rebirth" of 1933. The trauma of defeat and the burning thirst for revenge went right along with racism and dreams of an empire for the "master race." Propaganda became a mass weapon for mobilization and destruction. The waning of religion produced bitter clashes between militant secularizers and defenders of the churches. Ideological movements increased the tensions in the class structure which was finally disintegrating under the impact of military defeat and economic crises. The despair of the downward moving social strata made fascism an obvious choice. Add to this list the failure of popular government, from the confusion and mistaken actions of the beleaguered voters to the malfunctioning of the party system, in addition to the popular anxiety caused by the sudden demise of the monarchy, the last symbol of the passing of the seemingly conflictless traditional society — and you have explained the failure of the Weimar Republic. Still, there was no necessity whatsoever for Hitler to have inherited power at the moment when the general crisis was already beginning to wane. The inner compulsion of transitional German society toward National Socialism, not to mention the path from Luther to Hitler, is pure fiction. That Hitler did come to power was due chiefly to his demagogic and strategic abilities and to the criminal stupidity of the men who conspired to have him appointed Chancellor. Without Hitler, Germany would very likely have muddled through another decade or two with recurrent crises of one sort or another and then reached maturity without the horrid interlude of National Socialism and without World War II.

What is the sociological evidence that post-war West German society has indeed passed the transitional phase? It is in the features of the "new society," so similar to the features of other Western societies, such as the waning of class distinctions, the decline of ideology, the nature of the social elites, and the new individualism of the masses, as it expresses itself in their concentration on their individual pursuit of happiness. German society today has a social predisposition for democracy, which pre-Hitler Germany never had. The economic recovery and the subsequent economic growth helped bring about the development of the "new society" by producing the labor shortage and boosting the broad masses of Germans to the stage of mass consumption. It was not the chief cause, although it did "recapitulate" the industrial revolution, this time bringing about a real capitalistic development and an independent *bourgeoisie*. The chief cause may well have been the social mobilization of depression, totalitarianism, and war as well as the *de facto* equality of poverty immediately after the war. This is hardly a road to modernity that can be recommended to new nations, but it was evidently an effective shock treatment for the extreme case of adolescent rebellion of Germany.

One can gauge the progression of modernization also in the description given by the German sociologist Helmut Schelsky of the changing states of mind of German youth in the twentieth century: the first fifteen years of the century were characterized by the romantic rebellion of Youth Movement and *Wandervogel*, an idealistic state of mind described with great intuition in Eduard Spranger's classic, *Psychologie des Jugendalters*. The 'twenties and 'thirties saw the rise of a militantly political youth which found its outlet in paramilitary, "comradely" organizations and utopian movements of the extreme right and left. Schelsky calls German post-war youth "the skeptical generation," because it has shown little readiness to carry its hide to market for any great and glorious leader or set of ideas. It is characterized by its concentration on personal success, a "consumer mentality," and its desire for early marriage and family life. The greater commitment of the young to European integration and their abandonment of class consciousness and ideological thinking also can be called harbingers of the future. The values of the "new society" and especially of young people in Western Germany have been decried both in Germany and abroad as materialistic, mediocre, decadent, barren of moral commitment, and by worse epithets. German intellectuals above all have expressed their extreme dissatisfaction with all facets of the "new society." Yet, if we may come back to the image of the adolescent in violent rebellion, what has really happened is that he got married, took a job, and settled down. It is quite true that he did not, as some had hoped, embark on a brilliant career (he had already set the world on fire once), and he married a very average girl, Modernity, the sister of the wives of his older brothers. There may be many who feel let down and disappointed by this development, though in view of the past it would seem far more appropriate to heave a sigh of relief.

Transitional Remnants in West German Politics

There remains the question of where transitional elements still survive and what dangers, political or cultural, these elements may hold. To begin with, one should note that, even though the danger of a relapse into a traditionalistic revolt is always present when the process of modernization falters, today's Germans really have no traditions left to go back to. If the newly rich strata should go bankrupt, what would they fall back on? On their memories as post-war black marketeers, perhaps? There are no "cabinets of barons," as in the last days of Weimar, and no *Junkers* for them to bail out and to get their estates off the auction block. The old-timers who still dream of monarchy, the old refugees and expellees who reminisce about their homelands in the East, and the handful of neo-Nazis cold-shouldered by the "skeptical generation" are not only dying out and are heavily outnumbered, they are also very far removed from the predominant course of sentiment in the Federal Republic. The majority sentiment may indeed turn in many directions, but it is extremely unlikely to wax enthusiastic about any of these old-time dreams. Public opinion polls have given us an indication of the extent to which today's West Germans are satisfied with the position of their nation in the world, in spite of Berlin and the reunification issue. While only two-thirds of Frenchmen, one-half of Americans, and two-fifths of Englishmen have expressed satisfaction, more than six out of seven supposedly revanchist and irredentist West Germans have said they are satisfied with the position of their country in the world. The pollsters have also shown how the West Germans are attached to their present life. When asked at what time the country was best off, more than one-half in 1951 still felt it had been before 1933 and especially in the "good old days" before 1914, and close to another half named the pre-war years under the Nazis, while a mere one in fifty said it was now, under the new regime. When asked the same question in 1959, more than four in ten said "now," while less than three in ten were still dreaming of the days of the *Kaiser's* Germany and less than two in ten of the period from 1933 to 1939. In the winter of 1963–64, finally, 62 per cent said "today" and only one in ten and one in six, respectively, looked back nostalgically to the 1930's or the 1910's. This may seem like a rather prosaic measurement of allegiance, but, as a vote of confidence in modernity after half a century of transitional crises, it outweighs a thousand intellectual sand castles and utopias.

This is not to say that some segments of German society do not stand with at least one leg still in the transitional phase. Organized religion in post-war Germany, for instance, has played an ambiguous role in the religious revival that has had such profound importance in salvaging the mental and spiritual ruins of totalitarian corruption. There is a fine line of distinction between, for example, a "Christian cultural policy" and bigotry toward secular elements or other religions. The same line also divides the spiritual guidance of the young in German primary education, especially in denominational schools (*Bekenntnisschulen*), from obscurantism and denominational narrowness, and the laudable interest of the churches in social policy from playing politics in the pulpit. There is a great need in modern society for the vital spiritual force of religion, but political abuses of spiritual authority and sentiment belong strictly to the transitional phase. There is much to be said for the disestablishment of the German churches and their direct collection of dues from the faithful as an alternative to the present practice of having the state collect church taxes. A religion that relies too much on crutches stands in danger of becoming lame.

Another segment of West German society that is transitional, if not traditional in character, are the regional protest movements, such as the Bavaria Party, the DP in Lower Saxony, and smaller groups elsewhere. All of these have visibly declined in voting strength. The voting statistics have shown their clientele to be composed of farmers, small businessmen, craftsmen, and a motley collection of persons from many strata whose chief traits appear to be the way they move from one small right-wing group to another, including the neo-Nazi fringe, and their reluctance to accept a democratic party system and representative government. A study conducted by Erich Reigrotzki in the mid-'fifties revealed some tell-tale characteristics of workers voting for these small parties or for the FDP. They are politically disoriented and express in disproportionate numbers a sense of political powerlessness and a preference for a one-party system or no parties at all. This appears to be the very stuff of which the Nazi landslide was composed in the early 1930's.

There are, of course, also transitional elements in the three large, democratic parties. In the CDU/CSU there is the close link with the Catholic Church, which dates back to the days when German Catholics had to defend themselves against a hostile, Protestant government. The rapprochement with Protestantism was an enormous step toward modernity. The correspondence of CDU/CSU voters to a cross-section of the population testifies to the modernity of that party. But it still relies on such transitional fetters as regional elements, states' righters, tradition-minded farmers, artisans and small business, and the "pulpit support" of the churches. The Christian Democrats' increasing emphasis on the "Christian ideology" indicates that in recent years they have been retreating from modernity, a trend likely to be reversed by competition from the SPD. The latter party has moved with determination since 1953, and especially since 1957, to shed its transitional heritage as a highly ideological and class-bound workers' party. Both ideology and class-consciousness are typical transitional phenomena from the days when submerged and discriminated classes had to battle for a place in the sun and their frustrations bloomed into messianic hopes of deliverance. If we look at the de-ideologization of the SPD in conjunction with the German working-classes' gaining easy access to durable consumer goods, such as passenger cars and television sets, and with the rise of the values of individualism and the pursuit of happiness, the future of a modern SPD in a post-Marxian society seems bright indeed.

In this connection, it is also worth noting that the most numerous parts of West German society, blue-collar workers (47 per cent), rural laborers (4 per cent), white-collar employees in private industry (19 per cent) and government (6 per cent), in fact a good three-fourths of society, are about evenly split between the SPD and the CDU/CSU and give almost no support to any other party. Thus three-fourths of the population, whose lives have been revolutionized by the "new society," would be fully represented within the framework of a two-party system. Of the rest, the CDU/CSU receives the vote of the bulk of the farmers (11 per cent of total population) and a significant

portion of independent businessmen (11 per cent) which constitute its
safe edge in federal elections. The sprinkling of SPD supporters
among the professions (2 per cent) has more qualitative than quantitative significance.

It is among the remainder of independent businessmen and the
professions, not counting the volatile vote of politically disoriented
workers and others, that we find the basis of the FDP, *Bildung* and
Besitz, and an articulate opposition to a two-party system. *Besitz* is
the property-conscious commercial and industrial bourgeoisie, either
post-war or before, which either votes for regional parties or the
FDP, but finds the CDU/CSU "too leftish." *Bildung* are the educated
upper classes, including, in particular, the professions and the managerial elites of business and government whose higher education has
inculcated in them a wariness of both Christian Democratic clericalism and Social Democratic collectivism. Theirs is an elitism that shies
away from all identification with the toiling masses, whether SPD- or
CDU/CSU-inspired. There can be little doubt about the transitional
character and origin of the economic and cultural liberalism that mo-
tivates these elements today, even though they used to be the spear-
head of modernization and still have a very valuable function to fulfill
both in the cartel-ridden economics of Western Germany and in West
German politics, which can use every ounce of liberalism, regardless
of origin. The emergence of the economically conservative, but politically liberal Protestant leadership in the CDU/CSU and the new
course of the SPD now present FDP voters with reasonable alternatives, if their party fails to qualify for representation in the *Bundestag.*
In the meantime, this third party continues to complicate democratic
government in Germany.

The realm of *Bildung,* or higher education, is probably the largest
single stumbling block from the transitional past, if not from older
traditions. The social substance behind *Bildung* is the educational establishment of the public secondary schools, both the type based on
humanistic education and the natural science type, and the universities. In a society increasingly marked by the disappearance of social
distinctions, these nine-year secondary schools are entered by only
about 15 per cent of ten-year-old schoolchildren of both sexes. It has
often been claimed by German philosophers that a high development
of civilization is made possible only by deliberately delaying the
physical maturity of youth. German higher education achieves this

goal all too well by the absence of coeducation, of planned extra-
curricular activities, and of life adjustment, and by grueling academic
competition which further shows its resemblance to French higher
education. The rigors of competitive examinations and the exodus of
those leaving after the sixth year for a commercial or technical career
reduce the percentage of secondary school students graduating with
the coveted *Abitur* diploma to no more than 6 per cent of all schoolchildren. The *Abitur* is practically the only avenue to a university education, although in theory privately tutored youths could get in by
examination and there are night school courses for this purpose. By
the time the select few have acquired their *Abitur,* they have already
become the Brahmins of German culture by virtue of these nine years
of intensive, one-sided intellectual education which leaves them alienated from the life of man and of the society around them. Their
university years can do very little to change the attitudes formed during their teens and are unlikely to do so, since German universities
mainly concentrate on academic specialization and have remained
almost as impervious to reform as the secondary schools. The university graduate, the *Akademiker,* becomes a part of the educated establishment and very protective about his vested interests and status in
society. The professions and a considerable portion of the managerial
positions in business and government are reserved for *Akademiker* or
at least give preference to them, regardless of whether they have
proved themselves on the job or not. The teaching and administrative
staff of the secondary schools in some states is drawn exclusively
from university graduates, in sharp contrast to the teacher training of
the primary schools, and this, next to the vested interests of the whole
establishment, is the chief cause of the perpetuation of the system.

German university students show the effect of their secondary
training in various ways: they are introvert, aloof from the life of
their own society, unsociable, and given to a peculiar mixture of cultural idealism and crass opportunism. The post-war revival of the old
"student corporations," of which a very significant portion again wear
the old colors, engage in fencing duels, and express loyalty to pre-
democratic, transitional, or even medieval social and political ideals,
is a symptom of both alienation and opportunism rampant, for the
alumni of the student corporations can deliver the reserved jobs to
the newly graduating *Akademiker*. Political interest among university

students is relatively low considering their advantages of education and upper class background. The small minority that is politically active shows a typical transitional cast of mind, which tends to look at politics through ideological glasses — Socialist, Christian Democratic, Liberal, or neo-Nazi in persuasion, such as the 6000-member National Student Association outlawed in 1960–61.

It is not that the humanistic tradition of German education produces Nazis or ideological fighters of other persuasions, but that it leaves German students so alienated and maladjusted that they are either unpolitical or tend toward a curiously distorted view of contemporary politics. A recent sociological survey of student attitudes toward politics at the University of Frankfurt by Juergen Habermas and others brought out the full dimensions of this syndrome: close to one-half of the respondents expressed both democratic convictions and showed basically democratic attitudes of varying degrees of sophistication, while another 9 per cent were politically active, but ideologically oriented students, most of whose families were not part of the educated establishment and most of whom were studying the natural sciences. The other 43 per cent fell into two main categories: students of a quasi-platonic cast of mind which predisposed them to avoid politics with its political parties, compromises, and muddling through, almost to the point of favoring a kind of enlightened absolutism by philosopher-kings or experts; and unpolitical students who are either absorbed by their private lives and parochial interests or lost in the contemplation of ancient art, philosophy, or classical music — never modern art or music. The rest were students who are disaffected and resentful toward the present democratic Germany, chiefly because they are the sons or daughters of painfully denazified Germans. Many of these unpolitical and anti-democratic students come from *Akademiker* families and express the resentment of a declining old elite toward the "new society." The Habermas book pointedly quoted Thomas Mann's famous *Reflections of an Unpolitical Man* in which the author also gave a classic description of the battle between the heroic warriors of Germany and the merchants of the West:

> . . . for being German and being bourgeois is the same; if *Geist* is at all of bourgeois origin, German *Geist* is bourgeois

in a special way; German *Bildung* is bourgeois, the German
bourgeoisie humanistic — from which it follows that it is not
political as the Western bourgeoisie is and can become political only at the price of losing humanism.

This swan song of the educated bourgeoisie of Germany is curious
reading today, after the bourgeoisie fell for Hitler's barbarian hordes
and at a time when the gradual cultural and social decline of the educated elite in an egalitarian society is becoming a recognized fact.

Whither, German Democracy?

We have yet to mention the greatest remaining obstacle to Germany's
becoming truly modern. We have talked about the process by which
German society has in many ways left the transitional phase and arrived at modernity, although there are still segments and elements of
the past to be overcome. We have also seen that the arrival of the
"new society" in Western Germany created a social predisposition
toward democratic politics that had never before been present in Germany. But while the predisposition may be very important and necessary for democracy, it is not enough to make it a working reality. In
fact, the arrival of the "new society" elsewhere has clearly demonstrated that "new societies" contain new dangers to the freedom of
individuals and minorities — a pressure for conformity, the tyranny of
the majority, intolerance, and any number of other difficulties and
crises which appeared recently in such advanced societies as the
United States.

The chief safeguards against crises for fully developed democracies
are constitutional government and, to quote our Tory, Kenneth Stearn,
a well-functioning "game of politics." The institutions of constitutional democracy in the Federal Republic are generally well-designed
for optimal functioning and have worked reasonably well, although
there is always room for improvement. There have been many sug-
gestions for minor changes, but they would require a detailed presen-
tation of the existing institutional system. What is worth noting, however, is that Germany today seems to lack an experimental attitude
toward its governmental institutions. This appears to be not so much
because it has an authoritarian attitude toward such institutional ar-
rangements as the educational system of secondary schools and uni-

versities, or the distribution of power between the cabinet and the *Bundestag.* There is a widespread super-sensitivity to criticism which does not belong in a democracy. But the main reason why the nation seems reluctant to change its institutions arises from the peculiar fractioning of the German public into smaller, functionally divided publics of interlocking but unacknowledged responsibilities; thus only the narrowest of spheres is left for popular, democratic decision-making. With a matter like educational reform, for example, most Germans will tend to discount their responsibility for it and even deny that it has anything to do with politics. Instead, they will suggest that the question of whether or not reform is needed, or what kind of reform, should be decided by education experts and those dependent upon them; so the whole complex is left squarely in the lap of the self-perpetuating establishment of educated elites, parents, teachers, and educational administrators. As in many aspects of West German politics, the parties are considerably ahead of the general public in acknowledging their interest and responsibility for the whole field of public policy. The specialized "public" of any particular field, however, resents the intrusion of "politics" and the claims of the political parties.

As for the "game of politics," it will be remembered that the present West German party system is infinitely more stable and far more simplified than that of the Weimar Republic, with its multi-party system, rigid ideological camps, and militant movements. Thus the "game of politics" among the parties, especially in the making of public policy, is by and large quite satisfactory. But there is also another difference which is rarely mentioned: to put it in the form of a simple formula, the Weimar parties tended to make themselves the instrument of popular discontent against the state and were quite reluctant to take over governmental responsibility. The critics of the Weimar Republic who called it a "parties' state" (*Parteienstaat*) should really have vented their spleen on the "parties against the state." The Bonn Republic, by contrast, is truly controlled by the political parties who, far from representing popular discontent against the government, tend to have the paternalistic concern of a democratic government for the not-so-democratic people. This governmental attitude toward the people has an historic cause in that the post-war anti-fascist leadership of Germany felt an understandable distrust toward the masses, who had, after all, supported Hitler.

Today this democratic paternalism appears to be in urgent need of reform, if it is to maintain contact with the "new society" and give West Germans more civic responsibility. The widespread use of public opinion polls by the parties for the purpose of learning how to campaign successfully and which policies to adopt clearly demonstrates the need for the parties to have more public participation in their affairs. But public opinion polls are a poor substitute for direct consultation with the people. Even though the uses of town-meeting democracy or of initiative, referendum, and recall may be limited — there were some untoward experiences with the referendum in Weimar days — their introduction at this point could do wonders for German democracy. The political parties, moreover, would do well to abandon the exclusiveness of their card-carrying membership and to delegate responsibilities to a broader segment of their followers. Although there is no precedent for this in continental Europe or England, for example, they could turn over such a vital function as the nomination of candidates for legislative office to primary elections by the large number of faithful voters of the various parties. Such a procedure would also force politicians running for office to make more of an effort to consult and plead with their constituents. As long as there is no such expansion of partisan activity, the West German voters will be denied further education in democracy. Worse still, they will also be confirmed in their propensity to think of politics as just another specialized activity which should be left to the "political experts" in the parties. Democratic politics supplies a vital, unifying interest in all modern, pluralistic societies, and in Germany its unifying role is more indispensable than anywhere else, in part because pluralism has always been very deeply ingrained and unifying efforts have always been rather weak.

The passivity of the West German voter poses an even more serious problem. As Alfred Rapp put it in a recent book, *Bonn auf der Waage* (*Bonn on the Scales*), the Germans "do not think at all ill of democracy, but it rarely or never occurs to them that they themselves are that democracy." They have a quasi-platonic feeling that conceives of democracy as Socrates thought of virtue: as a matter of knowledge or belief rather than as something one does. But in addition to this bourgeois heritage there is also the enormous mutual distrust engendered by totalitarianism and by repeated political purges, first by the Nazis and then by denazification. An excellent comparative study of political participation in the United States, Great Britain, Germany, Italy, and Mexico was conducted recently by Gabriel Almond and Sydney Verba; it gives a sound conceptual framework for comparison and brings out the objective dimensions of the weakness of West German democracy in this respect. Almond and Verba place the development of contemporary democracy in the context of modernization. They show on the one hand the parochial, unpolitical attitudes found in Germany, especially among women, youth, farmers, and the undereducated, who are hardly aware of the existence of government; they contrast these with the politically disaffected who violently reject their government, such as Communist voters in Italy and, presumably, voters for the Nazi party in the early 'thirties. On the other hand, they show two types of positive political attitudes: the "orientation of the subject" of a modern state which arises with the incorporation of an area and its inhabitants into a modern, territorial state and includes an awareness of what government can do for its subjects; and "participant style" which means not only democratic participation in all kinds of organized functions, but also a distinct pride in such functions as voting or having a representative in parliament. As might be expected, Americans showed a highly developed "participant style" in the Almond and Verba study, while the Germans were relatively more parochial and showed a fully developed "subject orientation." Quite contrary to the stereotype of German authoritarianism, however, the British exhibited an equally well-developed "subject orientation" side by side with a full-blown "participant style." This illustrates the fundamental thesis regarding the modernization process that that study and this book present: parochial, subject, and participant attitudes are not mutually exclusive, "eternal attributes of national character," but rather successive stages of development superimposed one upon the other during the historical formation of territorial states and their subsequent democratization. There was an exception in the American case, where the "subject orientation" was historically skipped due to the circumstances of the New World. For present German democracy, this simply means that the Germans still have some way to go to build up a democratic tradition and to inculcate more participant style and civic consciousness in their citizens. Italians, by comparison, were found to be still

more parochial and considerably weaker both in subject and participant orientation than the Germans.

When details about German political participation in the Almond
and Verba study are compared with political life in the United States
and Great Britain, they are equally interesting. Germans turned out
to be about as well-informed about politics as the English-speaking
countries, in spite of the scandalously low information level of German women, but showed far less pride in their country and form of
government. From 80 to 90 per cent regularly turn out to vote, but
they appear to have a significantly lower sense of political efficacy,
especially in national affairs, though not in local government. They
were also more reluctant to discuss politics or join political parties,
and they got comparatively little satisfaction out of election campaigns or from the act of voting. Almond and Verba also discovered
that, while German men appeared to be about as prone to joining
organizations as Americans or Englishmen, they very rarely held
offices in them, and hardly any German women did. And Germans
were far less likely to form or join an informal group for political action. Students of comparative government used to joke that an American with a political grievance usually wrote to his Congressman, a
Frenchman would sit down and write a book, and a German would
go to his beer garden and discuss the matter endlessly with his cro-
nies, which gives a good idea of the effectiveness of political action in
the three countries. Almond and Verba present some evidence that
shows Germans prefer to complain to the administrative official in
charge or, if the grievance is very serious, to form or join a formal
organization, such as a party or pressure group. Judging from the private complaints of elective officials, West German voters have also
taken increasingly to writing letters by the basketful, a development
which has not been welcomed by the politicians receiving them, who
would themselves rather be philosopher-kings than listen to their constituents. Englishmen, by way of contrast, like to complain to their
elected officials or to form informal groups with neighbors and
friends. Americans also like informal groups, and they place great reliance on petitions and on "voting the rascals out of office." One main
reason why Germans are reluctant to form or join informal groups for
political action is that they do not trust each other. According to Almond and Verba, only about one-third as many Germans as Ameri-

cans felt that "people could be trusted" and almost twice as many agreed that "no one really cared what happened to you." When people feel that way about their neighbors, colleagues, and friends, they must indeed feel very powerless in relation to the organized forces of society and the state.

In the last analysis, there is Thomas Mann's unpolitical bourgeoisie still to be accounted for. It is difficult to understand why the political heritage of the ancient world developed so differently in the Western countries and in Germany. In the former, Greek and Roman thought, not unlike Protestant religion, appears to have been easily combined with the aspirations of the rising bourgeoisie for self-government and hence political participation. In Germany, however, classical thought seems to have been diluted by the political and social circumstances of the educated classes and the presence of princely absolutism into a quietistic faith characterized by political fatalism. German pride in an "inner freedom," comparable, perhaps, to the philosophy of Spinoza, is small compensation for the lack of interest in "external freedom." Instead of cultivating the public virtues of good citizenship, the German bourgeois cultivated his private virtues, his "inner life" (*Innerlichkeit*) and "beautiful soul," and followed the doubtful precept that "quiet and order are the first duties of a citizen" (*Ruhe ist die erste Buergerpflicht*). The effect of this quietism has lingered on among the bourgeoisie, if not among other classes of German society, for centuries, though it seems to have started to disintegrate, along with much of bourgeois civilization, toward the end of World War One. The relative passivity of present West Germans in politics, especially of the young, is more the result of insufficient political socialization in the home, the school, and elsewhere, than of historical traditions that have ceased to govern their lives in other ways as well. The failure to induct the new generations into the ways of civic participation is a typical example of the failure of emancipated man to take firm control of his new life.

What has been done about civic education in post-war Germany? Since the mid-'fifties, civics instruction has been introduced in various forms throughout the entire school system in all states. This in itself is a revolutionary fact which is likely to have a long-range influence on political socialization beyond the school years. There still is considerable discussion about how best to teach civics and concern over avoiding indoctrination or narrow specialization. What is most necessary, and what often is not recognized, is to teach democracy by practicing democracy in schools from an early age. Teachers in the secondary schools quite often teach civics as if it were Greek. And students from the educated upper classes, deeply steeped in the spirit of German humanistic education, quite often approach the subject as they would a theoretical field of knowledge such as Greek or algebra. Hence the need for basic educational reform.

There is also a need for secondary schools to promote direct contacts with other parts of society, such as party politicians, the world of the trade unions, farmers, practical businessmen, and so on, for the children of the educated classes grow up carefully sheltered from all these aspects of the real world. By emphasizing humanistic ideals, the schools seek to keep the students in Greek antiquity, as it were, and shield them from such sordid details of everyday life as the necessity for making a living. In addition, the schools have long been reluctant to teach contemporary art, contemporary music, and, until recent years, contemporary history. The American press has particularly mentioned this failure to teach recent history, which, by the way, it neglects to say is true of most European countries. It has done so because it has assumed German schools have been trying to gloss over crimes of the Nazi period. Actually the schools' attitude reflects a long-standing pattern of escapism that dates back to the nineteenth century and before. The teaching of recent history has been introduced meanwhile, although the general pattern of escapism still persists in the secondary schools.

A good deal of evidence has been amassed to prove that, since the end of World War II, the authority relationship between husband and wife, parent and children, boss and employee, and individual and government have become much different today than they were around the turn of the century. Women insist on equal rights (*Gleichberechtigung*), children on independence, employees take advantage of the labor shortage, and citizens have defied government authority from black-market days at the end of the war to the student riots and ban-the-bomb marchers of the last decade. Young soldiers in the new German army reveal a truculent awareness of their rights when ordered around by sergeants and officers. Even German intellectuals, whose humanistic tradition long isolated them from the feeling expressed by the masses that they would "not be pushed around," have lately begun to speak out against customs that make their country a *"Land der unbegrenzten Zumutbarkeiten"* (land of forever-letting-people-walk-over-you). But again, truculence and rebelliousness, necessary as they may be, do not accomplish the democratization of authority structures. In addition to the desire to assert themselves, the future citizens need to know how to participate in family and governmental decisions and to develop convenient and standardized procedures for asserting themselves and participating regularly in such decisions. German children need to grow up with the equivalent of Robert's *Rules of Order* and a bagful of democratic tricks and practices of organization and petition. German adult education and the universities, both of which are making a creditable contribution to popular civic education, need to step up their efforts and to emphasize more the procedures of democracy. As mentioned before in a different context, the electoral campaigns of the past decade and a half have been an education in democracy for the West German public. And if the political parties would solicit public participation more than they now do, they could provide far more intensive education in practical democratic politics.

It is evident that West German democracy is gradually evolving into a firmly established system after the Western model, although there is no lack of problems to solve and details to straighten out. Some years ago this writer concluded that the founders of the West German Republic had created a sturdy and stable framework within which future generations of Germans could develop the skills and satisfactions of democracy. We can now sound a similar note of optimism about the prospects for German democracy. It has come far since 1949, when the Western powers first lifted their tutelage. Over the years it has been greatly helped by factors beyond political control and manipulation — for instance, developments on the international scene and changes both in German society and German economy. As a result, Western Germany today is within reach of democratic maturity. All the country needs to do is to continue along the same road it has followed over the last twenty years.

The post-war period has also seen a notable change in German literature and social criticism. It has ceased being so obsessed with the

morbid and the Messianic aspects of German life and culture, and is
no longer so fascinated with the motes in other people's eyes. These
symbols of the cultural malaise existing during the transitional phase
of German modernization seem to be rapidly disappearing. Dissatisfied intellectuals today are generally hard-pressed to find things to
criticize. All that remains is the "undigested past," which has bedev-
iled West Germans in their international relations and in their internal reconstruction and adjustment. The most obvious embodiment of
that past, the one thousand members of Mass Murder, Incorporated,
and most other Nazi criminals have all been meted punishment
— that is, as much as punishment can ever achieve, which is very little.
The majority of Germans alive today were born too late to have been
involved with the Nazis. Even so, they are being constantly prodded
into recognizing the German past and to undertake methods of dealing with it, such as teaching contemporary history in the secondary
schools, which they might never have undertaken otherwise. The echo
of the Second World War, the "harvest of hate" engendered by the
misdeeds of the Nazi regime, continues to beat on German ears with
the regularity of an ocean tide. If it should ever flag, German intellectuals will keep it alive, or important elements in other countries will
do so for reasons of their own. And, in addition, the Soviet Union,
which routinely attacks Albania when it means to chastise Red China,
will continue to attack West Germany when it means the United States.
Finally, the occasional stirrings of the neo-Nazi fringe provide as effective an irritant as could be devised for arousing liberal sentiment in
West Germany. Individual cases, such as that of Hans Globke or the
affair of *The Deputy,* are raked over time and again in all their
extraordinary complexity, to no one's complete satisfaction, for the
paradoxes of real life just will not fit simple ideological, moral, or
even legal alternatives. "Digesting the past," after all, is not the same
as brooding about it. No one can turn his hatred of foul deeds committed against any living persons, guilty or partially guilty, without
running the danger of demeaning his own soul as well. If the experience of the Nazi years has taught us anything, it is that hatred of
human beings is the most destructive force known to man, a double-
edged sword that in the long run tends to maim or kill both the victim
and his persecutor.

In the last analysis, "digesting the past" means setting ghosts to rest and turning to the problems of the present and the future. The real test of Germany's moral recovery is not how anti-this or anti-that the Germans turn out to be. Anti-fascism and anti-Communism are quite sterile and unpromising without a positive commitment to the worthwhile tasks and challenges of today and tomorrow. It is not even enough to ask how well Germans of today acknowledge their responsibility for the past; it is much more important to ask what they are going to do with their future. Modern man cannot be obsessively concerned with the past. Such concern would sap vital energies which he needs to take firm hold of his life today. It can even be a form of escape, in sack and ashes, from the pressing responsibilities at hand. The past is prologue; now man must take control.

BIBLIOGRAPHICAL NOTES

The following bibliographical comments are not meant to be an exhaustive guide to the sources available, nor a complete list of the references used in the writing of this book. They are designed rather to draw attention to other significant writings, both in German and English, that may be of interest to the readers. Where appropriate, evaluative remarks have been added to the enumeration.

1: The Germans in History

It is hardly necessary to draw attention to the vast body of literature about German history and national character written by German nationalistic historians and intellectuals, nor to the contemporary literature in English, French, and German which attempts to deal with the problem of German wrongheadedness from a philosophical or ideological angle. Far less well-known are such scholarly accounts as Koppel Pinson's *Modern Germany* (1954), and many other historical studies of academic recognition. Among the innumerable German treatments of many different historical schools of thought, special mention should be made of Rudolf Stadelmann's *Deutschland und Westeuropa* (1948), which shows rare insight and a dispassionate understanding of the broad issues involved. Hans Kohn's *German History, Some New German Views* (1954) contains English versions of a number of representative, contemporary German historians who have reinterpreted the history of German national unification and the image of Bismarck. For an understanding of German society and the popular mind, as distinct from the writings of German intellectuals, there is no substitute for reading the innumerable diaries, memoirs, and biographies of Germans who have lived through the great transformation from traditional society to modernity. A conceptual scheme of a comparative character can be found in *The Passing of Traditional Society* (1957) by Daniel Lerner and others who have studied the process of modernization at various stages in the Middle East. A good glimpse of German society before 1914 can also be obtained from the anthropologist Robert Lowie's *The German People, A Social Portrait to 1914* (1945) and his more expanded *Toward Understanding Germany* (1954). See also David Rodnick's *Postwar Germans* (1947).

More specialized aspects are treated in the still very admirable *Imperial Germany and the Industrial Revolution* (1937) by Thorstein Veblen and in Leonard Krieger's *German Idea of Freedom* (1957), an analysis of German evasion of the Western concept of political freedom, as well as Klemens von Klemperer's *Germany's New Conservatism* (1957) and Fritz Stern's *The Politics of Cultural Despair* (1961). See also the recent book about the German youth movement, *Young Germany* by Walter Z. Laqueur (1962), and H. Plessner's *Die verspätete Nation* (1959). More general are also the classic *Die soziale Schichtung des deutschen Volkes* (1932) by Theodor Geiger and the discussion of the social basis of democracy in Seymour M. Lipset, *Political Man* (1959).

2: How Could They?

Only a decade and a half ago, the fourteen fateful years of the Weimar Republic, not to mention the rise of Hitler, were primarily a subject of virulent controversy among different groups and individuals trying to attach the blame to a single institution, group, or failing of German society. A good sampling of this controversy is given in John L. Snell, ed., *The Nazi Revolution* (1959), and Stephen J. Tonsor, ed., *National Socialism, Conservative Reaction or Nihilist Revolt* (1959). Only very few fairly objective treatments of the politics of Weimar antedate 1950, such as Arthur Rosenberg's *A History of the Weimar Republic* (1936), Konrad Heiden's *Der Führer* (1944), and Arnold Brecht's *Prelude to Silence* (1944). Since about 1950, however, the period prior to and leading up to the Third Reich has been subjected to a continuing scholarly assault from many aspects and by numerous individuals and research institutes. Among the most notable contributions in German are Karl Dietrich Bracher's *Die Auflösung der Weimarer Republik* (1955), and by the same author and others *Die National-sozialistische Machtergreifung* (1960); the publications of the official Kommission für Geschichte des Parlamentarismus und der politischen Parteien, such as Erich Matthias and Rudolf Morsey's *Ende der Parteien* (1960) and many other studies of particular political parties or phases; and the publications of the Munich Institut für Zeitgeschichte whose leading historians Hermann Mau and Helmut Krausnick can now be read in English, *German History, 1933–1945* (1959). Among the many other noteworthy books in German are Waldemar Besson's *Württemberg und die deutsche Staatskrise, 1928–1933* (1959), Theodor Eschenburg and others, *Der Weg in die Diktatur* (1963), and such studies of detail as Otto-Ernst Schueddekopf, *Linke Leute von rechts* (1960), H. H. Hoffmann, *Der Hitlerputsch* (1961), Wilfrid Daim, *Der Mann, der Hitler die Ideen gab* (1958), and Karl Buchheim, *Die Weimarer Republik* (1960), to mention a few. Particularly insightful from an analytical point of view among English language materials are such older works as Talcott Parson's *Essays in Sociological Theory* (2nd ed., 1958), Siegfried Kracauer's *From Caligari to Hitler* (1946), Harold D. Lasswell's earlier writings, and Sebastian DeGrazia's *The Political Community, A Study of Anomie* (1948). Of great merit among many detailed studies are also Klaus Epstein, *Matthias Erzberger and the Dilemma of German Democracy* (1959), Walter H. Kaufman, *Monarchism in the Weimar Republic* (1953), H. H. Gordon, *The Reichswehr and the German Republic* (1957) and the English translation of Edmond Vermeil's *Germany in the Twentieth Century* (1956). Valuable insights into the psychology of National Socialism are offered by such studies of prejudice as *The Authoritarian Personality* (1950) by Theodore Adorno and others, or, on a more popular level, G. M. Gilbert's *Psychology of Dictatorship* (1950), a report by the court psychiatrist at the Nuremberg trials, or Milton Mayer's *They Thought They Were Free* (1955), the story of ten average Nazis. Further notable analytical accounts include Rudolf Heberle's *From Democracy to Nazism* (1945), a study of rural Schleswig-Holstein, Alan L. C. Bullock's *Hitler, A Study in Tyranny* (1953), Hannah Arendt's *Origins of Totalitarianism* (1951) and *Eichmann in Jerusalem* (1962), Norman R. C. Cohn's *Pursuit of the Millennium* (1957), William Ebenstein's *Today's Isms* (3rd ed., 1961), and Carl J. Friedrich and Z. Brzezinski's *Totalitarian Dictatorship and Autocracy* (1956).

3, 4, and 5: An Economic Miracle?
The New Society of Western Germany,
and Americanization Apace

A great deal of the material used for these three chapters was found in current German newspapers such as the *Süddeutsche Zeitung, Frankfurter Allgemeine Zeitung,* or *Die Welt,* in weeklies such as *Der Spiegel, Die Zeit,* the numerous illustrated magazines, and German monthlies such as *Der Monat, Frankfurter Hefte,* or *Die Gegenwart.* Among English language books on the subject there are several that are very helpful even to a non-economist. Henry C. Wallich's *Main Springs of the German Revival* (1955) and Wolfgang Stolper's *Germany Between East and West* (1960) cover most of the ground and J. Frederick Dewhurst and others, *Europe's Needs and Resources* (1961), supplies the comparative perspective up to 1955. More recent comparative information about the various European economies and their standards of living can be gathered from the national monographs of OEEC, now called OECD, which also publishes economic statistics and occasional studies such as Milton Gilbert and others, *Comparative National Products and Price Levels* (1958). The Commission of the Common Market (EEC) also publishes some comparative statistics about member nations once in a while. Finally, there is occasional information in the English language press and at times whole issues or supplements such as the survey *Western Germany* of the *Financial Times* (March, 1960).

As for sociological insights, one of the best sources is Ralf Dahrendorf's *Gesellschaft und Freiheit* (1961), which contains most of the pertinent articles of the German sociologist, and also his *Soziale Klassen und Klassenkonflikt in der industriellen Gesellschaft* (1957). Of great merit also are Theodor Geiger, *Die Klassengesellschaft im Schmelztiegel* (1949), and H. Popitz and others, *Das Gesellschaftsbild des Arbeiters* (1957). For a comparative perspective R. Hoggart's *The Uses of Literacy* (1957) can be recommended for Great Britain and the Winter 1964 issue of *Daedalus, The New Europe,* for the other continental European societies. George Lichtheim's *The New Europe* (1963) is also a good general essay on aspects of the post-Marxian society there. Last, but hardly least important, W. W. Rostow's *Stages of Economic Growth* (1960) and Robert L. Heilbroner's *The Making of Economic Society* (1962) should be cited for conceptual support.

For information about the government policies throughout the period since 1948, the best sources are the two books by Ludwig Erhard, *Deutsch-*

lands Rückkehr zum Weltmarkt (1953) and *Wohlstand für Alle* (1951). There is also a great deal of detail in the annual reports of the federal ministries, entitled *Deutschland im Wiederaufban* or, since 1960, *Deutsche Politik*. Needless to add, there are also the official statistical yearbooks and other presentations of the *Statistisches Bundesamt* and the statistical offices of the *Laender*.

6: A Man Named Gruber

The fate of former Nazis since 1945, neo-Nazi activity, and suspicions about West German rearmament have been an object of misleading news items in the press to a greater extent than any other aspect of German affairs. This is due in large part to the air of sensationalism that has made Hitler and the Nazi war machine also a favorite subject of certain men's magazines, but in part also to the continuing propagandistic interest of various groups of persons, including those particularly involved in World War II or persecuted by the Nazis, and the Soviet Union. This circumstance detracts from the objectivity of some of the recent books on German affairs as well. Typical examples of Soviet propaganda are the numerous press statements, official accusations, and even films from Eastern European countries attacking, for example, the German NATO generals, Speidel and Heusinger. It is very rare that these propaganda fabrications contain any new and incriminating facts among their web of lies and gross distortions, nor do they ever mention the comparable figures for East Germany which is known to employ 17 former Nazi generals out of 30 leading officers. Another example is the *Dokumentation der Zeit* of the misleadingly named *Deutsches Institut für Zeitgeschichte* in East Berlin which likes to collect newspaper items about alleged infringements of the freedom of speech and the press in West Germany without, of course, even so much as a hint as to the complete absence of such freedom in Communist Germany. Among books in English that show very heavy bias, Heinz Abosch's *The Menace of the Miracle* (1963) is characterized by its obvious sympathy for the Communist regime of East Germany and the Berlin Wall. Just as biased, though for different reasons, is T. H. Tetens's *The New Germany and the Old Nazis* (1961), a compilation of incidents involving unreconstructed Nazis and neo-Nazi activity set against a background of spy stories and hints of global conspiracy. Tetens's book also goes into the foreign policy implications of considering Western Germany "still Nazi and always Nazi."

These implications have been spelled out in a more scholarly fashion in Fred Warner Neal's *War and Peace and Germany* (1962) and Gerald

Freund's *Germany Between Two Worlds* (1961). There are also several exceedingly critical accounts by West German authors, such as Helmut Hammerschmidt and Michael Mansfeld's *Der Kurs ist falsch* (1956), Reinhard M. Strecker's *Dr. Hans Globke* (1961), a collection of documents, or Erich Kuby's milder *Alles im Eimer* (1960). Distinctive efforts at reaching a balanced judgment are John Dornberg's *Schizophrenic Germany* (1961) and Terence Prittie's *Germany Divided* (1961), two journalistic accounts of considerable depth and evident long familiarity with the German scene. A balanced and scholarly account can be found in Alfred Grosser's *La démocratie de Bonn* (1957) which has meanwhile appeared in German as well. The social and political developments since about 1958 clearly separate the recent accounts from such earlier works as James B. Conant's *Germany and Freedom* (1958), Norbert Muhlen's *Return of Germany* (1953), or Charles W. Thayer's *The Unquiet Germans* (1957), as well as Grosser's earlier *The Colossus Again* (1955). One might be inclined to speak of a loss of innocence since 1958 even though this is actually the turning-point toward a more conscientious re-examination of the past by the German public. Earlier accounts simply took the integrity of the German post-war leadership and the necessity for German rearmament for granted.

The best survey of neo-Nazi activity in West Germany is Manfred Jenke's *Verschwörung von Rechts?* (1961) whose facts and figures in no way lend credence to the fears expressed by T. H. Tetens and sensational press accounts. There is also a recent report of the Federal Ministry of the Interior which gives facts and figures about the numerous groups of the right-wing fringe. In English, there is *The German Dilemma, an Appraisal of Anti-Semitism, Ultra-Nationalism and Democracy in West Germany* (1959) of the American Jewish Congress. Specifically dealing with neo-Nazi ideology are Hans Helmuth Knuetter, *Ideologien des Rechtsradikalismus im Nachkriegsdeutschland* (1961) and Enno de Vries's *Der Neonazismus in der Bundesrepublik Deutschland* (1956). Otto Buesch and Peter Furth, *Rechtsradikalismus im Nachkriegsdeutschland* (1957), deals only with the SRP.

On the problems of German rearmament, see also Karl W. Deutsch and Lewis J. Edinger, *Germany Rejoins the Powers* (1959), Hans Speier and Phillips Davison, *West German Leadership and Foreign Policy* (1957), and Hans Speier, *German Rearmament and Atomic War* (1957). For a glimpse of the German views, see also Eric Waldman, *Soldat im Staat* (1963), *Schicksalsfragen der Gegenwart* of the German Ministry of Defense, and Helmut Schmidt's *Verteidigung oder Vergeltung?* (1961) for the SPD position. Elizabeth Wiskemann's *Germany's Eastern Neigh-*

bors, Problems Relating to the Oder-Neisse Line and the Czech Frontier Regions (1956) and Zoltan M. Szaz's *Germany's Eastern Frontiers, The Problem of the Oder-Neisse Line* (1960) throw light on some of the border problems. There is now also an expanding literature in German about the problem of reunification.

7 and 8: The Post-war Metamorphosis of German Politics and Dummkopf, Vote for Adenauer

The material for these two chapters was gathered in large part from contemporary newspaper and periodical items as well as from the CDU yearbooks and convention protocols, all in German. Of great help were also the monographs by Hans Georg Wieck, *Die Entstehung der CDU und die Wiedergründung des Zentrums im Jahre 1945* (1953) and *Christliche und Freie Demokraten in Hessen, Rheinland-Pfalz und Württemberg, 1945–1946* (1958), and Ernst Deuerlein's *CDU/CSU 1945–1957* (1957), which also contains a good bibliography of further German sources. There is a wealth of material on Christian social theory available in German, of which we shall only pick one at random, Alois Schardt's *Wohin steuert die CDU?* (1961). Others can be found at all levels of sophistication and also in the form of periodicals of organized groups. In the English language, Arnold J. Heidenheimer's *Adenauer and the CDU* (1960) is indispensable to an understanding of the web of relationships that made up Chancellor Democracy. Michael D. Fogarty's *Christian Democracy in Western Europe, 1820–1953* (1957) and the English versions of Edgar Alexander's *Adenauer und das neue Deutschland* (1956) and Paul Weymar's *Konrad Adenauer* (1957) help to place the movement in its historical perspective. See also this writer's *Origin of the West German Republic* (1963), and such treatments of post-war politics as Edward H. Litchfield's *Governing Postwar Germany* (1953), Harold Zink's *The United States in Germany, 1944–1955* (1957), and many others.

For the broader setting of the Christian Democrats in the German party system, see especially Max Gustav Lange, ed., *Parteien in der Bundesrepublik* (1955), and Erwin Faul, ed., *Wahlen und Wähler in Westdeutschland* (1960), and Rudolf Wildenmann, *Partei und Fraktion* (1955); also the election studies, Wolfgang Hirsch-Weber and Klaus Schuetz, *Wähler und Gewählte* (1956) and Bernhard Vogel and Peter Haungs's *Wahlkampf und Wählertradition* (1963). Studies of the 1953 and 1957 elections are also available in English; James K. Pollock and others, *German Democracy at Work* (1955), and U. W. Kitzinger's *German Electoral Politics* (1960). See also *Modern Political Parties* (1956) by Sigmund Neumann who also wrote the classic *Die Deutschen Parteien* (1932). There are a number of excellent general sources about German postwar politics which, among other subjects, deal with the rise of Adenauer and the Christian Democrats. In addition to the materials already mentioned in previous chapters, there are in particular Richard Hiscock's *Democracy in Western Germany* (1957), Heidenheimer's *The Governments of Germany* (1961), Elmer Plischke's *Contemporary Government of Germany* (1961), and the sections on Germany in the standard textbooks on European governments. Finally, there are now an increasing number of journalistic accounts of German politics of high quality, beginning with Fritz Réné Allemann's *Bonn ist nicht Weimar* (1956), and more recently represented by Alfred Rapp's *Bonn auf der Waage* (1959), Guenther Scholz *In Bonn Schlägt's 12* (1961), and Winfried Martini, *Freiheit auf Abruf* (1960), to pick a few. Very noteworthy is also *Das Erbe Adenauers* by Ruediger Altmann, a young Christian Democrat.

The analysis of voting behavior in Chapter 8 is based largely on direct observation, newspaper accounts, and on the election studies cited above. Very helpful also was the doctoral dissertation (for Columbia University) of Juan Linz, *Social Bases of West German Politics* (1959), which evaluates public opinion materials collected in a German study at the University of Cologne under the direction of Erich Reigrotzki whose *Soziale Verflechtungen in der Bundesrepublik* (1956) is based on the same data. Useful information can be found in E. P. Newmann and Elizabeth Noelle's *Statistics on Adenauer, Portrait of a Statesman* (1962), in the public opinion data published regularly by EMNID, DIVO, the Institut für Demoskopie, the United States Information Service, and the Gallup Poll. There are also books about aspects of German affairs that contain compilations of public opinion materials, such as *Germany Rejoins the Powers* by Deutsch and Edinger, cited above, and Heinrich Sattcr's *Deutschland—ohne Feigenblatt* (1956). Electoral statistics for Germany are usually found in the official publications of the Federal and Land statistical offices. Richard Schachtner's *Die Deutschen Nachkriegswahlen* (1956) contains election returns by *Laender*. The election studies cited above also include some of the statistics.

9: The Opposition in the Wings

The material on the FDP and SPD presented here stems primarily from direct observation, contemporary newspaper accounts, and from the periodicals and other information issued by the two parties, in particular from the yearbooks, party convention protocols, and numerous other materials of the SPD. A list of SPD publications can be found in Fritz Saenger, *Soziale Demokratie* (1960). Beyond these sources, much can be found in the general accounts of German parties, politics, and elections cited for the previous chapters.

More specifically about the earlier history of the SPD are Carl Landauer, *European Socialism* (1959), Carl E. Schorske, *German Social Democracy, 1905–1917, The Development of the Great Schism* (1955), A. J. Berlau, *The German Social Democratic Party, 1914–1921* (1949), and Lewis J. Edinger, *German Exile Politics* (1956). The German literature about the earlier years of the SPD is quite voluminous and references can be found in Landauer, or in the standard history of German parties *Geschichte der politischen Parteien in Deutschland* (10th ed., 1960) by Ludwig Bergstraesser who together with Sigmund Neumann furnishes an excellent perspective on the SPD among the other German parties. See also now, *1863–1963, 100 Jahre Deutsche Sozialdemokratie* (1963), edited by Georg Eckert, and Karl Anders's *Die ersten 100 Jahre* (*1963*), as well as O. K. Flechtheim's new documentary collection on parties. Very illuminating is also *Soziologie der deutschen Parteien* (1955) by F. A. von der Heydte and Karl Sacherl which in a sense continues the tradition begun by Robert Michels's classic *Political Parties* (1915). Party programs, including those of the CDU/CSU, can be found in the collections of Wolfgang Treue, *Deutsche Parteiprogramme 1861–1961* (3rd ed., 1961), and Wilhelm Mommsen, *Deutsche Parteiprogramme* (1960). At the time of the 1957 elections Schimmelbusch & Co., Bonn, brought out a collection of five booklets, each with an introduction and program furnished by the SPD, FDP, BHE, CDU, and DP, respectively.

There is relatively little material about the early post-war years of the SPD except for Fried Wesemann's *Kurt Schumacher* (1952) and Willy Brandt and Richard Lowenthal's biography of *Ernst Reuter* (1957), the famous mayor of Berlin, and the general works on German parties and politics mentioned above. Among the latter, the section on the SPD in *Parteien in der Bundesrepublik* is particularly helpful. Lewis J. Edinger and Douglas Chalmers are soon to bring out books on the SPD. There is also a running commentary on the internal state of the party and on the progress of reform by Klaus-Peter Schulz, *Sorge um die deutsche Linke* (1955), continued in *Opposition als politisches Schicksal* (1958). For the economic policies of the mid-'fifties, see also Hans-Heinrich Zimdahl's *Wirtschaftssysteme und Parteiprogramme* (1953) and, by Carlo Schmid and others, *Grundfragen moderner Wirtschaftspolitik* (1957). Party publications such as *Sozialdemokratie und Bundeswehr* (1957), *Die Zukunft Meistern* (1959), *Kultur und Politik in unserer Zeit* (1960), *Sozialplan für Deutsch-*

land (1957), *Junge Generation und Macht* (1960), *Von Verkehrswirrwarr zur Ordnung* (1961), *Der Bauer in der Welt von Morgen* (1960) and *Soziale Demokratie* (1960), most of them materials from special conferences and the last-mentioned a commentary on the Godesberg Program of 1959, give perhaps a clearer picture of the programmatic upheaval within this party than a comparison of yearbooks and regular party convention protocols, or even of the Godesberg Program itself, with the *Handbuch Sozial demokratischer Politik* (1953). There are also critical appraisals of the new trend by writers close to the Christian Social tradition, such as Gustav E. Kafka's *Der freiheitliche Sozialismus* (1960) or Albrecht Beckel and Guenter Triesch, *Wohin steuert die SPD?* (1961). See also Willy Brandt, *My Road to Berlin* (1960). For a critique of SPD policy from within its own disavowed left wing, see the contribution of Wolfgang Abendroth in *Bestandsaufnahme* (1962), edited by Hans Werner Richter.

The latter book also contains much that fits into the pattern of hostility of West German intellectuals toward society and government. Another pertinent collection is *Die Alternative oder Brauchen wir eine neue Regierung?* (1961) edited by Martin Walser.

Materials on the FDP, not to mention smaller German parties, are almost non-existent in English with the exception of the general works on parties and politics cited above. There is an excellent article by Gerard Braunthal, "The Free Democratic Party in West German Politics," in the *Western Political Quarterly,* June 1960. In German there is little aside from the programmatic and periodical publications of the party itself which are not particularly plentiful. Reinhold Maier's *Ende und Wende* (1948) and Hans Bott's *Begegnungen mit Theodor Heuss* (1954) or Hans Heinrich Welchert, *Theodor Heuss* (1959), permit a glimpse into the world of ideas of the old-style Liberals, and Karl Georg Pfleiderer's *Politik für Deutschland* some insight into their foreign policy concepts. For a conservative point of view, there are some materials issued by the DP, especially during the 1950's, and books such as *Politik im Widerstreit* (1957) by Hans Joachim von Merkatz, a long-time DP leader and Federal Minister, or the writings of Hans Joachim Schoeps, such as *Konservative Erneuerung* (1958) or *Die Letzten 30 Jahre* (1956). Materials on the right-wing fringe groups have been mentioned in connection with Chapter 6. There is also *Die KPD in der Bundesrepublik* (1959) by Hans Kluth which follows the West German Communist Party until it was outlawed, and Carola Stern's *Porträt einer Bolschewistischen Partei* (1957). Also now, Hermann Weber, ed., *Der Deutsche Kommunismus, Dokumente* (1962) on the Communists of East and West Germany.

10. Whither, German Democracy?

In addition to previously cited materials, attention should be drawn to such gems as *Education for Democracy in West Germany* (1961) and *The Politics of Postwar Germany* (1963), both edited by Walter Stahl, which contain in spite of lapses in the translation a wealth of information about how West Germans today are grappling with the task of civic education on all levels and through all kinds of media. There are also a number of critical points of view discernible, such as the intellectual-humanistic camp which is represented, for example, by the literary writers' "group 47," or by the above mentioned contributions to *Bestandsaufnahme* or to the book edited by Martin Walser. Another example would be Karl Jaspers's *Freiheit und Wiedervereinigung* (1960). Then there is a group of political scientists who direct their criticism at specific institutions and procedures, such as O. H. von der Gablentz in *Die Versäumte Reform* (1960) or Theodor Eschenburg's *Institutionelle Sorgen in der Bundesrepublik* (1961), *Aemterpatronage, Herrschaft der Verbände,* and other writings. In this connection one should also mention the journalistic accounts again which are usually in part critical, as is the West German press. A critical attitude toward the privileged position of what we have called the educated establishment is most often to be found among writers close to the trade unions or to the SPD.

The comparative study of political participation by Gabriel Almond and Sydney Verba mentioned is *Civic Culture* (1963). The sociological study of the civic attitudes of Frankfurt University students referred to is *Student und Politik* (1961) by Jürgen Habermas and others, a fascinating piece of work although somewhat colored by what we have called the quasi-Platonic bias. And finally Helmut Schelsky's *Die skeptische Generation* (1957) is a sociological study of German youth since 1945.

INDEX

As a trained political scientist and a native-born German, the author is in an unusually favorable position to write such a book. It is based in part on the impressions he gathered on returning to Germany after an absence of seven years. The book will surely be both stimulating and essential reading for anyone concerned about the future of this important nation.

Peter H. Merkl is Associate Professor of Political Science at the University of California, Santa Barbara. He is the author of *The Origin of the West German Republic.*

Peter Viereck, *Mount Holyoke College*, says:

"A beautifully written, thoughtful book, seeking the complex truth rather than easy answers. Though occasionally overoptimistic about the decline of German nationalism, it is still the most searching book so far on the subject of German guilt."